Paying with Plastic

Paying with Plastic

The Digital Revolution in Buying and Borrowing

Second Edition

David S. Evans and Richard Schmalensee

The MIT Press
Cambridge, Massachusetts
London, England

MIT Press books may be purchased at special quantity discounts for business or sales promotional use. For information, please e-mail <special_sales@ mitpress.mit.edu> or write to Special Sales Department, The MIT Press, 5 Cambridge Center, Cambridge, MA 02142.

This book was set in Sabon by SNP Best-set Typesetter Ltd., Hong Kong. Printed and bound in the United States of America.

Library of Congress Cataloging-in-Publication Data

Evans, David S. (David Sparks), 1954–
Paying with plastic : the digital revolution in buying and borrowing / David S. Evans, Richard Schmalensee.—2nd ed.
    p. cm.
Includes bibliographical references and index.
ISBN-13: 978-0-262-05077-7 (hc.: alk. paper)—
978-0-262-55058-1 (pbk.: alk. paper)
ISBN-10: 0-262-05077-3 (hc.: alk. paper)—0-262-55058-X (pbk.: alk. paper)
1. Credit cards—United States. 2. Bandk credit cards—United States.
3. Electronic funds transfers—United States. 4. Electronic commerce—United States. 5. Consumer credit—United States. I. Schmalensee, Richard. II. Title.

HG3755.8.U6E94   2005
332.7'65'0973—dc22

2004055249

10   9   8   7   6   5

To Karen and Diane

Contents

Preface   xi

Acknowledgments   xv

1 **Plastic Cards**   1
   The Star   8
   The Main Characters   12
   Other Members of the Cast   14
   Behind the Stage   18
   The Foreign Cast   19
   The Thirteen Acts   21

2 **From Seashells to Electrons**   25
   The Evolution of Money   25
   Buy Now, Pay Later   45

3 **More Than Money**   53
   Dining on the Cuff   53
   1958   56
   The Birth of Co-opetition   61
   Regulation and Stagflation   67
   The 1980s' Spending and Debt Spree   75
   The 1990s and the Rise of the Debit Card   80
   The Golden Anniversary and Beyond   84

4 **From Gourmets to the Masses**   87
   The Growth and Diffusion of Payment Cards among U.S.
   Households   88
   Using Payment Cards to Execute Transactions   90

Credit Card Lending: Joys, Sorrows, and Controversies   95
Credit Cards and Entrepreneurship   107
Room for Growth   113

5 From Sardi's to Saks.com   115
Getting to Be Everywhere You Want to Be   116
Getting Cheaper and Better   119
Not Everywhere Yet   126
Paying for Plastic   129

6 It Takes Two to Tango   133
Multisided Platform Economics 101   134
Business Models in Multisided Platform Markets   142
Multisided Platforms and Price Setting in Payment Cards   149

7 Co-opetition and the Payment Card Ecosystem   159
The Co-opetitives   162
Cooperation, the Tragedy of the Commons, and the Role of
Rules   167
The Co-opetitives, the Go-It-Alones, and Payment Card
Ecosystems   175

8 System Wars   185
Weapons of War   189
And They Don't Take American Express   190
Master the Possibilities   199
The Card That Is Just Like a Check   205

9 Issuer Brawls   213
Who Are the Players?   213
Product Variety and Market Segmentation   216
Competitive Strategies   225
Market Structure   228
Market Performance   232
Debit Issuance   240

10 Backroom Battles   247
The Evolution of the Payment Processing Business   248
Who's Who in the Back Room   251
Market Structure and Performance   258

11 The Antitrust Wars   267

Harm to Competitors or Harm to Consumers?   272

Who's In, Who's Out?   275

Who Pays for Plastic?   285

Square Pegs and Round Holes   294

12 On the Brink   297

Technologies from the Exotic to the Merely Smart   298

E-Commerce, E-Payments, and M-Commerce   304

Shaking up the Marketplace   310

13 And They Don't Take Cash   317

Sources and Notes   321

Selected Bibliography   345

Index   353

Preface

In the last half of the twentieth century, payment cards—credit, debit, and charge cards—have quietly revolutionized how we pay for goods and services. If you bought this book over the Internet, you probably entered the sequence of digits from one of your payment cards. The electrons you set in motion precipitated the movement of money, mostly in the form of binary digits, between you, the merchant, and participants in the sprawling payment card industry. It is increasingly common to find merchants who do not take cash or checks, and increasingly rare to find merchants who refuse payment cards.

Payment cards have also revolutionized how we coordinate the timing of when we purchase goods and services and when we pay for them. The popular media often focus on how credit cards, by making it much quicker and easier to borrow, encourage people to spend beyond their means and get mired in debt. Although removing the hassle from the process of borrowing has allowed some people to borrow too much, credit cards have enabled many more of us to achieve a better standard of living. The millions of people who finance purchases on credit cards want to enjoy life earlier than their current incomes and savings permit. Credit cards enable them to do so.

This book is about the complex industry that lies behind the revolution in how we pay for and finance our purchases. But we have several other stories to tell. One is about how the entrepreneurs behind the payment card industry solved the classic chicken-and-egg problem. Consumers do not want cards that merchants do not take, and merchants do not want cards that consumers do not have. Another story is about how the payment card industry was shaped by the highly localized nature of the U.S. banking industry. Credit cards were developed by two associations, MasterCard and Visa, which now have thousands of members across the country—ranging from the smallest credit unions to the largest commercial banks—and indeed around the world. A further story concerns the legal battles that have embroiled these associations throughout their existence. In particular, 2003 was not a good year for the associations in the courts. The payment card industry looks to be in a time of upheaval. This is partly because the courts have shaken things up, partly because new competitors have appeared, and a bit because points of stress are emerging in the payment card systems themselves. At the same time, the Internet and mobile phones are changing how people buy things; e-commerce and m-commerce provide both opportunities and threats to the existing order. Only by looking back some years from now will we know whether all this is just a hiccup on a path of gradual evolution, or whether we have entered a discontinuity from which will emerge a very different industry.

We bring two perspectives to bear on the payment card industry. First, we examine the evolution of this industry through the lens of economics. We are particularly interested in explaining how economic forces have combined with institutional and technological ones to shape this industry, and in showing how competition works in an industry that does not fit neatly into any of the standard models used by economists. Second, our own introduction to this industry has come in part through consulting work we have done for Visa. We began working for Visa in 1991 when Sears (then the owner of the Discover Card) filed an antitrust lawsuit after Visa refused to let Sears issue a Visa card. We have since worked on most of the subsequent antitrust cases discussed later in this volume. We believe that the antitrust charges against the credit card associations often stem from a lack of understanding of how competition works in the payment card industry and from a failure to recognize the need for creative solutions to the special problems that affect this unique industry. This book explains how this industry works and argues that it works remarkably well. But we keep these views mainly in the background, and hope that we have provided a survey that card competitors and card phobics will find useful.

Although this is a second edition, it is so different from the first that we were tempted to change the title. We began the process of preparing this volume thinking that we would simply update the first edition—change the numbers to reflect more recent years, and modify the discussions here and there to hide the fact that the book was originally written in 1997 and 1998. We soon realized that was impossible for several reasons.

First, in five years time the industry had changed dramatically. There was tremendous consolidation of card portfolios as a result of bank mergers and the exit of banks from what had become a highly competitive business with scale economies, debit cards had become a central character, American Express had roared back as a significant player, the Electronic Funds Transfer (EFT) systems consolidated and became for-profit companies, and First Data Corporation was emerging as a major contender.

Second, the economics of multisided market platforms—a body of work that began with the insights of two French economists, Jean-Charles Rochet and Jean Tirole, in a paper that began circulating in 2001—provides a new way of looking at the payment card business and analyzing some of its characteristics. It turns out that payment cards are one of many products whose existence requires getting two distinct groups of customers—who need each other in some fashion—to use them. Examples include dating clubs, free television, computer operating systems, and shopping malls. Multisided market platform industries must design pricing, investment, and marketing strategies to "get both sides on board." The new economic theory as well as empirical studies of these industries both show that platform businesses often solve the chicken-and-egg problem by pricing very low to one side—in some cases below incremental cost. This new volume is thus tied together by two-sided market theory.

Third, we could not contain our curiosity as we delved into this industry again. For its economics, its institutions, its past, and its future, this is a fascinating industry, and we've deepened our discussion of several key issues. We hope you, the reader, come to share our fascination.

Acknowledgments

We are grateful for the help we have received over the years from many people. A number of people provided exceptional help with the research, including Richard Bergin, Kristin Brief, Irina Danilkina, Daniel Garcia Swartz, Melba Largent, Anne Layne-Farrar, Melissa Long, Sean MacLeod, Nese Nasif, Chris Nosko, Bernard Reddy, Ye Tao, and Elizabeth Wang. We are also indebted to Richard Epstein, Jean-Charles Rochet, Joanna Stavins, and Jean Tirole for many helpful comments and suggestions on the manuscript. We received many helpful comments and suggestions from several employees of MasterCard and Visa. Two individuals deserve our special thanks: Paul Allen, who encouraged our research and writing during his years as General Counsel of Visa, and Howard Chang, who has been our close collaborator on this and the previous edition and who has made numerous contributions to the book and to our thinking about this industry. We are also grateful to Visa for financial support as well providing access to data and information on the payment card industry. This book, of course, does not necessarily reflect the views of any of the people who have generously provided us with all forms of assistance, nor does it necessarily reflect the views of Visa or any other organization with which we have an affiliation.

1

Plastic Cards

It was necessary to reconceive, in the most fundamental sense, the nature of bank, money, and credit card; even beyond that to the essential elements of each and how they might change in a microelectronics environment. Several conclusions emerged: First: Money had become nothing but guaranteed, alphanumeric data recorded in valueless paper and metal. It would eventually become guaranteed data in the form of arranged electronics and photons which would move around the world at the speed of light.

—Dee Hock, former CEO of Visa

Look in your wallet. If you are like most Americans, you have at least one thin plastic card that you use to pay for things at many merchants. Take out one of those cards. The card you picked is about $3\frac{3}{8}''$ long by $2\frac{1}{8}''$ wide, weighs about a fifth of an ounce, has a magnetic stripe on the back, and has your name and a thirteen- to sixteen-digit account number embossed on the front. It is called a "payment card." Yours is one of more than 865 million payment cards in the hands of U.S. consumers in 2002. Once cardboard, now plastic, the card itself may become an anachronism. The digits—with their link to you—are what matters. How they are stored and transmitted is a detail.

If you have only one payment card in your wallet, it is probably a debit card. It will have the logos for several EFT networks, such as STAR, on the back and it may have a logo for MasterCard or Visa on the front. When you pay with this card, the funds are automatically deducted from your checking account.

Do you have a credit card as well? This will have the logo for American Express, Discover, MasterCard, or Visa on the front; if it is a MasterCard or Visa card, it will also typically have the name of the bank that issued you the card—Bank of America, for example—on the front. When you pay with a credit card, your purchase will appear on your next monthly statement. You can pay in full or finance your purchase over time. Perhaps you have a charge card—such as the American Express Corporate card. Your purchase will appear on your next statement, but you must pay in full and cannot finance your purchase over time.

Increasingly, you may have the option of receiving your salary on a prepaid card, which you can use to withdraw cash from an Automated Teller Machine (ATM) as well as pay for goods at retailers—an attractive option if your family is among the 13 percent of the U.S. population that doesn't have a checking account.

All told, in 2002, U.S. households used their 865 million debit, credit, and charge cards to pay for $1.7 trillion worth of goods and services. Around the world, 1.8 billion general-purpose payment cards were used to pay for $2.7 trillion worth of goods and services that year. (We adjust all dollar values in this book so they reflect purchasing power in 2002.)

Many U.S. wallets are bulging with other cards. You may have cards that allow you to pay at particular retailers—a Circuit City or Bloomingdale's card. While such store cards are numerous—there were 547 million in 2002—U.S. households only used them for $128 billion in purchases, or about one-thirteenth of what they put on the debit, credit, and charge cards that could be used at many merchants. You may also have a prepaid card—preloaded with money—that allows you to buy at a particular store such as Starbucks or to make long-distance phone calls (these types of cards are sometimes referred to as stored-value cards). In this book, we concentrate on general-purpose payment cards, which you can use at many different merchants.

You carry payment cards because you expect that many merchants will take one of your cards for payment. But they don't have to. In fact, unlike cash and checks, merchants *cannot* take your card for payment unless they have entered into an agreement with an agent of the same card logo that appears on your card. If you have an American Express card, you cannot use it unless the merchant has a contract with American Express. In 2002, out of the 5.3 million merchant locations that took MasterCard and Visa cards, about 2 million did not take American Express. And while "No Card Is More Accepted" than MasterCard—as its advertising says—you cannot use it, or Visa for that matter, at a Neiman Marcus store.

Merchants must pay a portion of each purchase made with a payment card to the firm that processes their card transactions. Yet most retailers have chosen to accept payment cards. And those who take one brand of card usually take many brands of cards. They don't have the bulky-wallet problem: although they may post many decals displaying the logos of the cards they accept, they can use the same equipment to handle many different kinds of cards and can often find a business that will process all of their card transactions for them. Merchants take cards because they know that customers have these cards and want to use them. Cards that few customers carry may not be worth the bother; the JCB card that is mainly carried by Japanese visitors to the United States, for instance, is commonly accepted in high-end stores in tourist destinations frequented by Japanese visitors, but has much less acceptance elsewhere.

That brings us to a fundamental feature of payment cards. Just as you cannot dance the tango without a partner, a payment card needs both consumers and merchants. This is what economists call a "two-sided platform market." Businesses in such markets need to get two distinct groups of consumers on board the platform. A frivolous example is the singles scene. Any business that involves getting men and women together has to get both groups of customers. A more serious example is operating systems for computers. Successful developers of operating systems, such as the Palm OS for handheld devices, go to great lengths to get both software application developers and users on board. Users want an operating system that supports lots of good applications, and software developers want to write applications for operating systems with lots of users.

And just as a nightclub with few women attracts few men (and vice versa), a card brand with few merchants attracts few cardholders (and vice versa). The strategies used to establish payment card systems, the economics of pricing payment cards, the business and operational problems faced by participants in the card business, and the business ecosystems that characterize this vast industry all turn on the two-sided nature of payment cards.

So does the evolution of payment cards since their birth in 1950. Early that year, Frank McNamara gave some cards to a few hundred people in Manhattan and talked some local restaurants into paying his company 7 percent of the meal tab billed to the Diners Club card. He got a small platform started. But the payment card industry did not experience a big bang. Rather, from these small beginnings, the industry has expanded slowly over time. Part of the story involves new card platforms coming into the business; Diners Club was followed by Carte Blanche, American Express, and BankAmericard within the decade. But more of the story is how these card platforms have nurtured the two sides of the market over time—with customers gradually attracting merchants gradually attracting customers. What might have looked like tidal waves at the time—Bank of America flooding its customers in California with cards or Sears offering most of its store cardholders a Discover Card—now appear as ripples in the ocean.

Much has happened in the last thirty years to make plastic ubiquitous. In 1970, a bit less than a generation after the industry's Manhattan birth, only 16 percent of households had payment cards, and we estimate that at most, 20 percent of retailers accepted them. With few households with cards and few places to use them, the average spending on plastic per household (across all households) was only a little more than $47 per month (about 1.5 percent of the average monthly household income). Today, most large retailers, supermarkets, and mail-order firms take plastic, along with a rapidly increasing number of fast-food restaurants, health-care providers and other businesses. And payment cards are the main currency for Internet transactions. Almost everything on Amazon.com and eBay is bought with digits taken from a payment card, either directly or through an intermediary such as PayPal that allows individuals to take credit cards. Most consumers make at least some purchases with a plastic card. And in 2002, the most recent year for which we have data, on average households charged $1,280 per month on payment cards (about 25 percent of their average monthly household income).

Indeed, payment cards have become a global common currency. For example, you can use your Visa credit or debit card in three hundred countries and territories at more than twenty-one million merchants. And many card systems in other countries have affiliations with

MasterCard or Visa so that travelers from those countries can use their credit or debit cards in the United States.

Still, more than fifty years after the payment card industry was born, 69 percent of payments made by U.S. households are made with cash or checks. Dee Hock's "guaranteed data" have a long way to go.

Although cash and checks may not be toppled for generations, if ever, payment cards have nonetheless wrought a revolution. Humankind has seen only four major innovations in the most routine aspect of economic life—how we transact with one another: the switch from barter to coin around 700 BCE; the introduction of checks by the Venetians in the twelfth century; the shift to paper money in the seventeenth century; and now the payment card. Let's be clear again, though—it is not the card, it is the digits, and as we will see, when it comes to the electronic transfer of funds, plastic cards are not the only game in town.

The industry behind this revolution, the subject of this book, is quite extraordinary. To see why, think about what has to happen for you to be able to buy a pair of shoes at the nearby mall using a payment card. You must have a card. Someone had to issue you that card, and in the course of doing so, may have worked with other companies that helped it determine whether you were a good prospect. It hired another company to manufacture your card, and it has probably lined up someone else to send you statements and collect your money.

To let you buy your shoes with plastic, the local store has to accept the card you have. That store has to have signed a contract that enables it to accept the card you present and ensures that it will be reimbursed for (most of) the price of your shoes. One business may sign the local store up and take care of everything, from installing the terminal equipment, to processing transactions, to settling up accounts. Alternatively, one business may sign the merchant up, and another may take care of the details after that. The business that installs equipment and processes the transactions works with other firms: manufacturers of card-processing equipment for sure, and perhaps other companies to assist in the processing and accounting work.

The card systems are the hubs in a vast interconnected network of businesses and consumers. After you present your card to a merchant, the clerk swipes the card through an electronic terminal near the cash register. Within seconds, the terminal connects to a computer miles away and verifies the willingness of the entity that issued your card to pay for your purchase. Over the course of a year, these computers process twenty-four billion transactions in the United States between the millions of merchants who take payment cards and the hundreds of millions of consumers who use payment cards. It is a tour de force.

This feat is all the more extraordinary because the computers have so many masters to please. Suppose you used your MasterCard credit card. MasterCard is an association of financial institutions—some issue cards, some service merchants, and some do both. The system has to transfer money to the merchant from the member that signed up the merchant. It has to transfer money from the member that issued the card to the member that signed up the merchant. The member that issued the card must obtain all the information necessary to bill the cardholder. And all along the way, the system works to collect and distribute various fees among the parties that have participated in each transaction.

How this complicated coordination takes place, and how the institutions developed to accomplish all this, is a story of how solutions to complex organizational and technological problems emerge and evolve in markets. And it is a story of how those solutions can deviate sharply from the look of competition in other industries, while nonetheless effectively delivering to consumers the benefits of intense competition.

Indeed, it is hard to find an industry that, on the surface, fits as poorly as this one does into the boxes that economists have developed for classifying industries. We have already seen one difference. This is a two-sided platform industry. Economists have shown that many of the usual rules of thumb do not apply in this case. Prices, benefits, and costs do not track each other as closely as they do in traditional industries. For instance, almost every card system loads the costs of conducting transactions on the merchant. The other distinguishing feature is the mixture of competition and collaboration among some members of the industry. MasterCard and Visa—two brands that account for 72 percent of all U.S. payment card transactions—are associations of financial institutions. Members *cooperate* in a few key areas that generate efficiencies for consumers and merchants—particularly in the design and operation of the vast computer networks that now enable transactions around the world to be completed in just a few seconds, as well as in advertising and some aspects of product development. Members *compete* along almost every other dimension—such as interest rates, fees, service, and innovative card offerings. This is called "co-opetition."

The payment card is inherently a two-sided industry. It is not necessarily a co-opetitive one. Over fifteen years after McNamara got restaurants and diners on board his platform, the payment card industry was dominated by large national firms: what we call the "go-it-alones." American Express was the leader, having surpassed Diners Club in the early 1960s. Both competed with Carte Blanche, which had been started by the Hiltons of the hotels. MasterCard was born in 1966 as a cooperative of banks that did not want to align with the existing systems. The Visa cooperative was born in 1970, after a franchise system established by Bank of America in 1966 collapsed. Co-opetition resulted: a vast landscape of competition surrounding tiny cooperative organizations. MasterCard's transaction volume per employee is more than twenty-nine times that of American Express.

Now ubiquitous and intimately part of our lives, payment cards have a fascinating past, present, and future—all determined, more so than in many industries, by the intersection of economics, business, law, technology, and public policy.

Ever wonder why your credit card bill comes from Delaware? You need look no further than the U.S. Supreme Court's 1978 *Marquette* decision, which allowed credit card issuers to get around state interest rate caps by issuing the cards in states without interest rate caps to consumers in states with interest rate caps. Delaware rolled out the welcome mat for credit card issuers, and jobs that New Yorkers might have filled went to Delawareans instead.

If you have spent time in France, you may be curious why most of the locals enter numbers into the terminal at the point of sale while you are asked to sign. It isn't a secret society. Most French have so-called smart cards that have a personal identification number (PIN) securely stored on a chip. The card device honors the card if the PIN that cardholders type in matches the PIN on the chip—no need to call the central computer to see if the card has been stolen. But it isn't that the French made a technological advance U.S. card companies couldn't make. Telephone connections are less expensive and more reliable in the United States than in France, so there was no business case for using smart card technology, which is more expensive than magnetic stripes, in the States. That may change as smart cards become cheaper and the technology becomes useful for services besides fraud control.

You might also consider how the card businesses make money. You pay little or nothing, at least not directly, for having a payment card that you can use to buy things. Your debit card comes with your checking account, and there are few additional charges for it. You may pay an annual fee for your charge card, but you get the benefit of the float on your purchases between the time you purchase and the time you pay; perhaps you also get other rewards, like airline miles. It is unlikely that you pay an annual fee for your credit card, and like charge cards, you get the benefit of the float and perhaps freebies from hotel discounts to free insurance. (Of course, if you have a credit card and decide to finance your purchases, you will pay finance charges. But transactions financed on payment cards account for only about 15 percent of the dollar volume of purchases.) This is a typical two-sided market—no different than Adobe giving away its reader software and charging companies for the production software, Microsoft charging developers little for its tools and making its money from computer purchasers, or your local television station showing you endless *Friends* reruns for free while making its money from advertisers.

And returning to Europe, the following is curious. Card associations— many affiliated with MasterCard and Visa—started in continental Europe shortly after they began in the United States. Yet different kinds of cards succeeded on each side of the Atlantic. Credit cards surged in the States; debit cards were available from the beginning, but they didn't take off. Debit cards grew rapidly in France, Germany, Portugal, Norway, and Sweden. Some convergence has taken place in the last decade, credit cards are still uncommon in Europe, but debit cards have blossomed in the States. Culture? Institutions? Technology? Historical accident? We touch on this puzzle, but we do not claim to solve it.

The Star

The star of our story is the plastic card you pulled out a few minutes ago. At least since the famous line in *The Graduate*, plastic has connoted all that is superficial and temporary in modern society. So it is a good idea to give our star an image makeover. It is really a peripheral device that gives you access to a vast global computer network. From the front, the card has some interesting features. Your account number is embossed at the bottom and identifies the card. Visa cards start with a "4," MasterCards with a "5," and Discover Cards with a "6." A "3" indicates a travel and entertainment (T&E) system, with a "37" for American Express, and a "38" for Diners Club and Carte Blanche. The remaining digits on the card identify additional details, such as the bank that issued your card and your account.

But it is the magnetic stripe (or magstripe) on the card's back that really makes it useful. That stripe holds most of the key information on your card account: your name, account number, expiration date, card type, and perhaps other details as well. That information gets sent from your merchant's terminal over telephone lines to a computer.

Magstripe is a quite efficient, but not terribly smart technology. Smart cards can be brighter. The French version mentioned earlier is not at the head of the class: it just holds the same information as the magnetic stripe in a more secure way—it is much more difficult to read the information off a smart card. But it is possible to download data and software onto the chip and create a card that does much more creative things. There are operating systems and applications for these cards just as for other chip-based devices. For now in the United States, smart cards are a technology—albeit a potentially powerful one—in search of an application that consumers want.

Star Performance

How does a payment card work in practice? The answer varies a bit according to the specific card. Let's focus on the most popular brand of card—Visa—and one issued by one of Visa's largest members—Bank of America. Figure 1.1 shows some of the important elements. Suppose you go to Best Buy to purchase a new MP3 player and you swipe your Visa card issued by Bank of America (the "issuer") through a card reader. The card reader takes data off the magnetic stripe on the back of the card. It combines this data with information about the merchant and the dollar value of the purchase to create an electronic message. It then dials the

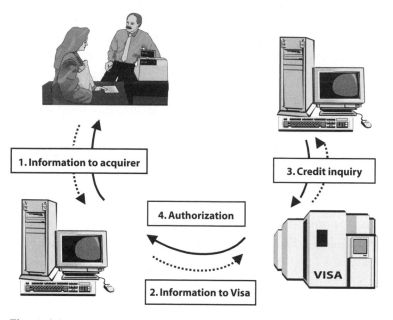

1. Information to acquirer

3. Credit inquiry

4. Authorization

2. Information to Visa

VISA

Figure 1.1
How do payment cards work?
Source: Visa U.S.A.

telephone number of a computer maintained by Best Buy's "acquirer" (the bank that handles its Visa transactions). Once connected, a message is sent to the acquirer's computer. This computer reads the message and figures out that you have used a Visa card. It dials up Visa's computer system (there are actually two that work in parallel just in case one of them goes down). After reading the message, Visa's computer knows to check with Bank of America's computer to see whether you have enough money on your credit line to cover the purchase. If you do, Bank of America's computer will send a message back to Visa's computer authorizing the transaction. Visa relays the message back to Best Buy's acquirer, which then sends a message back to the terminal at the store. The terminal prints out the receipt that you sign. Because the entire transaction was captured electronically, the main purpose of the receipt is to help resolve disputes when cards are stolen and signatures are forged. This authorization process usually takes just a few seconds.

Best Buy then automatically submits a request for payment to its acquirer, which in turn, sends it on to Visa's computer. The Visa computer passes on the request to Bank of America's computer, which posts the transaction to your account. Visa's computer consolidates this transaction with all the other Visa transactions and settles accounts among banks. For this purchase, Bank of America pays the acquirer, which then pays Best Buy. This process is typically completed within two to three days from the time you made your purchase. The Best Buy store receives about 98 percent of the amount charged for your MP3 player. The remaining 2 percent difference is called the "merchant discount," which is the fee paid to the acquirer for providing its services. The acquirer, in turn, pays about 1.7 percent of the purchase amount to the issuer, in this case Bank of America. That 1.7 percent "interchange fee" is set by Visa; MasterCard has a similar fee.

This process is the same whether you used a Visa credit or debit card until almost the end. With a credit card, the issuer compiles information on your charges over the course of the billing cycle (usually thirty days) and sends you a statement. The issuer expects full or partial payment typically within twenty-five days of the end of the billing cycle. With a debit card, the issuer simply deducts the charges from your checking account—generally within a day or two of the purchase. Your monthly checking account statement will then contain your debit card purchases as well as other account activity.

When you've used your debit card, you might have noticed that debit transactions can be authorized with a PIN or a signature. When you sign, you're making a signature debit transaction, which goes through either Visa or MasterCard, as just described. When you enter a PIN, you're making a PIN debit transaction, which goes through one of the EFT networks, such as STAR, NYCE, or Pulse. (EFT networks started out as ATM networks, later adding debit functionality for retail purchases.) Of course, you can enter a PIN only at a business that has installed a PIN pad, although some EFT systems have started to allow some insurance companies and other businesses to accept PIN debit transactions without requiring PIN authorization. Somewhat confusingly, at many businesses with PIN pads, you have to choose the credit rather than the debit button to make a signature debit transaction. (PIN debit and signature debit are also referred to in the industry as online and off-line debit, respectively. We don't use those terms since PIN and signature debit transactions are all processed electronically—or online, in common parlance.)

Banks that issue debit cards can enable their customers to use these cards with a signature (through agreements with MasterCard and Visa) and a PIN (through agreements with one or more EFT networks). Almost all debit cards can be used with a PIN, but only about 70 percent can be used with a signature. A Visa or MasterCard logo on the front tells you the card can be used for signature debit, while the EFT logos on the back tell you which EFT networks your card works on.

Some of the intricacies of the card transaction described above arose because issuers such as Bank of America are each a single node in a network of thousands of issuers and acquirers; they do not operate their own independent card system. If you had presented an American Express card or Discover Card, a few things would have happened differently. The merchant might have a direct line to American Express, especially if it is a larger merchant. In that case, the message created by swiping the card through the reader goes directly to American Express's computer for authorization, and the computer sends the response right back to the merchant. American Express takes on the role of both merchant acquirer and issuer here, thereby cutting two steps out of the message relay process described earlier. If the merchant does not have a direct line to American Express, the message goes to the merchant's processor, which then transmits the message to American Express, thereby cutting one step out of the process. Surprisingly, with the use of fast computers and reliable telecommunications networks, there is no perceptible difference between the speeds at which American Express, Discover, Visa, and MasterCard process transactions.

The Main Characters

American Express, Discover, MasterCard, and Visa are the major "brands" of signature-based payment cards—and together they account for 90 percent of all purchase volume on general-purpose payment cards. You can recognize them from their distinct logos. The four brands are also the major operators of payment card "systems." Each system consists of a distinct set of computers and rules for processing transactions, seeking verification, getting approval, transferring funds, and capturing billing information. The new kids on the block are the EFT networks.

These systems are the result of the merger and reorganization of banks' ATM-only networks. They account for the remaining 10 percent of purchases made with payment cards, but their share is growing. The largest of these new kids, the STAR system, itself accounts for 5 percent and is now slightly larger than Discover.

American Express is the oldest character here. It started in 1850 as an express company—sort of a cross between bicycle couriers and United Parcel Service. It introduced its first hit product, the travelers cheque, in 1891. Its first charge card, the American Express Green Card, was launched in 1958. In the late 1980s, it started a credit card, Optima. Initially a case study in poor product planning, Optima developed into a solid product by the mid-1990s. Its most recent hit, introduced in 1999, is the American Express Blue Card. This was the first significant U.S. smart card—the first general-purpose payment card with a computer chip on the card. Relying on the image of the chip, Blue was advertised as a "high-tech" card "custom designed for the 21st century consumer." In reality, however, Blue offered no tangible benefits unless used with a special chip reader, the card also had a traditional magnetic stripe on the back. Nevertheless, whether it was the card's high-tech imagery or attractive pricing, there were 2.2 million Blue Cards in the hands of U.S. consumers just over a year after its launch.

Discover is the teenager in this group. Sears, Roebuck and Co. introduced the Discover Card in 1985. This orange-on-black card became one of the greatest business success stories of the 1980s—helped by Sears's seventy-plus years of experience with a store card and its decision to offer the card to twenty-five million creditworthy Sears cardholders. By 1991, the Discover Card was accepted by more merchants than the American Express card. In 1993, Sears spun off its investment and credit arm into Dean Witter, Discover and Co., which later merged with Morgan Stanley, and the card continued to prosper. Though its growth slowed substantially after its initial success, Discover was still the fifth-largest issuer of credit cards in the United States in 2002. (Sears is no longer even in the store card business: it sold its card operations to Citigroup in 2003.)

Visa is the biggest of the players. Almost half of the general-purpose payment cards in the United States have the blue, white, and gold Visa logo on the lower right-hand corner, and almost all the merchants that take payment cards take Visa cards. Visa started in 1966 as the BankAmericard franchise system, although its origins date back to Bank of America's go-it-alone card program started in California in 1958.

MasterCard was started at the same time as Visa. Cards with the orange-and-red MasterCard balls are second only to Visa cards in abundance. In 1978, Visa overtook MasterCard with respect to the number of cards issued. MasterCard reversed its relative decline in 1992, after embracing novel card programs run by nonfinancial giants like AT&T. Then, in the late 1990s, MasterCard persuaded several banks—most notably Citigroup, which is the second-largest credit and charge card issuer in the United States—to shift their issuance toward MasterCard. As a result, MasterCard has made a big comeback in credit cards, nosing out Visa for the lead in terms of the number of cards and volume of outstanding balances in 2002, although it still trailed slightly in terms of the volume of credit card purchases. Beginning in the mid-1990s, however, Visa has built a big lead in signature debit cards.

STAR, by far the largest of the EFT networks, is a young character just coming onstage. It was started as an ATM system in 1984 and added debit capabilities two years later, although debit volume was unimportant until well into the 1990s. Through a wave of mergers and acquisitions in the late 1990s and early 2000s, a number of EFT systems including STAR, MAC, HONOR, and Cash Station became a single system operating under the STAR brand and owned by Concord EFS. Concord provides a range of processing services to merchants and financial institutions in addition to operating STAR. First Data Corporation (FDC), a "supporting player" discussed below that may be increasing in prominence, now owns STAR, following the merger between FDC and Concord in February 2004.

Other Members of the Cast

Although American Express, Discover, MasterCard, and Visa are the main characters in our story, the real action takes place in the constant competitive struggle for the consumer and the merchant. American Express and Discover are in the fray. MasterCard and Visa are too, but primarily through their members, who compete with each other as well as with American Express and Discover. And STAR is also in the mix, but its story is complicated and will thus be saved for later.

Let's look at a snapshot of the industry in 2002. Table 1.1 shows the top ten credit and charge card issuers, ranked by transaction volume in 2002. These issuers accounted for almost 80 percent of the total volume. Go-it-alones American Express and Discover were the first- and fifth-largest issuers respectively. The other eight issuers were members of the co-opetitives. Consider, for example, Citigroup, MBNA, and Bank of America.

Citigroup was the second-largest issuer with 14 percent and the largest of the co-opetitive issuers. In 2002, it had forty-five million MasterCards and thirty million Visa credit cards in circulation in the United States. It shifted allegiance toward MasterCard from Visa in 1998. (In addition to being a MasterCard and Visa issuer, Citigroup also owns two other card systems: Diners Club and Carte Blanche. As figure 1.2 shows, in 2002, relatively few Diners Club cards were issued or used in the United States; Carte Blanche was too small to plot.) Citibank, part of Citigroup, was the third-largest commercial bank in the United States with assets of

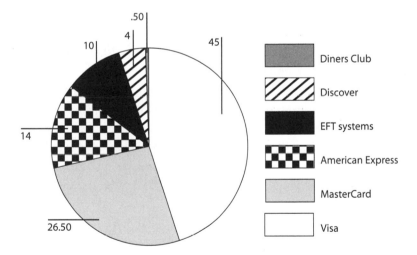

Figure 1.2
System share of U.S. general-purpose card purchase volume, 2002 (%)
Source: The Nilson Report (various 2003 issues).

Table 1.1
Top ten credit and charge card issuers, ranked by gross volume, 2002

Issuer	Volume ($ billions)	Share of industry volume (%)
1 American Express	234	16
2 Citigroup	204	14
3 Bank One	155	11
4 MBNA America	131	9
5 Discover	94	7
6 J. P. Morgan Chase	87	6
7 Bank of America	62	4
8 Capital One Financial	61	4
9 U.S. Bancorp	45	3
10 Household	37	3
Total (top ten)	*1,110*	*78*
Total (all issuers)	*1,432*	*100*

Note: Numbers may not add up to totals due to rounding.
Source: The Nilson Report (various 2003 issues).

more than $515 billion in early 2003. Like most MasterCard and Visa members, it provides checking account services to consumers along with many other depository and lending services. Payment cards accounted for about 20 percent of Citigroup's overall profits in 2002—almost as much as its retail banking operations.

MBNA was fourth-largest issuer, with 9 percent of credit and charge card volume. It was the second-largest issuer of MasterCards (twenty-seven million) and the fourth-largest issuer of Visa cards (twenty-five million). MBNA is an example of a "monoline" bank, one that is in business almost exclusively to issue payment cards. Started in 1981, it had $79 billion of outstanding credit card balances, but only $12 billion of ordinary consumer loans at the end of 2002. Many monolines have grown significantly in recent years. For instance, MBNA's share of credit and charge card volume increased from 4.7 percent in 1995 to 9.2 percent in 2002.

Bank of America, one of the credit card pioneers and currently the seventh-largest credit and charge card issuer, is now the leading debit card issuer in the United States. It has twenty-one million debit cards, with seventeen million of those offering signature debit functionality on the Visa system. Its prominence is partly a function of being the second-largest commercial bank in the nation. But it is also a result of Bank of America's decision in 1994 to make a big push in debit generally and its decision to issue debit cards to 90 percent of its checking account customers, rather than the 70 percent that is more typical in the industry. Bank of America also offers its customers the choice of debit cards with frequent flyer miles from U.S. Airways, Alaska Airlines, or AmericaWest.

Most of the 20 percent of credit and charge card volume not accounted for by the issuers listed in table 1.1 comes from banks that have local or regional card programs. For example, Virginia Credit Union in Indiana had the hundredth-largest credit and charge card program in 2002. But its cardholders had only $140.8 million in gross credit card volume, amounting to one-hundredth of 1 percent of the total industry credit and charge card volume. The large issuers compete with these smaller ones to get into your wallet and to be used by you to pay.

The go-it-alones act as their own issuers. They control the acquiring process, but they also rely on third-party firms to help. The co-opetitives have divorced issuing from acquiring: these are two separate business activities that are coordinated only through their common connection to the hubs. They have also allowed third parties—firms that aren't members of the co-opetitives—to do much of the work related to signing up merchants and processing their transactions. Many banks that sign up merchants and maintain relationships with them use third parties to do most of the back-office work. Table 1.2 shows the top ten merchant acquirers based on transaction volume in 2002. These acquirers accounted for 78 percent of the volume in 2002. Six of these acquirers are banks that belong to the co-opetitives including Chase, the largest acquirer. Four of these acquirers are third parties that have an affiliation with a co-opetitive member but essentially do all of the work. Two of the top ten acquirers have joint ventures with FDC. American Express does a substantial portion of its own acquiring through its Centurion Bank subsidiary, which ranks as the fifth-largest acquirer. (American Express is formally the acquirer on all of its transactions, but in some cases relies on third-party processors to do a large portion of the work.)

Table 1.2
Top ten general-purpose card acquirers, ranked by charge volume, 2002

Acquirer	Volume ($ billions)	Share of industry volume (%)
1 Chase Merchant Services	224	13
2 NPC	176	10
3 Paymentech	149	9
4 Concord EFS	146	9
5 Centurion Bank (American Express)[1]	138	8
6 First Data	130	8
7 Fifth Third Bank	110	6
8 Nova Information Systems	110	6
9 BA Merchant Services	71	4
10 Global Payments	68	4
Total (top ten)	*1,321*	*78*
Total (all acquirers)[2]	*1,692*	*100*

Notes: Numbers may not add up to totals due to rounding.
1. Acquired volume for Centurion Bank is an estimate.
2. Comprised of total industry bankcard volume (estimated by eighty-eight acquirers), total industry PIN debit volume, and total purchase volume for American Express, Diners Club, and Discover.
Source: The Nilson Report (various 2003 issues).

Behind the Stage

The payment card systems and co-opetitive issuers have found that there are important roles that others perform better. Signing up merchants; manufacturing, selling, and servicing card-reading terminals for merchants; switching transactions from the terminals to the correct card system; and doing much of the processing that results in the cardholder's receiving a bill are "backroom" roles that are now filled to varying degrees by third parties. These third parties include independent sales organizations (ISOs) that acquirers—including the go-it-alones on occasion—use to sign up merchants. (Even though many merchants already take cards, more than twenty-four thousand new merchants come into existence every year.) The third parties also include cardholder processors that do much of the backroom work for issuers, accounting for the processing on over 70 percent of cardholder accounts. Many of the cardholder processors are the same firms that process for merchants, as discussed above.

FDC has emerged as a significant player in the card business by piecing together many parts of the back room through acquisitions and by expanding in each of the major segments. It is the largest cardholder processor, sending out monthly statements to cardholders and collecting money from them; it processes 33 percent of all U.S. cardholder accounts. In addition to acting as a de facto acquirer for some merchants, as we just discussed, it is also the largest merchant processor—processing at least 32 percent of all merchant transaction volume. Many of these transactions result from the joint ventures that it has with banks—twenty-four as of 2003. And, as we mentioned above, it also owns STAR, by far the largest EFT system.

The Foreign Cast

Although the major characters described above play on a global stage, there are noteworthy regional differences.

The systems themselves differ outside the United States. MasterCard (which merged with Europay, a European bankcard association, in 2002) operates as a centralized global entity. Visa, on the other hand, has relatively autonomous regional organizations, each with its own board of directors. Visa U.S.A., Visa Europe, and other regional organizations belong to Visa International. Visa International functions for the benefit of its members, much as Visa U.S.A. does in the United States. American Express has a somewhat different business model outside the United States: in addition to issuing some cards on its own, it has franchised its card or entered into alliances with local banks that also issue its cards. Events discussed below may bring this model to the States. Discover has not gotten a foothold overseas, while Diners Club, which operates a small charge card program in the United States, has some successful national franchises overseas.

Even though the JCB card originated in Japan, consumers there use mainly cash and checks. Payment cards are used for less than 10 percent of consumer spending in Japan. This is probably in part because

Japanese credit cards are more cumbersome to use. Japanese cardholders have to tell the clerk whether they want their payment debited directly from their checking account or they want to finance the purchase. Not surprisingly, few individuals want to disclose publicly that they don't have the cash on hand to pay for something. Moreover, any credit that is extended has to be paid back on a prearranged schedule—for example, perhaps 10 percent of the amount each month.

Some other industrialized countries have their own bankcard associations such as Cartes Bancaires in France and Bankcard in Australia. Bank members also have affiliations with MasterCard or Visa so that their international cards are accepted by MasterCard or Visa merchants outside their countries, and so travelers can use their MasterCard or Visa cards within those countries; some systems also offer domestic versions that can only be used within the home country.

Additionally, there are credit card brands known elsewhere around the world that remain almost entirely invisible in the United States. JCB International, for example, is the second-largest card in Japan (after Visa) and the fourth-largest international card brand, with 10.4 million merchant locations, mostly in the Far East, and $35 billion in purchase volume in 2002. In the United States, however, only about 500,000 merchants currently accept the JCB card, while Visa and MasterCard are accepted at approximately five million outlets. (This may change, though, as JCB has recently reached an agreement to cooperate with American Express on merchant acceptance globally.)

The emerging economies are interesting as well. China and India, each with more than a billion people, are potentially huge but currently undeveloped card markets. China is ahead of India in this regard, with about 270 million cards issued. The vast majority of these are debit cards issued by four large domestic state-owned banks. The card acceptance technology is relatively immature—no single card reader can handle both the cards from the domestic banks as well as Visa and MasterCard cards. India has a minuscule six million payment cards issued. The lack of an existing infrastructure in countries such as China and India does offer one potential advantage. As industry commentators have noted, these nations can "leapfrog" more developed countries in their choice of technology. Unencumbered by past investments in card terminals and cards, card systems in both China and India are exploring the possibility of moving rapidly to smart cards rather than using magnetic stripe technology.

The Thirteen Acts

The star, main characters, and other actors will make repeated appearances in the following chapters. Here is a brief synopsis of the action.

"From Seashells to Electrons" (chapter 2) discusses payment cards as the fourth in a sequence of major innovations in how people pay for things, following the development of metallic coins in ancient times, the creation of checks in the Middle Ages, and the spread of paper money during modern times. Payment cards have resulted in the increasing use of digitally represented and electronically transferred money.

Although technological change in computers and reductions in communications costs made this revolution inevitable, it started in the United States at a time when the country had a highly fragmented banking system and a populace heavily dependent on paper checks. These factors have shaped the evolution of the payment card industry in the United States and influenced its evolution elsewhere.

"More Than Money" (chapter 3) traces how a few hundred cards for charging restaurant meals in New York spawned millions of cards for paying for and financing the purchase of goods and services around the world. The combination of payment and financing services on credit cards, along with other key innovations, resulted in the rapid growth in the number of merchants who took the cards and the number of consumers who used them.

Indeed, as we show in "From Gourmets to the Masses" (chapter 4), payment cards have spread through society and have benefited consumers from almost all walks of life. Only the wealthy had payment cards in the early 1950s; only the poor lack payment cards today. With the spread of payment cards, people can better coordinate their income and expense, smooth income and consumption over their lifetime, and even more easily start and finance a small business. (Of course, just as some people eat and drink too much at restaurants or drive too fast, some people take on more debt than they should.)

Merchants have benefited as well. Payment cards make buying easier for their consumers. Store owners and customers like payment cards because they are fast and because customers want to be able to use them. "From Sardi's to Saks.com" (chapter 5) looks at the growth of payment cards from the merchant side. It explains why merchants take cards, and it documents the growth and spread of merchant acceptance of payment cards over time.

"It Takes Two to Tango" (chapter 6) and "Co-opetition and the Payment Card Ecosystem" (chapter 7) are our economist's version of an intermission. Instead of champagne, we serve up some of the interesting economic characteristics of payment cards. Chief among these is the chicken-and-egg problem. No consumer wants a payment card if merchants won't accept it. No merchant wants to take payment cards if consumers do not carry them. This problem and the fact that the payment card industry has to cater constantly to merchants and consumers have wide-ranging economic implications. Chapter 6 explains that the payment card industry is one of many industries that face this two-sided problem and describes the economics of multisided platform industries. Chapter 7 examines the unique mixture of cooperation and competition that has characterized this industry since the mid-1960s. Through co-opetition, a minuscule amount of cooperation enables a massive amount of competition. We discuss why Visa and MasterCard, whose members compete with each other, have fared well in competition with American Express and Discover, which are unified firms with, in principle, much simpler decision-making processes.

The blood, guts, and gore come next, with three chapters that focus on competitive strife in various facets of the payment card industry. "System Wars" (chapter 8) explains how the card systems have competed with each other in two grand wars. American Express's war with MasterCard and Visa looked as though it was going to end in defeat for American Express in the late 1980s. But American Express fought its way back in the 1990s. The other war, between MasterCard and Visa, is less public because these systems have the same members, but it is no less serious than that with American Express. Visa had American Express and MasterCard on the ropes in the late 1980s, and the war between the two commonly owned associations continues in the early 2000s. The

1990s also saw the battle over debit between the associations and the EFT systems.

"Issuer Brawls" (chapter 9) goes into the trenches in which the individual issuers of cards fight for consumers. It documents the intense competition among issuers, and shows how it has benefited consumers through lower prices and higher quality. "Backroom Battles" (chapter 10) describes the nearly invisible, but extremely important struggles in the industry's back room. As we've discussed, the co-opetitives spun off various pieces of the payment card system over time. Third parties have put some of those pieces back together, added some new pieces, and created large, capable enterprises that now pose serious competitive threats to the associations and their members.

As with most U.S. industries, competition in the payment card industry takes place not just in the marketplace but in the courtroom as well, usually in the guise of antitrust litigation. "The Antitrust Wars" (chapter 11) describes two major wars that have influenced the shape and evolution of this industry. A major series of battles have been fought over how merchants and cardholders share the costs of payment cards. The $2.2 to $2.6 billion settlement between MasterCard and Visa on the one hand and a set of major retailers led by Wal-Mart on the other was at its heart about who pays how much. (The actual settlement was for approximately $3 billion paid over ten years; we have discounted back to 2002 dollars.) Another series of battles was over whether the go-it-alones could become members of the associations (the United States Court of Appeals for the Tenth Circuit agreed that the associations could say no) and whether they could enter into contracts with members to issue go-it-alone cards (the United States Court of Appeals for the Second Circuit said the associations could *not* say no).

"On the Brink" (chapter 12) looks to the future. It considers some of the reasons why the payment card industry may be at an inflection point—a time of rapid change that marks a sharp break from the past. Technological advances such as smart cards and fingerprint readers will greatly facilitate buying and selling over the Internet and mobile phones, and have set up forces that could change how payment cards are used (cards less, digits more). Dramatic changes—some of which have come from recent antitrust lawsuits—could also reshape the industry: the emergence of FDC, the consolidation of the EFT networks and their evolution into go-it-alone systems, and a court decision that allows member banks to terminate the loyalty contracts they had signed with the associations in order to enter into deals with the go-it-alones while continuing to belong to the associations.

"And They Don't Take Cash" (chapter 13) offers some concluding observations and conjectures about what is to come in the ongoing revolution in paying and borrowing.

Increasingly, financial transactions are taking place over electronic networks in which consumers and merchants are represented by series of numbers. Money is just an electronic picture, kept on some computer media, of what you owe and what you have. How long plastic will remain the physical form for recording and transmitting that series of numbers is both unknown and completely beside the point. The true revolution, the one that is sure to be even more important in the future than it is today, was the development of computer networks for exchanging electronic money.

2

From Seashells to Electrons

The use of coin, which has been handed down to us from remote antiquity, has powerfully aided the progress of commercial organization, as the art of making glass helped many discoveries in astronomy and physics; but commercial organization is not essentially bound to the use of the monetary metals. All means are good which tend to facilitate exchange, to fix value in exchange; and there is reason to believe in the further development of this organization the monetary metals will play a part of gradually diminishing importance.

—Antoine-Augustin Cournot, *Researches into the Mathematical Principles of the Theory of Wealth* (1838)

The manner in which people pay each other has seen few revolutions as fundamental as the spread of electronic money. E-money has altered *how* we pay for things: most of us now use plastic cards and their digits for many of our daily purchases. And it has altered *when* we pay for things: most of us defer some payments until our monthly charge or credit bills arrive, and many of us finance some purchases over time. History teaches us how significant both of these transformations have been.

The Evolution of Money

Perhaps the only more fundamental development in the history of money is the birth of money itself. Long before credit cards and checks, people found ways to pay for things they wanted.

Cash, Check, or an Ox?

For many millennia, people bartered—twenty of my arrows for two of your bushels of wheat; six of your vases for two of my loincloths. As civilization developed, people discovered the convenience of a unit of account, launching the first major transformation in the development of money as a means of exchange and a store of value. Over the next centuries, and today, money is still being transformed, but always with a focus on improving its convenience and usability as a unit of account, a means of exchange, and a store of value. *The Iliad* and *The Odyssey*, which appear to reflect customs around 850–800 BCE, refer to exchanges measured in oxen. A large tripod (an object with three legs serving as an altar or a sacrificial basin in ancient and classical times) was worth twelve oxen and a skillful female slave four. That didn't mean you had to pay twelve oxen for the large tripod; you could pay three skillful women or perhaps gold or silver worth twelve oxen.

An ox wasn't money because, although a fine unit of account, it wasn't a great means of exchange or store of value. Around two centuries later, the Lydians, building on a millennia-old tradition of using precious metal for exchanges, stamped out coins of fixed weights. Convenient to exchange, easily stored, and readily counted, these were the first money. It took industrialized societies another 2,500 years to accept that money was valuable even if not made of precious metal as long as people accepted it for exchange and used the same unit of account. Trust replaced metal.

Today, people exchange units of account—such as the dollar or the euro—which they convert into goods and services. Cash, checks, electronic transfers of funds among accounts, and payment card systems are ways of exchanging these units. Each is a medium for facilitating the exchange of value among buyers and sellers. And each is a variety of money.

Money, unlike air, is not a free good for society. It requires resources: producing physical money, processing checks, or keeping the books for electronic money. One way or another, people have always paid for the money they use. That is obvious for private payment systems such as checks and cards. It is less obvious, but nonetheless true, for government payment systems based on coin or paper—for instance, mints are usually impressive buildings with large staffs, and the "inflation tax" is one of the oldest levies. (The inflation tax is imposed when the government prints more money to buy things, the price level increases as a consequence, and the real value of money held by consumers and businesses therefore declines.)

History shows what it takes to have a successful medium of exchange. A large number of buyers and sellers must agree to use the same medium. To become a standard, the medium must be an efficient form of exchange—seashells worked better than oxen. Reliability is key as well—there may be episodes where, as Sir Thomas Gresham described, bad money drives good money out of circulation and into people's rainy-day stashes, but in the long run only reliable media of exchange survive. (Gresham, an adviser to Elizabeth I, was an early observer of this phenomenon, now known as Gresham's Law.)

Lydia, Florence, Boston, and Manhattan

Four major innovations have marked the history of money: (1) the birth of money in the form of metallic coins, (2) the creation of checks that promised payment in money, (3) the creation of paper money, and (4) the emergence of electronic money through payment cards and other methods.

According to Herodotus, perhaps not the most reliable of historians, the Lydians "are the first people on record who coined gold and silver into money, and traded in retail." For at least a millennium before the Lydians struck the proverbial first coin in the latter half of the seventh century BCE, people had exchanged precious metals. But the Lydian coins made it easier to quote a price that everyone could relate to the costs of other goods—they provided a unit of account. They also facilitated transactions among buyers and sellers—they provided a means of exchange. And buyers and sellers alike could hold coins as part of their assets—coins provided a liquid store of value. This first money spread east into the Persian Empire and west to Italy. (Other civilizations from India to China can lay claim to similar innovations; here we focus on the West.)

Governments became the main sponsors of currencies. While this served a noble purpose by making money a standard, it also generated profit: the difference between the value of a coin in exchange and the value of its metallic content is known as seigniorage. Many Greek cities debased the alloys in their coins to earn more profit. Athens, though, was known for the integrity of its money. For four centuries after Solon took office in 594 BCE, the silver content of the drachma remained roughly constant. Athenian coins became widely used in trade not only in Greece but also in a good portion of Asia and Europe, and this remained the case even after Greece was absorbed into the Roman Empire.

It took about two thousand years to have another event of such lasting importance as to merit being called a revolution: the development of checks. Among westerners, the Italians appear to get the credit for this one. The original invention was the "bill of exchange," developed in northern Italy around the twelfth century. The bill was a piece of paper issued by a bank that promised the recipient money—at that time, metal coins—from the bank. With this bill, a trader avoided having to carry heavy coins on a long-distance shopping expedition and risk their theft. Bills of exchange proved handy during the Crusades. They were the precursors of paper money—they were valuable only because the possessors of the bills trusted that they would get their funds.

Bills of exchange were also the basis for an innovation in the provision of bank credit. For example, say that a Florentine trader wanted to buy wool in London, to then sell to a weaver in Venice. The cash-strapped trader would go to a bank, which would give the trader a loan to buy the wool. But rather than giving the trader coins from its vault, the bank would provide a bill of exchange. The bill would then go to the trader's London supplier, who in turn collected from a branch or agent in London (possibly a certain number of days after the purchase, depending on the type of bill). By this time, the trader had returned from Venice and repaid the loan. The bank got a fee for the loan even though none of its coins went anywhere (although periodically the bank would have to settle up its transactions with its London branch). Bills of exchange and their descendants, checks, enabled banks to loan out more money than they had in their vaults. Timing was everything here, and it still is. If too many people cash their checks and withdraw their money at the same time, a bank quickly collapses.

Credit for another crucial revolution, paper money, goes to the Commonwealth of Massachusetts. In 1690, the colonial government needed to figure out how to pay for an unsuccessful attempt to capture the

French fortress in Quebec City. The commonwealth issued pieces of paper that promised redemption, later, in gold or silver coins. These pieces of paper circulated side by side with gold and silver coins, and were treated as if they were worth the gold or silver they promised. Issuing paper money and postponing its redemption became a regular way for the colonial government to pay for things. (Prices of goods, including gold and silver, rose so that both the purchasing power and the redemption rates of the notes collapsed—an early example of the inflation tax.) Other colonies caught on. So did the rest of the British Empire and later the world. As with Athenian coins, successful paper currencies have been based on the trust that the issuer will not debase their value.

Far lighter and easier to transport than gold or silver coins, paper money provided a convenient means of exchange and, although the ultimate unit was still gold or silver, a good unit of account. Gradually, over the next several centuries, paper money, usually but not always backed by precious metal, became a popular medium of exchange. Most industrialized economies relied on paper money by the beginning of the twentieth century.

At that time, the central banks of most industrialized countries guaranteed that people could convert their paper money into gold or silver. Of course, as long as people believed they could exchange their paper money for goods and services, and that their paper money would hold its value in terms of goods and services, they had little incentive to trade it in for metal. And by the last quarter of the twentieth century, all industrialized countries had effectively abandoned the pretense that their currency was tied to gold, silver, or anything else of intrinsic value. The successful introduction of the euro in early 2002 reinforced the point that "faith" is enough. You cannot convert the euro to gold or silver, and you have to trust a still loosely connected group of often bickering countries to maintain its value. Nevertheless, having a standard currency in Europe has reduced transactions costs and helped integrate European markets.

Between the time when paper money spread and the time when its knot with precious metals was definitely cut, there was another key innovation, the consequences of which are the focus of this book. In 1950, McNamara's charge card for restaurants in Manhattan was originally based on paper: the card was cardboard, and its use resulted in a paper trail from the merchant to Diners Club to the cardholder. Not for long, though; the computer revolution transformed cards into an electronic medium of exchange.

Today, money consists of a unit of account that is exchanged through several different payment systems. None of these systems is free. Each requires that society—through the government or private parties—spend resources to operate and maintain it. And each provides benefits to society by reducing the costs of exchanging value among buyers and sellers.

There isn't enough evidence to say that one of these systems is better than another, and that society should promote one over another. Some observers leap to conclusions that one system is superior without considering all of the costs or the benefits. Cash is sometimes said to be the best because it does not require card or check fees. Yet many of the costs of cash are hidden in the government's budget. And some of the advantages of checks or cards over cash are easily ignored. Buyers don't want to carry around large wads of cash, for instance, and sellers worry about security. Likewise, electronic exchange—via cards or other transfers—is sometimes said to be the cheapest. It may be in the long run. But past investments in cash and checks, whether wise or foolish in retrospect, may make those seemingly antiquated media appear efficient at the moment.

From the standpoint of individual buyers and sellers, each of these media has costs and benefits. The fact that most buyers and sellers use all of the available media suggests that different ones have advantages in particular circumstances. Coins don't work well with eBay, nor checks with vending machines. More important, the success of any particular medium depends on its value to both buyers *and* sellers. Buyers can't pay cash if sellers won't take it. Sellers can't insist on checks if people don't want to carry them. Madonna's American Express Black Card may be exclusive, but it won't get her a ham sandwich at Joe's Diner. Exchange media are multisided platforms: to be viable, they must get all sides on board. For that to happen, a platform has to make sure that each side gets benefits that exceed the costs, with enough left over to cover the cost of running the system.

Cash remains a major payment platform almost three thousand years after the Lydians started stamping coins. Visa staff estimated that in 2000, cash payments accounted for 19 percent of the value of consumer expenditures that involved payment (thus excluding items such as the "rent" that you pay yourself for living in your own home) in the United States, and significantly higher worldwide. Cash is hard to beat for its convenience in countries that aren't extensively wired. But even in those that are, buyers and sellers find cash attractive for many transactions. Checks have fallen out of favor in many countries, but remain popular in others—notably the United States.

Fifty years after its introduction, plastic accounts for 27 percent of the value of consumer expenditures in the United States, 22 percent in Europe, and 20 percent worldwide. (Another source puts the plastic share in the United States at 31 percent. Both these plastic shares include some cards, such as store cards, that do not fit in the general-purpose payment card category that is the focus of this book.) Like previous important monetary innovations, the electronic medium of exchange has spread slowly but surely—even in the United States, the country that gave birth to plastic cards and, with relatively heavy computer use as well as inexpensive and reliable telecommunications services, one of the environments most conducive to the spread of electronic money.

In the Land of the Dollar

Cash and checks account for the majority of all payments in the United States. One source estimates that in the year 2000, about 69 percent of consumer expenditures were paid for with cash and check, while another source puts it at 65 percent. Among industrialized countries, the United States is unusual not for its continued use of paper money but for the widespread use of checks.

To tell the story of cash and checks in the United States—and ultimately the story of payment cards—we must first explain why, until quite recently, this country has been populated by a large number of small banks.

America, Land of the Small Local Bank   The evolution of the banking system in the United States guided the evolution of the electronic payment card industry. Colonial America was primarily agricultural. Particularly away from the Atlantic coast, long-distance communications and trade were difficult and risky. Understandably, small business and property owners required the services of conveniently located banks. The local banks that developed tended to be small, just like the towns they served. Larger companies involved in European import and export trade often dealt with the big merchant banks in Great Britain and continental Europe; they had little need for such institutions in the British colonies. (We use the term "banks" in this book to refer to commercial banks, savings banks, savings and loan associations, and credit unions.)

Federal and state legislators prevented banks from operating in multiple states—and sometimes limited branching within a single state—for much of the first two centuries of the United States. There were brief spasms of exceptions toward the end of this period. In the early 1950s, banks evaded interstate banking restrictions for a while by forming holding companies that controlled several banks that each operated within a single state. Citicorp was thereby able to establish a national network of banks. Congress prohibited holding companies in 1956 unless states specifically allowed them to operate, although it allowed the few nationwide banks that had been established previously to continue to operate.

In 1966, a watershed year for the payment card industry, there were 13,821 commercial banks in the United States—70 per million people— and the 10 largest held 24 percent of all assets held by commercial banks. (Data going back to 1966 on savings institutions and credit unions are not available.) As we will see in the next chapter, the fragmented local banking industry of the 1960s shaped the evolution of the payment card industry in the United States and other countries.

Barriers to geographic expansion started falling in 1978 when Maine began permitting out-of-state bank holding companies. Most states followed Maine's lead over the next fifteen years, and by 1992, only Hawaii prevented out-of-state bank holding companies from operating. Consol-

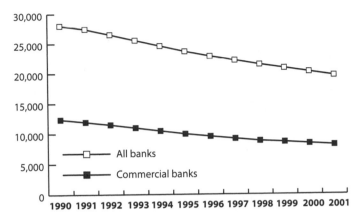

Figure 2.1
Number of banks in the United States, 1990–2001
Note: All banks include commercial banks, savings institutions, and credit unions.
Sources: Federal Deposit Insurance Corporation, *Historical Statistics on Banking;* and Credit Union Administration, *Annual Report* (various years).

idations have taken place as banks have merged with one another. Based on total assets held by commercial banks, the share of the ten-largest banks in the United States increased from 21 percent in 1990 to 40 percent in 2001. And as shown in figure 2.1, the number of banks in the United States fell significantly between 1990 and 2001. Nevertheless, even with these consolidations, in 2001 there were approximately twenty-eight commercial banks for every million people in the United States.

We can compare the United States with other countries in terms of all banks, including savings institutions and credit unions as well as commercial banks. In 2001, the United States had forty savings institutions and credit unions for every million people. (Our discussion of changes in U.S. banking over time relies on data covering only commercial banks because data on savings institutions and credit unions are not available before 1985.) The United States thus had a total of sixty-nine banks for every million people in 2001. As shown in figure 2.2, the United States has the highest number of banks per capita among the seven leading industrialized countries.

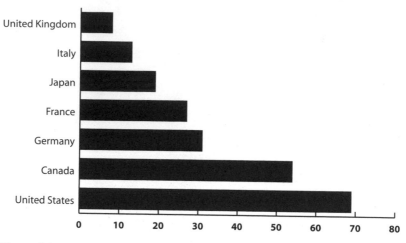

Figure 2.2
Banks per million people in the seven leading industrialized countries, 2001
Note: Data are reported for the G7 member countries.
Sources: Bank for International Settlements, *Statistics on Payment and Settlement Systems in Selected Countries* (April 2003); Federal Deposit Insurance Corporation; National Credit Union Administration; Insurance Information Institute; and U.S. Bureau of the Census, *Statistical Abstract of the United States: 2002.*

From Wampum to the Greenback   The widespread use of banks in the United States can be traced back to the earliest days of the country's history. Indeed, the history of cash, checks, and plastic in the United States is intertwined with the emergence of the banking system in colonial America. The first-known money on the North American continent was the "wampum" used by Native Americans. Wampum consisted of black and white seashells strung together like necklaces and was redeemed for things like beaver pelts. As colonial settlement progressed, the beavers scurried away, so the story goes, and wampum became hard to redeem. Shells were on the way out as the seventeenth century ended, and they ceased to be legal tender in the New England states in 1661. Various commodities were used as media of exchange including grain, rice, cattle, whiskey, and brandy. Tobacco was one of the most important and durable media. It lasted as legal tender in Virginia for 200 years and in Maryland for 150, until the U.S. Constitution stopped the states from having their own currencies. Massachusetts used paper money at times, as we noted above, as did some of the other colonies—all redeemable, at various rates depending on the time and the place, for silver or gold coins.

The Constitution gave Congress the power to coin money and regulate its value. And Congress followed the recommendation of Alexander Hamilton and passed the Mint Act in April 1792. The act identified the dollar as the basic monetary unit of the United States and defined the currency system on a decimal basis (cents, nickels, dimes, and quarters). The act also placed the United States on a bimetallic standard, with fifteen ounces of silver equivalent to one ounce of gold.

Paper money was the subject of considerable controversy and chaos until the Civil War. Several attempts at creating national banks fell afoul of politicians, and no national paper money took root. Many state-chartered banks issued notes that circulated like money, but there was no national standard. According to one account, "Thousands of notes were being printed and issued by hundreds of state banks. It was hard to know anymore what a dollar ought to look like, and the farther a dollar traveled from the bank that had issued it, the more gingerly it was treated by people who could not be expected to recognize the note or even the bank, let alone assess its reputation." One source estimates that by 1860, more than 1,500 state banks existed and about 10,000 different kinds of paper money circulated.

The Civil War brought about important changes in the U.S. monetary system. For one, the convertibility of paper money into specie (that is, gold or silver) was suspended in the early 1860s. Second, the National Banking Act passed by Congress in 1863 provided for the creation of nationally chartered banks and helped put the state banks out of the currency business. The national banks were authorized to issue notes, the so-called national bank notes, backed by government bonds. Third, the federal government issued "greenbacks" (or U.S. notes) to help finance the Civil War. By 1867 national bank notes and greenbacks were the two main components of the U.S. monetary stock.

In 1879 the United States resumed the convertibility of paper money into gold. The country went back and forth on the gold standard, and finally abandoned it during the Great Depression of the 1930s, although a modified gold standard (the so-called gold-dollar standard) survived until 1971 when President Richard Nixon famously "closed the gold window."

The monetary system that prevailed in the United States during the national banking era (that is, between the Civil War and World War I) was successful in terms of creating a uniform currency, but it was also unstable. Banking panics occurred in 1873, 1884, 1890, 1893, and 1907. Although since the late nineteenth century there has been a debate as to what caused the panics, the interpretation prevailing before the creation of the Federal Reserve suggested that none of the various forms of currency in circulation could adjust rapidly enough to temporary shocks in the demand for money, like those that occurred at harvest time. In this view, the underlying problem was the absence of a central bank, an institution that would provide funds at times when the demand for currency was unusually high.

The Federal Reserve System, created by Congress in 1913, was set up to address precisely this issue. Congress created a network of twelve regional Reserve Banks supervised by a Board of Governors located in Washington, D.C. All nationally chartered commercial banks had to become members of the Federal Reserve System ("member banks"), while state-chartered banks could decide whether or not to join. The Fed, as it is now called, assumed responsibility for regulating the overall money supply. In addition, the Fed and the U.S. Treasury maintain the currency system together. The Treasury makes the paper and coins, and the Fed allows banks to deposit used currency with them and get new currency at par. By 2002, the cost of supplying currency was about $582 million a year (in 2002 dollars), most of it accounted for by the cost of verifying and sorting deposits of used currency as well as the expense of replacing unfit bills with new ones. That's a small sum relative to the amount of currency and is about half what the Pentagon pays for a B-2 stealth bomber. The Fed, as we will see, also took charge of checks.

A Land Awash in Checks Today, most Americans deposit their paychecks at a local bank where they maintain a "demand depository account"—commonly called a checking account. The development of the modern checking system provides a preview of the later development of the payment card industry.

In 2001, 87 percent of all Americans had at least one checking account into which they could make deposits and on which they could write checks, according to the Fed's *Survey of Consumer Finances.* And although innovations in the financial services industry have enabled consumers to write checks against their money market or mutual fund accounts, most Americans still rely on their local bank as their primary financial institution.

The checking account at the local bank is the cornerstone of the finances of the typical U.S. household. That is no different from other countries. But households in many other industrialized countries make greater use of electronic methods for taking money out of their checking accounts—either with debit cards or electronic transfers. In France, for example, it is routine for a household to pay periodic bills—from a telephone bill to a mortgage—by allowing vendors to make withdrawals—via electronic transfers—from the household's checking account.

Americans, in contrast, make virtually all of their regular payments by check, although that is gradually changing. Americans are also more likely than the residents of many other countries to carry their checkbooks with them and write checks for a variety of purchases. For instance, checks were used for 23 percent of all U.S. supermarket and grocery store purchases in 2001. On average, Americans write more than 125 checks per year. By comparison, the French write 71 checks per year, Canadians 51 checks, Italians 10 checks, and Germans 4 checks.

Checks are such a pervasive—and in the global context, odd—part of the U.S. monetary landscape that it is worth examining how we got to this point. The history of checks is mainly about how banks have tried to reduce the costs of dealing with the inherently cumbersome processing of paper checks—giving money to the presenter of the check and getting the money from the bank on which the check is written—and the role of the Fed in this effort. We will also see in this episode a precursor to the interchange fee battles recently faced by payment cards, which we discuss in chapter 11.

By the mid-nineteenth century, U.S. banks issued and accepted three media of exchange: bank notes, drafts, and checks. Checks, our focus here, gradually displaced the less flexible notes and drafts. Like all payment media, checks have two sets of customers, both of which must be on board for the medium to work: those who are willing to pay by check, and those who are willing to accept checks for payment. A bank in an area can operate a check platform all by itself if its depositors write checks and local merchants accept them. To do so, it must have a way for merchants to get reimbursed. This is of course simple when merchants and consumers have accounts at the same bank. Checks are more useful if they are more widely accepted, however. So banks can offer more valuable checking services to their customers if their checks are accepted at more merchants. As a practical matter, that requires the cooperation of other local banks as well as banks far away. The manner in which banks cooperated on checks provides a preview of what was to come for payment cards.

There is one major difference. Banks faced a constraint on how they could price checks to people who write checks and people who cash checks—for convenience, call them check payers and check cashers. According to common law, which the United States carried over from England, cashers can get the amount of money on the face of the check if they present it in person at the payer's bank; but if they present it in any other way—say, by Pony Express—the payer's bank may pay less than the face value. That odd distinction created the incentives that shaped checking from the mid-nineteenth century through the early twentieth. The economics of two-sided markets (see chapter 6) would suggest that this constraint on pricing prevented banks from coming up with the right price structure—the one that best balanced the demand by payers and cashers—and may have led to pricing that was less than optimal from the standpoint of both society and the banking industry.

For now, though, we want to look mainly at how this distinction influenced practices and institutions for honoring checks. Banks close to one another tended to reach agreements to exchange each other's checks at par (that is, for face value). When it would be easy enough for check holders (consumers and banks) to present in person, they couldn't collect more than minimal exchange charges. Also, if banks charged each other for cashing each other's checks, the charges would tend to offset each other. So it made sense for everyone to agree to the simplest and thus least costly mechanism for exchanging checks. That resulted in the emergence of clearinghouses: banks sent clerks to a central location at a specific time where they were able to quickly and efficiently exchange checks drawn on each others' banks.

These clearinghouses were far more efficient than having banks send messengers to every other bank in town. For example, there were fifty-two banks clearing checks with each other at par in New York City in the early 1850s. Without any agreements, each bank would have had to send fifty-one messengers to arrange settlement, and each would have had fifty-one messengers coming to its door. Instead they agreed to deal with a single clearinghouse.

The Emergence of a National Checking Network Without railroads, that would have been the end of the story. But the country became increasingly integrated over the last half of the nineteenth century. Inter-regional commerce increased. Local banks received an increasing volume of out-of-town checks from merchants. The problem wasn't just how to present that check—in person or by mail. Checks drawn on distant banks were more likely to bounce: it was harder to know whether any particular check was legitimate, more difficult to collect from travelers, and harder for the law to catch a bad-check artist on the move. Hence, an out-of-town check wasn't worth as much as one drawn on a local bank.

Although at that time banks could not address the issue of the trustworthiness of the payer (the technology for check verification and guarantee was far in the future), they did attend to the clearing-and-collection concern by setting up the respondent-correspondent system. The respondent bank, often a smaller country bank, would clear its interregional checks through the correspondent bank, typically a city bank. Frequently, the correspondent would not charge explicit fees for its services (and would in some cases agree to pay exchange fees for checks cleared on the respondent), but instead make its money on deposits that respondents were required to hold with it.

Correspondent relationships tended to be organized by region. New England banks selected banks in Boston and New York as their correspondent banks, whereas midwestern banks selected banks in Cincinnati, Cleveland, and most commonly, Chicago. Most banks had at least one correspondent in New York. Furthermore, most banks also had relationships with between three and a dozen banks located in neighboring counties.

The overall result was a complex network—neither hub and spoke nor point to point. Each respondent-correspondent relationship was bilateral. Each correspondent, however, had many respondent relationships and was thus at the hub of a mini payment platform. The respondent banks at the spokes were also connected to a few other hubs. And the correspondent banks generally had relationships with each other to facilitate check clearing across the country. For example, a Cleveland bank and a Chicago bank might have an agreement to collect checks for each other at par within specified geographic limits. The correspondent banks were the intermediaries that helped solve the redemption problem for interregional checks. Any bank could sign up with a correspondent and thereby clear its interregional checks.

These late nineteenth-century interregional clearing systems have been subject to some criticism that has become relevant to modern-day payment systems. First, isolated country banks could charge exchange fees that exceeded their costs of remitting payment for a check drawn on them. Some commentators argue that these fees were therefore "excessive" and "monopolistic." We will see in chapter 6 that one needs to be careful in making these statements about two-sided market platforms. Each bank needed to establish fees for checking that were attractive to those who pay with checks and those who are paid by checks. All these fees help cover the costs of providing checking and making a profit. As with most two-sided platforms, prices generally don't track costs on either side of the market. Thus, banks today often don't charge transaction fees to customers who pay by check, even though processing each check costs the bank money.

The second and related criticism was that to avoid these exchange charges, some checks took a circuitous route before returning to the bank on which they were written. According to lore, there is one check that was drawn on a bank in Sag Harbor, New York, and was deposited in a bank in Hoboken, New Jersey, about one hundred miles away. It passed through eleven banks, traveled around 1,500 miles, and was in transit about eleven days en route to Sag Harbor. (Some researchers have argued that such anecdotal examples, although entertaining, were quantitatively insignificant. These instances didn't happen that often and didn't add much to costs.)

Finally, some critics suggest that the par rule should have been extended to situations where presentment was done remotely. While such a rule would have shifted costs from city banks to country banks—the battle over who pays is a common theme in payment systems—there would have been no obvious efficiency gain from doing so. City banks didn't refuse to accept checks from country banks, but would have preferred to pay less to collect. While exchange at par may seem natural, there is no reason to believe that it would have produced net benefits.

The Fed got into the business of check clearing starting around 1915, partly as a response to these concerns about nonpar banking. (For simplicity, we leave out some of the distinctions between actions taken by the Federal Reserve Board and those taken by the regional Federal Reserve Banks.) The Fed set up a national system for the clearing and collection of checks. The one key difference is that the Fed *imposed* check collection at par. In the first phase, in March 1915, the Fed announced a voluntary plan in which banks that chose to join would clear checks on each other at par. This plan proved unsuccessful; at its peak in October 1915, only one-quarter of the Fed member banks had joined, and more banks were leaving than were joining. This suggests that par exchange was not an attractive option for most of these banks.

The Fed changed its strategy in April 1916. It required Fed member banks to remit at par for each check that a Reserve Bank presented to them whether in person or not. Then the Fed turned its attention to nonmember banks. The Fed kept a "par list" of nonmember banks that were willing to clear at par and began an aggressive campaign to expand the list. The Fed accumulated the checks of nonpar banks to present over the counter for payment at par, thereby preventing them from collecting exchange fees. In some cases, the Fed even put nonpar banks on the par list without their consent. The number of non-Fed members on the par list grew from about 10,000 in December 1918 to over 19,000 at its peak in November 1920, with only about 1,700 nonpar banks left.

Following litigation that led the Supreme Court to impose limits on some of the Fed's actions to coerce banks to join the par list, many non-member banks withdrew from the Fed's system, and the number of nonpar banks reached four thousand by 1928. The number of nonpar banks later declined, especially in the early 1970s. As the economy expanded, one-bank towns became two-bank towns. The second bank could clear checks at par over the counter on behalf of out-of-town banks. By 1980, there were no nonpar banks left in the United States.

The Fed's role in the development of check clearing in the United States is controversial. Did the Fed help solve a market failure resulting from nonpar checks, or did it create one by forcing banks to clear at par? Most firms that operate two-sided platforms vary prices to the two sides to balance the two demands and to make sure they get both sides on board. The par rule in the context of the checking platform prevents firms from using prices to do that. One is tempted to say that it is only fair that a merchant who gets a check for $100 should be reimbursed $100. It is not that simple, though: someone has to bear the costs of the checking system, and the merchant is receiving a service just as the payer is. If you doubt this, ask yourself why it is fair that you receive Adobe Acrobat Reader for free to read PDF files, but that those who generate these files have to pay for the necessary software. And in fact, the par rule is much like the government telling Adobe that it can't give away its readers. The economics of two-sided markets we discuss in chapter 6 suggests that imposing par pricing for checks most likely causes a market failure and thus reduces social welfare.

After check-processing fees were eliminated in 1918, the Fed shouldered the burden of the clearing and collection process, underwriting the system and increasing the incentive to use checks. It did not charge any explicit fees for check clearing until 1980, at which time the taxpayers were, indirectly, shouldering about $500 million a year for the check system. The U.S. check system is as widespread and efficient as it is in part because of the subsidies it received from 1918 to 1980.

Many other countries have developed different systems for paying bills that don't rely on checks, and not surprisingly, people in those countries use checks less. Some of these are based on a "Giro," a consolidated bill payment scheme that is operated either by the post office, the bank system, or both. It originated in Europe in the 1800s, and made the shift from paper to electronic in the late 1960s and early 1970s. The Giro system plays an important role in, for example, the Scandinavian countries; in Norway, it accounts for 50 percent of the total number of noncash transactions and 95 percent of their value. Several countries have easy-to-use systems for having regular bills deducted directly from checking accounts. This is possible in the United States, but it is not yet nearly as widely used as in Europe.

Although one might claim that the absence of these alternative systems in the United States resulted in heavier check use, it is also possible that the early development of America's efficient check processing system has discouraged investment in these alternatives. U.S. banks initially had greater incentives to develop an efficient checking system because banks were smaller and more spread out than banks in other countries. Our fragmented banking system might be the root cause of our reliance on checks.

Several competing payment media have started curbing the U.S. appetite for checks. The share of consumer payments made with checks has fallen from 51 percent in 1990 to 41 percent in 2001, based on dollar volume. The remarkable growth of debit cards during that period—from irrelevance to challenging credit cards in importance—played a major role in checks' decline. People who want to pay with money in their checking account have a more convenient method for doing so—swiping a card rather than writing a check. The share of consumer payments made with a debit card has increased from 0.4 percent in 1990 to 7 percent in 2001. The electronic funds transfer system—the "Automated Clearinghouse" (ACH) system—has gained in popularity as well. Between 1990 and 2001 the share of consumer payments made through the ACH system increased from 0.8 to 3.6 percent. According to the Survey of Consumer Finances, the proportion of households using direct debit—an electronic transfer out of an individual's checking or savings account via the ACH system, generally to pay recurring bills—increased from about 22 percent in 1995 to about 40 percent in 2001. (Some industry sources put the 2003 number at about 50 percent.)

Debit cards and electronic fund transfers have been much more popular in less check-reliant industrialized countries. Debit cards were introduced widely in many countries in Europe starting in the 1970s. The percentage of cashless transactions paid with a debit card was higher in France and Sweden in 1990 than it was in the United States in 2000. Electronic fund transfers were also more popular than in the United States. For instance, the proportion of cashless transactions conducted as a direct debit was higher in Belgium, France, Germany, Japan, the Netherlands, and the United Kingdom in 1990 than it was in the United States in 2001. As figure 2.3 shows, the United States still trailed

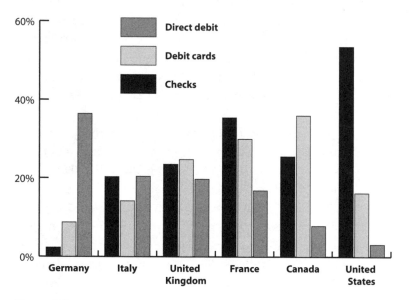

Figure 2.3
Use of cashless payment instruments in leading industrialized countries, 2001 (percentage of cashless transactions)
Note: Data reported for the G7 member countries as available. Data on Japan are not available.
Source: Bank for International Settlements, *Statistics on Payment and Settlement Systems in Selected Countries*, (April 2003).

many industrialized countries in the use of debit cards and direct debit in 2001.

Buy Now, Pay Later

The rise of payment cards changed not only how people pay for things but also when. That is why the most important transformation for the payment card was its integration with two ancient activities: lending and borrowing. This didn't happen overnight. Shortly after the launch of the Diners Club card in 1950, some banks tried to create a card that integrated payment services with lending. Most failed, and even the successes grew slowly. But over time, the products were improved and the problems were solved, and the credit card picked up steam in the 1970s. A revolution in bank lending, consumer borrowing, and merchant financing followed. It was a revolution waged amid the historical remnants of age-old efforts to regulate lending and borrowing by religious and governmental authorities.

People have borrowed from each other for at least as long as they have traded with each other—though like the first trade, the first loan is lost in time. One imagines a farmer in prehistoric agricultural times loaning his neighbor some seeds in return for a share of the future harvest. We do know that buying on credit predates primitive money; there is evidence of ancient lending in communities that had no medium of exchange or standard of value.

From the earliest recorded history, lenders have sought a return—interest—on their capital. Others have complained that interest is immoral, and for long periods of time in various parts of the world, civil or religious laws forbade interest or limited how much lenders could charge. Aristotle argued that making money from money is unnatural. And as is always the case when laws prohibit willing buyers from entering into deals with willing sellers, people have made efforts to evade the laws. The loan shark may not be the oldest profession but it is likely up there.

The earliest-known formal code of laws, set forth by Hammurabi in 1800 BCE, permitted lending but capped interest rates: 33.33 percent on loans of grain and 20 percent for loans of silver. There were other restrictions. Debt could be secured with the debtor or his wife, concubine, children, or slaves along with land and other capital. Slavery on default was limited to three years. The Greek Laws of Solon (about 600 BCE) eliminated previous limits on interest. But they also did away with slavery on default. The Twelve Tables, a codification of Roman laws around 443 BCE, set the maximum interest rate at 8.33 percent. The creditor could seize the debtor, but was also required to feed him. Interest was briefly banned in Rome around 342 BCE, but was then returned to its old maximum; the maximum was raised to 12 percent in 88 BCE and another half point in the fourth century CE.

The Bible was hard on lenders, and its language is still used to describe interest limits. Lenders were called "usurers," and lending was called "usury." The Old and the New Testament advocate zero-percent financing. In the Old Testament, Ezekiel 18:8 tells us, "He that hath not given forth upon usury, neither hath taken any increase. . . . He is just, he shall surely live, saith the Lord God." And in the New Testament, Luke 6:35 reads, "Lend freely, hoping nothing thereby." St. Bernardine in the early fifteenth century frowned on interest as well: "Accordingly all the saints and all the angels of paradise cry then against [the usurer], saying, 'To hell, to hell, to hell.' Also the heavens with their stars cry out, saying, 'To the fire, to the fire, to the fire.' The planets also clamor, 'To the depths, to the depths, to the depths'" (*De Contractibus*, sermon 45, 3:3). St. Thomas Aquinas said, "To take usury from any man is simply evil." In the Muslim world, the Koran prohibited usury even more strictly than the Bible. It precluded people from profiting on the exchange of silver or gold, and it also prohibited the use of bills of exchange.

Not surprisingly, given these harsh views, usury was a sin in Europe during much of the Dark Ages and the Middle Ages, and with the church so much a part of the state, there were laws against lending as well as the possibility of excommunication from the church for usury. The Capitularies of Charlemagne (800 CE) forbade usury "where more is asked than is given." In the twelfth century, the Second Lateran Council prohibited usury. Sidney Homer and Richard Sylla's survey of interest rates summarizes the period: "For long centuries the ordinary consumer loan, and, for that matter, the ordinary commercial loan, was opposed by effective popular and clerical censure and often by civil law."

It was never possible to eliminate an economic activity as basic and necessary as lending and borrowing. Thus, laws were often enforced only in egregious cases. Semantic and theological distinctions were made to permit some lending. Pawnshops existed openly. Usury laws mainly discouraged the development of lending institutions and capped interest rates, and as a result, held back the development of banking.

Hostility toward usury waned through the Renaissance with the growth of trade. With the Reformation, lending became more accepted in Protestant countries—Calvin and others rejected the extreme view of Aristotle and Thomas Aquinas—but Catholic countries came around more slowly. Finally, around the middle of the eighteenth century, commercial lending, which is essential for modern capitalism, emerged victorious throughout much of Europe. Most European countries repealed their usury laws between 1854 and 1867.

The United States stands out in two respects. It has maintained usury laws much longer than its European cousins. These laws date back to the country's beginning. Most of the colonies followed Maryland's lead in 1692 in capping rates at 6 percent. Two hundred years later, in 1881, only fourteen of the forty-seven states had repealed their usury laws, and many of these states eventually reinstated them. The typical ceiling remained at 6 percent. More than a hundred years later, in 1987, thirty-three states had legislated maximum interest rates for consumer loans. Today, twenty-nine states still do. Given how few other prices are regulated by law today, this is a remarkable historical legacy. And until well into the twentieth century—and we still see echoes today—borrowing money, especially by households, was considered bad form.

With this legacy, it is a paradox that along with its comparatively high rate of usage of checks, the second way the United States stands out is that it gave birth to the credit card, which is used far more in the United States than in any European country. The card builds on a tradition of buying on credit that dates back to the early days of the republic. One chapter in a late nineteenth-century memoir suggests that not much really changes: "Buy Now, Pay Later—Mama Discovers an American Custom."

Credit: Financing the American Dream?

The chest of drawers for the early nineteenth-century parlor, the sewing machine for the late nineteenth-century home, the radios and phonographs for the early twentieth-century household, televisions for the mid-twentieth-century family room, and an automobile for the garage—all were essential in their day to the American Dream. And Americans have been able to pay later for household durables that they buy now since at least the early years of the United States. As historian Lendol Calder details in his study of U.S. lending, *Financing the American Dream*, Cowperthwaite and Sons in New York sold furniture on installment terms by 1812. Other furniture dealers did the same during the nineteenth century. I. M. Singer popularized the installment plan in the last half of that century. It allowed suitable sewing machine buyers to put $110 down and pay $65 to $110 dollars a month plus interest (as always, in 2002 dollars). By the 1890s, Singer settled on $19 down and $19 a week for its sewing machine. By the turn of the twentieth century, at least in Boston, retailers were selling clothing as well as consumer durables on credit. According to one historian studying immigrants in the late nineteenth century, "The practice of installment buying initiated newcomers into the possibilities of immediate acquisition and familiarized them with the impatient optimism that characterized the American consumer."

Most retailers of durable goods sold them on credit by 1930; that year, 80 to 90 percent of furniture was bought on credit, as were 75 percent of washing machines, 65 percent of vacuum cleaners, 18 to 25 percent of jewelry, 75 percent of radio sets, and 80 percent of phonographs. Indeed, during the Great Depression, Montgomery Ward, Sears, Roebuck and Co., and other large department stores offered to sell everything on some form of installment plan. Of course, most households by this time were buying cars on credit. By 1920, consumers used credit for about two-thirds of car purchases. Dealers sold cars under two prices: the cash price and the "time price," which was generally 15 to 22 percent higher than the cash price, and included finance charges, dealer reserves, loss reserves, and insurance premiums. Installment contracts for cars were typically twelve to eighteen months long. By the time banks started introducing credit cards in the mid-1950s, Americans were accustomed to buying now and paying later. Many merchants financed purchases. And households had accumulated significant debt.

Since the 1950s, consumer debt has continued to grow. Figure 2.4 reveals some interesting facts about this process. First, the total of consumer credit outstanding has grown consistently since the middle of the century—real growth rates were 133 percent in the 1950s, 79 percent in the 1960s, 44 percent in the 1970s, 41 percent in the 1980s, and 45 percent in the 1990s. Second, consumer debt has grown at a slower pace since the spread of credit cards—the 133 percent growth in the 1950s is more than the 79 percent in the 1960s and almost three times the growth rate of the 1990s. Third, revolving credit (accounted for mainly by outstanding balances on credit cards) has replaced other forms of consumer debt—the share of revolving credit in total consumer credit increased

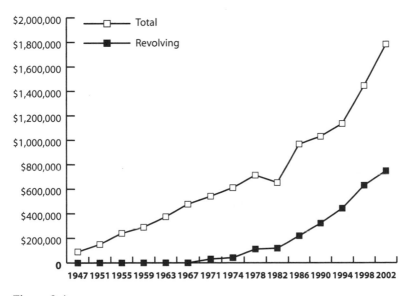

Figure 2.4
Consumer credit outstanding, 1947–2002 (not seasonally adjusted)
Note: Revolving credit includes balances outstanding on credit cards and other unsecured revolving lines of credit; nonrevolving credit includes secured and unsecured credit for automobiles, mobile homes, trailers, durable goods, vacations, and other purposes. Figures are in 2002 dollars.
Source: Federal Reserve Board, *Statistics: Releases and Historical Data.*

from zero in 1950 to about 4 percent in 1970, 16 percent in 1980, 31 percent in 1990, and 44 percent in 2000.

Credit: Dealing with the Devil?

Throughout its two-century life in the United States, the "buy now, pay later" concept has faced two major objections and one obstacle. The objections are that (1) it is just wrong for consumers to consume on credit, and (2) consumers are irrational to consume on credit based on the terms that lenders offer. And the obstacle is that lenders should not charge interest rates that are "too high."

Americans have never had a problem with borrowing to produce things, and capital markets helped finance the industrialization of the United States during the nineteenth and twentieth centuries. Borrowing to consume things was another matter. Benjamin Franklin's *Poor Richard* warned people about borrowing: "He who goes a borrowing, goes a sorrowing"; and "Be frugal and free." The major piece of financial advice given to households during the nineteenth and early twentieth century was "live within your means." One nineteenth-century adviser said the "trinity of evil" was "debt, dirt, and the devil." An early twentieth-century adviser noted that there "was no excuse for going in debt for the ordinary necessities of life." The Victorian ethos waned after the turn of the century—helped perhaps by inflation that eroded the value of savings. But even today, there is no shortage of opinion leaders and financial advisers who believe that buying on credit is bad for households and the economy.

For many decade, some commentators have argued that even if it isn't wrong in principle to consume on credit, Americans are foolish to do so on the terms actually offered by lenders. Already in the late nineteenth century, women in charge of managing the household budget were singled out. An 1884 editorial in *Scientific American* discussed "the curious processes of reasoning" that women used in deciding to buy a sewing machine on an installment plan. The author discovered the "psychological fact, possibly new," that women "will rather pay $50 for a machine in monthly installments of five dollars rather than $25 outright, although able to do so." Both sexes engage in this reasoning now. Many people pay interest on credit card purchases that is far higher than the interest they are earning on their savings. We examine this case against credit in more detail in chapter 4.

Banks, Merchants, and Consumer Financing

Whatever the view of its critics and proponents, consumer credit has become as American as apple pie, via merchants' financing programs and, later, credit cards, which made borrowing and lending of small amounts of money even more efficient. After credit cards became widely available, many merchants happily discontinued their lending programs, while a few with highly profitable programs continued to encourage their customers to use their store cards. Why did merchants offer financing in the first place? One possibility is that merchants had better access to capital than did their customers. Merchants could obtain capital—possibly from banks, but more likely from their own retained earnings—much more easily for financing sales than their customers could for buying, let's say, some furniture. Banks were not in the consumer lending business throughout most of U.S. history. Personal finance companies appeared in the late nineteenth century, but they were where consumers went to consolidate their merchant installment debt, not where they went for a small loan for a phonograph. Thus, providing financing was a service that merchants could perform more cheaply for their customers than customers could provide themselves. It made sense to offer this complementary service, particularly if one could do it better than the competition.

Some merchants *were* extremely good at lending; they were large enough to average the risks of default, and good at spotting and monitoring credit risks. Sears excelled. Others did not. We know from the credit card experience that lending is a complex business. We'll see later that even American Express initially blundered when it tried to provide credit cards to its charge card customers. And there are some scale economies so that smaller businesses found lending costly—although necessary given that consumers wanted to pay in installments and their competitors offered this option.

Credit cards provided a platform that made the borrowing and lending of small amounts of money more efficient. Cardholders received a small credit line that could be used at many merchants based on a single application for a card. These cardholders didn't have to fill out applications at many merchants and keep track of the bills, and they didn't have to make a trip to a bank or personal finance company to buy a specific item. Merchants benefited so long as the credit card issuers could provide loans to their customers more efficiently than they could. Many merchants applauded credit card programs and dropped their financing programs once customers had another alternative.

For example, Joseph Nocera tells us that when Kenneth Larkin, a Bank of America executive, visited a drug store in a small town hoping to persuade its owner to accept BankAmericard, the man received him as the savior of his business. In practice, Nocera explains, "A store owner who accepted the credit card was, in effect, handing his back office headaches over to the Bank of America." And banks could lend money without having a personal loan officer interview every consumer who approached them for a loan.

The convenience of payment cards for banks, merchants, and consumers is a product of a delicate balance that emerged after much trial and error. As we will discuss in chapter 3, getting the business model for lending money on the card platform right was tough work, and it took many years for the credit card industry to figure out how to do this profitably.

3
More Than Money

"Perhaps you would like to see what our credit cards are like," [Doctor Leete asks of his guest, Julian West]. "You observe . . . that this card is used for a certain number of dollars. . . . The value of what I procure on this card is checked off by the clerk, who pricks out of these tiers of squares the price of what I order." [Mr. West, from Boston, has awakened 113 years in the future, in the year 2000.]
—Edward Bellamy, *Looking Backward, 2000–1887* (1888)

The simple payment card has been around since at least the beginning of the last century. Hotels, oil companies, and department stores issued cards before World War I. In response to customer requests, Sears began offering lines of credit in 1910 to customers of "unquestionable responsibility," although the Sears card came more than a decade later. Some large retailers gave cards to their wealthier customers that identified them as having a charge account with the store. By the 1920s, several department stores allowed cardholders to pay off their bills in monthly installments. Metal "charge-plates" with embossed consumer information were introduced by department stores in 1928. During the 1920s as well, oil companies issued "courtesy cards" for charging gas. By the end of World War II, charge cards were no longer a novelty, but they were about as far from the cards of today as barter was from coin.

Dining on the Cuff

Restaurants did not issue cards. In 1949, Frank McNamara, the president of a New York credit company, was having lunch in Manhattan. A year later, as we mentioned earlier, he had a thriving business based on this experience. He was written up in *Newsweek* two years later: "Halfway through his coffee, McNamara made a familiar, embarrassing discovery; he had left his wallet at home. By the time his wife arrived and the tab had been settled, McNamara was deep in thought. Result: the 'Diner's Club,' one of the fastest-growing service organizations." (This is the earliest rendition of the story we've found. One journalist several years later gave the credit to Alfred Bloomingdale, then the president of Diners Club, and changed the meal to dinner.)

Following McNamara's epiphany, people began carrying charge cards in their wallets. McNamara and an associate, Ralph Schneider, started small. Beginning with $1.5 million of start-up capital, they signed up fourteen New York City restaurants and gave cards away to selected people. By the card's first anniversary there were 42,000 cardholders, each paying $18 a year for membership in the "club." And 330 U.S. restaurants, hotels, and nightclubs accepted these cards; they paid an average of 7 percent of the cardholder's bill to Diners Club. In March 1951, Diners Club handled $3 million of exchanges between cardholders and merchants, and reportedly made almost $60,000 in pretax profit. At that pace, it was handling $35.5 million in transactions annually. Unlike store cards, Diners Club cards provided a broader medium of exchange—one that extended to at least all the merchants in the club.

And that club expanded rapidly. In 1956, it had an annual transaction volume of more than $290 million. The card was accepted at nine thousand establishments, according to the *New York Times*, from Anchorage to Tahiti. By then its merchant coverage had expanded beyond restaurants to auto rental agencies and gift shops—almost the gamut of travel and entertainment locations. Two years later, Diners Club had an annual charge volume of more than $465 million, and earned gross profits of $40 million from merchant discounts and cardholder fees.

McNamara and Schneider had not only discovered the idea of a general-purpose payment card; they had also discovered a pricing strategy that got both merchants and cardholders on board, and thus has been followed by payment card systems since. By 1957, Diners Club had raised the cardholder fee to $26, but had left the merchant fee at 7 percent. It nevertheless continued to earn most of its revenues, about 70 percent, from merchants. Similarly, American Express currently earns over 82 percent of its revenues from merchants, excluding finance charges.

Diners Club faced competition soon after its entry. Information is spotty on some—National Credit Card, Inc., for instance, started its card program in 1951, operated in forty-two states, but had filed for bankruptcy by 1954. A 1955 *Newsweek* article referred to Trip-Charge with eighty-five thousand cardholders and nine thousand merchants after a year in business; it asserted that the founder, Sidney J. Rudolph, "is now a hairbreadth from realizing his hopeful company motto: 'Charge Everything Everywhere.'" Esquire and Duncan Hines both had travel and entertainment cards, which merged in 1957. *Gourmet* magazine had a club for diners, too.

Merchant coalitions were another source of competition. Hotel owners balked at the fee they had to pay on charge cards. In 1956, the American Hotel Association established the Universal Travelcard. It didn't charge participating hotels and rental car agencies any fee but billed cardholders the same $26 fee as Diners Club. The National Restaurant Association, with sixty thousand members, signed on. One might wonder how they could get by without the 70 percent of the pie from merchant fees that Diners Club received. Part of the answer is that they didn't do central billing. Each hotel billed its customers directly, although the card association did ensure payment. There was a railroad card and an airline card as well.

Some banks had also entered the payment card business by the 1950s, but their cards—sometimes called "shopper" cards—targeted a different cardholder and merchant base. These bankcards were typically held by "housewives," as the newspapers of the day put it, and could be used only at retail stores in the locality the bank did business. Franklin National Bank started one of the first shopper cards on Long Island in 1951, and one hundred or so banks—mainly small, suburban banks in the Northeast—followed. While one hundred may seem like a large number, one should keep in mind that in 1951, there were 13,455 commercial banks as well as many more credit unions and savings and loans. Banks generally charged retailers the then-standard 5 to 7 percent merchant fee. Cardholders reportedly didn't pay any direct fees and, as with the other card programs, were supposed to pay their monthly bill in full. These cards were thus charge cards, though the press of the day called them credit cards.

Of the early major entrants, only Diners Club survived the decade as a stand-alone company. It bought Trip-Charge in 1956 and Esquire's card program in 1958. The bankcards failed mainly because they had trouble signing up merchants, and only twenty-seven of the shopper cards were still in existence by 1957. The Universal Travelcard and the Gourmet Magazine Club card were swallowed in 1958 by a new competitor (American Express) that appeared during what became a critical year for the future history of the card industry.

Diners Club also expanded overseas in the mid-1950s, using franchise agreements to extend its reach to Europe. As in the United States, European hotel trade associations posed strong resistance to the travel and entertainment (T&E) cards, going so far as to expel members who accepted payment cards that required a merchant discount. Some hotels in England and Switzerland chose to flout the prohibition; they accepted the T&E cards and formed their own association. They also went a step further: the newly formed hotel association created the BHR credit card in the 1950s, which evolved into the EuroCard in the mid-1960s.

1958

Though planning had started years earlier, several competitors rolled out new cards in 1958. In September, Bank of America started a credit card in California. In October, American Express launched its national charge card, and Hilton Hotels spun off its hotel card into Carte Blanche.

Bank of America

California did not have restrictions on branch banking in 1958. With an economy larger than Japan's, California was able to support several large banks. Bank of America was the largest, with over six hundred branches throughout the state. It had started as Bank of Italy in 1904, founded by one of the greats of U.S. banking, A. P. Giannini. By 1958, Bank of America was the largest bank in the United States.

Despite its size, though, Bank of America was cautious about offering a payment card, even though one of its small competitors, First National

Bank of San Jose, had started a credit card in 1953. Bank of America considered introducing its own card in 1954, but initially decided that there wasn't a good enough business case. After studying the emerging industry over the next few years, it decided to introduce a credit card in 1958. Creditworthy customers would receive cards with limits of either $1,500 or $2,600; prior authorization would be required for purchases over $260; and a revolving credit option was available for some cardholders. Revolving credit was the innovation that distinguished this card from existing charge cards.

The bank conducted a market test in Fresno, California, in fall 1958. Three hundred retailers signed up initially, and every Bank of America customer in the Fresno area received a card. According to one study, "This mass mailing of 60,000 cards had been William's [the executive in charge of the effort] solution to the problem of how to convince retailers that enough individuals would possess a card to make their participation in the program worthwhile. His solution worked, for during the next five months another eight hundred Fresno-area retailers joined the newly named 'BankAmericard' program." Bank of America had planned to track the financial results of the card in Fresno before going statewide, but fear of competition persuaded it to accelerate the launch. It expanded throughout the state during the following year. By the end of 1959, twenty-five thousand merchants accepted the card and almost two million California households had one.

Things did not go well at first: fraud was rampant, the number of delinquent accounts was five times higher than expected, large retailers resisted joining, and echoing an old theme, "Public criticism came from those who viewed credit as a societal evil." The program lost $45 million in 1960. The bank worked on collection problems and reduced the merchant fee to as low as 3 percent to entice retailers. Delinquencies declined and the merchant base increased to thirty-five thousand in 1962. The card turned its first operating profit in 1961.

American Express

American Express started as an express mail company in 1850. Money was one of the things people wanted to move around the country, especially after the post–Civil War expansion of the rail network created national markets. Of course, people also wanted their money delivered safely. The U.S. Post Office developed the money order; American Express introduced a competing product. Both products were subject to theft, and neither was a good substitute for cash.

The travelers cheque, invented by an American Express employee, was a significant advance over the money order. The cheques came in multiple denominations just like cash and had the dual-signature system (sign when you obtain, and sign when you cash) that remains the major security device to this day. Initially, people could cash travelers cheques only at American Express offices; later, they could cash them directly at merchants. The major selling point for consumers was security: American Express guaranteed payment, but it also assumed responsibility for lost or forged checks. The product has remained a highly profitable one for American Express for over a century, although its popularity has declined steadily over the last decade. The profits all came from individuals. A consumer purchasing $500 in travelers cheques, say, would pay American Express a fee in addition to the $500, and American Express would continue to earn interest on the amount invested in the cheques until they were cashed. Stolen or misplaced cheques that were not cashed or replaced would be pure profit.

A hundred years after its formation in Buffalo, New York, American Express was the world's largest travel agency and operated the world's largest private mail service. Between its cheques and travel offices, it was profiting enormously from the boom in international travel following the end of the Second World War. The number of American Express travel agencies grew from fifty at the end of the war to nearly four hundred ten years later. The company sold approximately $6.5 billion worth of travelers cheques in 1951, and by the end of the decade claimed to control 70 percent of the U.S. travelers cheque business.

The Diners Club charge card was a new competitor for American Express. By 1953, American Express had begun planning its response. It considered buying Diners Club in 1956, but rejected the idea. The company finally entered the charge card industry on October 1, 1958, with 17,500 merchant locations and 250,000 cardholders. It achieved this scale quickly by buying the Gourmet Magazine Club card and the Universal Travelcard. Within seven months of launching its card operations, American Express had over 600,000 cardholders. By late 1960, it had a charge volume of over $500 million and 750,000 cardholders.

American Express adopted a slightly different pricing policy than Diners Club. It initially set its annual fee $1 higher (in 1958 dollars) than Diners Club's $5, thereby suggesting that it was the more "exclusive" card (in 2002 dollars, the American Express annual fee was $31 while the Diners Club fee was $26). But it set the initial merchant discount slightly lower than Diners Club's 7 percent: 5 to 7 percent for restaurants, according to their sales volume; and 3 to 5 percent for the recalcitrant hotel industry, depending on the hotel guest's charge level.

American Express struggled at first. Even a charge card involves extending credit for a time, and American Express, unlike the founders of Diners Club, had no experience doing this. By 1961, with losses mounting, it considered selling the business to Diners Club, but decided that such a sale might not pass muster with the Justice Department. Instead, American Express hired George Waters, later known as the "Father of the Card," to run its card operations. Waters started putting pressure on customers who had not sent their payments in on time. And he raised the annual fee to $39, and later to $48. Despite the increased fees, the American Express payment card system continued to grow. By the end of 1962, there were 900,000 American Express cardholders who could use their cards at 82,000 merchant locations. In 1962, almost four years after its launch, the card operation posted its first (small) profit.

Today, American Express accounts for 14 percent of the dollars transacted on payment cards. By that measure, it is one-third the size of the Visa system (see figure 1.2 in chapter 1) and one-half the size of MasterCard. Diners Club, on the other hand, has shrunk to almost nothing within the United States. The charge card pioneer spread itself too thin in the 1960s and early 1970s in an attempt to counter the inroads made by American Express. In particular, Diners Club tried unsuccessfully to follow the American Express model by expanding into travel clubs and travel agencies, but it lost money on both endeavors and lost sight of the newly emerging competition from the bankcards.

Carte Blanche

Hilton Hotels had issued a million charge cards for use at its worldwide hotel chain. After a failed attempt to buy Diners Club, it rolled its hotel card into a new general-purpose card company, the Hilton Credit Corporation, which distributed the Carte Blanche card. In 1958, it entered with a low merchant fee, 4.5 percent, which soon dropped to 4 percent. The 600,000-member National Restaurant Association, which had been complaining about the 7 percent fees charged by Diners Club and American Express, threw its official support behind the card. Nonetheless, as a result of issuing cards to the wrong people and an inefficient billing system, Carte Blanche became known in the trade as "Carte Rouge" for its steady losses.

What Happened to the Class of 1958

In 1960, a decade after the birth of the general-purpose payment card, there were three major national card systems. Diners Club, with 1.1 million cardholders, was still the biggest, but it faced competition from recent entrants American Express and Carte Blanche. These three, in turn, faced regional competition from BankAmericard in California and Chase Manhattan in New York City, though nothing else of significance. Chase Manhattan sold its card program to a subsidiary of American Express in 1962. This became the Uni-Card—a credit card that was available in the Northeast United States. It was sold back to Chase in 1969. Chase joined the BankAmericard association in 1972 and converted its cards to the BankAmericard brand.

Carte Blanche was sold to Citigroup in 1965. (Citigroup started as First National City Bank. In 1976, it became Citibank. Subsequently, the payment card operations were spun off into a separate subsidiary, Citigroup Global Consumer Group, which along with Citibank operates now under the Citigroup parent. For simplicity, we will refer to it as Citigroup regardless of the time period being discussed.) Pressured by an antitrust suit brought by the Justice Department, Citigroup sold Carte Blanche in 1968. The Justice Department was concerned that with Carte Blanche, Citigroup might limit development of the "Everything" credit card program it had started in 1967. When Citigroup quickly dropped the Everything card and had not introduced a replacement by 1978, however, the Justice Department relented, and Citigroup bought Carte Blanche back again. By that time, Carte Blanche's share of credit card volume had declined to less than 1 percent.

American Express moved past Diners Club to become the industry's volume leader in 1966. Diners Club continued to decline throughout the

1960s, in part because it lacked the travel offices that American Express used to distribute its card during the industry's early days. American Express also had a better T&E brand as a result of its travel offices and travelers cheques. Diners Club attempted to meet American Express head-on through travel and reservation system acquisitions, but it failed to make those profitable. Diners Club was sold to Citigroup in 1981. After the sale, Diners Club shifted its focus to affluent business travelers, trying to follow American Express's successful upmarket strategy. Diners Club had 8.5 million merchant locations worldwide in 2002, including 2 million in the United States. That year, it had 0.5 percent of U.S. general-purpose payment card purchase volume and 0.7 percent of general-purpose credit and charge card purchase volume.

And the statewide BankAmericard became the worldwide Visa card.

The Birth of Co-opetition

Another watershed year for the emerging payment card industry was 1966, which marked the start of a battle between three competing business models for operating payment cards.

American Express, Carte Blanche, and Diners Club were mainly used for travel and entertainment, and thus became known as T&E cards. They did not offer credit beyond the time it took to get cardholders their monthly bills, which had to be paid in full. Nor was there a link to cardholders' checking accounts. Many business travelers and wealthy households had one of these cards, but most Americans didn't. Data for 1966 are not available, but even by 1970 only 9.2 percent of households had one of the T&E cards.

Interstate banking regulations and other hurdles made it difficult for Bank of America to compete head-to-head with the three T&E cards. To take its card national, the California bank decided to franchise. In 1966, it announced that it would license its BankAmericard program to selected banks across the country. Each bank would operate the program independently using the BankAmericard name; merchants signed up by the franchisees would have to accept all BankAmericards, allowing consumers to use their BankAmericards at any participating merchant. Bank of America charged the franchisees a royalty of up to 0.5 percent of cardholder volume and an entry fee of about $113,000.

Unlike T&E cards, bankcards did not charge cardholders membership fees, earning revenue from finance charges and merchant discounts instead. For example, the Chase Manhattan Charge Plan, introduced in 1958, charged cardholders 1 percent of the revolved (that is, unpaid) balance every month, while charging merchants 2 to 6 percent of sales depending on volume.

The BankAmericard franchise was not limited to the United States. Major banks in countries such as Canada, Columbia, Italy, Japan, Mexico, Portugal, Spain, the United Kingdom, and Venezuela signed up as international BankAmericard franchisees around the same time as the domestic franchise system launch in 1966. In 1968, MasterCard also expanded internationally by forming alliances with EuroCard, the European card association mentioned earlier, and Banco Nacional in Mexico. The alliances allowed the MasterCard network and foreign networks to interoperate, but preserved each card as a distinct brand. In addition, MasterCard expanded in Asia by gaining member banks in Japan.

In the United States, within two months of the Bank of America franchising announcement, American Express, Carte Blanche, and Diners Club responded by offering their own franchise opportunities to banks. The American Express bankcard differed from the standard card: it offered a minimum $9,000 line of credit. American Express would split revenues with the banks: banks got a commission for signing up cardholders and revenues from credit provided by the card; and existing American Express cardholders could be converted to the bank program. American Express didn't charge additional franchise or licensing fees. Carte Blanche priced its franchise at $45 for every $4.5 million in bank assets, with a $22,625 minimum fee. Diners Club offered to franchise its card for $22,625 to banks with less than $4.5 billion of assets and for $45,250 for banks with $4.5 billion or more. While the historical evidence is sketchy, it does not appear that the various efforts at franchising these cards attracted any takers within the United States. (American Express also planned to franchise its Uni-Card credit card across the country in 1968. It had a million cardholders and eighteen thousand merchants in New England, New York, New Jersey, and Pennsylvania.

Instead of following through on those plans, though, it sold the Uni-Card program back to its original owner, Chase Manhattan, in 1969, and Chase converted these cards to BankAmericards in 1972.)

For many banks, there were significant negatives to the franchise system. Major banks, including Wells Fargo in California and Chase Manhattan in New York, were not eager to sign up to issue someone else's card. The successful franchise systems we're familiar with— McDonald's, the Athlete's Foot, or Mail Boxes Etc.—typically involve a prominent brand name with outlets operated by unknown local entrepreneurs. Although some franchisees can become quite successful with multiple locations, they generally have little ability or desire to promote their brand name over the franchisor's. This was not the case with the major banks.

Developing a proprietary card system was another option for banks. As we mentioned, Citigroup, in addition to owning Carte Blanche, had started its proprietary Everything card in 1967. Because Citigroup held a national banking charter and had customers across the country who were potential payment cardholders, it initially hoped to develop the Everything card into a national brand. Other banks found this option unattractive. While a national charter was, legally speaking, not necessary to issue credit cards around the country, some banks were reluctant to expand out-of-state.

Many banks found the answer in co-opetition. Banks *competed* for merchants and cardholders. Banks *cooperated* at the card system level by setting operational standards. Despite the dismal experience of the 1950s, many banks decided to start cards in the 1960s. They compared the problems of going it alone to the benefits of cooperation. They formed associations. Five banks in Illinois founded the Midwest Bank Card. By January 1967, nearly six hundred banks in Illinois, Indiana, and Michigan had joined; some of these issued one of the five original members' cards. There were also two Michigan associations. Other banks across the country followed. Three New York City banks started the Eastern States Bankcard Association in June 1967. The state and local banking groups began to develop ties with other groups. The Interbank Card Association started in 1966. Early on it included banks in Buffalo, Pittsburgh, Milwaukee, Seattle, and Phoenix. At the same time, several banks in California started the Western States Bankcard Association, issuing cards under the Master Charge service mark. By 1967, the California banks issuing Master Charge had joined the Interbank Association. By February 1968, Interbank had 286 banks in at least seven states.

It became apparent during 1968 that there were two competing national networks of banks: the BankAmericard franchise system, and the Interbank cooperative system. Banks—and groups of banks—started aligning with one or the other. "Just about every bank in the card field," said *Business Week*, "is convinced that it must join one or the other network." Bankers Trust in New York City went with BankAmericard and franchised the card to other banks in the New York area. Meanwhile, Citigroup converted its Everything card to Master Charge and joined Interbank. Chemical and Manufacturers Hanover joined that association as well. For the most part, the larger banks had chosen Interbank over BankAmericard. In contrast to the BankAmericard franchise model, Interbank charged only a "modest" entrance fee and a small annual fee to cover the operating costs of the joint enterprise. And as noted, banks would be selling a brand they jointly owned, rather than that of another bank. This was an important point for banks that harbored hopes of future national expansion when interstate banking restrictions were lifted—though in hindsight, that was still more than three decades away.

BankAmericard was not doing too badly by many measures. Under its franchise model, it had about 27 million cardholders and about 565,000 merchants by 1970, a sizable jump from 1.8 million cardholders and 61,000 merchants in 1966. But it was in the process of being overtaken by Interbank, which had attracted most major banks. And the franchisees were restless.

The franchisees quickly went from restless to rebellious. They had grown in importance to the system and wanted a voice in its future. In 1970, faced with this revolt as well as with operational problems, Bank of America agreed to convert the system into a membership-owned corporation: National BankAmericard, Inc. (NBI). NBI wasn't an ordinary stock corporation; instead, its members had voting rights that they couldn't buy or sell. Initially, NBI had 243 charter members, including

Bank of America, Bankers Trust, and First Chicago as well as numerous smaller community and regional banks.

The brief period 1966–1970 turned out to be critical for the future development of the payment card industry. Three alternative business models battled against each other. The go-it-alone model had been the one used by American Express, Diners Club, and Carte Blanche for charge cards. Bank of America adopted this model in California, Citigroup tried it with its Everything credit card, and American Express tried it with its Uni-Card credit card. Bank of America and the three T&E card companies tried the franchise model. Finally, the co-opetitive model was used by Interbank and many other associations of banks across the country. The web of interstate and branch banking restrictions played a crucial role in the battle among these models.

By the end of the 1960s, the franchise model was dead in the United States. And the go-it-alone companies and the co-opetitives had gone in different directions. Sticking to what they knew best, the go-it-alones decided not to issue credit cards. American Express had ventured into credit with its Uni-Card, but decided to get out and did not try again for twenty years, as we will see. The co-opetitives, on the other hand, focused on issuing cards with a revolving line of credit. (Debit cards were soon added, but took until the early 1990s to have an impact.) Today, the co-opetitives account for 71 percent of card volume.

The basic idea behind co-opetition was clear as early as the Midwest Bank Card. The five founding members competed with each other for cardholders and merchants in the Chicago area. They cooperated in two related respects. They agreed to make their systems "interoperable." A First National Bank of Chicago cardholder could use her card at every merchant who had signed up with any of the five banks. A Harris Trust Company merchant could accept as payment any card from these banks. What the banks lost in helping their competitors, they more than gained in making their own card more appealing to cardholders and merchants. Interoperability forced cooperation in another way. When a First National Bank of Chicago cardholder bought something at a merchant who was affiliated with Harris Trust Company, Harris Trust had to get reimbursed by First National. These banks faced the same problem as in the BankAmericard franchise: system cooperation was essential to process the slips of merchant receipts that were growing exponentially with the number of participants in the system.

The two national associations encountered similar issues to Midwest Bank Card, only on a grander scale. MasterCard—which started out as the Interbank Card Association in 1966, changed its acceptance brand to Master Charge in 1969, and finally became known as MasterCard in 1979—and Visa—which began as BankAmericard in 1958, switched to National BankAmericard, Inc. in 1970, and settled on Visa in 1976—took cooperation further than any of the regional associations. First, they established rules and processes for settling transactions. Part of this involved how the merchant and the cardholder banks divvied up the transaction proceeds. Some of the regional cooperatives had initially exchanged at par so that the cardholder's bank reimbursed the merchant's bank for the entire transaction and the cardholder's bank didn't get any of the merchant fees. (The banks may have simply been applying the check model of par exchange, which they soon found unsatisfactory for cards.) MasterCard and Visa both settled on an interchange fee—a percentage of each transaction that the merchant's bank gave to the cardholder's bank. (We discuss this further in chapter 6.)

Another area of cooperation was on the card brand. The banks that belonged to Interbank decided early on to use the Master Charge brand. That—and not the individual bank's name—is what was most prominent on the cards from the late 1960s and early 1970s. Visa replaced BankAmericard as the brand name for that system in 1976. The co-opetitive felt that "standardizing the somewhat confusing array of blue-white-and-gold cards issued under different names in twenty-two countries around the world" would lead to greater acceptance of the card. Focusing on the system's brand involved a trade-off basic to the co-opetitive model: choosing between doing things at the system versus the member level.

Overall, the co-opetitives chose to do most things at the member level. A few statistics are revealing. Association membership fees and dues for Visa and MasterCard, which cover the costs of the centralized operations, account for only about 1.5 percent of the total direct card-related expenses incurred by members of these systems. Visa's centralized activities are conducted by a staff of about 1,300 employees. To put this in perspective, these people comprise less than 0.5 percent of the total estimated employees involved in issuing Visa cards.

Regulation and Stagflation

American Express prospered during the 1970s. Between 1960 and 1977, real net income grew at an average annual rate of 16.6 percent. By 1977, American Express had eight million cardholders, bringing in $393 million in annual card fees. Its lead over Diners Club and Carte Blanche had widened dramatically. American Express had decided against offering a credit card and had unloaded its Uni-Card credit card. About 200,000 of its cardholders had "corporate cards"—cards that employers ask employees to use for expenses and that provide employers with detailed spending data. Sticking with charge cards, shunning credit cards, and focusing on corporate users was a profitable strategy for some time.

Meanwhile, American Express's credit card competitors—the banks that issued credit cards and the two associations to which they belonged—struggled during this decade of government regulation, volatile interest rates, and economic stagnation. The economy went through several severe recessions in the 1970s and early 1980s (see table 3.1). The economy also experienced accelerating inflation, jumping

Table 3.1
U.S. recessions, 1969–1982

Start	End	Duration (months)	Peak monthly unemployment rate (%)
December 1969	November 1970	11	5.9
November 1973	March 1975	16	8.6
January 1980	July 1980	6	7.8
July 1981	November 1982	16	10.8

Note: The National Bureau of Economic Research defines a recession as "a period of significant decline in total output, income, employment, and trade." *Sources:* National Bureau of Economic Research, *U.S. Business Cycle Expansions and Contractions*, <http://www.nber.org/cycles/> (accessed April 21, 2003); and U.S. Department of Labor, Bureau of Labor Statistics.

from 4.2 percent in 1972 to a peak of 9.4 percent in 1981. This led to an increase in (nominal) interest rates. (Economists distinguish between nominal interest rates, which are quoted by lenders, and real interest rates, which are lower than nominal rates by the rate of inflation. Real rates adjust for the impact of inflation on purchasing power over time; nominal rates tend to vary with the rate of inflation, all else being equal.) The one-year Treasury bill rate climbed from 4.89 percent in 1971 to 14.8 percent in 1981. As interest rates climbed, state usury laws made credit card lending a bad business proposition. Banks need a spread between the finance rate they charge consumers and their own cost of funds to cover their operational costs, including fraud and defaults, and make a profit. As inflation rose, that spread generally narrowed and even became negative in states with low caps on loan rates. Banks lost money on the credit they had already made available on cards and became unwilling to extend further credit in the face of these losses. Usury laws, and a Supreme Court decision about them, helped shape the card industry in the 1970s and beyond.

Usury Laws

Thirty-six states had usury laws in 1982. Some had caps that were so high, they didn't matter during times of normal inflation and interest rates—for instance, Georgia had a maximum of 60 percent. But others topped out at rates that made it difficult for banks, even in normal times, to make unsecured loans profitably. Arkansas, for example, had a maximum rate of 5 percent above the Federal Reserve discount rate, giving a maximum rate of about 12 percent at the time. Banks lived with their state caps by tailoring their credit card lending. Banks in states with high limits could extend credit to a wide range of people because they were able to charge finance rates that covered the inevitable defaults, late payments, and fraud. Banks in states with low limits raised their credit criteria for issuing cards and imposed higher membership fees. For example, because Arkansas imposed a low cap on consumer loan rates, banks in that state had to set their standards relatively high and offer credit to very few people in order to hold down costs. As a result, charge-off rates in Arkansas were low, but so was the use of credit cards.

(Charge-offs are credit card balances that have been written off as losses for tax purposes.)

Usury laws had a significant effect on the development of a national card industry because they limited the ability of banks to market their cards on a national or even regional basis. Interest rates that were lawful in one state were unlawful in another. A bank therefore couldn't market a card nationally or regionally and capture scale economies from wide distribution. The few banks that issued in multiple states had to incur the expense of administering multiple card programs with different terms in each state. This wasn't just an issue of processing extra paper; the banks had to adjust credit standards and collection criteria according to the finance charges they could assess in each state.

A Supreme Court decision changed the rules of the game in 1978 and helped create national competition for payment cards. First of Omaha Service Corporation, a subsidiary of First National Bank of Omaha, began to apply interest rates that were legal in Nebraska, but higher than the Minnesota rate ceiling to its Minnesota credit card customers. Marquette National Bank of Minnesota challenged this practice. The Supreme Court sided with First of Omaha. In *Marquette National Bank v. First of Omaha Service Corp.*, the Court ruled that as a national bank, First National Bank of Omaha "may charge interest on any loan at the rate allowed by the laws of the State where the bank is located." The Court also said that a bank's "location" refers to the state in which the bank is chartered, regardless of the states in which it solicits customers.

The *Marquette* decision led to three major developments. First, nationally chartered banks started issuing credit cards from states with less-restrictive usury laws. Citigroup, for example, moved its credit card operations from New York, which at the time had an interest rate cap of 12 percent on balances greater than $850, to South Dakota, which had raised its interest rate ceiling to 19.8 percent. Many other banks moved their operations to Delaware, which eliminated interest rate caps in early 1981. By 1987, many large banks legally resided in Delaware, including Bankers Trust, Chase Manhattan, Chemical, Manufacturers Hanover, Morgan, and Marine Midland.

Second, in an attempt to attract or retain such movable card operations, some states began to modify their usury laws. In 1980, the same year that Citigroup announced it would be moving its operations to South Dakota, the New York State Senate passed a bill that eliminated interest rate ceilings on most types of loans, except annual rates on credit cards, which remained at 25 percent. By 1988, the majority of states still had some form of an interest rate cap on credit card loans, but many had raised their ceilings.

Third, less balkanization from state credit restraints set the stage for marketing payment cards on a nationwide basis. Citigroup led the way in the late 1970s and early 1980s: it expanded nationwide through acquisitions and mass-mail credit card solicitations. Throughout the 1980s, many other banks launched national credit card campaigns as well, including Bank of America, Chase, Continental Illinois, First Chicago, and Manufacturers Hanover. By permitting nationwide competition, *Marquette* enabled issuers to realize scale economies in marketing and processing costs, thereby making payment cards more readily available to consumers across the country. Thus, even though Arkansas still caps interest rates at 5 percent above the Federal Reserve discount rate today, consumers in Arkansas have a wide range of card choices from national issuers.

Duality

Federal antitrust laws also had a major effect on the evolution of the payment card industry in the 1970s. Visa's rules initially prohibited MasterCard-issuing banks from issuing its cards or handling its merchant paper. In July 1971, one of Visa's charter members, Worthen Bank and Trust Company of Little Rock, Arkansas, filed an antitrust suit, claiming that Visa's prohibition amounted to an illegal group boycott. (We discuss this case in more detail in chapter 11.) While this case was eventually settled out of court, Visa remained exposed to similar lawsuits. In 1974, it asked the Antitrust Division of the U.S. Department of Justice for a business clearance review—in effect, a letter of approval for a rule that would prohibit dual membership by card-issuing and merchant-acquiring banks. After a year of consideration, the division declined to grant clearance, citing insufficient information. Without the division's support, Visa removed all restrictions on dual membership in mid-1976. The age of what has become known as "duality" began, and members of each system rushed to join the other.

Competition among issuers increased sharply as new members scrambled to sign up consumers for their second card. From mid-1976 to mid-1977, the number of cardholders increased by 11.7 percent for MasterCard and 13.1 percent for Visa—significantly higher growth than in preceding years. Banks that were previously exclusive to MasterCard could now sign up their merchants for Visa (and vice versa) as well as compete generally for merchants. Merchant acceptance grew sharply from mid-1976 to mid-1977, by 24.3 percent for MasterCard and 17.3 percent for Visa, again much higher than in preceding years.

One year after the restriction was removed, twenty of the nation's twenty-two-largest banks that issued cards had become dual. With increased system overlap, Visa and MasterCard twice discussed the possibility of merging system infrastructures in the 1980s, but decided against the move both times. With duality, the difference between Visa and MasterCard began to blur, at least as far as consumers were concerned. Some dual members offered common agreements, billing statements, and credit lines. And some used common advertisements for their dual cards.

Over time, almost all member institutions joined both associations, and the increasing overlap in membership led to some decline in competition between the two systems. As we explain further on, dual membership lost some of its appeal in the late 1990s, and a recent court decision may bring yet more changes on this front.

A Painful Decade for Card Issuers
The Visa and MasterCard associations had little trouble finding banks to join their still-fledgling associations in the 1970s. First, banks were afraid of being left behind. Many banks got into the card business to preempt or counter their competitors' plans. Second, there was a growing belief that credit cards were a stepping-stone to the "cashless society." Third, cards created an opportunity for cross selling. Many banks even felt that they could not offer their retail customers an acceptable menu of banking services unless they operated a card plan. And fourth, even

though achieving profitability would remain challenging, some banks had shown they could make money in the card business. The number of bank issuers grew from about 600 in 1971 to at least 1,750 in 1981.

The association model provided banks with opportunities to specialize that they didn't have with their earlier go-it-alone card programs. Banks could just issue cards, since those cards could be used at all merchants that were card customers of other members of the association. Or they could just handle credit card transactions for merchants (as acquirers). They could also do both—which is what most banks did in the 1970s—although some focused on issuing or acquiring.

Nonetheless, echoing some of the problems of the 1950s, profits did not come easily or quickly. The early 1970s were marked by substantial losses. As described in 1971 by the *American Banker*: "The top managements of many of the nation's large credit card issuing banks, though, are becoming increasingly disillusioned with the negative profit contribution of their card programs and are questioning whether they can afford to stay in the business." Wells Fargo lost more than $27 million between 1967 and 1970; Bankers Trust lost nearly $22 million in 1969 and more than $11 million in 1970; Riggs National Bank lost almost $4 million in 1970 (as always, these figures are in 2002 dollars). All told, bank credit card losses in 1970 rose 50 percent over 1969, to $440 million or 3.4 percent of the outstanding credit card debt.

There were a couple of reasons for the mounting losses. First, and perhaps most important, the credit card business was quite different from traditional types of lending. As one industry observer noted, banks entered the credit card industry "without being remotely prepared to solve the hundreds of problems, both large and small, that were bound to arise." Learning what worked and what didn't involved costly mistakes and inefficient practices. Second, banks did not have the luxury of starting out small while learning the business. As the *American Banker* reported in 1966: "Credit cards are not something a bank can 'feel its way into.' They require a big splash of publicity, much careful planning, aggressive selling and perhaps above all, the courage to continue as the losses mount."

The second reason behind the mounting losses of the early 1970s had its roots in the late 1960s. The "big splash of publicity" that banks used to enter the payment card industry often came in the guise of mass mailings of free, unsolicited credit cards. Banks typically drew names for the mailings from lists of depositors and customers with mortgage and installment loans. The mass mailings got the cards to lots of consumers, providing a sufficient cardholder base to attract merchants. But they also came at a price. Given the volume of consumers who received a free card in the mail and the rush to beat competitors' card offerings, the banks often did little more than a basic credit check, and some didn't even do that much. Moreover, they could not provide secure delivery of cards. Chicago postal clerks were caught hoarding unmailed cards to sell on the black market; small-time criminals stole cards out of mailboxes; even the Mafia got involved, trafficking in stolen cards and working with dishonest merchants to submit false sales slips. As a result of all this, the levels of fraud and defaults in the early 1970s were quite high.

(The economics of two-sided markets tells us that we should not be too quick to claim that these efforts were bad business, however. Many platforms invest in getting one or both sides on board; it is unclear whether banks could have ignited their platforms in some other way without incurring comparable losses.)

The Federal Trade Commission finally banned mass mailings of credit cards in April 1970. But in 1971, banks were still feeling the effects. Visa issuers' losses due to fraud were over 0.3 percent of total sales volume. (To put this in perspective, fraud losses were only 0.07 percent of volume in 2002.) Charge-offs for bankcards were also relatively high. In 1969, charge-offs for all bankcard plans were almost $230 million, or 2.4 percent of the total credit card loans outstanding. In 1970, a recession year, charge-offs for all bankcard plans were close to $440 million, or 3.4 percent of the total loans outstanding. Added to the turmoil of fraud and consumer delinquency were the thorny issues of how to coordinate the various banks in the system. Who was responsible for fraud and unpaid cardholder bills, and how would the various parties settle with one another? Recall that in the early 1970s, the newly formed bank associations did not have computer systems to smooth transactions; everything was done with paper and postage.

Although bankcard issuers had started to leave the red ink behind by 1972, they still found it difficult to earn the same returns from credit card lending as they did in their other lines of lending. From 1974 (the earliest year with available data) through 1980, the rate of return on assets (net before-tax earnings divided by assets) on credit card lending ranged from –1.61 percent (in 1980) to 3.09 percent (in 1977), for an average of 1.53 percent. In contrast, banks earned far higher average rates of return on other forms of lending over that same period: 2.26 percent on installment loans, 2.48 percent on real estate loans, and 3.04 percent on commercial loans. The discrepancies are especially surprising given that credit card loans are not secured with physical assets, whereas the other loan types are. Credit card loans were thus riskier to make, but earned banks a lower return throughout the 1970s.

And Yet, a Decade in Which Foundations Were Laid
Although the bankcard programs struggled in the 1970s, the associations to which they belonged laid the foundations for the modern electronic payment card systems. The associations established their brands—MasterCard and Visa—firmly in the minds of households and merchants. Both associations spent millions of dollars in the 1970s on national television ad campaigns, such as the 1974 "Relax—you've got a Master Charge" effort. Most important, they relied on the computer revolution to develop systems for quickly and efficiently authorizing as well as settling transactions among the growing numbers of merchants, cardholders, and members.

Visa built the BASE-I system using computers from Digital Equipment Corporation. The system allowed a merchant's authorization request to be transmitted over phone lines from the merchant to the cardholder's bank, with Visa providing backup when the cardholder's bank was closed. This went online in 1973. BASE-I cut the wait for a transaction authorization from four minutes on average to about forty seconds. It cost about $30 million to build, but it was estimated to have saved members over $100 million in fraud prevention in its first year of operation. Visa then set about building BASE-II, which computerized the entire transaction process and solved the other major member headache: the physical interchange of paper among members. BASE-II went online in 1974. MasterCard made similar investments to move its systems off paper and onto computers, with its own BankNet and I-Net systems.

The 1980s' Spending and Debt Spree

Let us take stock of the shape of the payment card industry in 1983—a year that marked the end of stagflation in the United States and the start of a long economic expansion. At least 1,500 companies ran credit or charge card programs in the United States. All of the companies with credit card programs were financial institutions that belonged to the MasterCard and/or Visa associations. Many issued cards with both brands; those that acquired transactions from merchants did so for cards from both associations. American Express was the major charge card company with 87 percent of all T&E cards; Carte Blanche and Diners Club, both operated by Citigroup, held the remainder. Table 3.2 lists the top issuers in 1983 of credit and charge cards by gross charge volume.

The payment card industry was poised for growth. Interest rate ceilings were no longer as serious a problem as they recently had been. Banks' cost of funds fell dramatically after the 1980–1982 recession, and usury laws were less prevalent, less severe, and after the *Marquette*

Table 3.2
Top issuers of credit and charge cards, 1983

Issuer	Volume ($ billions)	Share of total industry volume (%)
1 American Express	47.6	25.6
2 Bank of America	9.9	5.3
3 Citigroup	9.0	4.8
4 Diners Club/Carte Blanche	7.4	4.0
5 First National of Chicago	5.1	2.7
6 Chase Manhattan	4.8	2.6
7 Chemical Bank	3.6	1.9
8 First Interstate Bank	3.1	1.7
9 Manufacturers Hanover	2.9	1.6
10 Security Pacific National	2.6	1.4
Total (top 10)	*95.9*	*51.6*
Total (all issuers)	*185.9*	*100*

Note: Numbers may not add up to totals due to rounding.
Sources: The Nilson Report; Visa U.S.A.

decision, less important. Many banks had mature card programs with customers whose credit behavior they had observed for some time. The 1970 Fair Credit Reporting Act helped to ensure that creditors had access to accurate credit reports, increasingly at the national level. And the card industry had learned from experience how to reduce losses from card-holders who didn't pay their bills.

Credit cards were well-understood products that could make money for banks in several ways. Banks that issued cards charged membership fees. (Many banks had instituted these fees in response to a 1980 Federal Reserve requirement that they hold reserves against outstanding credit card debt.) They also earned income from merchants: they received a percentage of each transaction through the interchange fee, which was around 1.6 percent in the early 1980s. And from cardholders who revolved their balances, they received finance charges. Banks that acquired transactions from merchants earned revenue from fees that were usually based on percentages of transactions volume. (We discuss the economics of card issuing in chapter 9 and of card acquiring in chapter 10.)

As this picture suggests, the payment card industry grew dramatically over the remainder of the 1980s, during one of the longest peacetime economic expansions in U.S. history. Between 1982 and 1990, overall consumer spending rose from $3.4 trillion ($41,170 per household) to $4.8 trillion ($51,280 per household). Retail spending increased from $1.8 trillion ($21,380 per household) in 1982 to $2.3 trillion ($24,760 per household) in 1990. Restaurant spending almost doubled from $120 billion ($1,440 per household) to $225 billion ($2,410 per household). These increases naturally provided more opportunities to use payment cards. Dollar transactions on credit and charge cards increased from $155 billion in 1982 to $400 billion in 1990. Part of this increase reflected growth in spending on cards by people who had cards. The average monthly charge on cards increased from $268 per household in 1977 to $395 in 1992. (Data are not available from the early 1980s.) Another part reflected growth in the number of households with cards. The percentage of households with at least one card increased from 43 percent in 1983 to 62 percent in 1992. (More people started carrying multiple cards so the average amount charged per card did not increase as much as the average amount charged per household.)

People not only charged more, they borrowed more. Between 1982 and 1990, the total amount of consumer credit outstanding rose from $640 billion to $1,015 billion, and the average consumer credit outstanding per household increased from $7,660 to $10,880. Thus, the total consumer credit outstanding grew at an average annual rate of 6 percent. Credit card debt grew even faster: outstanding loans on credit cards grew at an average annual rate of 21 percent, from about $50 billion to $225 billion, increasing from $580 to $2,430 per household in 1982 and 1990, respectively.

Not surprisingly, the increased demand for payment and credit services, combined with a more favorable financial environment for payment card issuers, generated an enormous increase in the supply of payment card services. Existing issuers from Citigroup to American Express issued more cards. More important, banks that wanted to get into the card business could issue the established MasterCard and Visa brands, and the cards they issued could be used instantly at the millions of merchants who already took these two brands. Between 1981 and 1991, about 4,200 financial institutions became issuing members of the Visa association. (Legislation in 1982 that made more institutions eligible for federal deposit insurance expanded the pool of possible entrants.) Several of these entrants are particularly noteworthy, and we will discuss them shortly.

On the other side of card transactions, acquirers signed up more merchants during the 1980s—both new merchants who were part of the wave of new business formation and existing merchants who hadn't taken cards before. From 1982 to 1990, the number of U.S. merchants accepting Visa increased by 37 percent. By 1991, more than 2.5 million merchants accepted Visa cards. MasterCard experienced a similar growth in merchant acceptance.

The increased supply of card services for customers and merchants came from three other notable sources. Sears, Roebuck and Co. started the Discover Card in 1985 (and went national in 1986). Less than two years after the signature orange-and-black Discover Card was released, there were twenty-two million cards in circulation—more than Citigroup had accomplished after two decades—and $4 billion in receivables, ranking it third among all credit and charge cards in the United States. Over 700,000 merchants accepted the card by 1987.

Less than two years after the Discover Card launch and about twenty years after selling its credit card (the Uni-Card), American Express launched the Optima credit card. Yet what American Express thought would be a successful competitor to the bankcard issuers quickly turned into a disaster. Default rates skyrocketed and losses soared, costing the company hundreds of millions of dollars. This sophisticated company's problems make clear the complexity of the credit card business. American Express assumed that their charge card holders would be good credit risks—after all, they paid their bills on time. What American Express failed to recognize, though, was that many of these charge card holders were using their cards for company business for which they were reimbursed. They were less conscientious when they had to pay the bills themselves. There were enough defaults to sink the Optima card in red ink. By October 1991, during a recession that hit white-collar workers particularly hard, about 8 percent of Optima's receivables were charged off. The credit arm of American Express had to take a $327 million charge against third-quarter earnings in 1991, including $135 million to restructure the credit card operations and $191 million to add to credit loss reserves. In addition, about 1,700 employees were laid off. Altogether, American Express reported a 93 percent drop in its third-quarter income for 1991. By early 1992, Optima's credit losses topped out at 12 percent of receivables. American Express eventually turned its credit cards into a success in the 1990s, as we will see, but it wasn't easy.

Meanwhile, the pioneers of the payment card industry, Diners Club and Carte Blanche, had become marginal players in the United States by the end of the 1980s. Together, they had a share of less than 2.5 percent of payment card transaction volume.

In the 1980s, several significant entrants into the card business came in through MasterCard and Visa. Three giant nonfinancial firms—AT&T, General Electric, and General Motors—decided to get into the card business. MasterCard was much more enthusiastic about these nonbanks becoming part of its association than Visa was, so many of these firms issued MasterCards at first. These firms either bought banks that were members of MasterCard or Visa, or they entered into contracts with banks that were association members. Either way, it was the industrial giants whose names were prominently featured on the cards.

Many of the nonbanks' cards were tied to the business of the firm that sponsored the card. "We saw our relationships with twenty-two million calling–card customers in jeopardy," stated Paul Kahn, head of AT&T Universal Card Services Corp. Thus, AT&T linked its card to its primary business; the payment card could function as a calling card. A General Motors card allowed cardholders to accumulate points that could earn a rebate on a General Motors car. General Electric's card, however, had no such links. Instead, it offered general reward coupons that were redeemable at various retailers. The nonbank firms gained many cardholders and became some of the largest programs in the early 1990s. In fact, two of the top ten bankcard issuers in the early 1990s (by charge volume from 1991 to 1994) were nonbanks: AT&T Universal and Household Bank (which among other things, issued a General Motors card).

Some, but not all, of the nonbank card issuers were able to sustain this early growth. The General Motors card is still issued by Household and still enables cardholders to accumulate points toward a General Motors car. In 2002, General Electric Capital Financial was the fifteenth-largest issuer, by charge volume, of MasterCard and Visa credit cards. AT&T, in contrast, sold its card portfolio to Citigroup in 1998, though the AT&T Universal card still functions as an AT&T calling card.

Two other kinds of cards were introduced in the 1980s that were notable marketing successes. The first was proposed by one of the bank associations. In 1978, Visa introduced affinity programs that for the first time, allowed a nonmember's name or logo to be displayed on the face of the card. In 1980, however, Visa banned new affinity card programs, arguing that they tended to dilute the Visa brand, but it allowed the existing programs to continue. Five years later, faced with apparent payment card saturation, both Visa and MasterCard began allowing new affinity programs. After only one year, 296 clubs, charities, professional associations, and other nonfinancial organizations had developed Visa and MasterCard affinity programs. By 1989, there were over 2,000 affinity card programs in the United States, ranging from the Sierra Club to the National Football League to the UCLA Alumni Association. Affinity cards involving for-profit companies are also known as "cobranded" cards.

The other new type of card was introduced by Citigroup. Citigroup and American Airlines announced the AAdvantage bankcard in April 1987, marketing it to about six million members of American's AAdvantage frequent-flier program. At the time, AAdvantage was the largest-frequent flier program, and Citigroup was the largest credit card issuer in the United States with fifteen million cards issued. The card had a $50 annual fee and credit lines of up to $50,000, which led some industry expert to assume that Citigroup was "competing for the same kinds of customers as American Express Co.'s Green and Gold Cards." By early 1993, about 1.5 million AAdvantage credit cards were in circulation.

These three payment card innovations in the 1980s—the nonbank issuers, affinity and cobranded cards, and frequent-flier rewards cards—each contributed to a dramatic rise in consumer card use over the decade. By 1991, there were almost twice as many cards per household compared to five years earlier.

The 1990s and the Rise of the Debit Card

In 1990, almost 65 percent of payment cards in the United States offered revolving credit. And most households used credit cards for consumer purchases. Charge cards were used mainly for business expenses. Although ATM cards were common—accounting for about 31 percent of payment cards—and were technically debit cards (usable at those few merchants equipped to accept PIN debit), consumers hardly ever made purchases with them.

This mix of cards was quite different from that in other industrialized countries. Banks in most European countries, for instance, issued debit cards more often than credit cards. Some of these cards were deferred debit cards: the charges were accumulated and then deducted from the cardholder's checking account at the end of a monthly billing cycle. Others deducted charges right away. Credit cards were much less common. For example, virtually all cards in France and 83 percent of all cards in Germany were debit cards. In Japan, credit cards resemble Europe's deferred debit cards: consumers agree to pay the card balance at the end of the month, and issuers are authorized to directly debit a customer's account to pay the total outstanding shortly after the last day of the payment cycle.

Debit cards had been around in the United States since 1975, but they were rarely used. That changed in the 1990s as a result of two developments. After several false starts, the Visa association found a way to ignite debit cards—to get its members to issue them and households to use them. Since most of these debit cards required the cardholder to sign an authorization slip, we call them signature debit cards here. (For technical reasons, they are also called off-line debit cards in the industry.) The other development came from outside the payment card industry. Bank associations transformed ATM cards into debit cards during the 1990s by persuading merchants to install equipment to accept them. Since these cards required cardholders to enter their PIN, we refer to them as PIN debit cards. (The industry also refers to them as online debit cards.)

The contracts that merchants entered into with Visa acquirers required them to take all Visa cards—debit cards as well as credit cards. From the standpoint of the merchant, Visa's debit cards worked just like its credit cards and didn't require any additional equipment or training. But Visa didn't have the other side of the market—the cardholders—because banks hadn't been interested in issuing these kinds of cards. As we describe in more detail in chapter 8, Visa embarked on a campaign to convince banks that they could make money from debit cards and to convince cardholders to use these cards. Visa made a commitment to promote a new debit card brand—Visa Check—through extensive national advertising. Around the same time, Visa staff tried to convince banks that the interchange fee revenues they would receive from transactions on the cards they issued would make these cards profitable. (Visa's debit card interchange fees were set slightly lower than its credit card interchange fees at the time.) MasterCard followed with a similar product and strategy after initially pursuing an unsuccessful PIN debit strategy.

The bank associations that ran the EFT (then ATM) networks faced a different business problem: they had gotten many cards into the hands of households, but didn't have merchants who were willing to take those cards. During the 1980s, banks had installed ATMs and issued cards to their customers that allowed them to take out cash and conduct other banking transactions. Associations of banks formed that enabled customers of one bank to use their cards at the ATMs of other banks. The EFT networks didn't have a system for authorizing card transactions by signature. But they could authorize and settle transactions if merchants had PIN pads that were connected to the ATM switches. And most of the EFT systems required banks to allow ATM cards to be used for retail transactions. To get merchants on board, the EFT networks had to convince merchants to install PIN pads. They did this by setting an interchange fee that was much lower than that charged by the card associations. This resulted in merchants with PIN pads paying a much lower merchant discount for PIN debit transactions than for signature debit transactions.

Most banks chose to put the marks of either MasterCard or Visa (for signature debit) and the EFT networks (for PIN debit) on the same card. This resulted in synergies between signature and PIN debit. The existing base of ATM cards made it easier for banks to issue Visa Check cards, while the Visa Check promotions helped persuade people to carry and use these cards—in both modes—for paying for things.

The efforts to increase debit card use, by both Visa and the EFT networks, were successful by the end of the decade. Today, debit cards account for 29 percent of both all payment cards and all payment card volume. Of the $490 billion worth of transactions on debit cards in 2002, 66 percent by value were signature debit and the remainder were PIN debit.

While the rapid growth of debit cards was by far the most notable change in the payment card industry in the 1990s, four other developments deserve mention. The first was a financial innovation known as "securitization," which enabled credit card lenders to sell credit card debt to other institutions that could consolidate many different kinds of debt from many different lenders. Credit card issuers could use securitization income to expand their businesses. Securitization also allowed assets to be moved from the card issuers' balance sheets, thus lowering the capital reserves they were required to hold. In addition, credit card issuers could reduce their risk from cardholders defaulting on payments—a particular worry in the event of an economic downturn.

Without securitization, an individual issuer, especially those that focused on credit card lending, had difficulty diversifying away their risk exposure. Securitization allowed lenders to diversify their risk and thus to extend credit deeper into the pool of relatively risky consumers (that is, consumers with poor credit histories). Industry experts estimate that $61 billion in retail and bank credit card loans, roughly 10 percent of outstanding balances on store and bank credit cards, were securitized in 2001. (This development came later than, but is similar to, the securitization of mortgages. Most mortgage lenders resell their loans to companies that consolidate loans from many lenders and then diversify the risk through complex financial arrangements.) Securitization also made it easier for companies to both enter credit card lending (because they could diversify their risk) and get out of the business (because they had a market for the loans they had made).

The second key development occurred in the banking industry. We saw in the previous chapter that legislative changes resulted in a massive consolidation of banks. This had effects on the payment card industry. Consider the fifty-largest banks ranked by total assets in 1990. Through mergers and acquisitions, these fifty banks were consolidated into eighteen banks by 2003. For example, Chase Manhattan took over Chemical Bank in 1996. Bank One acquired First USA and First Chicago in 1997 and 1998, respectively, and Bank of America—one of the largest bank credit card issuers—merged with NationsBank in 1998. This automatically led to consolidation among payment card issuers. Moreover, there was substantial consolidation within the card industry through portfolio sales. AT&T Universal sold off its portfolio to Citigroup in 1998, for instance, and MBNA purchased the SunTrust Bank portfolio in 1999. Additional shifts have occurred as some issuers have substantially increased their share of sales volume. For example, MBNA more than doubled its share of Visa and MasterCard credit card volume from 4.5 percent in 1990 to 10.8 percent in 1999. The payment card industry became more concentrated—the top ten bankcard issuers accounted for 74 percent of Visa and MasterCard volume in 1999 versus 44 percent in 1990—although as we discuss later, it is still less concentrated than other major industries.

A third development concerns the co-opetitives. During the 1990s, each co-opetitive began aggressively encouraging its members to dedicate themselves to one association at the expense of the other association. By the end of the 1990s, both MasterCard and Visa began to offer formal partnership programs, providing benefits to banks that agreed to focus their card business on just one system. One could argue that this marked the effective end of duality, but an antitrust decision, discussed in chapter 11, may pose a challenge to the partnership programs and result in the associations blending together again.

Finally, one can't talk about the 1990s without talking about the Internet. At least in the United States, payment cards have been essential for online commerce. In this country, 95 percent of Internet purchases are made with payment cards. In the United Kingdom and Australia, cards were used for 90 percent of online purchase volume; in France, the figure is 80 percent. In many other countries, however, cards are used far less often for online transactions. Scandinavians use payment cards for 50 to 60 percent of Internet purchases. In Austria, Germany, Holland, Italy, Japan, and Spain, payment cards account for only around one-third of online volume. Account-to-account (A2A) payments are the main competitor to cards for worldwide online payments. In an A2A payment, money is transferred directly from the payer's checking account to the payee's checking account via electronic transfer. (We discuss A2A payments in more detail in chapter 12.)

The Golden Anniversary and Beyond

The general-purpose payment card turned fifty in 2000. Despite all the talk about the cashless society, this electronic method of payment still accounts for less than half of all retail transactions, and only 27 percent of all consumer expenditures—this excludes implicit consumption that doesn't involve payment, such as the rent you pay yourself if you own your home. Cash and checks haven't disappeared. The move to electronic money has been gradual, but steady. Figure 3.1 shows the purchase volume of general-purpose payment cards as a percentage of consumer expenditures in the United States from 1970 to 2002.

The payment card industry has evolved through incremental changes that persuaded more individuals and businesses to rely on this method of payment. There have been some drastic innovations—McNamara's

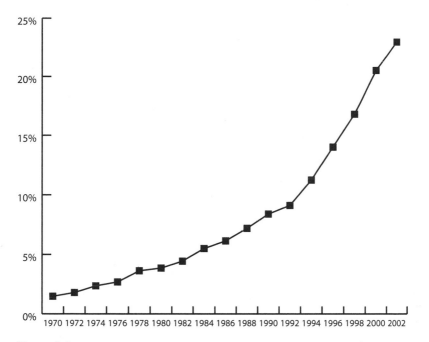

Figure 3.1
Purchase volume on general-purpose payment cards as a percent of consumer expenditures, 1970–2002
Note: General-purpose payment cards include credit, charge, PIN debit, and signature debit cards.
Sources: Bureau of Economic Analysis; and *The Nilson Report* (various 1970–2003 issues).

initial insight, and the idea of bundling revolving credit with a payment device, just to mention two. But less drastic innovations have also been important in aggregate. These include the use of computers to reduce the time it takes to complete transactions, the development of credit-scoring techniques to identify and then monitor creditworthy customers, securitization, and bundling airline rewards and other features onto cards. As we start the new millennium, however, we can't say breathily that the cashless society is right around the corner.

4

From Gourmets to the Masses

Credit is the latest ally of the devil. It is the great tempter. It is responsible for half the extravagance of modern life. The two words "charge it" have done more harm than any others in the language. They have led to a vast amount of unnecessary buying. . . . They have created a large and growing sisterhood and brotherhood of deadbeats. They have led to bankruptcy and slow pay and bad debts. They have raised the cost of everything.

—Irving Bachellar, *Charge It!* (1912)

This little strip of plastic, and the unique global partnership that supports it, has transformed the way we shop. The way we pay our bills. The way we bank. The way we travel. The way we *live*.

—Paul Chutkow, *Visa: The Power of an Idea* (2001)

Once targeted only to the Bloomingdale's set, plastic cards are now used throughout society—by college students and retirees, by the unemployed and hopeful entrepreneurs, by many of the poorest households and most of the wealthiest. Advances in credit-scoring techniques have enabled credit card issuers to make cards with at least some revolving credit available to a wide range of households. In 2001, about 73 percent of U.S. households had at least one credit card. Virtually all households with charge cards also had a credit card. And 40 percent of households with neither credit nor charge cards used a debit card in 2001. Furthermore, prepaid cards are beginning to make it possible for the poorest members of society—workers who are paid in cash or who can't open a checking account, and people on welfare—to pay with a convenient plastic card. Almost everyone has electronic money—just in time for shopping on the Internet or their cell phones.

This chapter explores how payment cards have spread through U.S. society in the last fifty years, how they have affected consumer spending and borrowing, and whether cards are financial junk food. (Some of the research in this chapter is based on the Federal Reserve Board's *Survey of Consumer Finances* [*SCF*]. The *SCF* has reported charge and credit card ownership in the United States since 1970, debit card ownership since 1992, and debit card use since 1995. The endnotes for this chapter discuss the strengths and weaknesses of these data, and why the *SCF* data are not always consistent with other data we report.)

The Growth and Diffusion of Payment Cards among U.S. Households

In the 1950s, payment cards were extremely exclusive even though they had annual fees of only $25 to $30. Cards were only useful during this period for paying at upscale restaurants, hotels, and other travel and entertainment destinations. By the end of the decade, you could put a night on the town in Manhattan on your Diners Club card, but you were out of luck if you wanted to put a lightbulb on it. Naturally, only the well-heeled—upscale shoppers and corporate travelers—would want one of these cards.

And in those days before sophisticated credit checks and the constant monitoring of spending and payment, the T&E cards only wanted well-heeled cardholders. For instance, Diners Club would only consider applicants who earned above the median wage. American Express had similar income requirements, and both firms required evidence of a steady employment history. In addition to an income requirement, an application for membership was judged on a person's credit rating in the community.

At the start of the 1960s, only 7 percent of households had either a credit or a charge card. Using the *SCF*, figure 4.1 tracks the growth of credit cards and their diffusion across the income distribution beginning in 1970. (The lowest 20 percent of incomes are in IQ1; the highest are in IQ5.) We see that while poorer households are less likely to have cards in any given year than wealthier households, they have had impressive gains in card ownership. For example, the proportion of households in

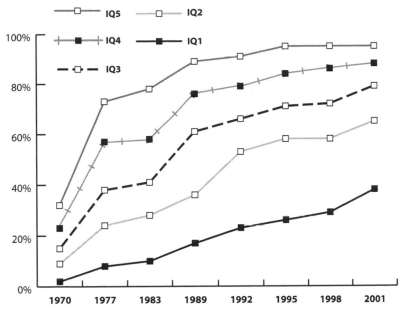

Figure 4.1
Percent of households with at least one credit card by income quintile, 1970–2001
Note: Income quintiles calculated based on cumulative income distribution for each year. IQ1 is the lowest income quintile.
Source: Federal Reserve Board, *Survey of Consumer Finances* (1970–2001).

the bottom-income quintile with credit cards grew from 2 percent in 1970 to 38 percent in 2001.

Overall, between 1970 and 2001, the percentage of households with credit cards more than quadrupled, from about 16 percent to almost 73 percent. In the meantime, the percentage of households with charge cards went down and up several times with a trough in 1977 (at about 8 percent) and a peak in 1989 (at about 13 percent). As we noted in chapter 3, though ATM cards were in widespread use in the 1980s, their use as debit cards was unimportant until around 1990. About 53 percent of households had debit cards in 1992, when the *SCF* first asked about this, and coverage had increased to almost 70 percent by 2001.

Cards have spread from wealthier to poorer people as well. The median income of households with credit cards was about 47 percent higher than the median income of all households in 1970, but only 28 percent higher in 2001. Among the 20 percent of households with the lowest incomes, about 2 percent had credit cards in 1970 while about 38 percent had them in 2001. Poorer people have benefited especially from the growth of debit cards. Debit card ownership in the lowest-income quintile went up from about 26 percent in 1992 to almost 43 percent in 2001. About 20 percent of households in the lowest-income quintile owned a debit card as their only type of payment card. Debit card use is growing more rapidly among poorer households, and differences across income classes in the use of payment media are likely to continue to diminish. Among households who had neither credit nor charge cards, poor households were about 42 percent as likely to use debit cards as the general population of households in 1995, but this number increased to 73 percent by 2001.

Prepaid cards are also beginning to give low-income households greater access to the convenience of plastic. In 1999–2001, for example, government agencies carried out a pilot program that relied on smart cards to deliver welfare benefits. The so-called Health Passport Project used smart cards to distribute benefits to more than 20,000 persons enrolled in the Women, Infant, and Children program. Participants, essentially low-income women and their children, used the smart cards to receive food at retailers, store medical information (lead screenings, immunization records, doctor's appointments), and check into clinics. Payroll cards are another version of prepaid cards. Their use has grown especially among companies with large proportions of temporary, part-time, or immigrant workers who wish to avoid check-cashing fees.

By 2001, households were more likely to have a payment card than they were to have a computer or own a home. People were still less likely to have a card than a telephone, but the gap was closing quickly.

Using Payment Cards to Execute Transactions

Most of us rely on many different payment mechanisms. The people we pay dictate some of our choices. We can neither pay with cash over the Internet nor pay our mortgage with a payment card. But many of our choices are the result of our weighing the costs and benefits of different ways of paying for the purchase at hand. Most of us will use cash for small purchases and cards for larger ones. Much of this is dictated by what's happening in our daily lives—whether it has been convenient to get cash out of an ATM, whether we have remembered to bring our checkbooks, and what our credit limits allow us to charge on various cards.

Most cardholders pay little or nothing for having or using cards. Debit cards usually come with checking accounts at no additional charge. The average annual fee for bankcards that have a fee is almost $44, but about 85 percent have no fee, and the benefit from not having to pay until the end of the billing cycle covers much of the average annual fee for those cards that have one. Not only are all cards costless to use (card issuers never charge transaction-related fees, with some limited exceptions for debit cards), but many cards even offer rewards such as airline frequent-flier miles for using them.

Payment cards have provided three major transaction-related benefits to cardholders. First, they have reduced the amount of money that people have to keep in checking and savings accounts because they enable people to manage their money better. Second, they have reduced the amount of time people need to spend in completing transactions for which they would have used a check. And third, and perhaps most important, they have enabled cardholders to benefit from several products and services that could not exist without cards.

Interest Savings from Better Money Management
People hold cash and checking deposits, as opposed to less liquid assets with higher returns, for two primary reasons. One is to manage regular transactions: households receive income in lumps—a biweekly or monthly paycheck, for example—but make purchases almost continuously. The other one is the "precautionary" motive of wanting to be prepared for unpredictable expenses—a serious family emergency, or an unexpected chance to purchase a discounted winter vacation on the island of Nevis. Even if households don't actually use them to borrow, credit and charge cards provide a way for households to satisfy their transaction and precautionary demands for money, thereby reducing

the need to have cash on hand or in checking accounts—that is, cash balances.

If consumers do not borrow, they must have money in their checking accounts to pay their payment card bills, but they can nonetheless reduce their need for cash balances; they may hold funds in higher-yielding assets until it comes time to pay their card bills. For example, they can write a check from a money market account or transfer money from savings to checking. We used the *SCF* to examine the effect of payment cards on checking account balances (respondents were asked for their average checking account balances in the previous month) as a percentage of total financial assets, holding constant other factors that could affect cash balances (such as income, age, and education). The results, summarized in table 4.1, show that holding payment cards is associated with a substantial reduction in checking account balances. (Holding store cards or gas cards had no such effect.) The payment card effect is also "statistically significant"—it is measured with enough precision that we are confident that there really is a relationship.

By reducing the need for cash balances, general-purpose charge and credit cards provide a benefit to consumers. According to the *SCF*, approximately 77.4 million households carried credit cards and 11.2 million households carried charge cards in 2001. The estimates in table 4.1 imply that on average, households with credit cards reduced their checking account balances by 3.8 percentage points (as a percentage of total financial assets) and households with charge cards did the same by 1.5 percentage points. (For the most part, the group of households with

Table 4.1
Reduction of checking account balances through payment card ownership

Payment card	Reduction in checking account balance as percent of all financial assets (%)	Amount by which owning payment cards reduces checking account balances ($)
Bank credit card	3.8	1,568
Charge card	1.5	619
Total reduction	5.3	2,187

Note: Estimates are statistically significant at the 5 percent level.
Source: Federal Reserve Board, *Survey of Consumer Finances* (1983–2001).

charge cards is a small subset of the group of households with credit cards, but the statistical analysis behind table 4.1 accounts for this fact.) For households with credit cards (with median total financial assets of $42,583), this 3.8 percentage point decrease translates to roughly $125.2 billion in reduced checking account balances. For households with charge cards (with median total financial assets of $145,887), the 1.5 percentage point decline implies a $24.5 billion reduction in balances. If these households had invested those reduced cash balances in a one-year T-bill security, which had an average interest rate of 3.84 percent in 2001, they would have earned an accumulated interest of $5.8 billion in that year.

The estimates in table 4.1 are averages across all households, including some who occasionally carry balances on their credit cards at interest rates above those they can earn on liquid assets. The story is more complicated for these households, as we discuss below. For the roughly half of all households who always or almost always pay off their balances, however, the analysis above applies directly, and the cash management benefits are clear.

Time Savings in Completing Transactions

Payment cards can save cardholders time. Different studies provide different estimates of how long it takes people to pay with various payment instruments at the counter. And as we are all aware, there is a lot of variance across merchants depending on their particular equipment and setup—not to mention their clerks. There is agreement that credit cards are faster than checks, but there is disagreement as to how much faster. The answer will almost certainly vary by retail category and other variables. One industry source suggests that the difference in favor of cards is as large as fifty-six seconds (that is, seventy-three seconds for checks versus seventeen seconds for cards). Whether cards are as fast as cash is also a matter of dispute. To use cash, of course, requires spending some time getting it. This is easier today with the proliferation of ATM machines and cards, but for the card industry's first few decades it required trips to the bank window. Time savings of only a few seconds per transaction become worth quite a bit when billions of transactions are involved.

To get a rough idea of the magnitude of the time savings for consumers, consider some simple calculations. (There are also time savings on the merchant side.) Checks accounted for 24 percent of point-of-sale transactions that didn't involve payment cards in 2001. Let's assume that 24 percent of payment card transactions at the point of sale would be made by check as well if there were no payment cards. Then, an additional 6.4 billion transactions would have been conducted by check instead of by card in 2001. Let's say that payment cards were 56 seconds faster than checks and as fast as cash, once the trip to the ATM is taken into account. People would have then spent an extra 358 billion seconds (or 99.6 million hours) in 2001 as a result of using checks instead of cards. If people valued their time at the average hourly wage in the U.S. economy, $17.18, then using checks instead of cards would have cost them the equivalent of $1.7 billion. Note that this just accounts for the time the individuals conducting the payment card transactions saved; the calculation does not take into account the time the persons waiting in line behind them saved. For example, if on average two people waited in line, then the savings in 2001 amounted to $1.7 billion × 3 = $5.1 billion.

New Products and Services

Some products and services available to cardholders either would not exist in the absence of payment cards or would involve significantly higher transactions costs. Consider renting a car. No rental car company is thrilled with the idea of people they don't know and can't locate driving off with a $25,000 vehicle. Securing car rentals with a card has been popular since the early days of charge cards. Rental car companies would have to develop different ways of obtaining collateral if payment cards didn't exist. Today, it is all but impossible to rent a car without a payment card. The same holds true for many other companies that rent durable equipment.

Similarly, Internet commerce would have had a much harder time without electronic money in the form of payment cards. Just think how much more convenient it is to order books from Amazon.com with your payment card rather than by sending in a check or paying COD. (We will see the benefits from the merchant's perspective in the next chapter.)

Credit Card Lending: Joys, Sorrows, and Controversies

The amount of credit available through cards has grown dramatically in the last thirty years, and at least $4 trillion was available in 2001. Available credit grew by at least 800 percent since 1970 since the number of cards grew by that much and, on average, the credit available on each card increased substantially as well. At the same time, credit card borrowing has become available to an increasingly wider portion of the socioeconomic spectrum. Some have argued that the growth and democratization of credit has improved living standards. As Joe Nocera puts it, "Americans were tired of going without. So rather than wait and save, they took out personal loans or bought on the installment plan. And when they saw that nothing bad happened as a result, they did it again, adding the television loan to the refrigerator loan to the auto loan. . . . Thus did Americans begin to spend money they didn't yet have; thus did the unaffordable become affordable." Others have worried that easy credit card lending has led otherwise responsible households to take on ruinous levels of debt. Consumer debt is not a new source of concern, as we saw earlier. History teaches us that lending/borrowing is one of the most controversial exchanges between consenting adults.

The Growth and Democratization of Credit

The growth in credit has come from increases in both the number of households who have cards and the average amount of credit that is available on those cards. The total credit card loans available (adjusted for inflation, as always) divided by the number of U.S. households increased 146 percent between 1989 and 2001, at an annual growth rate of about 7.8 percent. This reflects two trends. First, the average credit card loan available to U.S. households with cards increased 90 percent over the same time period, at an annual growth rate of about 5.5 percent. Second, the number of households with cards increased from 52.1 million to 77.4 million—an annual growth rate of about 3.4 percent— as the fraction of households with cards rose from 56 percent to 73 percent.

At any time, of course, households in aggregate use only a portion of the credit available to them. Among households with cards, the total outstanding balances—that is, the amount of money that households owe to the credit card lender—represented 12 percent of available credit in 1989 and about 10.6 percent in 2001. Adjusted for inflation, these balances grew at an annual rate of about 7.8 percent over that time period.

In general terms, credit availability and use have increased across all income categories. To show this, we have divided households into five income quintiles based on their rank in the income distribution for each year for which we have data. Figure 4.2 shows the average amount of credit available for households with cards in each category (with IQ1 again including the 20 percent of households with the lowest incomes, and IQ5 including those with the highest incomes) over time. Figure 4.3 tracks the evolution of average outstanding debt for households with cards by income quintile. (The debt-outstanding information is available earlier than the line of credit information.)

Credit cards have likely increased the overall amount of consumer borrowing somewhat by providing a more convenient platform for lenders

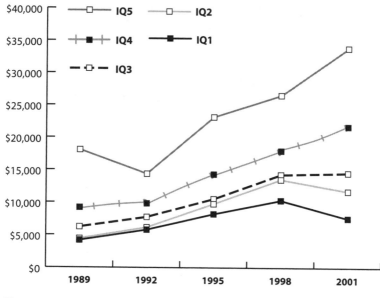

Figure 4.2
Average credit available for households with cards, by quintile, 1989–2001
Note: Figures are in 2002 dollars. IQ1 is the lowest income quintile.
Source: Federal Reserve Board, *Survey of Consumer Finances* (1989–2001).

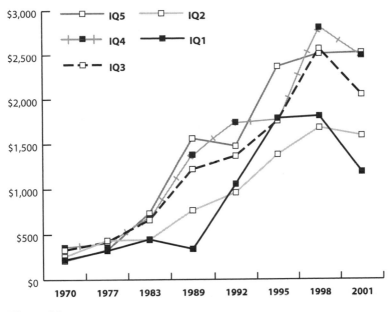

Figure 4.3
Average debt outstanding for households with cards, by quintile, 1970–2001
Note: Figures are in 2002 dollars. IQ1 is the lowest income quintile.
Source: Federal Reserve Board, *Survey of Consumer Finances* (1970–2001).

to lend and borrowers to borrow. Nevertheless, credit card loans have almost certainly also substituted for installment loans, store card loans, and other methods that consumers have used for financing purchases. As a proportion of total consumer credit, credit card loans increased from about 4 percent in 1970 to about 42 percent in 2002.

The Joys and Sorrows of Borrowing

It seems that for nearly as long as people have been walking upright they have been borrowing—and that for just as long they have been chastised by others for doing so.

People borrow to smooth the timing of income and consumption over their lifetimes. Income tends to increase until middle age, then level out, then decline toward the retirement years, and finally, often drop dramatically when people leave the workforce. Sometimes income drops dramatically for short periods when workers move between jobs. There is no reason why anyone would want their level of consumption over time to track their income exactly. So borrowing, including on credit cards, is a way of using future income to pay for immediate consumption. There's a related reason for borrowing: many goods provide benefits over time—from clothes to televisions to automobiles. If people want to smooth the net benefits they get over time, they may want to dedicate future income (through borrowing) to paying for durable goods purchased today that provide benefits in the future.

In making these sorts of choices between present and future consumption, many of us would rather consume now as opposed to later. We value the present more than the future and are willing to pay to pull future consumption toward the present. Part of this is risk—we don't know whether we will be around in the future. But there is more going on.

A Curious Process of Reasoning   Many people who borrow, on credit cards or in other ways, don't have to. That is, they have liquid assets that are earning interest at lower rates than they are paying credit card lenders. For example, some people might put a $700 digital camcorder on their credit card and revolve a balance on it for several months at 18 percent interest, even though they have several thousand dollars in savings accounts earning only 2 percent interest.

One explanation for this seemingly imprudent behavior is that people worry about finding themselves in financial difficulty from a sudden change of circumstances—the loss of a job, say, or an unexpected expense. While credit limits on credit cards are in fact rarely reduced for customers in good standing, this may not be generally known, and it is not unreasonable to worry that a drastic change of circumstances could put your ability to borrow at risk. If you empty your savings account to pay for a home theater system, you may thus worry that you would be unable to borrow to put food on the table or (via a cash advance) pay the rent if you lose your job. Moreover, even the thought of borrowing for food or rent if times get tough is upsetting to some people. So you may decide to leave some money in the bank or some other liquid account and borrow to buy your new digital camcorder.

A related puzzle concerns how people use credit and debit cards. Many people have both debit and credit cards in their wallets. When they go to the supermarket, they pay for their groceries with the debit card. The money comes right out of their checking account. If they had used their credit cards, they wouldn't have to pay until the next billing cycle. If they paid their bill on time, they would earn a little interest on the float and maybe some reward points as well. At the same time that some of these people are passing up a free loan on their grocery purchases, they are financing a new set of tires on their credit cards at 13 percent interest. Psychologists have explained this behavior in terms of mental accounting and budgeting: many people apparently feel that one way to avoid financial trouble is to pay over time (by borrowing) only for things that yield benefits over time, like tires or a memorable vacation.

Economist Lawrence Ausubel has discovered what seems like another puzzle in some of the data we've been using for this chapter. The *SCF* asks people how much money they have borrowed on credit cards, and since this is a random sample of the population, we can use their answers to project how much money the U.S. public overall has borrowed. It turns out that what people say they have borrowed is quite a bit less than what they actually did borrow, which we know from other sources. Since people underestimate what they have borrowed in the past, Ausubel argues, perhaps they underestimate what they will borrow on their credit lines in the future and therefore are less sensitive than they rationally should be to the finance rates they are being charged. While no doubt some consumers fit this pattern, the roughly 36 percent of card-owning households who did not borrow at all in 2001 clearly do not. Moreover, the intense competition among low-rate cards (with offers to switch balances) seems to suggest that lenders believe that cardholders who do revolve are in fact sensitive to interest rates. It seems that in responding to surveys, consumers systematically understate things they are not proud of, and we doubt that one can infer much more from their underreporting of borrowing than from their underreporting of beer consumption or television viewing.

Some recent theories (including what is known as the "hyperbolic discounting" literature in the emerging field of behavioral economics) explore consumers' use of commitments (for example, not having ice cream in the freezer) to deal with self-control problems. The argument here is that consumers try to prevent themselves from splurging in the future by tying up their wealth now in assets they can't quickly liquidate—like equity in a house. But they hold credit cards, in part for insurance against economic adversity, and when the future comes they can't stop themselves from using their cards to splurge. There may be an element of truth in this for some consumers, though surely not all, but the theory remains controversial, and its prescriptions for policy are far from obvious. Even if the theory is correct, one would need to weigh the importance of the "temptation cost" of credit cards against the value of these cards in providing consumer financing and relaxing borrowing constraints that make consumers better off. We suspect that for most consumers, for whom splurging is not a major problem, the temptation cost pales in comparison to the financing benefits—but that is a question for future research.

The expansion of credit card use has made these issues more visible, but they are not fundamentally new, as we saw in chapter 2. Since the early 1800s, U.S. consumers have been criticized for accumulating debt, and the increasingly popular use of installment loans in the second half of the nineteenth century led to especially severe criticism of consumer borrowing. Women were chastised for engaging in the "curious process of reasoning" that led them to pay significantly extra for installment purchases when they had the money to buy the good outright. This history suggests that caution is advisable in the face of claims that credit cards have driven consumers to irrational borrowing. People valued the lending services provided by the installment loans that became widely available in the late nineteenth century as well as by the credit cards loans that became available in the late twentieth century. We don't think enough is known about how and why people borrow to conclude that irrational borrowing is a widespread phenomenon.

"Goes a Sorrowing"   Many commentators through the centuries have nonetheless worried that people's uncontrollable urge to borrow will bring ruin on them. People will borrow too much and go "a sorrowing," as Benjamin Franklin warned. Calder's study of nineteenth-century lending, discussed in chapter 2, found the same worries about installment lending leading people astray as we hear today about credit cards. At the turn of the twentieth century, *Keeping Up with Lizzie* and *Charge It!* were popular morality tales about the evils of spending and going into debt. (These inspired a comic strip called *Keeping up with the Joneses.*) Several generations of commentators have worried that reckless borrowing by those with weak wills would mire the public in debt and, in the process, drag down the U.S. economy. Some headlines illustrate this concern: "Running in Debt" (*New York Times,* 1873); "Borrowing Trouble" (*New York Times,* 1877); "Debt Threatens Democracy" (*Harper's,* 1940); "Is the Country Swamped with Debt?" (*Business Week,* 1949); and "Never Have So Many Owed So Much" (*U.S. News and World Report,* 1959).

Recent newspaper stories about credit cards echo the "[credit] is the great tempter" theme of *Charge It!* A typical one concerns someone who got their first credit card when a high school senior and filed for bankruptcy five years later because of an inability to make payments on $25,000 of debt spread among five credit cards. And echoing the concern of economists and politicians, the popular media have also expressed concern that debt—much of it from credit cards—is overwhelming the public and sinking the economy. Some examples that extend the series of headlines above include: "Debt May Be Drag on Recovery" (*Seattle Times,* 2002); "People are Borrowing to Maintain Lifestyles; Debt Could Swallow up Consumer, Say Experts" (*San Francisco Chronicle,* 2001); and "Paying the Piper: Hangover May Loom for Americans Who Enjoyed Credit Boom" (*Wall Street Journal,* 2000).

To see how severe the sorrowing problem actually is, however, and to judge whether it is getting worse over time, it is helpful to examine a few statistics. For all families in 1989, their total debt amounted to 15.8 percent of their total assets. This figure rose to around 16.5 percent during the 1990s and then declined to 12.3 percent in 2001. This does not suggest that credit cards are driving total borrowing to unreasonable levels. Additional data are provided by the Federal Reserve Board's *Household Debt-Service Burden,* an estimate of debt payments as a percentage of disposable (that is, after-tax) personal income that is available from 1980 to the present. Figure 4.4 shows this series for nonmortgage debt and total household debt including mortgage debt.

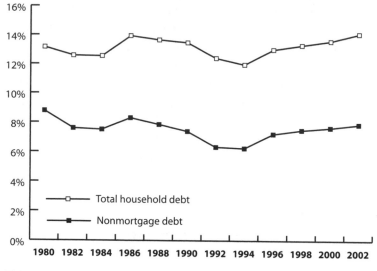

Figure 4.4
Household debt payments as a percentage of disposable personal income, 1980–2002
Source: Federal Reserve Board. *Household Debt-Service Burden.*

Credit card use has expanded enormously since 1980 (the purchase volume grew more than tenfold, and outstanding loans increased by a factor of thirteen), but this has clearly not driven the burden of household debt skyward, out of control.

Now let's look at credit cards in particular. Between 1992 and 2001, Visa cardholders charged $3.6 trillion on their credit cards. During that same period, Visa issuers had to write off $114 billion as a result of people not paying their bills. So a measure of the worst kind of debt problem works out to three cents on every dollar charged.

Some observers have also suggested that the rise in credit card debt has increased bankruptcies. Credit cards may increase bankruptcies simply because they enable people to accumulate more debt. But credit cards may also help avoid bankruptcies by providing people with a source of credit to get them over temporary financial crises such as unemployment. There is no conclusive evidence either way.

People may overextend themselves without going into default, of course. Yet it is hard to say objectively when someone has "borrowed too much"; one person's excessive credit card debt is another's must-have fifty-inch plasma screen television with surround sound. Some statistics from the *SCF* on household debt in 2001 nevertheless provide some insights. About three-fourths of all households with cards and balances would have needed no more than 11 percent of their annual income to pay their credit card debt in full, and half of all households with cards and balances would have needed no more than 4 percent. On the other hand, about 1 percent of households with cards and balances would have required at least 80 percent of their annual income to pay off their credit card debt.

These figures accord with those on defaults as well as our intuition and personal experience: credit cards are like many things in life. The great majority of people use them responsibly; a small percentage of people don't. By way of comparison, nearly 10 percent of people in the United States have problems with excessive alcohol consumption, nearly 23 percent are smokers, and 24 percent are overweight.

Another worry about credit cards that one sometimes hears is that because people can borrow more easily to get what they want, they are saving less, and thus in the long run, reducing investment and slowing economic growth. There is no doubt that the usual measure of household savings—personal savings as a percentage of disposable personal income—has declined substantially since the early 1980s, as figure 4.5 reveals.

But no serious analysis of which we are aware finds that credit cards played a major role in this decline. A key determinant of household spending—and hence of household savings—during this period was the rapid increase in households' assets. Despite the steep stock market decline after 2000, real household assets grew by about 4 percent per year on average between 1980 and 2002. If these large capital gains are added both to the usual measure of income used in figure 4.5, which increased at about 3.2 percent per year over this period, and to savings, it is not clear that the personal savings rate declined at all. Moreover, the Federal Reserve's flow of funds data indicate that the decline in some measures of the savings rate mainly reflected declines in household asset purchases—which is not unreasonable behavior when the value of assets you already own is rising rapidly—rather than an

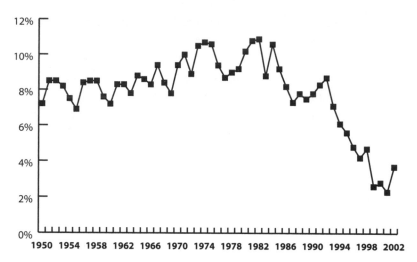

Figure 4.5
Household savings rate (personal savings as a percentage of disposable personal income), 1950–2002
Source: Bureau of Economic Analysis, "Personal Income and Its Disposition," national income and product accounts tables.

increased propensity to take on debt. If credit cards played any role at all in the decline in (some measures of) personal savings, it was almost certainly a minor one.

The Joys and Sorrows of Lending
There are two reasons why lenders tend to be wary of anybody looking for a loan. Both stem from what economists call "asymmetric information": borrowers know more about the likelihood that they will repay than do lenders. First, lenders face an "adverse selection" problem. The most avid customers for debt tend to be the least creditworthy, and no lender ever knows enough to judge creditworthiness perfectly. The people to whom a lender does not want to lend are exactly the ones who are most eager to borrow. In addition, lenders also face a "moral hazard" problem. When consumers procure large loans, the money allows them to spend more than without those loans or to take other risks, thus increasing the likelihood of default.

These problems are compounded by a moral and policy choice we have made. For most people, the major asset they have is themselves and their ability to work and earn income. Most societies long ago banned slavery as a way to settle debt. Lenders cannot easily attach future earnings. And bankruptcy provides debtors with various other protections. Lenders thus have limited collateral for many personal loans.

Faced with these problems, lenders in all credit markets sensibly engage in "credit rationing": they limit the amount they are willing to provide to individual borrowers. Sometimes that limit is zero. When these limits affect individual borrowers, such people face "liquidity constraints." A household is usually said to be liquidity constrained when lenders refuse to make it a loan or offer it less than the amount it wishes to borrow at the going interest rate. A variety of studies have suggested that roughly 20 percent of U.S. households are liquidity constrained. As might be expected, constrained households are typically younger than average, are less wealthy, and have smaller accumulated savings. Of course, more households would be constrained if they tried to increase their debt significantly.

Lenders have historically dealt with adverse selection and moral hazard problems in a variety of ways in addition to credit rationing. An obvious technique is seeking collateral—a house, a car, or a television. In 1960, at least 73 percent of bank loans were secured, including mortgages with houses as collateral, car loans, and personal loans collateralized with bank deposits. Another technique is lending based on relationships. Retailers, finance companies, automobile dealers, and banks generally lent money to people with whom they had personal contact. Bank officers, in particular, would meet with and size up customers who came in for a personal loan.

Credit card issuers fairly quickly learned the risks of granting unsecured credit, especially to people they didn't know. This was a new form of lending and an especially risky one, as we saw in the previous chapter. Some of the risks are just part of the business and remain so to this day. Card issuers extend credit and then weed out late payers over time. Eventually, they have a portfolio of people who they know tend to make loan payments on time. Other risks were reduced as lenders learned how to better target good credit risks and spot problems. Most important, the improvement of credit-scoring techniques has made it possible to lend more money to more people with less risk than ever before.

Credit-scoring techniques are computerized methods for determining the likelihood that candidates for a card will pay their bills and for monitoring cardholders' use of their credit lines. The computer revolution has made it easier to collect and process data on peoples' bill-paying habits. More data have become available as a result of this revolution and the fact that the credit-paying habits of an increasing number of people have been observed over long periods of time. And finally, the statistical techniques for credit scoring have improved considerably.

The credit-scoring system developed by Fair, Isaac and Co. is the most widely used system in the banking industry. Some banks, however, have started using in-house scoring systems in addition to commercially provided scores. The main motivation behind this step was a belief that third parties could not keep up with the pace at which cardholders changed their behavior. A recent credit-scoring tool developed by a Milwaukee bank uses some unconventional methods (such as tracking rent and utility payments) to determine creditworthiness. To take another example, a system called SureView, developed by Experian, focuses on the subprime bankcard market (that is, people who have not yet established a credit history or want to repair a damaged one). Using several factors, which Experian keeps secret, SureView confers a score from 1 to 999 on each account. The system monitors subprime borrowers over a twelve-month period as opposed to the traditional twenty-four-month period because SureView has found that the behavior of subprime borrowers tends to change faster than that of prime cardholders.

Issuers are using credit-scoring models to predict cardholder behavior more accurately before a card is issued. This has permitted banks to avoid issuing credit to applicants who present extremely high credit risks as well as allowing for the expansion of the possible cardholder base by more carefully considering a wider range of variables in addition to income. As the market for issuing credit cards to persons with unblemished credit histories has become saturated, aggressive issuers have been able to expand their card operations by issuing to customers with problematic credit histories. Although these customers represent higher levels of credit risk, they are also often willing to pay higher fees and interest rates in return for the convenience of credit cards. More sophisticated credit-scoring models have enabled banks to differentiate among high-credit-risk customers and to take into account likely borrowing behavior in predicting customer-specific profitability. This in turn has made it profitable to spread credit card ownership from upper-middle-class to lower-middle-class households. And together with intense competition among issuers, this spread was one of the contributors to the dramatic increase in the amount of credit available to households during the 1990s.

Credit Cards and Entrepreneurship

Aside from the Internet bubble of the late 1990s, when justaboutany-business.com could get venture financing, it has been notoriously hard for entrepreneurs to get funding for new businesses. Many small business owners have turned to credit cards as a source of financing in the short run. There are many popular stories about this.

When, for example, Brett Hatton established Four Hands, a furniture importing business in Austin, Texas, in 1996, he and his wife had to use as many as eight credit cards to finance their start-up. By 2001, Four Hands had $8.2 million in sales. Today it employs thirty people, its clients include Crate and Barrel as well as other high-end retailers located in the United States and other countries, and it ranks twenty-fourth on the list of *Inc.* magazine's top one hundred inner-city companies.

When Mark Fasciano and Ari Kahn started their software company, FatWire, in 1996, each of them contributed $20,000 from their credit cards to pay for the equipment and services that the company needed. In 2001, the company was named to Deloitte and Touche's Fast Fifty list of rapidly growing technology firms in the New York metropolitan area. The company now generates $10 million in annual sales, and its newest clients include Crown Media, Hallmark Channel, Bank of America, Andersen Windows, and Aventis Behring.

Business successes like these have helped make the U.S. economy dynamic and prosperous. Of course, for each success story that makes the papers there are a multitude of failures that don't, and even some of the successes don't amount to much. But the tiny fraction that succeed in a big way create important new products and services. The ones that stay small, and even the ones that fail, help the economy too. They help make labor markets more flexible—it is easier for them to expand and contract than larger firms—and they provide many goods and services that are more efficiently produced by small units. The vibrancy of small businesses in the United States is often mentioned as one of the reasons why this country has had a significantly lower unemployment rate than many other industrialized countries, especially those in Europe, and why the United States has been the source of much of the information technology revolution. The small business segment of the U.S. economy accounts for about half the private gross domestic product. Small businesses provide most workers with their first jobs and initial on-the-job training in basic skills, and they employ more than half of the private-sector workforce.

The stories above illustrate two key facts about small businesses. First, the fact that entrepreneurs borrow on their personal credit cards suggests that financing a business is difficult: entrepreneurs face liquidity constraints just like other households, but more severe. Entrepreneurs tend to resort to credit cards for financing when other sources of credit are unavailable. Second, the ability of entrepreneurs to use personal credit cards shows that this source of financing provides an increasingly large pool of capital for small business start-ups. The $4 trillion of credit that was available to the U.S. public in 2001 was just as available to people to start their own businesses as it was to buy stereo equipment. Indeed, in 2001, almost 20 percent of all credit card financing was available to households headed by someone who had their own business.

Stories about how credit cards helped people start successful businesses do not show that credit cards are a crucial source of financing any more than stories about how people started successful businesses in their garages show that having a garage is key to business success. This section therefore examines the role of credit cards in financing small businesses. In addition to analyzing the *SCF* data, we use the 1998 *Survey of Small Business Finances* (*SSBF*). The *SSBF*, which was conducted by the Federal Reserve Board of Governors, provides detailed information on the use of credit cards by small businesses. Together, these data sources paint a broad and deep picture of how small businesses use credit cards. The *SCF* data offer information on households headed by individuals who have their own business. These self-employed individuals may have a sole proprietorship, own their own corporation, or belong to a partnership, but most self-employed individuals operate extremely small businesses. The *SSBF* data provide information on approximately 3,550 businesses that have fewer than five hundred employees.

Small Business Financing

If you wanted to start a business, where could you obtain financing? First, you could dig into your personal savings. If your coffers were only half full, you might look to friends, family, or a local bank for a start-up loan. But if your friends and family couldn't help or if your application for a bank loan was denied by at least two banks, you might try to obtain a loan guaranteed by the Small Business Administration (SBA). If you were operating a more sophisticated business, you might also try obtaining equity investments from venture capital firms or other investors. In 2002, $18.2 billion of venture capital was provided to U.S. businesses.

Obtaining capital from any of these sources is difficult because lenders want assurances that their funds will be repaid. Lending to businesses is inherently risky, but lending to small businesses is especially so. Most small businesses fail within a short span of time. In fact, less than half of new firms remain in operation five years after their birth.

Although friends and family do not necessarily require a high rate of return on their loans, they are often financially unprepared to lay out the large sums of money necessary to get a business off the ground. And most requests for venture capital are denied: venture capital firms fund no more than 1 percent of the proposals they receive. To even consider obtaining a traditional loan from a bank or funds from a venture capital firm, borrowers must be able to prove they are a good risk. To obtain a bank loan, businesses must typically be prepared to provide several years of financial statements, information on existing debts along with accounts receivable and payable, lease details, projected future income streams, and signed personal financial statements. To receive a loan backed by the SBA, borrowers must be able to prove their good character as well as their expertise and commitment to business success, and borrowers are expected to contribute a large portion of their own funds to prove their dedication to the venture at hand.

Adverse selection and moral hazard lead business lenders to ration credit. A number of studies have found evidence of liquidity constraints for small businesses. Surveys that indicate that obtaining financing is one of the major obstacles to establishing a small business buttress this evidence. Indeed, evidence from the 2001 *SCF* suggests that almost one-fourth of all self-employed respondents who had applied for loans in the previous five years were either denied credit or not granted all the credit for which they had applied.

The Use of Credit Cards by the Self-Employed

Credit cards offer the self-employed a convenient payment mechanism and a convenient and easily accessible way to borrow. The *SCF* provides information on the use of credit cards by households headed by self-employed individuals, but it supplies no details on whether the card was actually used for business purposes. The *SSBF*, however, reports that 46 percent of small businesses in 1998 used their owners' personal credit cards to finance the business, indicating the importance of credit cards and credit lines to small business owners.

By 2001, approximately 10.7 million self-employed households (that is, households headed by a self-employed person) had a credit card. These households accounted for about 86 percent of all self-employed households. They accounted for about 20 percent of all credit card loans available and about 16 percent of all credit card loans outstanding. The average credit card loan outstanding for households headed by a self-employed worker increased by about 2,200 percent between 1970 and 2001—it grew by a factor of almost twelve between 1970 and 1989, and then almost doubled between 1989 and 2001. The average credit line for self-employed households increased by 60 percent between 1989 and 2001.

The fact that the self-employed now have access to a large volume of credit on their personal cards does not tell us whether and to what extent they use that credit for their businesses. To help address this issue we have compared credit card use by people who work for themselves (the self-employed) and people who work for someone else (wageworkers).

Table 4.2 reports the additional number of cards and additional balances held by self-employed households compared with those for similar wageworkers (that is, those of similar income, education, and age, among other factors) between 1970 and 2001. In 2001, compared to households headed by wageworkers, self-employed households carried about $2,600 more in balances and had a slightly larger number of cards. This was not always so. In 1970, for example, table 4.2 shows that self-employed households were likely to have slightly fewer cards and to carry somewhat smaller balances than similar households headed by wageworkers, although the differences were not statistically significant.

Credit Card Use by Firms with Fewer Than Five Hundred Employees
We now turn to an analysis of the use of personal and business credit cards by businesses with fewer than five hundred employees. As with the preceding analysis, this one focuses only on cards that provide a credit line and excludes charge cards like the American Express corporate Card. But it also includes a type of card we have not discussed before: the business card, which is offered by American Express, Visa, and MasterCard.

Table 4.2
Differences between cards and balances of self-employed households and similar wageworker households, 1970–2001

Effect of self-employment		
Year	Additional cards	Additional balances ($)
1970	−0.09	−547
1977	0.02	−41
1983	−0.09	−98
1989	0.19*	1,268*
1992	0.37*	769*
1995	0.24*	1,771*
1998	0.25*	3,147*
2001	0.14*	2,667*

Note: *Indicates statistical significance at the 5 percent level.
Source: Federal Reserve Board, *Survey of Consumer Finances* (1970–2001).

Issuers provide credit to small businesses through this card. (American Express offers a "Business" line of credit cards, and also offers small business versions of its Blue and Delta Skymiles cards.) For example, if you opened a small business in the Boston area and banked with Citizens Bank, you would probably receive an application for a loan as well as an application for a business credit card with a line of credit. As a result, small business owners can finance business purchases on either their personal credit card or a business credit card, if they can get one. While banks see small business credit cards as a growth area, they are still careful about issuing them, often declining applications from start-ups and/or requiring the business owner to be personally liable for loan repayment.

Our analysis is based on data from the 1998 *SSBF*, which asked small businesses several questions about credit cards and distinguished between personal and business cards. In the *SSBF* sample, 46 percent of firms' owners used their personal credit cards to help pay for business operations, which effectively provided them with a short-term loan, and 12 percent carried balances on those cards beyond the grace period. A smaller, but still sizable, 34 percent used business credit cards, with 5 percent carrying balances. And 12 percent used both sorts of cards. Overall, 68 percent used some kind of credit card in 1998 to pay for business expenses, with 16 percent carrying balances.

Firm size was also a significant determinant of whether owners used their personal cards to pay for business expenses, as figure 4.6 shows. Bigger firms were more likely to use business credit cards and less likely to use personal credit cards.

The availability of business credit cards appears to make it easier for businesses to expand. And by helping to meet expenses during bad periods, credit cards may also sustain firms and, in the long run, help turn a small employer into a large one. Indeed, David Blanchflower, David Evans, and Andrew Oswald have found that firms with business credit cards grow more quickly than firms without business credit cards. Part of this correlation almost surely arises because more successful firms are more likely to be approved for business credit cards. But the faster growth may also result from business credit cards helping to make capital more readily available to smaller firms.

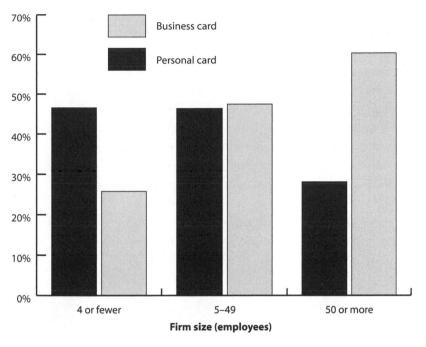

Figure 4.6
Card usage by firm size, 1998
Source: Federal Reserve Board, *Survey of Small Business Finances* (1998).

Room for Growth

At many points during the last fifty years, industry observers have marveled at how pervasive plastic cards have become. The *New York Times* wrote in 1956: "It showers flowers, garners gifts to bring home, and provides a variety of services for the traveler in places where he doesn't know a soul. It's all done with cards. Air travel credit cards, car rental travel cards, diners' club cards, credit cards for hotels, check-cashing credit cards, cards for this and cards for that." And it wrote in 1969: "Everybody is talking about the emergence of the great Cashless Society—not because there isn't much cash around today, but because credit cards seem to be doing away with most needs for it." Indeed, as we have shown here, payment cards have become one of the most commonly used products in the economy—beating out the computer, though still short of the telephone. But the glass is still at least partly empty, as noted earlier.

More than a quarter of U.S. households had neither a credit nor a charge card in 2001. Almost 32 million households were not conducting transactions with a payment card of any sort in 2001—about 14.5 million households owned but did not use credit or charge cards, and among the households who owned neither credit nor charge cards (about 28.6 million), about 17.3 million did not use debit cards. Although about 75 million households used their credit, charge, or debit cards in 2001, cash and checks remained important media of exchange. Some households don't have payment cards, many sellers still don't take them, and households continue to find other media more convenient to use in many settings. Acceptance by sellers and the convenience of using cards have dramatically increased over time and will continue to do so. And as we will see in chapter 12, new card products and technologies will fuel a continuing increase in the use of payment cards.

5

From Sardi's to Saks.com

The [credit cards] are a new burden in our industry—a tax. And they don't bring in more business—not in my experience.
—Philip Rosen, owner of New York City's exclusive Café Chambord (1958)

"You'll be the savior of my business," [he exclaimed] when told of BankAmericard's plan. The costs associated with managing his 4,500 [store] accounts were dragging him under.
—Drugstore owner in Fresno, California (1958)

Merchant acceptance of payment cards has expanded like ripples in a pond since McNamara cast the first stone. One day, a few brave merchants in a category take cards; soon most do. Over time, new categories of merchants take plastic. Some of the most recent are convenience stores, fast-food restaurants, and Web-based retailers.

Are cards accepted everywhere that you want to be? It only seems that way; there are many payments for which plastic still isn't taken. Some taxis honor payment cards, but most don't. Neither do most landlords or mortgage lenders. Nor does the babysitter. But past experience suggests that plastic will expand into these and other areas in which cash and checks remain the sole coin of the realm.

From Major's Cabin Grill (the birthplace of Diners Club), which forked over 7 percent of the tab to Diners Club in the early 1950s, to 7-Eleven, which paid around 1.5 percent to Discover a half-century later, many merchants have believed that the benefits from taking plastic exceeded the costs. And part of the explanation for the expansion of cards is that merchants' benefits have increased while merchants' costs have fallen. Taking cards is more valuable because more customers have them, clerks spend far less time processing transactions, and computerized billing and payment have improved. Merchant fees and other costs of taking plastic have plummeted.

Yet merchants complain about having to take a haircut every time a customer whips out plastic instead of a wad of cash. Indeed, organized merchant boycotts of payment cards have occurred repeatedly since hotels banded together in the mid-1950s to refuse to accept Diners Club, and they show no signs of abating. Most recently, various coalitions of retailers around the world have used the legal system to secure reductions in what they pay for taking plastic. These are classic symptoms of a two-sided market—"Let the other side pay"—but merchant complaints have also led to a debate over whether there is too much plastic.

Getting to Be Everywhere You Want to Be

The spectrum of merchants who take plastic for payment has widened considerably over time. It began with upscale restaurants in 1950, and expanded through the decade to hotels, car rental agencies, and other travel-related businesses. American Express persuaded retailers with heavy patronage from travelers to take their cards, and in the 1970s it convinced upscale department stores such as Saks Fifth Avenue. American Express cards were attractive because the cardholders had the "businessman, traveler-tourist, and expense account profile" these merchants found appealing.

Later on, credit cards brought in many other retailers, from hardware to clothing stores, where more typical households shopped. Larger retailers were leery of credit cards because these cards competed with their profitable store cards. They started taking credit cards only when many households had one of these cards and wanted to be able to use it for payment. As J.C. Penney's CEO explained, the nationwide department store chain finally decided to take Visa cards in 1979 because "we recognized that we had fifteen million active accounts, while all Visa members have thirty-five million active accounts. . . . It seems logical to expect that a good number of people who don't carry our card but who have Visa accounts would use Visa cards in our stores if they had the chance."

Plastic cards have spread from merchants who cater to the wealthy to those who cater to the poor. Even bail bondspeople take plastic these days. But cards have also spread to merchants who sell small-ticket items and to those with relatively low margins. Only about 5 percent of supermarkets took plastic in 1991, while by 2003 almost all did. To make this happen, the co-opetitives and go-it-alone systems took steps to reduce supermarkets' merchant discounts, and the EFT systems persuaded supermarkets to install PIN pads. The fraction of fast-food restaurants that took plastic cards has also increased; there were around 40,000 locations (out of a total of around 120,000) that accepted payment cards in 2002, up from 24,000 in 2001. And in March 2004, McDonald's announced plans to accept all major payment cards at its stores.

Web-based businesses are of course a natural for payment cards. Many of these dot.coms are virtual extensions of existing brick-and-mortar firms: Saks has Saks.com. Others, like Amazon.com and eBay, lead only a virtual existence. These Web merchants take payments almost exclusively through payment cards. The dollar volume of Web-based transactions increased at an annual rate of 54 percent between 1998 and 2001, and amounted to $30 billion in 2001.

In 1959, about 162,000 U.S. merchants took one or more payment cards. By 1971, this figure exceeded 820,000, implying an average annual growth rate of over 14 percent. By 2002, more than 5.3 million merchants took payment cards. This implies an average annual growth rate of about 6.2 percent since 1971.

Part of this growth has resulted from the increase in the number of merchants in the economy. If all restaurants take cards and the number of restaurants increases, there is an increase in the total number of merchants who take cards. It is useful to adjust the figures on merchant acceptance by the growth in merchants over time. For example, there were about 27 percent more merchants in 2002 than in 1971. When we adjust for the growth in merchants—that is, if we view growth in card acceptance as growth that is in addition to the growth in the total number of merchants—the average annual growth rate from 1971 to 2002 becomes a smaller but still impressive 5.4 percent.

As table 5.1 shows, by 2001, payment cards had become widely accepted in a broad range of merchant categories.

Table 5.1
Plastic share of dollar volume by merchant category, 1996 and 2001

	1996 (%)	2001 (%)
Total retail	31.8	46.2
Automotive	22.7	37.5
Food/grocery/drugstores	17.9	38.3
Drugstores	22.3	39.9
Grocery/supermarkets	17.2	38.7
Department stores	60.5	66.9
Specialty stores	41.8	55.9
Apparel stores	54.9	65.1
Hardware/home improvement stores	42.0	53.4
Travel and entertainment	42.1	47.9
Restaurants	25.0	35.9
Fast-food restaurants	1.8	5.3
Mid-priced restaurants	28.6	43.9
High-priced restaurants	51.0	60.8
Travel	68.9	74.7
Airline companies	84.5	88.2
Car rental agencies	86.8	89.6
Hotels/motels	80.0	80.7
Entertainment	19.1	25.0
Tickets	36.5	39.3
Movie theaters	3.4	12.9
Services/recurring expenditures	4.5	8.0
Insurance services	0.4	3.5
Utility/telephone	0.7	3.4
Phone company	1.0	5.5
Health care	17.5	25.1

Source: Visa U.S.A.

Getting Cheaper and Better

Merchants typically contract with an acquirer working on behalf of a card system (the acquirer may be the system itself in the case of the go-it-alones). The acquirer agrees to provide authorization services (using the card systems' computer networks) for all cards carrying the logo of each system it represents and to reimburse the merchant within a set number of days for all charges that have been authorized. The merchant is typically guaranteed payment even if a cardholder never pays their bill or if the card is stolen—so long as the merchant follows the authorization procedures agreed to (such as comparing signatures on the slip and the card). The acquirer typically also provides related services to the merchant such as periodic billing information that can be integrated into the merchant's accounts payable system.

The merchant pays a fee for these services—the merchant discount. In the case of the co-opetitives, this can be thought of roughly as the system's interchange fee plus other costs that the acquirer has to cover. (These are sometimes shown separately on the merchant's bill.) In addition, the systems typically impose some other requirements on the merchant. Until recently, the merchant had to accept every card that carried the logo of any system with which the merchant had a contract. This provision—sometimes known as the "honor-all-cards rule"—prevented a merchant from taking cards only if the cardholder didn't have cash, from taking cards from some kinds of customers but not others, and from picking and choosing among different kinds of cards offered by the system. Chapter 11 discusses a retailer lawsuit against the co-opetitives that resulted in an agreement by the co-opetitives to permit U.S. merchants, beginning in January 2002, to accept a system's credit cards without having to accept its signature debit cards.

Another card system rule prohibits merchants from imposing surcharges on customers who use payment cards. Merchants may give discounts for cash or checks if they wish, but they may not add separate charges for using plastic. This is known as the "no-surcharge rule." Card systems appear to have imposed both these restrictions on merchants since the early days of the industry.

The Basic Economics of Taking Plastic

You have finally realized your lifelong ambition of opening a hardware store in Minot, North Dakota. In addition to figuring out which brands of sledgehammers and duct tape to stock, you have to decide how you are going to let people pay and then arrange to implement each of the payment mechanisms you agree to accept. Should you take checks in addition to cash? Which, if any, brands of payment cards should you take? You cannot answer these questions without considering what forms of payment your customers would like to use, what forms your competitors are accepting, the costs of taking various forms of payment, and other factors.

Let's assume that like most retailers, you have decided to take cash. What about checks? You might get more business by taking checks, but you have to worry about bounced or fraudulent checks. Bad check costs amounted to $6.14 billion in the United States in 2001. To address this, you might pay for a check verification service or restrict check acceptance to customers you know or those who are in-state. (Some large retailers with a lot of check use, like supermarkets, set up their own check programs requiring customers to apply for check-writing privileges.)

Next, you consider whether to accept payment cards. As with checks, you may get some additional sales if you take plastic. Some of your customers may not be carrying cash or their checkbooks when they stop by your store, or they may avoid your store because they like to pay with plastic and your competitors take it. So when considering benefits, you need to take into account the volume of these "incremental sales" as well as the profits you will earn on them.

Your additional sales depend on the extent to which your customers have payment cards. Like J.C. Penney, many merchants started taking cards only when enough of their customers carried them. Even today, you probably won't take a JCB card because the Japanese tourists who typically carry this card seldom frequent Minot hardware stores. Your incremental sales also depend on how your customers use their cards. People are more likely to want to use plastic for large transactions because they are less likely to have sufficient cash on hand, and they may be particularly likely to use credit cards if they want to finance the purchase. Cash is commonly used in small transactions but not for large ones, while the opposite is true for payment cards and checks, as figure 5.1 shows. If you plan on stocking a wide selection of expensive tools and gadgets in addition to nuts and bolts, you would expect that many of your customers would like to use their cards.

The value of the additional sales you get from accepting payment cards depends on how much you mark up the goods and services you sell. You will care much more about making an additional sale if you make a $20 profit on it than if you make a $2 profit. Across major retail categories, the average margin (measured as the difference between revenues and the cost of goods sold) in 2000 varied from 12 percent for car dealers to 44 percent for clothing and accessories stores. Hardware stores have an average retail margin of 34 percent, so you can pick up some significant extra profits if taking cards increases sales.

There are other benefits as well. Most acquirers provide your store with convenient billing information. Cards, unlike checks, are

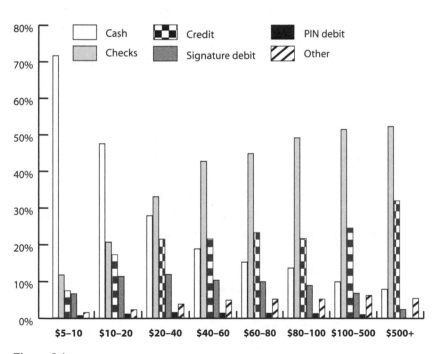

Figure 5.1
Payment methods by transaction size, 2001
Source: Visa U.S.A.

guaranteed not to bounce, and you don't have to worry about pilferage or theft as you do with cash. Credit cards also enable your customers to finance their purchases and may thus encourage them to buy more. Historically, many larger stores found that it was profitable to provide customers with installment loans or store credit cards. But it was never efficient for a single hardware store to operate such a program. It comes as little surprise, then, that smaller stores generally took credit cards well before the major department stores.

Of course, you also have to consider the potential cost of accepting payment cards. There are fixed costs incurred in setting up payment card acceptance, including purchasing one or more card readers, setting up phone lines, and training staff. To accept PIN debit, you have to incur the additional cost of a PIN pad, which is not needed for signature debit, credit, or charge cards. These fixed costs don't depend on your volume of payment card transactions, so you must have a large enough volume of such transactions to cover these costs. As well, you will incur variable costs—merchant discounts—when you take cards. These costs vary depending on the card. For a $100 purchase, they range from 41¢ for PIN debit cards to $2.64 for American Express (based on industry averages; we don't have available rates specific to hardware stores).

You also need to consider differences in processing transactions. Each payment mechanism takes time at the checkout counter—tying up your clerks and making your customers wait in line—and other processing costs. Both have proven hard to pin down, though numerous studies have tried. But as we discussed in chapter 4, based on casual experience and some evidence, cards seem to take slightly more time than cash and significantly less time than checks. Customers don't like to wait in line, but having more checkout lines to make them happier increases costs.

Merchant Competition

At this point, you are almost in a position to compare the value of taking one or more different kinds of plastic. (Many acquirers offer bundles of several cards, all of which work with a single card reader and will appear on a single statement.) But there is still one important element missing in the calculus: what your competitors are doing. If most of them have decided to let customers pay with plastic, then you will be at a competitive disadvantage if you don't accept plastic as well. Perhaps by avoiding the cost of payment cards you could offset this disadvantage by offering lower prices. In practice, as we saw above, plastic tends to either become almost universally accepted or ignored within a particular merchant category.

That is not a surprising result in competitive markets. Casual observation suggests that merchants attempting to sell roughly the same goods to roughly the same customers tend to offer roughly the same amenities, all of which cost something to provide. Most restaurants have public toilets, restaurant decor reflects the prices on the menu, many stores have free customer parking, and your hardware store, like others, is probably open on Saturdays. Businesses that compete directly often have advertising campaigns that also compete directly, even if they don't name each other. Almost every merchant incurs the costs of advertising and amenities mainly in hopes of attracting customers from other stores. Of course, in the aggregate, merchants would be better off if none of them had to do any of this, but then shopping would be much less pleasant (or for some of us, even more unpleasant).

This sort of nonprice competition, which includes competing by accepting checks and payment cards, has a curious feature: it can be socially excessive. Consider advertising. If merchant A's advertising simply shifts business from merchant B to A, the gain to A is likely to substantially outweigh the gain, if any, to society as a whole—that is, to all merchants, including B, and all consumers in aggregate. With a few more assumptions, one can argue that merchants as a group tend to advertise more than would be optimal from the standpoint of society as a whole. This "market failure" has been almost completely ignored in policy circles for one simple reason: even if there is too much advertising in theory, it is not clear how in practice one could ever calculate the optimal amount of advertising, let alone attain it. One might tax advertising spending, for instance, but a tax that is too high would do more harm than good, and there is no way in practice to know how high is too high.

It is interesting that basically the same argument is taken seriously by some policy makers when it is made in the more complex context of merchant acceptance of plastic cards. The contention here is that merchant

A benefits much more than society as a whole by accepting MasterCard, for example, because by so doing merchant A steals business from merchants B, C, . . . and Z. Thus, merchant A will find it profitable to accept MasterCards even when the costs to society as a whole from that merchant doing so outweigh the benefits. And so, most likely, will merchants B, C, . . . and Z. Since the more merchants accept MasterCard, the more attractive MasterCards are to consumers, the end result could be too many transactions on MasterCards relative to the theoretical optimum. Moreover, so the simplest argument goes, since merchants are overeager to accept MasterCards, the MasterCard system will likely maximize its members' profits by setting excessive interchange fees.

Of course, as in the case of advertising or merchant acceptance of checks, there is no way in practice to calculate what the ideal interchange fee or merchant discount should be. Furthermore, more complete economic models show that the profit-maximizing merchant discount may be below the socially optimal discount, so that reducing the discount may make society as a whole worse off.

For Merchants, Cards Have Gotten Better

From the standpoint of the merchant, taking payment cards has become more valuable. More potential customers have these cards and want to use them for buying and financing more things than in the past. Out of every one hundred households, twenty-one had one or more payment cards in 1970, forty-five in 1983, and eighty-four in 2001. The number of customers with card-based credit lines has also increased: from sixteen in 1970, to forty-three in 1983, to seventy-three in 2001. All payment card systems have developed increasingly sophisticated computerized systems for authorizing and processing transactions, and acquirers have been able to offer better billing and accounting services to merchants over time.

The performance of payment cards relative to other payment media has also improved. The amount of time that it takes to complete a transaction is one of the most important attributes of a payment system. There have been slight improvements in completing cash transactions over time—for example, cash registers now tell a clerk how much change to give. And there have also been some improvements in taking checks. But there has been a dramatic decrease in the amount of time it takes to process a card transaction. Visa, for instance, cut the time it took to authorize a transaction from four minutes to forty seconds with the implementation of BASE-I in 1973, as noted earlier, and it is down to just a few seconds today. Merchants have also used increasingly sophisticated technology to cut processing times. For example, Cinnabon, an Atlanta-based bakery that sells hot cinnamon rolls in malls and airports, found that installing new card terminals that had an "always on" connection decreased card processing times to three to five seconds from the twelve to twenty seconds it previously took using dial-up equipment. Decreases in transaction time reduce both the time clerks need to spend processing transactions and the time customers need to wait in line—thus making customers happier and more eager to come back.

Cards Have Also Gotten Cheaper
The costs of taking payment cards fell rapidly from the early 1950s through the early 1990s. In the last decade, merchant discounts for the major cards have remained roughly constant or increased slightly. But the cheaper PIN debit cards have taken an increasing portion of payment card transactions. Figure 5.2 shows the trend in merchant discounts as an average across the major systems: Visa, MasterCard, American Express, Discover, and the PIN debit systems.

The cost of authorizing and settling payment card transactions has declined as a result of decreases in the costs of telecommunications and computer processing. Following the breakup of AT&T in the mid-1980s, the Consumer Price Index for interstate toll calls declined by 43 percent from 1984 to 2003. The price of computer processing has declined because of rapid technological progress. The Consumer Price Index for information processing fell by 82 percent from 1991 to 2003, and the Producer Price Index for computers decreased by 85 percent over the same period.

The fixed costs of taking payment cards have also declined over time. Merchant terminals have gotten cheaper and better. Back in the early 1980s, it cost about $970 to purchase a dial-up terminal. Far more sophisticated terminals with integrated printers and PIN pads for PIN debit can now be purchased starting at about $190.

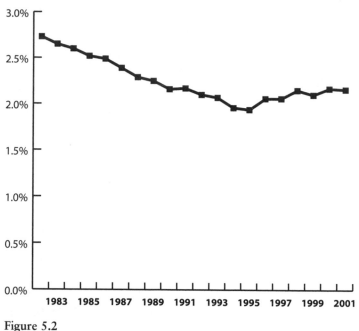

Figure 5.2
Average merchant discount rate, 1982–2001
Note: Weighted by purchase volume.
Source: Visa U.S.A.

Not Everywhere Yet

So many merchants take payment cards that we tend to think they all do. In fact, there are many transactions for which sellers don't take plastic. It is helpful in this context to divide transactions into the categories now used in discussing Web-based businesses: business to consumer (B2C), business to business (B2B), and person to person (P2P).

B2C

Payment cards have been used mainly for transactions between firms and their customers. There remain many businesses in which most firms do not yet take plastic. While data on merchant acceptance by merchant category are not generally available, we can look at the usage of cards at different types of merchants. As table 5.1 above shows, payment cards account for less than 10 percent of consumer spending in several merchant categories. Overall, such industries accounted for 42 percent of all consumer spending. (This total includes some industries such as insurance where the acceptance of payment cards is likely high even though the usage is relatively low.) Card use is particularly low at service industries such as professional services and real estate brokers, where there is likely potential growth for card acceptance. In addition, landlords and mortgage and other lenders generally don't take payment cards, although they do typically offer customers the option of having payments automatically deducted from their checking accounts through the ACH system.

Still, payment cards continue to penetrate merchant categories that have historically relied mainly on cash and checks for payment. An interesting case is the U.S. Postal Service, which agreed in 1995 to accept all major payment cards, including PIN debit. For the postal service, taking incremental sales from its competitors was not a big factor since it has a statutory monopoly over first-class mail. Rather, the postal service believed that plastic would offer substantial savings over the costs of processing cash and check transactions. It believed these savings, forecasted to reach almost $30 million by the third year, would permit it rapidly to recoup the up-front investment of $65 million in equipment and training.

Cable-television providers, health clubs, schools, apartment management companies, and day-care facilities, among others, have started to accept cards for paying recurring bills. Visa reported an increase of 26 percent in such payments to $39.9 billion in 2002. That was only about 4.6 percent of all recurring payments, though. (If other payment card systems had recurring payments in the same proportion as Visa, since Visa accounts for 45 percent of all card transactions, the total volume of recurring payments on cards would be $88.6 billion, or 10.2 percent of the total.)

B2B

Card systems have recognized that businesses as well as consumers spend money. In total, U.S. companies spent an estimated $8.2 trillion on B2B transactions in 2001. One type of B2B transaction is when the company's employees buy goods and services. Employees have long used personal and corporate cards to pay for T&E expenses incurred on behalf of the company, and this was crucial to the development of the T&E cards. Most companies' employees also make a lot of high-volume, low-dollar transactions—stocking up on office supplies, for instance. American Express, MasterCard, and Visa now offer purchasing card programs that allow businesses to handle these transactions more efficiently.

Purchasing cards can help businesses streamline their purchasing operations by replacing paper invoices and purchase orders, and they are potentially important for Internet-based B2B transactions. These cards can also help businesses monitor and control spending, as well as prevent employee abuse of cards, by providing detailed reporting. Firms can also choose to restrict where their employees can use the cards and how much they can charge. Annual transaction volume on purchasing cards was around $115 billion in 2002. Many of these transactions are at merchants who already take payment cards, but card systems are also trying to expand merchant coverage. MasterCard, for example, sets interchange fee incentives for transactions over $4,500.

P2P

Individuals also send money to each other—typically in small amounts. If the two parties are in the same place, cash is an option. If not, then traditionally people paid each other with checks or money orders, but this has started to change. One of the few Internet success stories has been eBay, the online marketplace, and one of the reasons for its success has been PayPal. Individuals running microbusinesses (or trying to clean out their garages) on eBay had to have a means of accepting payment. Checks took time to clear and were risky, cash wasn't feasible for Internet transactions, payment cards were too much hassle for tiny businesses and infeasible for individuals, and money orders imposed costs on the sender. Providing payment for eBay and similar transactions turned out to be the "killer app" for PayPal, the only success story among a flood of new payment systems that started during the dot.com boom. We discuss this further in chapter 12.

Paying for Plastic

Together, merchants and cardholders have to not only cover the costs of providing payment cards but also enable the suppliers in this industry to earn a competitive rate of return. Since the birth of the industry, payment card systems have recovered most of the costs of providing transaction services from merchants. Cardholders pay next to nothing for using cards for transactions only, as long as they pay their bills promptly and in full. This reflects the fact that payment systems operate in a two-sided market: they need to attract a suitable mix of consumers and merchants, just as singles bars need to attract a suitable mix of men and women, and newspapers need both advertisers and readers. As we describe in the next chapter, in two-sided markets, the price charged to each side—and thus the fraction of the total cost that each side covers—results from a more complex interplay of economic forces than in traditional one-sided markets.

Merchants would like to pay less for the services payment cards provide, and of course, so would cardholders. Periodically, merchants have taken their desire for lower prices to the point of organizing group boycotts against plastic. As we mentioned earlier, in the mid-1950s, hotels were vociferous in their objections to the 7 percent merchant discount charged by Diners Club and the slightly lower rates charged by its competitors: "Outside promoters have been pressing hotels to recognize their new cards and then pay them a commission of 7 percent of the guest's bill. These outsiders are trying to chisel into the hotel business as 7 percent partners." In 1959, Seattle restaurants, unhappy about Diners Club's merchant discount and the time that it took to be paid, tried to assess a 5 percent surcharge to customers paying with their credit cards. Diners Club dropped these restaurants as a result. In the early 1990s, American Express endured a well-publicized boycott, the Boston Fee Party, which we describe in chapter 8.

Merchants have also attempted to enlist regulators and courts to secure reductions in their costs. For instance, in 1997, a pan-European association of retailers asked the European Commission to force Visa to lower its interchange fees, and several national associations have pursued similar efforts. These associations argue that the co-opetitives have engaged in price-fixing by establishing an interchange fee—an issue we take up in chapter 11. In 2003, MasterCard and Visa settled a lawsuit brought on behalf of all U.S. merchants who took their cards (a class of about four million retailers was certified by a federal district court in Brooklyn) by paying around $2.2 to $2.6 billion (in present discounted value) and agreeing to some changes that the merchants claimed would reduce their fees for signature debit cards (there will be more on this in chapter 11).

The controversy over paying for plastic involves more than the understandable desire of one party to pay less. As discussed above, some commentators have claimed that competition among merchants induces them to take too much plastic. Merchants don't have any choice but to take cards, so the argument goes, because most consumers want to use them and because most other merchants take them. No single merchant could drop plastic unless its competitors did so too.

Some commentators focus on the cost-benefit implications. They note that once a merchant has agreed to take cards, that merchant has no way to encourage consumers to use the payment devices that impose the least cost on the business. Merchants can't add a surcharge for plastic, and the amounts involved (basically the merchant discount) are probably too small to make it economical even if they could. (Merchants seldom add surcharges in countries that allow them to do so.) Customers don't pay for using plastic, and many get more rewards the more they use their cards. The result is that customers use plastic when cash (or maybe even a check) would be cheaper for the merchant.

A proper cost-benefit analysis wouldn't consider only the merchant's costs, however; all parties' benefits are equally relevant, as are all costs incurred by consumers and other parties. Unfortunately, research on the costs and benefits of different payment systems is undeveloped. Many of the studies that purport to address the efficiency of cash, checks, plastic, and other payment media treat costs inconsistently and ignore many of the benefits of these media. Daniel Garcia Swartz, Robert Hahn, and Anne Layne-Farrar find that because the literature focuses on costs for a handful of groups, it provides only limited guidance on the desirability of substituting one payment instrument for another. In particular, costs from just one side of the market are misleading when used to argue that payment cards are costly for society as a whole. When all parties to a transaction are considered and when benefits are included in the accounting, Garcia Swartz, Hahn, and Layne-Farrar maintain that "payment cards appear competitive with other forms of payment available to consumers."

Other commentators note that since the merchant can't impose surcharges to cover the higher costs of payment cards, a business must recover these costs in higher prices to all customers, and cash and check users thus end up paying higher prices to cover the cost of their card-using fellow customers. Of course, most people use plastic for some transactions and cash for others, so the distinction between cash and card customers is blurry. Moreover, card customers end up paying higher prices to cover the costs of bad checks and pilfered cash. And in practice, for competitive reasons, businesses typically offer customers many other amenities that some customers use and others don't, such as parking, paper bags, toilets, customer service representatives, warranties and guarantees, drive-through windows, mints and fortune cookies, and shopping carts.

Still other commentators have argued that because competition induces merchants to be overeager to take plastic, social welfare (reflecting the combined interests of all consumers and merchants, and considering all costs and benefits) would be improved if merchant discounts were lower and plastic were used for fewer transactions. As we discussed above, however, more complete analyses indicate that this contention has not been well substantiated. (It is also worth noting that the basic assertion that competitive considerations lead to merchant overacceptance of plastic cards, which is socially harmful, requires the assumption that all other payment systems are priced optimally. As chapter 2 discussed, we know that this assumption is not true for checks, for example. Furthermore, competitive considerations surely affect the decision to accept checks as well as to accept plastic.) Researchers who have studied the issue generally conclude that there is no way to regulate merchant discounts that will generally increase social welfare.

At the most basic level, the claims that too many merchants take plastic strike us as a tempest in a theoretical teapot. Since merchant discounts are relatively low in fact, and since the payment card industry appears to be performing well by any conventional measure, it seems highly likely that even if this problem is present in theory, it is too small to worry about in practice—particularly when there is no proposed solution that isn't as likely to make matters worse as to make them better.

6

It Takes Two to Tango

A successful credit card program requires the participation of not just customers but store owners as well.... It was a chicken-and-egg dilemma. Which came first, the customers or the merchants?

Rather than recruit cardholders, he decided to create them. He would mail cards to anyone who did business with Bank of America, free of charge.... Fresno's shop owners knew for a fact that, on the day the program began, some 60,000 people would be holding BankAmericards. That was a powerful number, and it had its intended effect.

—Joseph Nocera, *A Piece of the Action* (1994)

Hiromoto Fukuda started a new kind of dating club, the Tu-Ba Cafe, in Osaka a few years ago. Men and women sit on opposite sides of a glass divide. If a man sees a woman he likes, he can ask a waiter to carry a "love note" to her. Like the long-lost inventor of the half-price frozen margarita for women, Fukuda knew he needed to get his pricing right. So the Tu-Ba Cafe charges men $100 for membership plus $20 a visit, and lets women in for free. That helps ensure there are enough men for the women and enough women for the men. Singles settings around the world have different prices, but most of them seem to agree that women need encouragement.

McNamara operated a different kind of club. He offered a way for customers and merchants to get together and do business with each other. If an individual consumer had dinner at a restaurant belonging to the club, he could put the meal on his Diners Club tab, and Diners Club would pay the restaurant directly. McNamara recognized that it takes two to tango: without enough cardholders, merchants wouldn't want to show up at his club, and without enough merchants, neither would cardholders. He figured that the merchants were like the men and that the patrons were like the women in a dating club, so he loaded the charges on the merchants. As we saw, American Express ran with this pricing model a few years later and made a fortune. A lot of other long-forgotten payment card companies from the 1950s didn't.

Bill Gates didn't call Microsoft a club, but his fortune rests on a formula that gets his two customer groups to meet up. Microsoft operating systems have always provided ways for two kinds of customers to work with each other without going on a date: computer users and applications developers. Gates discovered that providing access to Microsoft's operating systems for free to applications writers while charging end users for the operating system got both groups on board his platform. (Of course, most end users buy operating systems preinstalled on computers by hardware manufacturers.) By stimulating the supply of applications for its operating systems, Microsoft made computers with those systems more attractive to end users. Palm used the same approach to make its operating system the leader in handheld devices. This formula doesn't work for everything that uses chips, however; successful providers of video game systems make their money from games and game developers, not from sales of the video game console.

These are all examples of multisided platforms. Each business is built around a platform that enables distinct groups of customers to get together: the dating club, card authorization and settlement systems, and an operating system code. Multisided platform businesses have common features that help us better understand the individual cases. This chapter explains their workings, and much of the remainder of the book shows how basic attributes of multisided markets affect business decisions and competition in the payment card industry. (As we noted earlier, economic research on this topic originated from the work of Jean-Charles Rochet and Jean Tirole.)

Multisided Platform Economics 101

Platform businesses tend to arise in markets that have three characteristics:

1. There must be two or more distinct groups of customers.

2. There must be some benefit from connecting or coordinating members of the distinct groups.

3. An intermediary can make each group better off through coordinating their demands.

The examples we started this chapter with all had these three characteristics. For instance, dating clubs provide a service to men and women, who benefit from meeting each other, and offer an efficient way for men and women to connect. Operating systems vendors work to attract applications developers with a large population of computer users and to get end users on board with a large set of attractive applications. (The "distinct groups" of customers may be the same customers in different roles—for example, an eBay customer may be both a buyer and a seller.)

The fact that circumstances permit a platform to exist does not mean that it will exist or that it will be the only way customers are served. IBM had an operating system for its early mainframe computers, but made no effort to make it a platform in the way Microsoft did with MS-DOS or Windows. And although you can try to find your true love on Yahoo! Personals, you might prefer taking a walk in the Boston Public Garden. Like many business successes, platforms come into existence when someone realizes that consumers have a need that is not being well met and sees a way to meet it. That is how the payment card industry started, with the proverbial apple being McNamara's missing wallet.

Internalizing Externalities for Fun and Profit

As a practical matter, multisided platforms tend to arise when a stronger version of the second condition applies. Most platform businesses have what economists call "indirect network externalities." Let's begin with "direct network externalities." They arise when the value each customer places on a product increases with the number of other customers using that product. Instant Messaging is an example (or is it?—read on). The value each Instant Messaging user places on Instant Messaging increases with the number of other users because a larger group of users, all else being equal, will increase the chances that one user will want to communicate with another. The term "externality" refers to the fact that each user throws off a benefit that is captured by other users. Indirect network externalities arise when the value each customer places on a product increases with the number of other people using the product because that increases the production of complementary products. Someone who uses a personal digital assistant (PDA) with the Palm OS benefits when there are more users, not because it helps them directly, but because more Palm users stimulate the supply of applications written for the Palm. And of course, the power of these indirect network effects is exactly what McNamara discovered. As a *Time* magazine article noted in 1958, Diners Club "built up a roster of 17,000 restaurants, hotels, motels and specialty shops that were glad to pay them a 7% fee for the business of their 750,000 members."

Businesses can generate profits for themselves and benefits for their customers if they can figure out ways to "internalize" these externalities. If the business benefits from higher profits when it increases the externalities, then it has an incentive to harvest more of them—the business captures the benefits that are thrown off by each individual because it can charge more to other users. And that is what most platform businesses do. (We focus on businesses in this chapter. Standard-setting, informal coordination among market participants, as well as government mandates, can also sometimes help internalize externalities, as we discuss generally in chapter 7.) Dating clubs, for example, bring men and women together in one place. That makes each man available for every woman to consider, and each woman for every man. It harvests indirect externalities because on average each additional man or woman makes the place more interesting (that is, provides benefits) to every other woman or man. Payment card systems offer a mechanism for merchants and customers to use a common payment device that benefits both; systems with lots of merchants are more attractive to potential cardholders, and systems with lots of cardholders are more attractive to merchants.

Payment Cards' Multisided Relatives

Most businesses are not multisided platforms. Coca-Cola isn't, for example. Its entire business is driven by the price that consumers will pay for soft drinks. That price determines the prices Coca-Cola charges distributors and that they charge supermarkets. And it affects how much Coke is willing to invest in advertising and other promotions. It is possible to divide Coke's customers into separate groups, such as old and young or male and female. But there is no potential benefit from matching or coordination between such groups. The same is true for General Motors. Like Coke, it has no prices to balance. Its business decisions and relationships with its vast network of suppliers and distributors are determined solely by what consumers are willing to pay for its cars. These single-sided businesses might vary their prices according to the demand by various customer segments, but they do not engage in the fundamental balancing act that characterizes multisided platforms, where relative prices help harvest externalities.

Many significant businesses are multisided platforms, as the cases considered so far suggest. It is helpful to divide them into three categories, examples of which are shown in table 6.1.

Market makers are businesses that match buyers and sellers. P2P exchanges such as auction houses like Sotheby's, securities and futures exchanges such as NASDAQ, and matchmaking services such as Yahoo!

Table 6.1
Examples of multisided platforms

Market makers	Audience makers	Demand coordinators
• Auction houses such as Sotheby's	• Over-the-air television such as WPIX in Chicago	• Financial data and analysis delivery services such as Bloomberg
• Securities and futures exchanges such as NASDAQ and the Chicago Mercantile Exchange	• Newspapers and magazines such as the *Wall Street Journal* and *Vogue*	• Video game system producers such as Sony
• Matchmaking services such as Yahoo! Personals	• Directory services such as the Yellow Pages telephone directory	• PDA operating system producers such as Palm
• Shopping malls	• Internet portals such as CNet	• Payment cards such as Diners Club

Personals facilitate transactions between buyers and sellers. Shopping malls are an interesting case. Malls help customers and retailers meet each other. Customers value having multiple shops in the same location because this reduces their transportation and search costs. Retailers value being in a place that attracts many customers and also from being near stores that sell complementary products that may increase demand for their goods, such as a hosiery store next to a shoe store.

Audience makers are businesses that match audiences to advertisers. Examples include free television like WPIX in Chicago, newspapers like the Wall Street Journal and magazines like *Vogue*, and Internet portals such as CNet. Many of these platforms provide content that attract readers and sell space to advertisers. Although it is often said that consumers don't like advertising, in practice many consumers clearly value at least some advertising because it provides them information. The Yellow Pages are a platform for businesses and customers. Customers use these directories to identify and learn about businesses that supply them with products or services. Within limits, the more businesses that are listed, the better off consumers are. Businesses value these directories because they provide a convenient way to inform potential customers. They value placement in these directories more if they reach more customers.

Demand coordinators are platforms that coordinate the production of complementary products, yet do not engage in market making or audience making. Bloomberg, for instance, offers dedicated proprietary computer terminals with services that include news, data, analytics, research, order routing, and trade execution for people in the financial community who subscribe to the service. The company coordinates the demands of financial analysts and traders who want specialized, up-to-date financial information with firms that provide that information in real time. Sony coordinates computer game players and game writers. Palm is a demand coordinator for operating systems for PDAs, and it illustrates the tension between integration and using a multisided platform to develop an area. The Palm Pilot initially came with a bundle of hardware, an operating system, and applications. Once it reached a critical mass, Palm started working closely with developers to create more applications based on the Palm OS. Later, it licensed the Palm OS to other equipment manufacturers. It is now an OS-based platform like Microsoft. But just as Microsoft is partly integrated into the applications part of the platform, Palm remains partly integrated into the hardware portion of the platform. Bloomberg, too, is partially integrated: when the service debuted in 1982, it provided subscribers with the hardware, the software, and the in-house content; now the content is supplied by both internal and external sources. Payment cards are a demand coordinator as well—Diners Club, for one, sold different kinds of transaction services to merchants and cardholders, and needed to coordinate their demands to have a system that served either.

The Pricing Balancing Act

In single-sided markets, the price usually tracks the costs and the demand for a product pretty closely. Firms figure out what their unit cost will be and then mark the product price up—a little if there is a lot of competition, and more if there is little competition. Particularly in stable markets, this is not rocket science. Many industries have rules of thumb. Retail stores often mark up the cost of goods sold by about 100 percent.

In multisided markets, pricing is more complicated because of feedback effects between the distinct customer groups. If you charge women the same price as men to enter your singles club, you will not get enough women; then the men will not come; and then all of sudden you will have an empty club. Many Internet publications discovered that viewers deserted in droves when they attempted to charge them, although some did make the successful transition to paid subscriptions plus advertising.

Multisided platform economics shows that it may make sense for firms to charge low prices to one or more groups or even pay them to take the product. And that is what multisided businesses do. As noted earlier, Adobe gives away the software that reads PDF files and charges for the software needed to create them. Bloomberg charges subscribers a monthly fee for its proprietary terminals, but it gets little revenue from the information providers that use the Bloomberg platform to reach subscribers (subscribers pay for some of these services, but Bloomberg typically does not take a cut). Microsoft and most other computer operating system developers charge software developers little, if anything, for access to the operating system; they even provide help for free. Video game systems make their money from the sales of games (both from the license fees from games developed by others as well as from the sales of their own games) rather than consoles, on which they even sometimes lose momey. Magazines, newspapers, and television broadcasters typically earn the preponderance of their revenues from advertisers. Businesses in multisided markets often subsidize one side of the market to get the other side on board—sometimes explicitly by charging low or negative prices. At other times subsidies are less apparent, as when the platform makes significant investments in one side and does not charge for it. Table 6.2 shows some examples.

The economics of pricing for multisided platform businesses has another key implication. In single-sided businesses, the principle that the

Table 6.2
Revenue in selected multisided platforms

Industry	Multisided platform	Category	Sides	Side that is "charged less"
Real estate	Residential property Brokerage	Market makers	• Buyer • Seller	Buyer
Real estate	Apartment brokerage	Market makers	• Renter • Owner/landlord	Typically renter
Media	Newspapers and magazines	Audience makers	• Reader • Advertiser	Reader
Media	Network television	Audience makers	• Viewer • Advertiser	Viewer
Media	Portals and Web publications	Audience makers	• Web surfer • Advertiser	Web surfer
Finance	Proprietary terminals	Demand coordinators	• Trader/analyst • Content provider	Content provider
Software	Operating system	Demand coordinators	• End user • Application developer	Application developer
Software	Video game system	Demand coordinators	• End user • Application developer	Application developer
Payment card	Credit card system	Demand coordinators	• Cardholder • Merchant	Cardholder

one who causes the cost should pay the cost is good advice—for businesses as well as policy makers. For example, a car buyer "causes" the cost of manufacturing the car and thus pays the full cost. That principle usually does not make any sense in multisided markets, however. Often, a product cannot exist unless several different customers use it simultaneously. They all "cause" costs and benefits. That is true even if it is possible to identify costs that increase as a result of an additional user on one side—for instance, the cost of printing another copy of the Yellow Pages. Economists have shown that the best prices—from the standpoint of either the business maximizing profits or policy makers maximizing social welfare—involve complex relationships between the demand responsiveness of each side, the interdependencies between these demands, and the marginal costs.

Is There Anything New Here?

Multisided platforms have a number of features that economists have examined before. Yet traditional learning does not deal with the role of intermediaries in internalizing network externalities. Most businesses have distinct customer types: retirees, households, or businesses, men or women. But multisided platforms differ in that they must serve two or more distinct types of consumers to generate demand from any of them. Hair salons can cater to men, women, or both. Heterosexual dating clubs *must* cater to men *and* women. For hair salons, the ratio of men to women doesn't matter much; for dating clubs, it is absolutely critical.

Most businesses in single-sided and multisided markets engage in price discrimination because it is possible to increase revenue by doing so, and because in the case of businesses with extensive scale economies, it may be the only way to cover fixed costs. A dating club may charge men a higher price just because they have more inelastic demand and because it is easy to identify consumers on the basis of gender. But businesses in multisided markets have an additional reason to price discriminate: by charging one group a lower price, the business can charge another group a higher price; and unless prices are low enough to attract enough of the former group, the business cannot obtain any sales at all.

Like firms in multisided markets, many firms in single-sided markets sell multiple products, and there is an extensive economic literature explaining why they do so. The standard explanations for why firms produce multiple products probably apply to many of the platforms discussed here. But firms that make multiple products for several one-sided markets (for example, General Electric makes lightbulbs and turbine engines) or several complementary products for a distinct set of consumers (for example, IBM sells computer hardware and services) do not secure profit opportunities from internalizing indirect network effects.

The study of network effects is a well-trodden field in economics. Hundreds of articles, as well as many books, have been written in the economic and business literatures. It is fair to ask how market platform economics and network economics differ. They start with the same observation. Many technologies have network effects. But then they take rather different turns.

Many people got a few basic strategic messages from the work on network economics, particularly after it had been boiled down for popular consumption. First, he with the biggest market share wins— price low, build a market share. Second, he who's first wins—get in fast, build share. Proponents of this view emphasized tipping—you build up a critical mass and then the whole market flocks to you. And they stressed lock-in—once you get everyone on your network, no other network can get in. As Brian Arthur, an author of several influential papers in network economics, put it, "You want to build up market share, you want to build up user base. If you do you can lock in that market" (1994). This is a nice, simple theory. But it is hard to find many businesses that succeeded by following it. Unfortunately, many dot.com entrepreneurs and investors thought this theory was the path to great riches. Only a few made it very far down that path before reality closed it off and supposedly locked-in buyers left en masse.

Business Models in Multisided Platform Markets

Now consider the messages from the multisided markets literature. First and foremost, there's no magic elixir. Even with network externalities on your side, making a platform a success is hard work. Businesses have to get the pricing structure right; they must balance the demands of the various customer groups and nurture the several sides of the market. It isn't that building share isn't good. It is that getting the balance right is far more important. Platform markets don't tip quickly because, as a practical matter, it takes time to get things right. And the first entrant often doesn't win in the end; many other firms may come in and successfully tweak the pricing structure and business model. For example, eBay is a successful B2B exchange now, but many earlier B2Bs failed. These B2Bs tried a big bang strategy: make substantial investments in a platform and hope that both sides show up when the platform opens for trading.

Getting All Sides on Board

An important characteristic of multisided markets is that the demand on each side vanishes if there is no demand on the other—regardless of the price. Men will not go to dating clubs that women do not attend because they would not be able to get a date. Merchants will not take a payment card if no customer carries it because no transactions will materialize. Computer users will not use an operating system that does not have the applications they need to run (except in those circumstances where they plan to write all their own applications). Sellers of corporate bonds will not use a trading mechanism that does not have any buyers. In all these cases, the businesses that participate in these industries have to figure out ways to get both sides on board.

One way to do this is to obtain a critical mass of users on one side of the market by giving them the service for free or even paying them to take it. Especially at the entry phase of firms in multisided markets, it is not surprising to see precisely this strategy. Diners Club gave its charge card away to cardholders at first—there was no annual fee, and users got the benefit of the float. The mass mailings of cards by banks in the 1960s may have also reflected this strategy. Netscape gave away its browser to many users, particularly students, to get a critical mass on the computer-user side of the market. Microsoft is reportedly subsidizing the sales price of its Xbox hardware to consumers to get them on board.

Another way to solve the chicken-and-egg problem is to invest in one side of the market to lower the costs to consumers on that side of the market. Microsoft provides a good example of this. As we saw earlier, it invests in applications developers by creating and providing tools that help them write applications software using Microsoft operating systems as well as by offering other assistance that makes developers' jobs easier. By investing in this manner, multisided market intermediaries are able to cultivate (or even initially supply) one side, or multiple sides, of their market in order to boost the overall success of the platform.

Providing low prices or transfers to one side of the market helps the platform solve the chicken-and-egg problem by encouraging the benefited group's participation—-which in turn, due to network effects, encourages the nonbenefited group's participation. Bernard Caillaud and Bruno Jullien refer to this strategy as "divide-and-conquer." Another effect of providing benefits to one side is that this assistance can discourage the use of competing multisided platforms. For example, when Palm provides free tools and support to PDA applications software developers, it encourages those developers to write programs that work on the Palm OS platform. That also automatically induces those developers to spend less time writing programs for other operating systems. (See the discussion of Palm below.)

Pricing Strategies and Balancing Interests

Firms in mature multisided markets—those that have already gone through the entry phase in which the focus is on getting the various sides on board—still have to devise and maintain an optimal pricing structure. In most multisided markets, companies seem to settle on pricing structures that are heavily skewed toward one side of the market. Table 6.2 summarizes the pricing structure for some multisided markets. Bloomberg appears to earn a substantial majority of its revenues from end-user subscription fees, for instance, and real estate brokers usually earn most or all of their revenues from sellers.

Two other factors influence the pricing structure. There may be certain customers on one side of the market—Rochet and Tirole refer to them as "marquee buyers"—who are extremely valuable to customers on the other side of the market. The existence of marquee buyers tends to reduce the price to all buyers and increase it to sellers. A similar phenomenon occurs when certain customers are extremely loyal to the multisided platform firm—perhaps because of long-term contracts or sunk-cost investments. For example, American Express has been able to charge a relatively high merchant discount as compared to other card brands, especially for its corporate card, because merchants viewed the American Express business clientele as extremely attractive. Corporate expense clients were marquee customers who allowed American Express to raise its prices to the other side of the market: merchants. Marquee customers—in the guise of popular stores often called "anchor tenants"— are important for shopping malls as well; by attracting customers, they make a mall more attractive to other stores. The decline of a marquee store can sound the death knell for an entire mall. For example, the Mountain Farms Mall in South Hadley, Massachusetts, was once anchored by Zayre, a discount chain store that was popular in the 1950s and 1960s in that state. As Zayre's popularity fell, shoppers moved to other malls and Mountain Farms spiraled down to what is known in the business as a "Dead Mall."

Discerning the optimal pricing structure is one of the challenges of competing in a multisided market. Sometimes all the platforms converge on the same pricing strategy. Microsoft, Apple, IBM, Palm, and other operating system companies could have charged higher fees to applications developers and lower fees to hardware makers or end users. Most discovered that it made sense to charge developers relatively modest fees for developer kits and, especially in the case of Microsoft, to give a lot away for free. Getting the pricing balance right, however, requires considerable care. For example, in 2000, Yahoo!'s Internet auction site was second only to eBay in terms of the number of listings. Sellers found the site appealing because unlike eBay, Yahoo! did not charge sellers a fee for listing their products. In 2001, Yahoo! changed its pricing strategy and began charging a fee. Its listings dropped by 90 percent as sellers presumably moved to the larger venue, eBay. The price change affected Yahoo!'s buyer-side market as well, since buyers were now left with little to bid on.

Though some economists have argued from theory that network markets will necessarily tip toward whoever gets a lead (because network effects beget more demand, which begets network effects), real-world multisided platform markets do not appear to do so. The explanation may stem from the practical complexity of determining the optimal pricing structure for all sides. Many successful multisided platform firms have evolved gradually, developing customers on both sides through a process of trial and error. For example, eBay began as an auction site for one type of item—PEZ dispensers—and gradually expanded to the twenty-seven thousand item categories that can be found there today.

Multihoming

Customers on at least one side of a multisided market often belong to several different networks—a phenomenon that is known as "multi-homing." Take personal computers. Individual computer users almost always use a single operating system, and by far the preponderance of them use a Microsoft operating system. Software developers, however, usually write software for several operating systems. In 2000, 68 percent of software firms developed software for Windows operating systems, 19 percent for Apple Computer's operating systems, 48 percent for Unix operating systems including Linux, and 36 percent and 34 percent for proprietary non-Unix operating systems that run on minicomputers and mainframes, respectively. The fact that these figures add up to 205 percent indicates multihoming is common. Table 6.3 shows that multi-homing is common in many multisided industries. This is important because the availability of substitutes on one side affects the ability of the network to load charges on that side.

Sometimes unrelated platforms evolve into intersecting ones, which target one or more groups of customers in common. In chapter 8, we discuss such an intersection conflict between the EFT's and co-opetitives' debit card systems. Platform competition can be fierce when either group of customers is price sensitive because they have other alternatives. The *Houston Chronicle* may have 81 percent of the newspaper readers in Houston, but that doesn't mean that it can exercise a great deal of pricing power. Advertisers have many other ways of getting messages to readers, so they are sensitive to prices. And while readers may not have many newspaper alternatives, they do have other ways of getting the news, and having a lot of readers is what makes advertisers pay.

Scaling

Many successful multisided firms seem to adopt a fairly gradual entry strategy in which they scale up their platform over time. Many payment

Table 6.3
The presence of multihoming in selected multisided platforms

Multisided platform	Sides	Presence of multihoming
Residential property brokerage	• Buyer • Seller	Uncommon: Multihoming may be unnecessary since a multiple-listing service allows the listed property to be seen by all member agencies' customers and agents.
Securities brokerage	• Buyer • Seller	Common: The average securities brokerage client has accounts at three firms. Note that clients can be either buyers or sellers, or both.
Newspapers and magazines	• Reader • Advertiser	Common: In 1996, the average number of magazine issues read per person per month was 12.3. Also common for advertisers: for example, AT&T Wireless advertised in the *New York Times*, the *Wall Street Journal*, and the *Chicago Tribune*, among many other newspapers, on August 26, 2003.
Network television	• Viewer • Advertiser	Common: For example, viewers in Boston, Chicago, Los Angeles, and Houston, among other major metropolitan areas, have access to at least four main network television channels: ABC, CBS, FOX, and NBC. Also common for advertisers: For example, Sprint places television advertisements on ABC, CBS, FOX, and NBC.
Operating system	• End user • Application developer	Uncommon for users: Individuals typically use only one operating system. Common for developers: As noted earlier, the number of developers that develop for various operating systems indicates that developers engage in significant multihoming.
Video game console	• Game player • Game developer	Varies for players: The average household (who owns at least one

Table 6.3
(continued)

Multisided platform	Sides	Presence of multihoming
		console) owns 1.4 consoles. Common for developers: For example, in 2003, Electronic Arts, a game developer, developed for the Nintendo, Microsoft, and Sony platforms.
Payment card	• Cardholder • Merchant	Common: Most American Express cardholders also carry at least one Visa or MasterCard. In addition, American Express cardholders can use Visa and MasterCard at almost all places that take American Express.

card systems, for example, started in one city or region before expanding nationally. It is often difficult to predict just what the right technology and operations infrastructure will be. Therefore, the multisided firm may find it advantageous to establish efficient buyer-seller transactions and balanced pricing first, and make large investments only after the platform has been tested. For instance, eBay expanded outside the collectibles market only when users started listing such items for sale. Other platforms such as Palm and Yahoo! have expanded gradually and methodically, building up customers on both sides of their markets.

Economics, Strategy, and Making a Living in Multisided Platform Markets

Markets hardly ever cooperate by following simple textbook rules exactly. In traditional markets, however, the classic truisms can at least serve as a starting point for more nuanced analysis. That's why how-to books on starting your own small business can offer reliable advice like "charge X times the cost in sector Y." For example, one guide advises that the markup is generally 40 percent of the retail price in hardware stores and that for jewelry it ranges between 400 to 800 percent.

By contrast, multisided platforms—especially those in new markets—all too often require clean-sheet planning. With multiple yet interdependent business constituencies to serve, costs offer little guidance for pricing strategies. By the same token, early entry may yield first-mover advantages or provide an instructive failure that simplifies the search for successful strategies by businesses that follow. And in light of constituent interdependence, changes in the business environment may have multisided effects that are difficult to anticipate.

Along with greater challenges go greater rewards to the nimble and the better capitalized. Many of the great companies of the modern era—think of eBay, American Express, Microsoft, and Cisco Systems—have prospered precisely because they have excelled at making multisided platforms work to their advantage.

Multisided Platforms and Price Setting in Payment Cards

McNamara gets credit for creating the modern payment card because he had the inspiration to turn the charge card from a single-sided product into a two-sided platform. Stores had allowed people to buy now and pay later since at least the early nineteenth century. Retailers started using charge cards in the early twentieth century as a convenient device for identifying and keeping track of customers with accounts. Installment loans and charge cards helped retailers sell things, but they were all part and parcel of a single-sided market—retailers selling goods and services to customers. These instruments may also have resulted in different customers paying different prices—for example, early on Sears charged credit customers more —depending on the terms of payment and finance charges.

McNamara turned the charge card into a two-sided platform by recognizing the opportunity to create a new payment device that could be used by many customers at many different merchants. Payment cards had been a vertically integrated activity engaged in by individual merchants. McNamara's idea was to vertically disintegrate payment cards from the merchant and offer a program many of them could use. While this insight seems obvious in retrospect, it was not so at the time.

The pricing model developed by McNamara and his partners formed the basis for the modern payment card industry. For transaction services, the merchant contributes most of the revenue and the cardholder receives the service for little or nothing after taking the float and other benefits into account. This point is worth emphasizing because of the far-reaching consequences it has for the business strategies followed by the payment card systems, but also because of its role in much of the litigation that has enveloped the payment card industry during the current decade. Based on the available data, the share of American Express revenues coming from merchants has been between roughly 65 to 80 percent over the last four decades. And the share of MasterCard/Visa member revenues coming from merchants has been between roughly 60 to 75 percent during that same time. (Data are not available for all years. We should note that meaningful and consistent comparisons across time are difficult, as the share of revenues coming from merchants is affected by the mix of credit, charge, and debit volume, which has varied both across systems and time. Credit cards present an additional complication because certain revenues may be attributable to the financing rather than the payment function. We have excluded finance charge revenue from these calculations, assuming that they represent revenues associated with the financing function. Revenues from service fees, such as for late payment, are more difficult to apportion between the payment and financing functions, although such fees have not generally been at significant levels in the industry until recent years. For MasterCard and Visa, we have counted half of service fees as revenues from cardholders attributable to the payment function. For American Express, service fees are not reported on a sufficiently disaggregated basis to be incorporated in these calculations. Despite these difficulties in getting precise estimates, the numbers suggest broadly that as far as transaction services are concerned, the merchant has consistently provided the greater share of revenues to the system.)

Two-Sided Pricing Strategies by Go-It-Alone Systems

The go-it-alone payment systems have two basic pricing instruments to manage the two-sided markets in which they compete. They can choose the merchant and cardholder fees to conduct the balancing act central to all multisided markets and to compete against overlapping or intersecting systems. A significant part of the competition in the payment card industry over the last fifty years has involved the strategic use of merchant discounts (and for the co-opetitive systems, interchange fees).

Diners Club entered with a zero cardholder fee, which it raised when it had gotten the critical mass of cardholders necessary to attract merchants. Various competitors in the early 1950s tried lower merchant discounts, but these did not generate a sufficiently larger number of merchants to get more cardholders, and without more cardholders, merchants didn't have much incentive to take the cards, even with a lower discount.

American Express came in with a lower merchant discount and slightly higher customer fees than Diners Club. Bank of America, which started as a go-it-alone system, entered the California market with a merchant discount comparable to that of American Express, but it had a different business model. While American Express and Diners Club were targeting travel and entertainment establishments patronized by high-spending and often well-heeled customers, Bank of America went after a much broader group of retailers where cardholders could use credit cards. Its merchant discount was 5 percent, while American Express had a sliding scale ranging from 3 to 7 percent.

When Discover entered, it offered merchant discounts that were substantially lower than those charged by acquirers for the co-opetitives and by American Express. Initially, it had no merchant acceptance beyond Sears (which owned it) and had to persuade merchants to take another card brand. The lower merchant discount and the fact that the card was offered to twenty-five million creditworthy Sears cardholders helped Discover attain merchant acceptance that exceeded that of American Express's within eight years of its inception, and that today is almost equal to that of the co-opetitives.

The go-it-alones have also varied their merchant discounts to penetrate additional merchant segments. American Express eventually decided that it needed to expand its merchant base to compete with the co-opetitives. It lowered its merchant discount for retail segments that had resisted accepting American Express, such as gasoline stations.

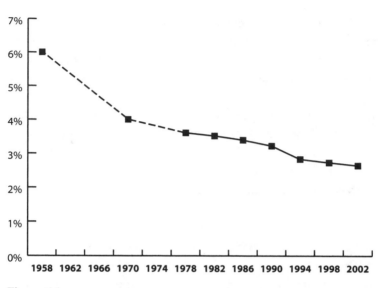

Figure 6.1
American Express average discount rates, 1958–2002
Sources: American Express, *Annual Report* (various years); Bernstein Research, *The Future of the Credit Card Industry*; and various trade press.

Figure 6.1 shows how the average level of American Express's merchant discount has varied over a forty-five-year period.

Interchange Fees and the Co-opetitives

In the 1950s and early 1960s, most banks—even large New York City ones—could not create platforms large enough to harvest efficiently the indirect network externalities discussed above. Their geographic footprints were too small as a result of branch and interstate banking restrictions. One exception was BankAmericard in California. The co-opetitive structure enabled banks to create platforms large enough to provide enough value through network effects to attract cardholders and merchants. These co-opetitives, however, which as we saw in chapter 3 emerged in many parts of the country in the mid-1960s, had two related business problems.

In these co-opetitives, banks pooled their cardholders and merchants together under a single brand. Thus, cardholders from one bank could use their cards at merchants signed up by another bank. To make this work, the co-opetitives needed a set of rules. Who would bear the risk that cardholders wouldn't pay their bills? Who would bear the costs incurred in serving merchants in that case? And who would bear the costs incurred by issuers? The answers to those questions affected the gains to trade that banks received from one another in the co-opetitives. Balancing the competing interests of banks was of primary importance in the early days of the co-opetitives, as we discussed in chapter 3.

The co-opetitives faced another problem—one that was far less apparent to them in the early days. The go-it-alone systems had two strings to pull to balance the demand of cardholders and merchants. Without more authority, the co-opetitives had no way to influence the relative prices paid by the two sides. The price level as well as structure would be whatever resulted from the competition between banks for merchants, on the one hand, and cardholders, on the other.

The interchange fee emerged early on as part of the solution to the first problem and over time became the solution to the second one as well. Without an agreement on interchange fees, it is unclear a coopetitive card system could function successfully. The evolution of the interchange fee at Visa and its predecessors is instructive.

Bank of America started as a go-it-alone system. It set cardholder fees and merchant discounts on its own. When it created a national franchise system, however, it needed to decide what to do when cardholders from one franchised issuer used their cards at a merchant affiliated with a different franchised acquirer. It decided to have the acquirer pay the full merchant discount to the issuer. Acquirers didn't earn any profits—or even cover their costs—on those transactions. Aside from reducing the incentives to acquire rather than issue, this arrangement obligated acquirers to report merchant discounts accurately to issuing banks. Issuers sometimes doubted that this was done, and the conflict and ill will created by this scheme was one of the reasons the Bank of America franchisees quickly became unhappy.

In addition to the mistrust between issuers and acquirers, the settlement process became more and more cumbersome. Initially, a merchant had to make a phone call to get authorization for large transactions. To save time, the merchant could accept transactions below a "floor limit," commonly around $200, without calling. Each card transaction generated a card slip that had to go from the merchant to the acquirer, then to the issuer, and finally to the cardholder. Such a system was inefficient and conducive to fraud. Moreover, increases in the number of merchants, cardholders, and transactions bogged this "interchange" of transactions down in paper.

After the franchisees' revolt, Visa (then NBI) instituted several changes that addressed the former franchisees' issues. First, it set a formal interchange fee that was uniform across members and thus not linked to the merchant discount fees charged by individual acquiring banks. This eliminated any incentive to misreport those fees. The initial interchange fee Visa set in 1971 was 1.95 percent. The first formal methodology for setting the fee, developed by Arthur Andersen in 1973, identified two components of credit card operations: the financing function, and the payment function. (At that time, fees other than finance charges on credit cards were uncommon, both because most states prohibited such fees and because cardholders appeared unwilling to pay fees even in states that permitted them.) The payment function was referred to as the "merchant servicing" function because its primary beneficiary was assumed to be merchants. The methodology assumed revenues to the system would come either from finance charges or merchant fees. The ostensible purpose of the interchange fee was to reimburse issuers for costs that were not attributable to the financing function. So for example, the cost of funds for providing the grace period would be part of the interchange fee, while the cost of funds for providing revolving credit beyond the grace period would not. Issuers would be reimbursed for the merchant-servicing-related costs on transactions that were interchanged (that involved another bank). And as we discussed above, both Visa and MasterCard built computer systems that approved—or "authorized"— card purchases to speed up the process and reduce fraud. These systems automated both the authorization of transactions at the time of sale and the bookkeeping among members to settle transactions at the end of the day.

To complement the newly established interchange and authorization systems, the associations developed rules that basically concerned both who got what and who was responsible for what. For example, the associations negotiated rules for how to handle fraudulent charges or charges on which consumers default. As long as the merchants met certain terms, such as properly authorizing transactions and checking card numbers against a list of known fraudulent accounts (this process is automated now), the system guaranteed payment. If a transaction turned out to be fraudulent or a consumer refused to pay for it, the issuing bank was responsible for the charge.

The interchange methodology was revised substantially in 1981. By then, cardholder fees had become much more common, and it was believed that cardholders valued the payment function associated with cards rather than just the financing function. So rather than viewing the payment function as solely related to servicing merchants, this was now something of value to both sides. As before, costs were apportioned between the financing function and the payment function, but now issuers would share in paying for the costs of the payment function on interchanged transactions. In the framework of multisided markets, we see that the balance struck by Visa changed to accommodate changes in the value that cardholders and merchants placed on the system. When cardholders began to see more value in the platform, the methodology shifted to a more merchant-friendly approach. In addition to the new accounting scheme, Visa instituted lower interchange rates for merchants who moved from paper to electronic processing. All of these factors— the new interchange methodology, the new lower rates for electronic transactions, and as a consequence, more and more merchants switching to electronic processing—combined to lower the average interchange fee for Visa throughout the 1980s, from an average of 1.7 percent in 1982 to 1.3 percent in 1989.

The interchange fee is a cost to acquirers that must be covered by the fees they charge merchants. As a result, the merchant discount for Visa and MasterCard includes the interchange fee. With intense competition among acquirers and thin margins in recent years in the United States, the interchange fee seems to be passed on to merchants. That is, changes in the interchange fee lend to changes in the merchant discount. (In the United States, large merchants typically pay an acquirer fee plus the interchange fee; the effect on smaller merchants may not be as direct or immediate. Also, different business and institutional arrangements lead to different results in different countries.)

Likewise, the interchange fee is a benefit to issuers; it is a source of revenues to offset their costs. Although it is harder to document, intense competition among issuers means that the interchange fee is largely passed on to cardholders in the form of lower fees and/or better features. Indeed, that is the reason why issuers can profitably provide low-fee or no-fee cards with various rewards even to individuals who do not revolve balances.

Over time, the co-opetitives had to keep three considerations in mind in setting their interchange fees. The first consideration is the role of acquirers and issuers as members of the association. This was not an issue when banks did both acquiring and issuing, so that interchange fees and expenses roughly balanced out for most members. It became more of a problem as banks specialized in either acquiring or issuing. And it became less of a problem as the association became more concentrated in the hands of banks that had delegated much of the arguing business to third-party firms.

Second, there is the concern about competition between the co-opetitives for members. This has become a particular issue recently as MasterCard and Visa have fought for near-exclusive arrangements with banks, and as membership duality has become less important. We discuss this in more detail in chapter 8.

Third, and foremost, is the effect of the interchange fee on cardholder versus merchant demand. To see this, consider what would happen to prices under different interchange fees given the intense competition in issuing and acquiring. In 1983, before the explosive growth of credit cards, the Visa interchange fee was 1.6 percent, the average merchant discount rate was 2.3 percent, the average annual cardholder fee was $16.86, and charge volume per account was $1,720. If the interchange fee fell to zero, the merchant discount rate would have fallen to 0.7 percent (assuming interchange fees were fully passed on to merchants)— a fifth of that being charged by American Express at the time—and the cardholder fee would have had to almost triple to $44.38 to keep the average issuer's revenues constant. (Changes in finance or other charges might have occurred in addition to or instead of a change in the annual fee, and the overall level of card ownership and usage would likely have declined.)

Multisided Competition among Nonoverlapping Platforms

Payment cards provide a fascinating example of competition among multisided platforms based on different business models. We explore the business dynamics of this in more detail in chapter 7. Here, we will simply lay out the conflicts in the language of multisided platforms.

The original go-it-alone systems (Diners Club and American Express) had a different business model than the original co-opetitive systems (MasterCard and Visa). The go-it-alone systems were based on charge cards, which extended a loan for up to thirty days. The co-opetitives bundled another service with the charge card: the possibility of revolving credit. Revolving credit substituted for installment loans for cardholders and installment lending by merchants.

Let's put competition within the co-opetitives aside and assume for a moment that credit cards were provided by another go-it-alone system. The go-it-alone credit card provider receives incremental profit from lending when it adds another cardholder or merchant to the system. That gives it an incentive to have an overall lower price level for the transaction services it offers to cardholders and merchants. Moreover, credit cards can do everything charge cards can do for consumers and more. The charge card system therefore has a problem unless it can come up with a competitive advantage over the credit card system or unless it can segment the market so that it is focusing mainly on individuals who do not want to finance. The pricing pressure becomes more severe when the go-it-alone credit card system becomes a co-opetitive because rather than being one of several firms setting prices, competition within the co-opetitive forces the price level down. As the co-opetitives expanded, American Express faced serious pressure from both merchants and cardholders. It faced the least pressure in corporate cards—these are targeted at people who do not finance (businesspersons on expense accounts)—and where the additional services that could most easily be provided by an integrated issuer-acquirer like American Express were important.

The EFT networks also had a different business model than the co-opetitives. They had a base of cardholders consisting of bank checking account holders who had been issued ATM cards. They realized that they could make additional profits by using their authorization and settlement systems (which they had originally built to handle ATM withdrawals by customers of one bank from ATMs of others) and their base of card-holders to conduct transactions at merchants. But they needed merchants. Not surprisingly, they set interchange fees that were close to zero both because that was necessary to get merchants on board and because they could do so profitably since they already had a viable platform that provided ATM services. And just as competition from credit card systems placed the charge card systems in a pricing predicament, competition from EFT systems put debit pricing pressure on the co-opetitives.

The collision of these two-sided platform businesses has made the system wars fascinating to watch, but brutal for the participants.

7

Co-opetition and the Payment Card Ecosystem

Whether it be customer, supplier, complementor, or competitor, no one can be cast purely as friend or foe. There is a duality in every relationship—the simultaneous elements of win-win and win-lose. Peace and war.
—Adam Brandenburger and Barry Nalebuff, *Co-opetition* (1996)

The Shell gas station on Memorial Drive near our offices in Cambridge, Massachusetts, has twelve card logos on its self-service pump. We can pay for our gas by inserting a card with any of those logos into the card reader on the pump. To make that happen, all of the cards whose logos are on display—though issued by competing payment systems—must be the same size to fit in the reader, use the same magnetic stripe technology from which the reader can extract information, and have a series of digits encoded on the stripe that tells the computers connected to the reader how to route the transaction through a maze of companies that are involved in paying the merchant and billing the cardholder. Lots of companies within the payment card industry must work together to make this happen. Some of these companies are business partners, while others compete fiercely. Cooperation among thousands of businesses around the country, and many more around the world, makes it possible for Shell to offer and its customers to use these various payment options.

The standardization of equipment, technology, and protocols has also made it easier for businesses to become part of the payment card industry. Discover could make its new card in 1985 both compatible and interoperable with all of the existing cards. Like most card issuers, it went to a supplier to have millions of Discover Cards stamped out—all the same size and shape, and all with the same kind of magnetic stripe, as the other card systems. In this regard, Discover's entry was much easier than MasterCard's and Visa's twenty years earlier or American Express's almost thirty years earlier.

For companies not wishing to take the go-it-alone route, the co-opetitives provide a platform that makes it particularly easy to participate in the vast interconnected payment card networks. They each provide a brand, an authorization and settlement system, and a set of rules that enable businesses to issue cards, service merchants, and engage in a variety of other payment card activities. A medium-size issuer, with eighty thousand accounts and $4.5 billion in assets, can join Visa and pay around $1.5 million in membership fees over the first five years; the fees for a large issuer, with 1.5 million accounts and $45 billion in assets, are about $95 million over the same period. These fees are only about 3 to 4 percent of issuer revenues, with less than half of that attributable to fees faced only by new entrants. Such issuers are thereby able to issue Visa-branded cards and use the association's computer network for authorizing and settling all their transactions. Moreover, their cards become immediately accepted by Visa's entire merchant base. Likewise, acquirers can join Visa for a relatively modest fee. Fees paid by new entrants amount to less than 0.5 percent of revenues.

Cooperation among competitors has proved important for the health and growth of the payment card industry. We think of American Express and Visa as mortal enemies—and indeed, they have battled fiercely both in the marketplace and before antitrust authorities. Yet these opposing systems have been working together on developing standards for smart cards. There is a long history of such cooperation. In 1968, for example, both the go-it-alone and the bankcard issuers insisted that the American National Standards Institute develop common standards for payment cards, which it did in 1971. These standards included the card dimensions, the location for the signature panel, the format for embossed characters, and a consistent account numbering system. By the time American Express had introduced the first smart card—American Express Blue—in 1999, American Express, MasterCard, and Visa had agreed on standards that guaranteed that their smart cards would all work at the same point-of-sale terminals.

This sort of cooperation is common in network industries because it often benefits all parties. Railroads had to agree on standard-size tracks in the nineteenth century so their passenger and freight cars could run on each other's tracks. Telephone equipment manufacturers and networks have always had to coordinate to ensure that connections between a caller and a receiver functioned properly whether or not they dealt with the same phone company. And gasoline producers, working through standards-setting institutions, agreed on specifications for the octane grading of so they could reduce the number of brands offered at the pump, reduce their marketing costs as well as the costs of installing and maintaining pumps and stations, and provide consumers with a dependable system of determining the quality of the gasoline being purchased. Many modern industries are based on interrelated products that must work together.

Sometimes, standardization is the result of an explicit agreement. There were more than 270 formal standard-setting committees operating under the American National Standards Institute in 2003. At other times, market forces play the same role by leading firms to converge to compatible technologies and practices. For example, the intense battle of standards for VCR designs between Sony's Betamax and JVC's VHS in the 1970s and 1980s was settled in part by consumers' preference for the longer-playing VHS tapes. While Sony worked to lengthen Betamax playing times, JVC was able to secure key industry alliances and line up a broader offering of prerecorded VHS tapes. This, in combination with the longer playing time, led consumers to prefer the VHS standard. In general, firms selling complementary products—like VHS tapes and the VCRs that play them—commonly have strong commercial incentives to make their offerings work well together. On the other hand, there are always strategic tensions between cooperation and competition, and individual firms, particularly industry leaders, sometimes choose not to coordinate with competitors on common standards even when doing so might make all firms and consumers better off in the aggregate.

Although the existence of cooperation among competitors in the payment card industry is not surprising, a close look at the co-opetitive systems reveals much that is at least highly unusual. These systems are sometimes compared to joint ventures like the National Football League or to cooperatives like Ocean Spray in cranberry products. But in important respects they are unique. They are more extensive than any other cooperative organization in the world—Visa alone has about twenty-one thousand members worldwide—accounting for $1.6 trillion of transactions in 2002. Yet the brain that manages this complex organism is small by comparison—Visa International had about six thousand employees that same year. And being open to new members, co-opetitives have an unusual dynamism; the success of the system has stimulated substantial entry over time.

The Co-opetitives

What Makes the Co-opetitives Different
The co-opetitives are different from the go-it-alones and other firms with which most readers are familiar.

You cannot buy stock in MasterCard or Visa. They are not publicly traded, so you can't buy and sell shares on the New York Stock Exchange or anyplace else. Any qualified financial institution can become a member of the MasterCard or Visa association. Once a member of Visa, it receives a certain number of votes that it can cast in order to influence how the association is run. Its votes are roughly proportional to its volume of Visa transactions (the date on which it became a member and other factors may also affect the number of votes it receives). A Visa member can vote periodically for the associations' board of directors. The preceding three sentences also described MasterCard until it was reorganized as a stock rather than a membership corporation on July 1, 2002, thus formally separating membership from ownership. As of this writing, the reorganization does not appear to have affected MasterCard's operation as an open, not-for-profit association, but this could change in the future. The directors of both associations almost always come from senior management at the member banks. (They are often CEOs.) The board appoints the management of the association, and the management reports to the board.

Compare this with the go-it-alones, which are owned by typical U.S. corporations. You can buy shares in the parents of both American Express and Discover on the New York Stock Exchange. And like most public corporations, the shareholders of parent companies for American Express and Discover elect the board of directors. American Express has entered into licensing and franchise arrangements with certain banks outside the United States, and it says that it intends to do so with banks in the United States—if a recent court decision that strikes down MasterCard and Visa prohibitions against this is sustained on appeal. The licensees and franchisees, however, do not get to vote on how the American Express card system is run or who manages it, nor do they get to select the members of the American Express board of directors.

The members of the co-opetitives and the shareholders in the parents of the go-it-alones are the ultimate "owners" of the systems. But there are two key differences between them. The co-opetitive members obtain services from the co-opetitive: in particular, they issue cards and acquire merchants over the co-opetitive's network, and they use its trademark. The shareholders do not generally have any business relationship with the go-it-alones; they just own stock. Moreover, while American Express shareholders have always expected to receive income from their shares—in the form of dividends and/or capital gains—the financial institutions that hold voting shares in Visa and MasterCard have had no such expectation. (In the case of MasterCard, this may change, as we noted above.)

How the Co-opetitives Are Organized

The members of the MasterCard and Visa associations have established organizations that conduct various activities on their behalf. These organizations focus on operating the authorization and settlement system, brand advertising, and research and development. They do not engage in issuing or acquiring themselves; those activities are left entirely to the members. In contrast, American Express and Discover generally keep the operation of the system, issuing, and acquiring all under common ownership and management. As we discuss in more detail below, the MasterCard and Visa organizations are a fraction of the size of the American Express and Discover organizations (adjusting for differences in the volume of transactions) because the bankcard organizations focus only on a narrow set of tasks on which the co-opetitives' members have agreed to cooperate. On everything else, they compete.

The co-opetitives are operated on a break-even basis. They do not collect profits and consequently do not distribute dividends to their members. The members are assessed various fees that are designed to recover the costs of engaging in the cooperative activities as well as to provide working capital and a cushion for unexpected expenses. Member fees are mainly based on volume. For Visa U.S.A., advertising and marketing constitutes the largest category of expenses, followed by the costs associated with running its processing infrastructure—these are two of the centralized activities that the co-opetitive conducts on behalf of its members. In contrast, American Express and Discover are typical corporations that seek to maximize their profits and return value to their shareholders through dividends and stock appreciation. Like the co-opetitives, American Express and Discover advertise heavily and operate processing systems, but unlike the co-opetitives, these proprietary systems participate directly in the issuing and acquiring businesses.

MasterCard International, based in Purchase, New York, is the organization established by the MasterCard members. MasterCard has centralized the operation of its global card system, keeping more of the decision making under the control of MasterCard International rather than its regional offices. Visa International, based in San Francisco, is the organization set up by Visa members. Visa has, compared to MasterCard, decentralized the operation of its global card system, allowing individual regions more autonomy. In the United States, Visa U.S.A., also based in San Francisco, is responsible for most of the activities on which members have agreed to cooperate.

To illustrate how the two co-opetitives are organized, it is helpful to describe Visa U.S.A. in more detail. The board of directors is comprised primarily of representatives from member banks, typically CEOs or other senior executives, as well as the CEOs of Visa U.S.A. and Visa International. The largest Visa members have the right to appoint directors, while other directors are elected by a vote of the other member banks. There are also provisions to guarantee representation of small issuers on the board. In total, there are typically about fifteen directors on the Visa U.S.A. board. In addition, there were a small number of working committees that drew on member employees. For example, the debit issuer committee provides feedback and advice from Visa members on the debit side of the business. Visa U.S.A. has an organizational chart that is similar to those for many companies: there is a CEO and various departments that are responsible for operational, legal, and financial matters.

The key difference between the co-opetitives and regular companies, however, is that the co-opetitive management has to build support among members with different objectives for major business initiatives. While support from board members is important, as they hold formal authority, support from other large members is also crucial. For instance, in the early 1990s when MasterCard's management contemplated the development of a rewards program that would be available to all members, the larger issuers that had their own proprietary rewards programs were unenthusiastic. In particular, Citigroup and First Chicago, which were not on the board, were resistant, and the management dropped the initiative. In addition, because board members are elected, they can also be voted off the board if they don't follow the interests of members that account for a substantial proportion of volume (and thus of votes). This process is unlike that followed in equity-based corporations in which shareholders play a passive role and are interested in management decisions only insofar as they affect share appreciation and dividends.

Although ownership and control rests in the hands of the co-opetitive members, the importance of individual members has fluctuated widely over time. First, co-opetitives have had liberal membership policies since their formation. Although they have prevented the competing go-it-alone systems from becoming members, the associations have allowed essentially any financial institution to join—and as we have seen, many thousands have. Second, the intense competition among issuers and acquirers has resulted in significant shifts over time in the transaction volume of members. Third, mergers and acquisitions have resulted in abrupt share changes. Fourth, efforts by the co-opetitive organizations to encourage loyalty have resulted in members' changing which co-opetitive brand they primarily issue. These changes in the relative importance of members have resulted in changes—both subtle and dramatic—in the missions of the co-opetitive organizations.

Fitting a Square Peg in a Round Hole

A key feature of the co-opetitives is that they facilitate competition among banks in issuing and acquiring. Banks didn't set up the co-opetitives because they were unusually fond of competition, of course. But operating outside a bank's geographic region was difficult: banks commonly solicited cardholders from their depositor base, and one of their goals in acquiring was to form relationships that might generate other sorts of business from merchants. Given that banks had limited geographic scope in those days because of restrictions on interstate operations and, in many states, the locations of branches, and perhaps because expanding nationally would have been a risky proposition requiring large amounts of capital, no bank made a serious attempt at a national go-it-alone system. The closest they could come was to set up a franchise system—the approach Bank of America took—and reap profits from royalties paid by other banks. But as we have seen, that approach foundered. A co-opetitive was the only way banks found to establish a viable card platform on a national level.

They came up with an exceptional solution to an uncommon set of business problems. Many observers seem unable to resist the temptation to force the co-opetitive organizations into one of two more-familiar conceptual boxes. One is the manufacturer-distributor model. In this box, the co-opetitive organization is like the manufacturer and the members are like distributors: General Motors is to its dealers as MasterCard is to its member banks. Yet co-opetitive members own and control the co-opetitive, while distributors neither own nor control the manufacturers. Moreover, the co-opetitives operate on a break-even basis in providing services to their members, while manufacturers try to maximize the profit they obtain from sales to their distributors. The other conceptual box is the franchise model. But franchisees don't get to vote on how the franchisor will operate, and franchisors don't seek merely to break even. (And as mentioned in chapter 3, it was precisely the failure of the franchise model that gave birth to the co-opetitive that became Visa.) Although the co-opetitives do bear similarities to cooperatives in other industries, attempts to find close analogs are apparently doomed to failure. The payment card co-opetitives just are what they are.

Cooperation, the Tragedy of the Commons, and the Role of Rules

Most large businesses are publicly owned, for-profit corporations like the parents of the American Express and Discover Card systems. Their internal operations are based on command and control. A CEO dictates how the business functions, subject only to oversight by a board of directors elected by the shareholders. Most large businesses have a single clear objective: to maximize shareholder value. In practice, of course, decision making involves building a consensus, office politics affect decisions, all CEOs delegate some decisions, and most businesses try to be good citizens even if it lowers their profits. Nonetheless, the goal of shareholder value imposes significant discipline on discretion and the delegation of authority within the firm.

Few significant businesses are cooperatives that closely resemble the organizations that lie at the heart of the co-opetitive systems. Cooperatives are run by their member-owners. But those members do not have a common objective; each is interested in maximizing its own individual profits, not the sum of all members' profits. Sometimes cooperation helps them achieve that goal, and sometimes it doesn't. Cooperatives function effectively only when their actions benefit most members. Members won't support efforts that harm them, so the only efforts that garner support are ones that make many members better off. And unless there are penalties for exiting, only members who believe that the cooperative is benefiting them individually will remain members.

In this section, we examine three problems faced by cooperatives. First, like any productive organization, cooperatives are constantly threatened by the ugly specter of opportunism. Second, like any institution based on voting and consensus building, cooperatives can be destabilized by differences among important members. Cooperatives also face special handicaps when competing with for-profit corporations. For these three reasons, cooperatives are seldom tried in most industries and often fail when they are attempted. Despite these serious problems, though, the payment card cooperatives have prospered, and the co-opetitives of which they are the heart have competed effectively with the go-it-alone systems. We address this apparent puzzle in the next section.

Opportunism

Opportunism results in the tragedy of the commons. A village maintains a green where sheep can graze. You benefit when you take your sheep to the commons, but your sheep reduce the amount of grass available for my sheep. The same is true for me and every other member of our village. If too many of us take our sheep to the common to graze, the grass will disappear. Then none of us will be able to nourish our sheep there. So each of us acting for our own benefit can cause a result that makes all of us worse off. This same basic problem can occur in many domains. Fishing provides an important modern example. In many parts of the world, fleets of fishing boats, each rationally maximizing its own catch, have seriously depleted fish stocks and thus threatened the viability of the fishing industry. But the tragedy of the commons is not limited to sheep and fish. If too many broadcasters crowd onto the unlicensed radio spectrum, the signals can interfere with one another, and all broadcasters will suffer. Similar issues arise with the industrial use of public bodies of water. Each company uses the water with its own profits in mind, not taking into consideration the overuse and pollution problems it creates for other firms and citizens.

The presence of a commons does not make tragedy inevitable. Rules can prevent it. Interestingly, the same individuals who act opportunistically may be willing to back the necessary rules because they prevent others from acting opportunistically. Hence, the villagers may agree to fine herders who let their sheep graze on the commons for more than an hour, even though each villager would like to graze her flock all day long. Likewise, we might all vote at our local town meeting for a strict policy of keeping dogs on leashes, even though in the absence of that policy we might each let our dogs run free. We agree to the policy because we are better off if everyone, including us, follows it. Groups—from villages to clubs to cooperatives to nations—adopt rules like these all the time: each member agrees to give up his right to act opportunistically (in certain ways specified by the rules) in exchange for every other member's agreeing to do the same.

The payment card co-opetitives face several problems that arise from opportunistic behavior, and like other groups, they have developed rules aimed at curbing such behavior.

Negative Externalities   The co-opetitives have invested billions of dollars over the years in building the MasterCard and Visa brands, which as a consequence, are recognized worldwide. Problems arise when members harm the shared brand in the course of pursuing their individual interests. One example of this occurred when a Visa member wanted to issue an affinity card associated with Hooters, the restaurant chain that highlights its buxom waitresses. Another example occurred when Citigroup wanted to emphasize its own brand on the front of the card and relegate the Visa brand to the back. Both of these situations placed the group interest in conflict with a member's interest. And in both cases, the co-opetitive enforced rules that protected what it viewed as the group's interest. In the second example, however, MasterCard changed its rules on branding to accommodate Citigroup—at least implicitly deciding that it expected the gain in system volume to outweigh the loss of visibility.

Free Riding   The cooperatives create value for their members largely through the indirect network effects we discussed in chapter 6. Problems arise when some members try to benefit from the indirect network effects created by other members without contributing anything in return—either helping to defray the cost of creating these effects or generating effects from which other members might benefit. Free riding is a particular problem with the introduction of new card products. The banks that help introduce these products early on generate indirect network effects that increase the value of these products for subsequent entrants. In addition, by testing the waters of the market they provide information for other members on whether consumers value these products. Examples include Visa's efforts to popularize debit cards and corporate Visa cards in the 1990s. In both cases, management was able to limit free riding by developing a consensus among members to invest group resources in products that initially benefited only a handful of individual members.

Loyalty   Cooperatives generally face several difficulties that result when the interests of individual members are not aligned with those of the group. One circumstance is just a variant of free riding. Some members may partake in the benefits of the cooperative when it is doing well, but leave and let the other members bear the cooperative's fixed costs when it isn't doing well. That behavior can make it difficult for cooperatives to make long-term investments: all members benefit if the investment succeeds, but the most loyal members get stuck with the costs if it doesn't. Agricultural and electricity cooperatives have dealt with this problem by imposing charges on members who leave; the charges cover investments and reduce the likelihood of financial instability resulting from member departures. After being hit with huge bills resulting from litigation in the first half of 2003, Visa passed a rule to impose an exit fee on members who withdrew substantially from its debit system to ensure that they could not impose their share of these bills on others. MasterCard, which adopted other devices to deal with this problem, protested this policy in court.

Another problem arises when members have divided loyalties. This occurs when members of a cooperative can also earn income by competing with it—perhaps by working with a competing cooperative or for-profit firm. This problem also reduces the ability of the cooperative to undertake long-run investment and planning. Most groups have rules that prevent or deter divided loyalties—for instance, most societies promote fidelity within marriages, social clubs pursue cohesiveness by only taking members sponsored by other members, businesses don't allow key employees to work for other firms, and franchisors often don't let franchisees work for competing franchisors. Even universities restrict professors' outside activities to prevent the creation of divided loyalties.

MasterCard and Visa have faced troubling loyalty issues from the beginning. Efforts to make members loyal to the cooperatives have resulted in several antitrust cases that we examine in chapter 11. The *Worthen* case involved a MasterCard member that wanted to become a Visa member and a Visa rule that prohibited this. The *MountainWest* case concerned a rule that prohibited Sears, American Express, and the owners of other competing systems from joining Visa. The Justice Department case involved a rule that prohibited members from issuing the cards of the competing go-it-alone systems.

Big Guys and the Holdup Problem

The divergent interests of large and small banks and the ability of large banks to extract concessions have posed challenges for the co-opetitives, especially in recent years. Citigroup, for example, has long sought to emphasize its brand over the co-opetitive's brand. It advertised its card as "Not Just a Visa; a Citibank Visa" in an attempt to create some differentiation. Its decision to align itself with MasterCard, in part because MasterCard was willing to change its rules to allow issuers to move the MasterCard acceptance logo to the back of the card, reflects the same strategic thrust. Smaller issuers, on the other hand, generally want the association to do more so that they can do less. They don't have the scale to do their own brand advertising, or to develop a platinum card or rewards programs. There are thus fairly predictable differences between big and small issuers' objectives—that is, in the actions they want the co-opetitives to undertake. Less obvious heterogeneity in strategies and interests give rise to similar differences among large issuers and among small issuers. The more varied the objectives of the membership, the more difficult it is to build consensus as well as to pursue *any* mission consistently and effectively.

The adverse effects of heterogeneity are increased when there are several important members. If all members are small relative to an organization, none can affect what happens other than by voting, and nobody's individual vote matters much. It's like an ideal New England town meeting. Residents may have different objectives; any one is likely to approve of some town decisions and disapprove of others. But with only one vote among many, no individual can affect those decisions much. The town will roll along, and decisions on any issue will generally reflect the preferences of those near the political center. At the other extreme, in organizations with only one important member and many small members, the important member will usually get their way. Consider a sailing club in which one member covers half the costs and one hundred members together each cover the other half. If the important member doesn't like a club decision, they can probably reverse it by threatening to leave, whether or not they are formally an officer or director of the club. Less-important members may or may not like the club's policies, but the club is likely to do a good job of making the important member—and those who share that member's preferences—happy.

Now imagine a waterfront club with, say, three members, each of whom pays a third of the club's dues. Suppose that the club will fold if any one member leaves, and the remaining members will be stuck with the cleanup costs. Now suppose the members can't agree on what the club should do: one likes sailing, one likes fishing, and one likes water-skiing. It is easy to predict that meetings will be loud, that there will be many threats to leave, and that the club is unlikely to do anything well—or even to survive. In a situation like this, members can engage in threats and other forms of *strategic* or *opportunistic behavior* in an attempt to change the behavior of others, and such behavior can be quite disruptive. With a hundred equally important members, in contrast, individuals' threats won't work and won't be tried; with only one large member, explicit threats are unnecessary and generally won't be observed.

Even if none of our three club members is inclined to threats, there is an additional source of instability that becomes more significant as the numbers become smaller: interests and incomes change, and people add and drop club memberships all the time. With a thousand members, this random churn is probably harmless, but in our three-person example, it is likely to be fatal to the club at some point.

Clearly, things are not this precarious in most real associations, but stability is often a significant issue, particularly when there are significant members. Often, members who don't share the same goals as most members of the group can leave without having much effect on the group because every member is small relative to the group. People change towns when they disagree with school system funding or change tennis clubs if they don't like wearing whites all the time. If a town's problems are sufficiently severe and widespread in effect, the decisions of many people to move away might be destabilizing, but the decisions of a handful of individuals are not important. Large members tend to destabilize the group when they leave, though, since the group loses financial support, network effects, or other significant assets. When large companies leave towns over tax disputes, they can send the town into an economic death spiral. If the most prominent members of an academic department leave, they can make it hard for the department to attract other prominent individuals, which reduces the prestige of all members of the remaining group. Citigroup's decision to leave Visa for MasterCard in 1998 resulted in a loss of 1.6 share points in co-opetitive credit and charge card volume for Visa over the succeeding four years (about a quarter of Visa's total decline relative to MasterCard), and raised the costs for the remaining

Visa members, who then needed to support the fixed costs of the system on a smaller volume.

In many settings, big players can "get their own way" or capture more of the benefits of the group for themselves by strategically threatening to leave. A number of companies played this game with New York City throughout the 1990s. The city was concerned that the loss of these companies would lead other companies to leave and would ultimately cause serious harm to the tax base. Sports teams are notorious for using this kind of pressure tactic to extract more concessions from city governments. Starting in the late 1980s, the Chicago Bears football team demanded a new and improved stadium—the historic, but dated, Soldier Field did not have any of the luxury boxes that have become so crucial for raising team revenues—and threatened to leave the city if it did not get one. Chicago's mayor finally capitulated after a decade of negotiating, and Soldier Field underwent a $632 million renovation. Visa encountered the problem of strategic behavior for several years with Citigroup and several other banks that together accounted for over 65 percent of the co-opetitive's volume in 1997. This coalition of banks threatened to leave and start its own system unless the cooperative made a number of changes on branding strategy, product development, and membership fees, among other things. Ultimately, as we have discussed, Citigroup made good on its threat, throwing much of its support and volume behind MasterCard.

During the last decade, the co-opetitives have seen a significant increase in the concentration of card volume (and therefore voting rights) as a result of bank mergers and decisions by many banks to get out of this highly competitive business. Figure 7.1 shows the trend in the concentration of volume within the co-opetitives.

As figure 7.1 illustrates, the top ten credit card issuers have captured an increasingly larger share of sales volume: from just over 50 percent in 1992 to over 75 percent in 2002. Looking at the top twenty-five issuers shows much the same trend: the share of volume rose from 70 percent in 1992 to around 85 percent in 2002. As the big bankcard issuers got bigger, the problems of instability and lack of cohesion got more serious. Small bank and large bank interests were even more divergent, and the threats to leave one association for the other implied a greater loss for

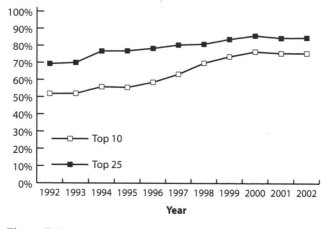

Figure 7.1
Share of credit card charge volume of top bankcard issuers, 1992–2002
Source: The Nilson Report (various issues). 1993–2003.

the system left behind. Consolidation has played an important role in changing association policies, in particular the decision by both Master-Card and Visa, examined in the next chapter, to institute partnership programs to encourage member loyalty.

Cooperatives and For-Profit Firms

Disloyalty, free riding, and opportunistic behavior are greater problems for cooperatives when they compete with for-profit firms since cooperatives face constraints on their actions that for-profit firms do not. Cooperatives have incentives to treat members alike to maintain cohesion and reduce opportunistic behavior. For-profit firms can enter into special deals with partners and keep the terms of those deals secret from other partners. Furthermore, cooperatives often operate on a break-even basis, and thus cannot raise capital by issuing equity and may find it more difficult to sell long-term debt. Financially healthy for-profits, in contrast, generally have ready access to investment capital.

Cooperatives have another reason to place a higher value on obtaining loyalty and reducing free riding when they are competing with forprofit firms. For a cooperative to pursue particular investment or business strategies, it must get the approval and cooperation of its members. Divided loyalties and free riding can make it difficult for a cooperative to achieve the degree of consensus necessary to pursue any coherent strategy effectively. For-profit firms do not face these problems (or at least not to nearly the same degree) since all decision makers in principle share a common objective.

Cooperatives can employ strategies to reduce their vulnerability to competition from for-profit firms or other cooperatives. For example, cooperatives have devised methods to prevent competitors from engaging in strategies that lead to a "run" on the membership or leave members with "stranded assets." Many agricultural cooperatives can delay returning the retained earnings of departing members, reducing their financial instability along with the incentives for members to leave. Long-term contracts protect electric cooperatives against large, destabilizing capital outflows. The courts have recognized the possible "snowballing" effect that could be brought on by a large member exiting an electric cooperative and have denied exiting members the right to sell their cooperative assets. Patrick Rey and Jean Tirole have shown that imposing rules or fines that make it harder for members to exit helps avoid a tragedy of the commons problem. Without such penalties, cooperatives would tend to invest too little in activities that make all members better off because of the uncertainty over whether members will be around in the future to share in the investment cost. (Rey and Tirole show that cooperatives will tend to adopt "weak exit penalties" as a result of balancing the tragedy of the commons problem, on the one hand, and the possibility that members might have a much better offer from outside the cooperative, on the other.)

The Co-opetitives, the Go-It-Alones, and Payment Card Ecosystems

The preceding section shows that compared with the for-profit go-it-alone systems, the payment card co-opetitives have some significant competitive handicaps. They are unusually complex joint ventures, including extremely heterogeneous participants. Joint ventures generally do not fare well. One study found that almost 30 percent of manufacturing joint ventures collapsed within three years of forming, and nearly half had dissolved after five years. A survey of multiple studies reports that, in general, between 30 and 50 percent of joint ventures experience unplanned changes or dissolutions. And apart from Ocean Spray, Ace Hardware, and the New York Stock Exchange and other securities exchanges that have not yet become stock corporations, there are few successful joint ventures or cooperatives in other industries.

Yet despite these handicaps, the co-opetitive payment systems have attracted thousands of U.S. members in the last three decades—along with substantial investment capital—have come to account for about 72 percent of payment card transactions volume in the United States, and have built a strong record of innovation. To understand the complex and somewhat unusual competitive interactions between the co-opetitives and the go-it-alone systems, it is useful to introduce the notion of "business ecosystems."

Business Ecosystems

Many industries involve tightly interconnected networks of organizations, technologies, consumers, and products that can be usefully thought of as ecosystems. These industries include payment cards, discount retailing, computers, automobiles, complex assembled goods like consumer electronics, and telecommunications. In these "distributed industries", the management of activities not under the direct ownership and control of any particular firm is important to that firm's performance and flexibility. Many activities—such as research and development, manufacturing, or sales—that are core functions for all firms in some industries are performed in distributed industries through a network of external partners.

The similarity of distributed industries to biological ecosystems suggests that a number of lessons from biological ecosystems can be applied to business networks. Crucially, members of both will tend to share a common fate, so many ecosystem characteristics such as stability, longevity, and productivity will also be found in successful business networks. If, say, General Motors were to return to auto industry leadership, a host of suppliers, partners, and distributors would share in its prosperity. Similarly, we would expect well-functioning networks of firms to adapt to many external shocks, to exhibit the specialization of individual firms and the capability for innovation at the network level, and to have structures that vary from industry to industry. Marco

Iansiti and Roy Levien summarize this in their book *The Keystone Advantage*:

Biological ecosystems provide a powerful analogy for understanding business networks. Like business networks, biological ecosystems are characterized by a large number of loosely interconnected participants who depend on each other for their mutual effectiveness and survival. . . . The ecosystem metaphor is not simply a colorful way of portraying the richness of interactions and connections among firms in business networks; it explicitly highlights key features that business networks share with ecosystems and that conventional theories about markets and industry structure often fail to capture: loose coupling between network participants, mutual dependencies, and complex relationships of cooperation, leverage, and exploitation.

The danger with analogies, of course, is that they may be taken too far. There are clear and significant differences between biological and business ecosystems. Unlike most members of biological ecosystems, businesses are capable of rational thought, of such activities as strategic planning and design. Also, business networks are in continuous competition for members, and some firms (for example, software vendors such as Adobe Systems that produce applications for both Apple Macintosh and Windows-based computers) belong to two or more competing ecosystems at the same time. It is important to point out that we are simply arguing that biological ecosystems can provide some specific and powerful insights to the different roles played by firms in certain industries.

All organizations in distributed industries are not equal. Most business ecosystems have a small number of organizations that are more richly interconnected than the vast majority; these are called "hubs" or "keystones." Microsoft plays this role in the personal computer industry, for instance; its ecosystem includes a vast array of hardware and software producers that must interact with Microsoft regularly on standards development and other technical issues, as well as their own suppliers and distributors. Similarly, there are relatively few automobile producers in the world, but each of them interacts with a host of suppliers, partners, and distributors. Economies of scale (as in automobiles) or network economies (as in personal computers) normally tend to drive industries to have only a few hubs. The benefits of decentralization and competition for innovation and cost reduction tend to lead to ecosystem complexity, and to require communication and coordination.

The payment card industry can be usefully seen as consisting of a set of complex business ecosystems in which both the co-opetitives and the go-it-alones play critical roles as hubs. The industry has four major hubs—American Express, Discover, MasterCard, and Visa—that maintain branded authorization and settlement systems. Each hub has connections with the many other participants in its ecosystem, some of which (for example, the makers of point-of-sale terminals) also belong to other ecosystems. These participants include the ultimate consumers of payment card services—merchants and individuals—as well as a web of businesses that help provide these services—bank acquirers, issuers, processors, and equipment manufacturers. As discussed previously, bank acquirers sign up merchants, install point-of-sale terminal equipment, capture the transaction data, and route it through the credit card network to obtain approval. Processors authorize the customers' transactions, provide a tally of these transactions for the merchants, and transfer funds to the merchant to cover the card purchases. Issuers provide cardholders with the payment card and settle their accounts. Equipment manufacturers make the terminal equipment. Finally, as we noted above, for certain tasks best done on an industry-wide basis, in particular the determination of technical standards, the hubs connect with each other.

Together, the four hubs take up a surprisingly small amount of space in the industry. In 2002, they handled over $2.7 trillion in transactions yet employed only fifty-three thousand people. The go-it-alones, American Express and Discover, handled $12.3 million and $4.1 million, respectively, in transaction volume per employee. In contrast, the co-opetitives, Visa and MasterCard, handled $262 million and $192 million per employee, respectively. The large difference between the two hub types, as shown in figure 7.2, underscores an important fact: the co-opetitives and the go-it-alones are organized in fundamentally different ways. Most of the work in the Visa and MasterCard systems is done at the member level.

MBA students learn that for any business strategy to be effective, it must be consistent with the organizational structure that is to implement it. Competition between the co-opetitive and go-it-alone ecosystems offers a striking illustration of this principle, as we will now show.

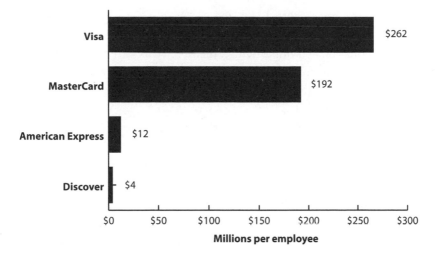

Figure 7.2
Worldwide purchase volume per employee, 2002
Sources: American Express and Discover Card, *Annual Reports*; and the Securities and Exchange Commission's filings for Visa U.S.A., Visa International, and MasterCard.

The Co-opetitive Ecosystems

The co-opetitives' key innovation is their organizational structure. As Bennett Katz, Visa's longtime chief counsel, describes this structure, "Visa is the hub; the spokes are the banks. . . . Visa doesn't have a life of its own. In fact, it's the largest joint venture in the world today." The co-opetitives' open structure makes it easy for banks to issue credit and debit cards, and thus encourages growth, but by reducing the entry barriers it facilitates competition in both issuing and acquiring. This intense competition, in turn, ensures that consumers, not bank shareholders, capture most of the benefits the industry produces.

Visa and MasterCard work with their members to set essential standards, and they run the railroads—the processing, authorization, and settlement systems—that allow transactions to be executed in the blink of an eye. These systems have been improved substantially over the years through research and development as well as investment projects approved and financed by members. As we discussed above, the need to build the support of heterogeneous, competing institutions for major system-level initiatives both limits the scope of what can be attempted (most members must see benefits) and may limit the speed with which the associations can act. In particular, member banks are generally reluctant to share customer data with each other, and some may resist changes in the associations' networks that will require investments in the banks' own computer systems.

Beyond basic operating standards, the associations have not dictated how members may use their systems in issuing or acquiring, nor have they much constrained members' relationships with their customers. Rather, the co-opetitive systems and brand names have served as platforms, considerably enhanced over time, on which association members have been able to build their own differentiated product offerings. This resembles the way Apple and Microsoft have made their operating systems available as platforms to other firms that produce applications software. Similarly, while both associations have engaged in system-level marketing and advertising, they have done little (apart from protecting the system trademarks) to constrain the marketing activities of their members. This lack of central control coupled with a diverse membership means that at any time there is likely to be considerable experimentation, but nothing that looks like an association-wide product or marketing strategy. Successful member innovations, such as cobranded cards, are generally copied by others, though usually with a lag that makes innovation profitable.

Neither Visa nor MasterCard, nor their members, are integrated into the production of the information technology hardware on which their systems rely (including, for instance, computer networks and point-of-sale terminals), and much of the software they use is produced by others. The resulting competition among specialized technology providers has benefited both the co-opetitives and consumers. Faster and cheaper processing technology has increased merchant acceptance, improving cardholder convenience. Improved technology has lowered the time at the point of sale needed to complete a transaction from minutes to seconds.

The open, competitive structures of the co-opetitives turned out to be ideal to capitalize on network effects. To appreciate how strong these effects are in the payment card industry, one has only to listen to the advertisements from the systems about who has the most merchants and to read the claims to merchants about how many cardholders each system has. The co-opetitives were set up in a way that enabled them to capture network effects rapidly. Open membership in the associations expanded the number of businesses that could seek cardholders and merchants on behalf of the associations' brands. Vigorous competition among issuers and acquirers drove prices down and expanded output. While issuer and acquirer profits were not particularly high on average (as we illustrate in chapters 9 and 10), they were high enough to attract the capital needed to expand the systems.

In part because of their different structure, the for-profit go-it-alones adopted a fundamentally different strategy that made considerable profits for a while, but obtained fewer network economies. As platform providers, MasterCard and Visa adopted something like the low-price, high-volume strategy that Microsoft took with its operating system. American Express, as we now discuss, adopted something more like the high-price, low-volume strategy that Apple employed, although with far less devastating consequences.

Go-It-Alones' Ecosystems

By performing more system activities under common ownership and management, the ecosystems in which American Express and Discover are hubs avoid both the need to manage webs of contracts and the need to build consensus among competitors for system-level actions. On the other hand, the centralization of decision making seems to reduce experimentation and, by reducing diversity within the ecosystem, may reduce the system's ability to recover from external shocks. And when the hub makes a strategic mistake, the consequences are more serious when the system is more centralized.

As a payment system hub, American Express has elected to control almost the entire relationship with the cardholder with virtually every card that carries its name. American Express signs up its own cardholders and merchants (although it also relies on third-party acquirers), has installed its own software, and processes its own payments. Even American Express leaves some commodity tasks to third-party firms, however. For example, payment cards, computer hardware, and point-of-sale terminals are manufactured by outside firms.

American Express's control of almost the entire marketing budget of its ecosystem allows it to respond in a coordinated fashion to changes in market conditions. For instance, when consumer spending slackened off in the early 1990s, American Express increased its focus on small business charge cards. More recently, it only took four months to launch the Blue Card, the first in the United States with an embedded chip, after developing the final idea for the product. In addition, American Express collects a tremendous database of consumer purchasing information. The associations collect less data because no single bank owns the entire transaction—the issuers and the acquirer will generally be different banks—and banks are reluctant to share customer data. For a fee, American Express shares its information with corporations for expense tracking and with merchants to monitor consumer-spending habits. American Express's database allows it to send out precisely targeted offers to consumers based on information gathered in card transactions.

On the other hand, American Express's ability to move its entire ecosystem rapidly in the same direction works against it when it chooses the wrong direction. With the benefit of hindsight, it would seem that American Express and Diners Club misjudged the promise of payment cards early on. American Express in particular was well situated to establish a system that could have dominated the industry in the United States and perhaps abroad. Yet it chose to maintain its high-price, low-volume model for many years. It also decided until recently not to offer a credit card—a decision that was perhaps driven by its unwillingness to lower its merchant fees to get the larger merchant base needed for this product. And it decided against seeking partnerships with banks until recently.

In the mid-1980s, American Express started recognizing the quandary it was in. But the ship was hard to turn. Harvey Golub, then American Express's CEO, describes some opportunities it missed:

Sometime around 1985, American Airlines asked us if we were interested in creating a frequent-flier card with them. We said brusquely, "no thanks" because we were afraid it would hurt our basic card business. They went ahead and launched the American Airlines Advantage card in partnership with Visa and Citibank. It was a tremendous success and hurt our business.

Five years later, before AT&T entered the card business, it offered to work with us to develop a joint credit card. Once again we said "no thanks." We thought it would hurt our card business. They launched the universal card anyway with MasterCard and Citibank. It was a success, and it hurt our business more than it would have if we participated.

This story has parallels to Apple Computer's fall from industry leadership. Like Apple, American Express insisted on operating a proprietary network and permitted no one else to use it. Apple controlled the entire stack, including the hardware, the operating system, and many applications. This strategy gave Apple, like American Express, a number of technical advantages, but it has not performed well against Microsoft's effective co-opetitive strategy. Microsoft licenses its operating system and developer tools to a wide variety of software vendors and hardware manufacturers. Competition between the software developers and the hardware manufacturers has spurred both the diversity of their products and the productivity of their manufacturing and distribution systems.

Discover, too, was a success story in its early years. Its selling point for cardholders was the absence of an annual fee coupled with cash-back rewards. Its selling point for merchants was a merchant discount that was slightly lower than the co-opetitives' and much lower than American Express's. Both cardholders and merchants could thus give Discover a trial at minimal cost. Just five years after its launch, it had become the third-largest credit and charge card issuer with a 5 percent share of transaction volume, and it had a merchant base comparable to that of American Express. Discover found it difficult, however, to build on that initial success on the cardholder side. It didn't have American Express's premium merchant discount available to offer better rewards to cardholders, nor did it have the prestige of the American Express brand. While it continued to expand its merchant base, it has been to date a one-trick pony on the cardholder side, and its share of payment card transactions has slowly declined since the mid-1990s.

In recent years, American Express has begun to add members to its ecosystem. The first major cobranding initiative taken by the company was an integrated electronic service offered through America Online in 1995. More significantly, American Express launched cobranded cards with a number of companies, including Delta Airlines, ShopRite, Starwood Hotels, and Fidelity Investments.

American Express's historic go-it-alone strategy seems to have slowed its expansion overseas. For example, Sumitomo Bank began issuing BankAmericard cards (the forerunner of the Visa card) in Japan in 1968, while American Express didn't issue cards in Japan until 1980. Here again, American Express's strategy seems to be changing. In 1997, American Express announced that it was seeking bank partners around the world. American Express has thus far indicated that it will select a small number of partners, often forming exclusive agreements in each country. As of late 2003, it had sixty card-issuing partnerships in sixty-three countries (there were a total of eighty agreements, as some banks had agreements with American Express in multiple countries), including GE Capital in France, Samsung in Korea, Sumitomo Bank in Japan, and AMP Bank in Australia. (The co-opetitives have not permitted their members to enter such alliances in the United States, although unless it is overturned by the Supreme Court, a 2003 appeals court decision discussed in chapter 11 will require them to do so.)

American Express is now a highly profitable public corporation. In 2002, the division that runs American Express's payment cards, Travel Related Services, earned $2.1 billion in profit—80 percent of the company's total profit. It is the largest card issuer in the industry, as measured by transaction volume, and is still the sole owner of the entire transaction process for most of its cards.

Both the co-opetitive and go-it-alone strategies have been around since the beginning of the payment card industry. As we have seen, the advantage of the co-opetitive business model is that it allows a wide variety of firms to move their ecosystem forward through competition and innovation, disciplined by common standards. The key disadvantage is the difficulty of maintaining cooperation among competing firms with different strategies and divergent interests. In contrast, the classic go-it-alone strategy provides a unity of purpose throughout the system, and facilitates translating the benefits of scale economies and systemwide exchange of information into profits. But the go-it-alones' dependence on a single management team may reduce experimentation and increase ecosystem vulnerability to external shocks. It will be informative to follow these contrasting and evolving strategic approaches as the payment system industry continues to face interesting times.

8

System Wars

It started in Boston—a skirmish that turned into a rebellion that routed one of the great payment card systems. Boston was in a recession during winter 1991. Unemployment in the metropolitan area was the highest since 1982, and personal income had fallen back to 1986 levels. Housing prices had declined by 27 percent since their peak in 1987. Jasper's, an expensive seafood restaurant near Boston's waterfront, and other premier restaurants in town were hit especially hard. They tried to trim expenses to stay in business.

Some restaurants found the fees they had to pay to American Express particularly irksome. Every time a patron took out her American Express card to pay, the restaurant saw an average of 3.25 percent of its revenues slip away. That is what American Express took off the top of the bill as its merchant discount. If the patron pulled out a Visa or MasterCard, the restaurant would pay only 2 percent of the check. Of course, the restaurant might lose some customers if it did not accept American Express—but how many?

So that winter, Jasper White, the owner of Jasper's, and other restaurateurs asked American Express to shave its merchant discount, just as they had gotten discounts and concessions from other suppliers. American Express refused. It is not hard to see why. Merchant fees accounted for two-thirds of its revenues from the American Express card. Cutting its merchant discount by even half a percentage point would cost American Express at least $470 million annually (as always, in 2002 dollars) and eliminate its card profits. The only way it could make up that revenue would be to raise the annual fee it charged cardholders, but that increase could drive cardholders away since the annual fee of $66 for American Express's lowest-priced Green Card was already three times the average for Visa and MasterCard.

American Express argued that the valuable cardholders it delivered to merchants justified its high merchant discount. With its "Membership Has Its Privileges" advertising campaign and other brand-positioning efforts, American Express had sought to cultivate elite customers used to living large. At the beginning of the backlash, one of American Express's marketing executives explained to a Boston interviewer, "Especially in troubled times, if there's one segment that continues to spend, it's American Express cardholders."

Perhaps they would indeed keep spending, but they no longer had to use their American Express cards to do so. By the early 1990s, most American Express cardholders had one or more credit cards from MasterCard or Visa, which they could use at virtually all the places that took American Express charge cards, including the rebellious Boston restaurants, and many more places that did not take American Express. Merchants' risk of losing high-spending American Express cardholders if they didn't take American Express was less serious than it used to be. As one of the ringleaders of the Boston revolt says he put it to American Express: "You guys just don't get it. This isn't the eighties anymore. Times have changed."

Visa and Discover soon took advantage of American Express's plight. Visa offered to pay any legal expenses the Boston restaurants incurred in their fight with American Express. Discover, the newest payment card system, sent a marketing team to Boston offering a merchant discount of 1.5 percent—less than half that charged by American Express. Discover boosted its coverage of Boston restaurants from 23 to 78 percent.

The Boston Fee Party was underway. By April 1991, more than 250 Boston restaurants were threatening to drop the American Express card. (Only a few, including Jasper's and Biba—another upscale Boston eatery—actually did.) Soon, restaurants across the country were threatening to do the same. Although the Boston restaurateurs represented only a small fraction of the 120,000 restaurants that took the American Express card nationwide, the press was merciless. The *Boston Globe* wrote a scathing piece critiquing the elitist attitudes of American Express and its cardholders. Faced with mounting pressure, American Express relented. It announced that it would negotiate merchant discounts individually with merchants. That soon led other merchants, including Land's End and U-Haul, to seek discounts.

American Express lowered its average merchant discount dramatically over the next few years: from 3.22 to 2.74 percent between 1990 and 1996. (This didn't wipe out profits as American Express also lowered its costs over this period and spending per card rose.) Of course, American Express did not drop its merchant discount solely because of the rebellion in Boston. For several years, Visa's television advertisements had attacked American Express. The televised stories of consumers paying for good times with their Visa cards always ended with the sober warning, "And They Don't Take American Express." The slogan had had an impact. American Express's share of credit and charge card spending had dropped from 26 percent when the advertisements first aired in 1985, to 22 percent in 1991 when Jasper White's rebellion took place.

The Boston Fee Party was a very visible battle in the wars that have raged between the card systems ever since Diners Club started wrestling with imitators in the early 1950s. The go-it-alones have waged war with the co-opetitives. The co-opetitives have waged war with each other, even though they have had the same members for many years. Both the go-it-alones and the co-opetitives have waged an increasingly intense war with the EFT systems. And of course, all these systems have fought in the überwar between cards, cash, and checks. Figure 8.1 shows the results of these struggles. We see the demise of Diners Club and the birth of Discover and the EFT networks over this period. We also observe the growth of Visa over the past three decades, which appears to have come

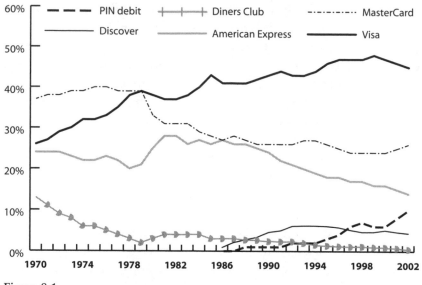

Figure 8.1
Systems' shares of payment card purchases, 1970–2002
Source: The Nilson Report (various issues).

at the expense of MasterCard and American Express, as well as cash and checks.

This is the first of three chapters that will discuss competition in the payment card industry. The next two examine competition among issuers and among acquirers. Many of these issuers and acquirers belong to the co-opetitive systems. They compete with each other as well as with the go-it-alone systems. The struggles between the systems are the focus here. The distinction between these struggles and the battles among issuers and acquirers is worth dwelling on because it is not obvious. The Boston Fee Party was about system competition. The merchant discount results mainly from decisions made at the system level; those same decisions also affect the numbers of merchants and types of industries that accept cards. Likewise, Visa's advertising strike against American Express was planned by the Visa association, acting on behalf of its members, not by individual issuers or acquirers. American Express's ups and downs, however, have resulted from both competition with issuers and acquirers that belong to the co-opetitives as well as with the co-opetitives themselves.

Weapons of War

Many weapons have been used in the competition between the systems. Three are of particular note.

Pricing

The go-it-alone systems determine prices for cardholders and merchants directly. American Express can alter its merchant discounts and card-holder fees whenever it wants. It can vary both the level of prices (the average total price that cardholders and merchants combined pay for transactions) and the structure of prices (the shares of the total price that cardholders and merchants each pay). The co-opetitives influence prices for cardholders and merchants indirectly. Given total system costs, the competition among issuers and among acquirers determines the level of prices. The more intense the competition, all else being equal, the lower the total price paid by merchants and consumers together. The co-opetitives determine the structure of prices through the interchange fee. In effect, a higher interchange fee shifts costs from issuers to acquirers and generally results in cardholders paying a smaller share of the total price, while a lower interchange fee generally results in merchants paying a lower discount, and thus a smaller share of the total price. Merchant discounts and interchange fees in turn affect competition among payment systems, on the one hand, and cash and checks, on the other.

Product Quality

Payment systems establish several key product features that consumers and merchants care about. (Issuers and acquirers determine other features that we discuss in the next two chapters.) Most important, they create and operate the networks for processing transactions. Faster and more reliable networks are more appealing to cardholders and merchants. The reduction in the amount of time that cardholders and merchants have to wait to consummate a transaction has made payment cards more competitive with cash and checks over the years. Although the systems have all progressed at roughly the same pace over long periods, different strategic choices have from time to time given some systems relatively short-lived advantages over the others. That is particularly true for the co-opetitives, which are always competing with each other for volume from their common members. The systems also compete by developing new card products, such as corporate cards, and new card technologies, such as smart cards.

Advertising

Through the years, the leading payment card systems have engaged in extensive advertising and marketing campaigns, as all television viewers know. These advertisements provide information—hard and soft—about the characteristics of the payment cards issued by the system. For example, Visa with its "Visa—It's Everywhere You Want to Be" campaign highlighted that many merchants take its card. Discover's "It Pays to Discover" campaign advertises the fact that its card has a cash-back bonus feature. The futuristic television ad for American Express's Blue showing the card being twisted into different shapes brands Blue as a flexible card for technically savvy consumers. American Express, Discover, MasterCard, and Visa spent about $780 million on card-related advertising in 2002. All but Discover were among the top one hundred brand advertisers in the first half of that year.

And They Don't Take American Express

The changing fortunes of American Express in the payment card industry illustrate the competitive interaction of the systems and the strategic use of the weapons described above. American Express had been in business for more than a hundred years when Diners Club presented American Express with a challenge and an opportunity. Diners Club was targeted to travel and entertainment businesses and their patrons in the United States and abroad—the same kinds of customers who used travelers cheques.

But Diners Club also demonstrated that charge cards were a profitable and popular product. American Express already had extensive experience selling a similar payment method to upscale households and merchants, and it augmented this by acquiring Universal Travelcard and the *Gourmet* magazine card programs that had followed in the footsteps of Diners Club. Largely because of these acquisitions, it had 17,500 merchants and 250,000 cardholders already in place when it entered the card business in 1958. By the mid-1970s, the American Express card had become dominant in the travel and entertainment sector, with more than seven times as many cardholders in the United States as Diners Club, its closest competitor in this category.

The American Express card also had prestige: it was carried by the economic elite, and was widely accepted by upscale restaurants, hotels, rental car companies, stores that relied on tourists, and other travel and entertainment–related businesses. Card membership was highest for well-off households and lowest for the poorest households. In 1978, almost 50 percent of households with annual incomes greater than $57,400 had American Express cards (as always, in 2002 dollars). According to data from the Federal Reserve Board's *Survey of Consumer Finances*, 26 percent of households in the top income quintile had charge cards in 1977, versus only 4 percent of the remaining 80 percent of households. (By this time, 85 percent of the gross volume on all charge cards was from American Express cards.)

American Express would burnish this image in the next decade. In 1975, it started its classic "Don't Leave Home Without It" advertising campaign, which emphasized the value of the card for charging purchases at merchant locations around the world. Around the same time, American Express began running its "Do You Know Me?" television advertisements. These ads featured American Express cardholders who were famous for something, but whose faces were not well known to the public. One of the classic advertisements featured William Miller, an obscure congressman who had run for vice president alongside Barry Goldwater's presidential bid in 1964. The pitch was that unless you're better known than Miller, carrying an American Express card would enhance your prestige.

By the time these ads ran, 68 million cardholders could charge their purchases at 1.2 million merchants on MasterCard and Visa cards. By 1978, households charged nearly $100 billion worth of goods and services on the co-opetitive cards, four times as much as on American Express cards.

American Express nonetheless prospered by focusing on upscale merchants and cardholders. By the start of the 1980s, its average merchant discount was almost 50 percent higher than the Visa/MasterCard average: 3.6 versus 2.5 percent. And American Express charged cardholders an annual fee of $68 for its standard Green Card and $89 for its Gold Card—more than twice the average annual fee charged by issuers on MasterCard and Visa cards. It mounted a new advertising campaign in the mid-1980s to emphasize the elite nature of its card products. "Membership Has Its Privileges" first hit television viewers in March 1987. The stock market crashed in October of that year.

By the mid-1980s, you *could* leave home without it, and merchants would be happy if you did. By 1986, 60 percent of American Express cardholders had a MasterCard or Visa card. Those cards were accepted at almost all the same places as American Express cards and at about 1.4 million merchants who did not take American Express cards. If you paid with your American Express card instead of your MasterCard or Visa, the merchant paid an extra 1 percent on average. Not surprisingly, merchants who accepted American Express cards sometimes encouraged patrons to use another card.

The other major go-it-alone system, Discover, appeared on the scene in 1985, emphasizing value rather than prestige. Discover was initially operated by a Sears subsidiary, Dean Witter, and its initial cardholder base was built from the twenty-five million holders of Sears store cards. Discover's advertising slogan, "It Pays to Discover," reminded people that Discover charged no annual fee and gave cardholders a cash rebate based on their purchase volume. On the other side of the market, Discover charged even lower average merchant discounts than the bankcard systems. The combination of a large cardholder base (twenty-two million cards issued after two years) and a low merchant discount enabled Discover to build a large merchant base rapidly. By 1992, Discover accounted for 6 percent of payment card volume. While many holders of Sears cards were not the sort of prestige-conscious highfliers who American Express courted, many of those highfliers were also concerned with value, and were attracted by Discover's cash rebates and large merchant base. Discover's entry made American Express's high-cost model increasingly visible to merchants and consumers alike.

Also in 1985, Visa launched an advertising campaign that highlighted the fact that American Express was not accepted at many merchants who took Visa. Each commercial featured a particular merchant and said, "Visa. It's Everywhere You Want to Be." Its tagline was: "And They Don't Take American Express." Consumer perceptions of the different card brands changed remarkably after these ads started airing. At the beginning of 1985, about 35 percent of consumers thought Visa was accepted at more merchants, compared with 28 percent for American Express. By the late 1980s, the percentages shifted to between 45 and 50 percent and 20 percent, respectively. And by the mid-1990s, nearly 70 percent of consumers said Visa had the greater merchant acceptance, while only 5 percent of consumers said American Express.

American Express's share of payment card volume (including credit, charge, and debit) had been roughly steady at 26 to 28 percent during the early to mid-1980s, but it declined thereafter. Since 1993, American Express's share of credit plus charge card volume has hovered around 20 percent, while the rise of debit cards in the 1990s reduced its share of total payment card volume to 14 percent in 2002.

Survey evidence confirms that Visa's commercials contributed to American Express's decline in the late 1980s and early 1990s by making cardholders and merchants more aware that this "prestige" card wasn't accepted many places. More important, it started becoming apparent that American Express cards were not a good deal. For cardholders, Discover, MasterCard, and Visa were cheaper, accepted at more merchants, and provided revolving credit. For merchants, American Express was significantly more expensive than most alternatives. That higher price had been justified on the grounds that American Express's elite cardholders would produce additional sales, but that rationale didn't work if those cardholders were willing to pay with their bank credit cards instead. The Boston Fee Party was a public manifestation of the tightening of this constraint by the early 1990s.

American Express's business model made it difficult for its charge card platform to compete with the credit card platform adopted by its competitors. It earned most of its revenue from merchants. If American

Express reduced its relatively high merchant fees to increase acceptance, it would have to make it up on the cardholder side or take lower profits. But if it raised prices to cardholders, it would increase the gap between its fees and those of its competitors. Of course, it could try to be more like the competition by issuing credit cards; so long as there were profits to be made on the extension of credit, those cards made it possible to charge lower fees to both cardholders and merchants. It had gotten out of that business in the late 1960s, and as we discussed in chapter 3, its attempt to reenter in the late 1980s had not gone well.

American Express was thus in serious trouble in a number of areas by the early 1990s. Its flawed introduction of the Optima credit card in 1987 had resulted in large losses from unexpectedly high charge-offs, adding to other severe losses in its Travel Related Services division. The Boston Fee Party had generated a lot of bad publicity, as had scandals involving senior management. Several analysts believed American Express was in a precarious position. One industry observer opined, "I don't see how they can survive. Everybody is offering what they're offering, but with more bells and whistles. What do they have that the banks can't offer just as efficiently?"

American Express still had a formidable card asset: its corporate card program. Many corporations required their employees to use American Express cards to pay for expenses. These corporations received reports that helped to monitor travel and entertainment spending and to identify areas where savings could be obtained. American Express provided data that allowed companies to compare how much they were spending on travel relative to their competitors as well as to identify employees who were in violation of corporate travel policies.

MasterCard and Visa had a hard time competing with American Express's corporate program. The co-opetitives were at a technological disadvantage—a price they paid for in their decentralized structure. American Express automatically had data on both the cardholder and the merchant because it dealt directly with both as a go-it-alone system. A co-opetitive issuer did not have automatic access to data on the merchants with whom its cardholders used their cards (except for merchants who the issuer happened to serve as an acquirer). And the co-opetitive systems were designed for cards issued to consumers, for whom seeing the merchant name and dollar amount on the bill is generally sufficient. In principle, the co-opetitive systems could always have required acquirers to transmit much more detailed merchant information and restructured their processing infrastructures to accommodate this, but most members were not interested in issuing corporate cards, and would thus oppose incurring these costs.

Some individual issuers attempted to issue corporate cards on their own. U.S. Bancorp started issuing corporate cards on the Visa system before Visa had developed a corporate product by getting the necessary information directly from major travel and entertainment merchants. While this was not as comprehensive as the merchant data American Express had, it was enough for U.S. Bancorp to launch a credible corporate card program.

By the early 1990s, about five million U.S. businesspeople had American Express cards, and were required to use them at many travel and entertainment settings. Restaurants, hotels, and other merchants who served businesspeople risked losing sales if they stopped taking American Express cards. (American Express did not offer merchants the option of taking only its corporate cards.) The corporate card was important to American Express. Recognizing the strategic importance of a strong competitive product, the Visa management persuaded its members to allow it to invest significant sums in a competitive corporate card program, even though only a few members were likely to issue corporate cards.

The American Express corporate card made predictions of the T&E card giant's death premature. The company started making radical changes in its business strategies to compete with its card rivals after Harvey Golub became CEO in 1993. These strategies were typically two-sided. They entailed increasing the number of cardholders to persuade merchants that the card would lead to incremental sales that would justify the high merchant discount, and broadening the set of merchants who took the card to persuade cardholders that it was worth carrying and using.

American Express introduced a variety of credit card–based products under the Optima logo, several designed to compete with the increasingly popular affinity cards issued by co-opetitives. The introduction of the Membership Miles (now known as Membership Rewards) program in 1991 also allowed American Express's charge card holders to earn frequent-flier miles from a variety of airlines (and now provides rewards from car rental firms, hotel chains, and other merchants). This program has strengthened its card offerings.

Over time, American Express's advertising has shifted from emphasizing the elitist nature of its card to stressing the comparative advantages of its card products over those of the other systems. American Express's "Do You Know Me?" campaign, as mentioned earlier, relied on famous, if not necessarily recognizable, personalities to build a high-end image for the card—important people carried the card, which itself conveyed status. The "Membership Has Its Privileges" campaign again emphasized the benefits of "membership" (American Express's term for cardholders) in an exclusive club. American Express's "Do More" campaign, started in 1996, was less elitist, focusing instead on the usefulness of the card, and showing how the company had broadened its offerings beyond the charge card to include credit cards, cobranded cards, and cards for students and senior citizens. American Express's most recent "Make Life Rewarding" campaign, launched in 2002, again highlights the ways the card can make life easier or more enjoyable, and also attempts to cross sell other American Express products such as its travel services and financial advisers.

American Express reduced its merchant discount and increased its investment in expanding merchant acceptance during the 1990s as well. This was done selectively. Travel and entertainment merchants who depended on corporate travelers were still charged significantly more than for MasterCard and Visa. Other segments such as supermarkets were offered about the same merchant discounts as the co-opetitives charged. American Express also offered low merchant discounts to a few large retailers.

In 1999, American Express and Costco, a "wholesale club" retailer, announced that they would be partnering to offer American Express consumer credit and corporate charge cards that also functioned as Costco membership cards on Costco's rewards program. This offered both companies an opportunity to expand their customer base, as only 15 percent of American Express cardholders were shopping at Costco, and Costco had twenty-seven million members worldwide at the time. As a result of the partnership, American Express became the only payment card to be accepted at Costco, which had only accepted Discover for the previous eight years. Industry estimates suggested that the merchant discount paid by Costco to American Express was as low as 1.1 percent. (When Costco formally stopped accepting Discover, Discover sent its cardholders a coupon for half off the price of membership at Costco's competitor, Sam's Club.)

American Express has also successfully marketed its cards to a wide range of consumers. It captured the imaginations of younger consumers with its American Express Blue Card. This smart card contains a chip and can be used with a reader attached to a computer to conduct Internet transactions with a greater degree of security (and in a much cooler way) than simply entering the card information manually. The Blue Card works just like any other when used at brick-and-mortar merchants, however, and there has been little tangible consumer benefit from the chip to date. Consumers generally face little or no liability from fraudulent use of any kind; security breaches in Internet transactions (as opposed to cards used fraudulently at Internet merchants) have not been a material problem compared to other types of transactions; and one survey found that only 0.6 percent of Blue cardholders were using the chip to secure online transactions in any case. Nevertheless, Internet security seems to have been an effective selling point, as were Blue's futuristic look, attractive pricing (no annual fee and a 0 percent introductory interest rate followed by 9.99 percent), and the appeal of having a card with a chip. Regardless, two million individuals signed up for the card within six months of its introduction in September 1999.

These strategies paid off. As American Express became more competitive, its share of credit plus charge card volume stabilized after 1993. The number of American Express cardholders increased from 19.6 million in 1993 to 25.2 million in 2002. The number of merchants taking American Express doubled from 1.6 million in 1993 to 3.2 million in 2002. While more merchants still take MasterCard and Visa, American Express covers almost all of the card spending of its cardholders; it is accepted at merchants who account for about 96 percent of the total card spending of its cardholders, up from less than 70 percent around 1991. As a result of its success in getting both sides of the market back on board, American Express in 2002 was the largest issuer of payment cards in the United States, as measured by purchase volume.

Another American Express strategy is notable, though it has not yet had an impact in the U.S. market. American Express sought alliances with banks that belonged to the co-opetitives. MasterCard and Visa prohibited their members from issuing American Express cards in the United States, though not in most other countries. This led to an antitrust suit, which we discuss in chapter 11. American Express's 1997 agreement with Banco Popular de Puerto Rico, the largest bankcard issuer on the island, provides an example of these alliances. This nonexclusive licensing agreement authorized Banco Popular to issue a card that (because it bore an American Express logo) would be honored by American Express merchants, but that was branded primarily as a Banco Popular card. In 2002, a quarter of Banco Popular's card accounts were American Express accounts, and they outnumbered its MasterCard accounts.

As of October 2003, American Express had sixty alliances of this basic sort. The number of American Express cards issued outside the United States has grown from 12.3 million in 1996 to 22.2 million in 2002. The additional 9.9 million cards constitute, however, only 1 percent of all payment cards issued outside the United States on the Visa, MasterCard, American Express, JCB, and Diners Club systems.

In the United States, unlike the co-opetitives, American Express does not plan to allow a large number of institutions to issue its cards or any to acquire merchants for it. Rather, it has decided to enter into strategic alliances with a few select banks. MasterCard and Visa have argued that this approach was designed to divide their member banks, and thus, to weaken the co-opetitives as system-level competitors. A key basis for this claim is a speech given to bank executives at the 1996 Credit Card Forum by then American Express chair Harvey Golub. He stated that Visa is "actually run for the benefit of a relatively few banks and the association staff—rather than in the interest of all of its members." He maintained that Visa had failed the majority of its members by "spending money that you've contributed on things that don't particularly benefit you; subsidizing a few individual banks who compete against you; and deciding what products you can and can not offer to *your* clients."

Golub then proceeded to discuss four Visa practices that he alleged were not in the interests of many banks: (1) Visa's advertising attacks on American Express's merchant coverage; (2) Visa's payments to support cobranded cards; (3) Visa's lowering of interchange fees, which forced down American Express's merchant discounts; and (4) Visa's development of corporate and purchasing card systems as well as travelers cheques. These investments all had effects on American Express.

Although Golub's speech did not lead to either a rebellion among Visa members or decisions to reduce the investments that helped the Visa system compete with the American Express system, American Express's efforts to lobby the Clinton Justice Department to bring an antitrust case against Visa and MasterCard were more successful. Again, we explore this case in detail in chapter 11.

Master the Possibilities

Despite appearances, Visa's main target in its "It's Everywhere You Want to Be" advertising campaign was not American Express. It was Master-Card. MasterCard was Visa's closest competitor at the start of this campaign. In 1985, the year the Visa campaign started, Visa had 43 percent of all payment card volume, and MasterCard was in second place with 28 percent, just ahead of American Express. Moreover, surveys indicated that consumers viewed MasterCard and Visa as almost indistinguishable in important respects. That view was well founded: both card brands were accepted at almost all the same locations, they provided similar services, and they had almost the same member banks. American Express, on the other hand, offered a charge card rather than a credit card, and it had positioned itself as the high-quality brand with no (explicit) limit on how much could be charged on an American Express card in any one month.

Visa wanted to differentiate itself from MasterCard. To do so, it focused its advertising on comparisons to American Express that attempted to enhance Visa's prestige by invoking and challenging American Express's position as the industry leader in upscale markets. As Visa's advertising agency put it to a committee of Visa members responsible for advertising, they would use American Express as a "straw man," with MasterCard as the ultimate target. Visa executives discussed the "halo effect" of positioning American Express as Visa's primary competitor instead of MasterCard. If successful, this strategy would also allow Visa to increase its share of travel and entertainment spending, American Express's stronghold for many years.

The effects of Visa's advertising campaign on consumer perceptions of MasterCard are striking. Prior to the advertisements, when consumers were asked which card brand was accepted at more merchants, 35 percent said Visa and 28 percent said MasterCard. By 1994, almost three times as many consumers said Visa as said MasterCard (69 versus 25 percent) even though MasterCard and Visa were accepted at almost exactly the same locations in the United States. Before the advertisements, when consumers were asked which card brand was the best overall card, 40 percent said Visa and 35 percent said MasterCard. Seven years after the advertisements started airing, 59 percent of consumers said Visa and only 22 percent said MasterCard.

Whether Visa's advertising increased its share and the extent to which it did so at the expense of MasterCard rather than American Express is hard to know. It is difficult to separate the effects of the advertising from the effects of many other dimensions of competition between the two systems as well as competition from other systems. In particular, a major market event took place in the payment card world contemporaneous with Visa's advertising campaign: the entry of Discover in 1985. Discover grew to capture about 5 percent of all payment card volume by 1991. Over the same period, Visa's share increased by 1 percentage point, while MasterCard's declined by 2 percentage points, about a fifteenth of its 28 percent share in 1985. If consumers had viewed Visa and MasterCard comparably, there would have been no reason to expect that Discover would have been more successful in taking share away from MasterCard than from Visa. Visa's advertising campaign thus likely played a significant role in Visa's ability to maintain its share in the face of Discover's entry.

Visa's advertising strategy left MasterCard little room to respond. "MasterCard Is Everywhere, Too" would not have helped, and MasterCard offered no real advantages over Visa that it could use to sway consumers. MasterCard relied on celebrities to tout its product in its

"Master the Possibilities" campaign that began running shortly after Visa's "It's Everywhere You Want to Be" campaign started. When Visa began positioning itself as a player in the travel and entertainment market, MasterCard decided to focus on traditional markets such as department stores.

The most intriguing aspect of Visa's strategy is that it was used at all. Because of membership duality, the same banks that owned Visa also owned MasterCard. In 1986, for instance, MasterCard accounted for 25 percent of the transaction volume of the ten-largest Visa issuers. To the extent that Visa's costly advertising campaign—which members were paying for through association fees—only took a share from Master-Card, it would only move business from banks' MasterCard columns to their Visa columns.

It is understandable that the Visa management would want to make its brand more successful. But why would the banks on the Visa board have approved this subtle attack on MasterCard? First, the advertising campaign did not just take a share away from MasterCard. This was not a zero-sum game. The ads also took a share away from American Express, as we saw above. In addition, it helped make Visa a premium brand. Even though the campaign hurt MasterCard, having two differentiated brands was likely better for banks than having two that were indistinguishable in consumers' minds.

Although overlapping membership has affected competition between the co-opetitives, MasterCard and Visa have nonetheless waged war against each other, as this advertising strike indicates. One of the first battles was over duality itself. MasterCard was larger than Visa in the early 1970s, and it was happy to grow further by allowing Visa members to join. Visa opposed duality, and in 1971 it passed a bylaw prohibiting dual membership. Under government pressure (as we discuss in chapter 11), however, Visa began to unwind dual membership restrictions in 1975 and eliminated all of them in 1976. Ironically, Visa turned out to be the main beneficiary from this leveling of the playing field between the two co-opetitives. Visa's share of card volume increased from 32 percent in 1975 (as compared to 40 percent for MasterCard) to 43 percent by the launch of the "Everywhere You Want To Be" campaign ten years later.

By 1990, when its share of card volume had fallen to 26 percent, MasterCard needed to take serious action. It considered some advertising strategies that involved direct attacks on Visa, but its board rejected these. The record is mixed on whether the MasterCard board rejected them because of concern over their effectiveness or because its members also had stakes in Visa.

Opportunity knocked for MasterCard in 1990. AT&T decided that it wanted to issue a credit card and, through a bank with which it had signed a contract, started issuing its AT&T Universal Card in 1990. Most of these were Visa cards. Yet Visa was not sure that it wanted issuers that were not banks and established a moratorium on nonbank issuers after AT&T's entry. MasterCard saw an opening, and it courted AT&T as well as other nonbanks such as General Motors and General Electric, which offered their own cards in 1992. Although Visa rescinded its moratorium by early 1992, the nonbanks came to issue mainly MasterCard cards. By 1994, these firms were large MasterCard issuers, accounting for about 25 percent of all MasterCard dollar volume, and AT&T had become the largest MasterCard issuer.

Nonbank issuers provided only temporary relief for MasterCard, however. There were no big new entrants after the initial wave, the nonbank issuers haven't grown as fast as others in recent years, and some—notably AT&T—have exited. (One can still get an AT&T Universal Card that functions as a calling card, but it is basically an affinity card issued by Citigroup.)

Another long-standing form of competition between the co-opetitives may tilt the playing field back toward MasterCard. Since the advent of duality, MasterCard and Visa have competed with each other by trying to persuade members to issue more of their system's cards and fewer of the other system's. Part of this competition involves advertising and other marketing actions intended to make each system's cards more attractive to customers. Some issuers give cardholders a choice of brand, and these strategies naturally lead customers to take the brand they see as superior. Other issuers promote a single card brand, and they are likely to promote the one they believe potential customers will find more attractive. Another part of this competition for issuers involves selling them directly on the benefits of one system over the other. The MasterCard and Visa cooperatives both have "account representatives" who, in effect, sell the brand to members.

In addition to advertising and brand marketing, the co-opetitives' managements develop new products and services that members can use to get more cardholders or to persuade cardholders to use their cards more. For example, both MasterCard and Visa now have a prepaid payroll card that members can offer to companies and their employees. Both also offer smart card platforms for their members to use.

On the cost side, the system managers seek ways to make card processing cheaper and more reliable. In 1992, for instance, Visa introduced PaymentService 2000 (PS 2000). PS 2000 provides for more information to be passed through on authorization messages, including the full detail from the magnetic stripe on the back of the card, which allows the issuer to check the card's validity and reduce fraud losses. In addition, PS 2000 lowers the frequency of transactions that are "charged back" (that is, a refund is requested from the merchant), which are costly for all parties.

Since the mid-1990s, however, competition between MasterCard and Visa for credit card volume has become increasingly for the long-term "dedication" of members—their agreement to concentrate on one brand of credit card instead of the other—rather than the kinds of incremental gains, such as bidding for a major issuer's next round of solicitations, each focused on in the 1980s. Part of the motivation for this shift may be the general rise in issuer concentration in the industry during the 1990s, which we discussed in chapter 7. Issuer concentration also increased in each association. The ten largest Visa issuers accounted for 42 percent of Visa cards issued in 1990, and the ten largest MasterCard issuers accounted for the same percentage of MasterCards issued. By 1998, the shares of the ten largest issuers had risen to 71 percent and 67 percent, respectively. Another factor may be the rise of debit; debit cards have been nondual since 1990, and the two associations began to pursue different debit strategies shortly thereafter.

In an important sense, the emergence of widespread dedication represents a turning away from duality. Ironically, just as the emergence of duality favored the weaker system, then Visa, the recent turning away from duality seems also to have favored the weaker system, now MasterCard.

The systems have used three techniques in competing for members' dedication. First, Visa and MasterCard have reduced system fees to members who agree to dedicate themselves to the system. Since 1999, Visa has had in place its Partnership Program to encourage dedication. Participants typically must agree to generate 90 percent of their total credit card volume through Visa and 100 percent of their signature debit volume on Visa cards. In return, they receive substantial discounts on their membership fees. MasterCard has offered similar incentives to its members in return for commitments to issue predominantly on Master-Card. About two-thirds of all bankcard volume comes from issuers dedicated to one brand or the other. (Unless reversed by the Supreme Court, a recent antitrust decision, which is stayed during an appeal as this is written, may alter this situation. As discussed in chapter 11, the decision requires MasterCard and Visa to allow their members to sign contracts to issue American Express cards and, if they do so, to renegotiate their dedication agreements. This decision will also establish duality indebit cards.)

Second, the systems have competed to offer higher interchange fees to their members. Since interchange fees amount to about twenty-five times the membership and processing fees paid by issuers, this can be a critical factor in choosing a system. From 1995 to 2002, average interchange fees for MasterCard and Visa have increased from 1.3 percent of the purchase amount to 1.7 percent.

Third, MasterCard and Visa have offered special deals for the largest issuers. For example, MasterCard made a big effort in 1999 to sign up Citigroup, which had long issued mainly Visa cards. MasterCard not only offered discounted dues to Citigroup but also agreed to allow Citigroup to move the MasterCard logo to the back of the card, leaving the entire front for use by Citigroup. After Visa was unwilling to accede to Citigroup's desire to move the Visa logo to the back, Citigroup announced its switch to MasterCard in February 1999. In general, MasterCard appears to have been more willing than Visa to allow dedicated banks to promote their own brands relative to the system brand.

MasterCard and Visa have also continued to compete with advertising. After struggling to find a response to Visa's ongoing success with its "Everywhere You Want to Be" advertisements, MasterCard finally had a hit with its award-winning and often-parodied "Priceless" campaign, launched in late 1997. The two co-opetitives have continued to engage in system competition through innovation as well. And both systems have continued to improve the efficiency of their respective processing systems. Visa has also developed systems to help members with fraud detection and prevention, through services such as the Cardholder Risk Identification Service, which attempts to identify fraudulent activity by comparing card usage to known patterns of fraudulent behavior. MasterCard introduced a system called Riskfinder that is intended to provide similar functionality to its members.

Of the top ten bankcard issuers in 2002, five were dedicated to Visa, three to MasterCard, and two had not aligned firmly with either system. MasterCard's relative success in this competition for loyalty, as well as along other dimensions, has led to its resurgence in the credit card business. In 1998, before dedication agreements, MasterCard accounted for 42 percent of bank credit cards, 35 percent of purchase volume, and 41 percent of outstanding balances. By 2002, these figures had risen to 51 percent, 42 percent, and 51 percent, respectively. These numbers imply that the average outstandings per card in each system were essentially equal in both years, while the average purchase volume per MasterCard credit card was 76 percent of the Visa average in 1998 and declined slightly to 71 percent of the Visa average by 2002.

The Card That Is Just Like a Check

During the 1990s, debit emerged as an important theater of the system wars. The two credit card systems struggled to both promote their brands to consumers and persuade banks to issue their debit cards. (Since 1990, banks have been prohibited from issuing both MasterCard and Visa debit cards as a result of an antitrust settlement the co-opetitives reached with fourteen states. Thus, MasterCard and Visa have competed for debit card issuers since then, just as they have been competing for credit card issuers in recent years.) During this decade, a new set of system warriors appeared to challenge MasterCard and Visa: the EFT systems. The struggle among these systems resulted in explosive growth in debit volume: from less than 3 percent of payment card transactions in 1990 to 29 percent in 2002. In absolute terms, the volume of debit transactions per household rose by 5,000 percent over this period.

The struggle for debit card volume also provides an interesting illustration of competition in two-sided markets. The EFT networks had developed substantial bases of cardholders who used their cards to withdraw cash or obtain other services at ATMs, thus reducing banks' need for tellers. Of course, the same cards could be used to pay for transactions at retailers, but that required merchants to install PIN pads so that cardholders could enter PINs, as they did at ATMs.

Please Sign

By the mid-1990s, Visa (and subsequently MasterCard) was poised to make a splash in the debit card arena. Much as the strength of the EFT networks came from the existing ATM cardholder bases, the strength of Visa lay in its existing merchant base. As we described in chapter 5, by the mid-1990s Visa had substantially increased its penetration in several key retail segments, including supermarkets, a particularly important segment for debit card use. Visa's strength also came from its signature-based technology—merchants could take credit and debit cards over the same system—and from having upgraded its processing capabilities in the early 1990s. Yet Visa still had its mark on only 11 percent of ATM cards in 1994.

Banks had to be convinced to issue debit cards with Visa debit capability (or to add Visa debit capability to existing ATM cards). Around 1993, Visa undertook a major campaign to convince the top fifty banks to issue its debit cards. It developed financial analyses that showed banks the benefits from higher interchange fees and transaction volume on signature debit versus PIN debit transactions. Visa's interchange fee on debit was much higher than the EFT networks' interchange fees—about 37¢ versus 8¢ on a typical $30 transaction. Visa argued that with such fees, debit cards could be issued profitably. (This interchange fee differential, and the honor-all-cards rule that combined credit and signature debit under one platform, were the central issues in the recent *Wal-Mart* case, discussed in chapter 11.)

Visa also invested in a processing facility in Denver that made it easier for issuers to operate their debit card programs by providing a single unified platform for processing both signature and PIN transactions. And Visa worked to help issuers encourage cardholders to activate and use their Visa debit cards.

As an important part of the sales pitch, Visa pointed to the massive advertising and marketing campaign it was going to undertake. Most consumers were unfamiliar with using debit cards to make retail purchases. Visa's solution on heride was to invest heavily in marketing and to eliminate the use of the term "debit," which consumers often associated with debt. To increase consumer awareness of its debit products, Visa launched a campaign in 1993 for "The New Shape of Checking," and developed brochures and held forums to let consumers know how to use the expanded capabilities of Visa's debit cards.

As part of this campaign, Visa came up with a new name for its debit card: Visa Check. Its advertising campaign told consumers that they could use Visa Check cards anywhere Visa cards were accepted and in the same way as any other Visa card. In addition, the choice of Visa Check as the name, along with the advertising campaign ("The Card That Works Like a Check"), told consumers that the value of transactions would be deducted from their checking accounts, much as with the use of paper checks. But unlike paper checks, as the advertising campaign emphasized, consumers did not need identification. The campaign made this point using well-known, albeit diverse, personalities including former senator and presidential candidate Bob Dole, Oscar-winner and sometimes new age mystic Shirley MacLaine, premier NFL cornerback and part-time outfielder Deion Sanders, and the lovable but temperamental Daffy Duck. The advertisements were all set in stores where each personality was recognized and acclaimed, but where their personal checks were not accepted without proof of identification.

All told, Visa had invested more than $268 million by late 1998 in advertising, marketing, and processing facilities in support of Visa Check. Between 1990 and 2002, the number of Visa Check cards in circulation increased from 8 million to 128 million. The purchase volume for Visa Check cards grew at an even faster rate, from 87 million purchases and $6.3 billion in 1990 to 6.5 billion purchases and $248.1 billion in 2002, with almost all of the growth after 1995.

MasterCard initially focused its debit efforts on PIN debit with its Maestro brand. Seeing Visa's success, however, it started to focus more on its signature debit card, MasterMoney, in the late 1990s. By that time, many issuers had already signed up with Visa, and as noted above, banks could only issue debit cards on one of the co-opetitive systems. While MasterCard lags noticeably behind Visa in debit, it has still achieved substantial growth. In 1990, fewer than 1.5 million MasterMoney cards had been issued, and they generated $840 million of volume on 14.5 million purchases that year. By 2002, more than 47 million MasterMoney cards had been issued, and they generated $70 billion in volume on 1.7 billion purchases.

Figure 8.2 shows the growth of signature debit (total Visa Check and MasterMoney) cards and purchase transactions from 1990 to 2002.

Please Enter Your PIN
By the mid-1990s, the EFT networks, which had introduced PIN debit in the 1980s, were on the verge of both rapid growth in PIN debit trans-

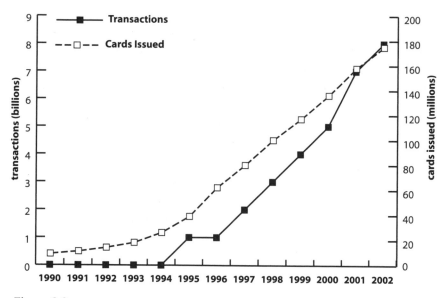

Figure 8.2
Bank signature debit cards and purchase transactions, 1990–2002
Source: The Nilson Report, (various 1991–2003 issues).

action volume as well as substantial restructuring of networks and ownership. As of 1995, the top ten systems were Interlink, STAR (then known as Explore), MAC, Most, Honor, NYCE, Pulse, Accel, X-Press 24, and Magic Line. All of these were owned and controlled, either directly or indirectly, by their respective member financial institutions or a subset of those institutions. Interlink was and is owned by Visa, which is in turn owned by its member institutions. (MasterCard's PIN debit system, Maestro, was not in the top ten.) Most of these networks were regional in scope. The largest, Interlink, was national, but STAR, the second largest, was only in twelve West Coast and Rocky Mountain states. Smaller networks, such as Magic Line and Cash Station, operated in only a handful of states.

In 1995, even though there were 190 million PIN debit cards in the hands of U.S. consumers, they were scarcely used other than as ATM cards. PIN debit purchase volume per card was only $99 that year. And PIN debit accounted for only 2.7 percent of all payment card purchase volume that year, though this was quite respectable growth from just 1.2 percent at the start of the decade.

One key to PIN debit growth has been the expansion in merchant acceptance. Much as signature debit needed more cardholders to go with MasterCard and Visa merchants, PIN debit systems needed merchants to go with their ATM-focused cardholders. The problem was that merchants couldn't rely on their existing equipment; they had to install PIN pads so that cardholders could enter PINs to authorize transactions. A strong incentive for merchants to install PIN pads was the flip side of the incentive for banks to issue signature debit: the interchange fee. Since the interchange fee on PIN debit was much lower than on signature debit, merchant discounts for PIN debit were also much lower. Every $30 transaction a merchant could switch from signature to PIN debit meant about a 30¢ savings. Just one such switch a day would pay for the $100 cost of a PIN pad in less than a year. The fact that PIN pads were becoming cheaper also helped make the case. (These calculations are illustrative, but they oversimplify matters somewhat, as merchants also incur additional costs to install PIN pads and train their employees. Most merchants still haven't chosen to accept PIN debit, suggesting their benefits may be particularly low and/or their costs may be particularly high.

Moreover, in many retail environments—such as high-end restaurants—it may be inconvenient to have a PIN pad that is accessible to the consumer.)

In addition to creating a stronger incentive to install PIN pads, Visa's signature debit efforts also increased PIN debit usage in other ways. Consider a consumer who has seen a Visa Check advertisement and, as a result, decides to use her Visa Check card instead of a check. Of course, her Visa Check card is also her PIN debit card on STAR or some other network. If she goes to a PIN pad merchant, she often will be asked to press either "Credit" or "Debit." If she (understandably) chooses "Debit," she will be asked for her PIN, thus authorizing a STAR transaction, even if she thinks she is using her Visa Check card. *Her* cost is usually the same either way, but her choice of "Debit" typically saves the merchant money. PIN debit systems have undertaken some local promotional efforts—such as billboard and radio ads and in-store promotions—to encourage consumer use, but they pale in comparison to Visa and MasterCard's signature debit advertising.

As a result of these factors, the PIN debit systems experienced tremendous growth in the 1990s, especially in the latter part of the decade, and in (at least) the early years of the following decade. The number of PIN pads installed increased from 53,000 in 1990, to 529,000 in 1995, to more than 4 million in 2002. PIN debit volume grew from $3.5 billion in 1990, to $18.7 billion in 1995, to $162.2 billion in 2002, or about 10 percent of total payment card volume.

The EFT systems have also undergone a radical structural transformation. Of the top ten systems we listed in 1995, seven have been absorbed into either STAR or NYCE. STAR is the largest PIN debit system; in 2002, it held a 53 percent share of transaction volume and its logo was on 51 percent of PIN debit cards. NYCE is the third-largest system; in 2002, it accounted for 12 percent of transaction volume and its logo was on 22 percent of PIN debit cards. The Justice Department dropped its objections to the merger between Concord EFS (which owned STAR) and FDC (which was the majority stakeholder in NYCE) after FDC agreed to divest NYCE following the merger.

The STAR and NYCE systems are not only large but also represent an important and relatively new type of card system. Neither STAR nor

NYCE fit neatly in the co-opetitive or go-it-alone categories we described earlier. They are like the go-it-alones in that they are typically for-profit entities in the business of making money for their shareholders (who are regular investors, not banks), yet they do not issue or acquire directly. They are like the co-opetitives in depending on thousands of issuing and acquiring banks, yet they are not controlled by those banks; the banks are generally not shareholders and do not have any voting rights. We saw in the early history of card systems that the Visa co-opetitive system arose in large part because banks did not want to sell someone else's brand. STAR and NYCE face this same problem: do banks want to be part of a system they do not own or control?

Interlink, Pulse, and Accel remain the only PIN debit systems in the top ten in 1995 not since absorbed into STAR and NYCE. (Accel, the sixth-largest system, is a for-profit entity like STAR and NYCE.) Pulse, in particular, has publicly promoted itself to banks as an alternative to nonbank-owned, for-profit systems such as STAR and NYCE. Pulse's slogan is "The Power of Ownership." Pulse started in Texas and is now national. It is the fourth-largest PIN debit system behind STAR, Interlink, and NYCE, with 10 percent of PIN debit volume in 2002. It is, like MasterCard and Visa, a co-opetitive operating on a not-for-profit basis. Pulse points out to banks that in nonbank systems, banks lose control over the systems' fee structure, rules, and strategic direction. Pulse also argues that nonbank systems are more costly for banks in terms of membership and access fees. Whether Pulse or Interlink will be successful in selling members on the benefits of bank-owned systems, or whether STAR will remain the leading PIN debit system, remains to be seen.

The impact of the *Wal-Mart* settlement, discussed further in chapters 11 and 12, also remains to be seen. As part of the settlement, starting in 2004, MasterCard and Visa will allow merchants to take their credit cards without also taking their signature debit cards or vice versa. Given the popularity of signature debit cards with cardholders, however, it is not likely that the co-opetitives will need to lower their debit card interchange fees much to maintain merchant acceptance. But time will tell.

9

Issuer Brawls

And while the law [of competition] may be sometimes hard for the individual, it is best for the race, because it ensures the survival of the fittest.
—Andrew Carnegie, "Wealth" (1889)

Although the advertising jabs among the card networks make for amusing diversions during *The Simpsons*, what ultimately determines who wins is which issuer gets you to carry its card and to use it when you shop. Issuers are more likely to get your attention through your mailbox than your television; Americans received five billion direct mail solicitations in 2001 from issuers hoping to get their cards in consumers' wallets and get balances switched from their competitors. Virtually all of this public competition for consumer spending and borrowing has been among issuers of credit and, to a lesser extent, charge cards. That competition is the focus of this chapter. But there is a quieter competition going on to get you to use the ATM card you already have to pay for things. Many banks give checking account holders ATM cards that can also be used as PIN- and signature-based debit cards. The last part of this chapter looks at how debit cards are shaking up competition among issuers as well as systems.

Who Are the Players?

If you can afford to buy this book, you almost certainly get frequent requests in the mail to apply for new cards, often with the guarantee that your application will be approved. Your magazines and newspapers are studded with advertisements for more new cards with yet more new features, complete with handy application forms for your convenience. And when you stand in line at your bank or many other locations, you are faced with a pile of applications for new cards. Solicitations for credit and charge cards now come from four distinct kinds of card purveyors: go-it-alone issuers, monoline banks (credit card specialists), depository institutions (ordinary banks), and nonfinancial companies. Of the top fifty credit and charge card issuers (based on charge volume) in 2002, there were three go-it-alone issuers, seven monoline banks, thirty-two depository institutions, and eight nonfinancial companies. These fifty issuers accounted for approximately 90 percent of credit and charge card total volume.

Go-It-Alone Issuers

The single-issuer networks accounted for about 26 percent of the dollar value of transactions on the credit and charge cards of the fifty-largest issuers in the United States in 2002. As shown in table 9.1, American Express was the largest issuer of cards in the United States, based

Table 9.1
Top credit and charge card issuers, 2002

Total charge volume (%)		Total outstandings (%)	
1 American Express	16	Citigroup	16
2 Citigroup	14	MBNA America	12
3 Bank One	11	Bank One	11
4 MBNA America	9	American Express	8
5 Discover	7	J. P. Morgan Chase	8
6 J. P. Morgan Chase	6	Discover	7
7 Bank of America	4	Capital One Financial	6
8 Capital One Financial	4	Bank of America	5
9 U.S. Bancorp	3	Providian Financial	3
10 Household Bank	3	Household Bank	3
Top ten	78	*Top ten*	79
Top twenty	87	*Top twenty*	91
Top fifty	90	*Top fifty*	94

Note: Numbers may not add up to totals due to rounding.
Source: The Nilson Report (various 2003 issues).

on dollar volume. (In 2001, one estimate suggested that over 40 percent of American Express's volume came from its corporate charge cards.) Discover was the fifth-largest issuer based on credit and charge card volume.

Depository Institutions

Depository institutions—banks or near-banks such as credit unions that offer checking account services to consumers and, generally, a range of related services—account for the largest portion of credit and charge card volume: 50 percent of the charge volume of the top fifty issuers in 2002. (We have excluded from the calculations in this paragraph banks that principally provide credit cards and offer limited depository services; they are covered by the discussion of monoline banks below.) Of the top ten issuers in 2002, five were depository institutions. One of them was Citigroup, the second-largest issuer and the largest co-opetitive card issuer, whether measured by dollars outstanding, number of cards issued, or dollars charged. (The landscape will be somewhat shaken up assuming the merger between S. P. Morgan Chase and Bank One is consummated, with the merged firm becoming the largest issuer in the industry.) Although most MasterCard and Visa credit cards are issued by banks that offer checking accounts and other consumer banking services, most of these cards are issued to consumers who do not purchase those services from the issuing bank. In fact, in 2001, only 17 percent of all MasterCard and Visa credit cards were issued to cardholders who had at least one other banking relationship with the issuing bank.

Monoline Banks

The term "monoline" refers to an issuer that engages wholly or primarily in issuing credit cards. Although some monoline issuers are chartered as credit card banks (some with charters that do not allow them to accept consumer deposits), others are chartered as standard depository institutions. MBNA, for example, is a nationally chartered bank just like Citigroup. Yet MBNA is often referred to as a monoline because credit cards are its primary business. Monoline banks accounted for approximately 17 percent of the charge volume of the fifty largest issuers in 2002. MBNA had the largest program of the monolines, and was the fourth-largest issuer and the third largest co-opetitive card issuer, based on charge volume. The other leading monolines in 2002 were Capital One and Providian.

Nonbanks

In 2002, one of the ten largest issuers was a nondepository institution affiliated with a giant nonfinancial corporation. Household Bank, the issuer of the General Motors card, was in tenth place. (Household could also be classified as a monoline bank, but we have categorized it with nonbanks because the General Motors card portfolio has been a substantial portion of its business. The General Motors card could also be characterized as a cobranded card—the line between a cobranded program versus one operated by a nonbank is not always precise.) Sears's MasterCard program (separate from its store card program), the next-largest nondepository credit and charge card issuer, was in fourteenth place. Together, nonbank issuers accounted for about 7 percent of the charge volume of the top fifty issuers in 2002. Just a few years ago, these institutions were much more important. They accounted for about 11 percent of the total industry charge volume in 1997. That changed dramatically when AT&T decided to sell its card program to Citigroup in 1998. It will change further when the sale of Sears's MasterCard portfolio to Citigroup (as well as its store card portfolio), agreed on in mid-2003, is completed.

Product Variety and Market Segmentation

Competition among payment card issuers takes place along two dimensions. Each issuer tries to get consumers to carry its card, either in addition to or in place of cards from other issuers. Each issuer then tries to get consumers who carry its card to charge more purchases on it and, for credit cards, to carry greater balances. Issuers are, of course, also trying to get consumers to switch their payments from cash, checks, and other media, such as store cards.

Several factors on the demand side and the supply side of the payment card industry drive competition within these dimensions. On the demand side, the diversity of consumer tastes for making payments in various ways, and for obtaining financing for those payments with unsecured loans, shapes payment card products. On the supply side, competition is driven by differences in expected profits from providing services to consumers whose various usage patterns and levels of credit risk are uncertain prior to issuing them a card and may change during their card ownership. These factors affect the revenues received and the costs incurred over the course of the relationship between the issuer and the cardholder.

Product Differentiation

Competition among card issuers is shaped by a fundamental fact: consumers are different from one another—they have varying preferences for buying and borrowing, and varying sensitivities to card fees, finance charges, and noncash perks like airline miles. Card issuers compete with each other—and identify profit opportunities—by tailoring their cards to meet the preferences and demands of different groups of consumers.

The result is that payment cards are "differentiated" products, like restaurants, rather than "homogeneous" or "commodity" products like red #2 winter wheat. You probably cannot name even two restaurants that are exactly alike, particularly when you take into account differences in location. Nobody thinks automobiles are homogeneous products either. In markets like these, prices of competing products can differ somewhat because buyers have different preferences, and advertising, location, product design, and research are often important dimensions of competition.

At first blush, credit cards and charge cards might seem like a commodity product: they all allow you to buy and borrow. A closer look reveals much heterogeneity among consumers and, as a result, considerable product differentiation among cards. As we saw in chapter 4, for instance, some consumers use their payment cards mainly as a convenient substitute for cash and checks; they write one check at the end of each month instead of many during the month and always pay their card bills in full. These "transactors" prefer low annual fees while "revolvers," who regularly maintain outstanding balances on their credit cards, prefer low interest rates. (Transactors comprise about 46 percent of households with cards, but account for about 68 percent of charge volume.)

Consumers differ along other dimensions as well. Some consumers are willing to pay an annual fee for a card that permits them to earn frequent-flier miles, for example, whereas others particularly enjoy using cards with the logo of their favorite college or pro sports team. Some regularly use their cards to obtain cash advances; others never do so. Similar differences exist with respect to all the many features that payment cards provide (or elect not to) and the many sorts of fees that they impose (or elect not to).

On the other side of the market, some banks issue cards primarily as a service to their depositors, while others market aggressively on a national basis and try to segment the markets by offering a range of products, each tailored to a different set of interests. Table 9.2 shows the differences among a sample of "typical" programs for top issuers as of May 2003. Many of these specific cards may no longer exist by the time you read this, but there will likely be other, similarly diverse offerings available. Cardholders are sometimes offered different fee rates based on their creditworthiness, payment histories, and profitability potential.

Now let's look at a few of the other dimensions along which payment cards differ: card fees, the interest rates, the amount of credit provided, the service fees, and special card features.

Card Fees   In a recent consumer survey, "no annual fee" was the prime credit card selection criterion for one-third of all respondents. And credit card issuers have tended to eliminate annual fees on credit cards in recent years. The cards that still charge these fees are usually rewards cards, as table 9.2 suggests. For example, Bank of America issued a Visa card that offered mileage rewards on America West and carried a $75 annual fee. Rewards cards without annual fees are also available.

Finance Charges   More than 30 percent of respondents in the consumer survey mentioned above said that a low interest rate on purchases was their prime card selection criterion. Eleven percent of respondents claimed that their main criterion was a low interest rate on balance transfers. Table 9.2 reveals that interest rates charged can vary substantially, from 7.99 percent to over 23 percent for different cards, likely depending in part on differences in creditworthiness standards.

The Amount of the Credit Line All credit cards come with a limit on the amount that the cardholder can charge. All other things being equal, cards with larger credit lines are more valuable to consumers but riskier for issuers. An issuer may attempt to differentiate its card offers by extending higher lines of credit than other issuers to similarly credit-worthy applicants. The development of "platinum" bankcards in the mid-1990s resulted in offers of relatively high credit lines, sometimes with promises of $100,000 credit limits. By the end of the first quarter of 2002, 32 percent of households held platinum credit cards. In 2001, mail offers of platinum cards accounted for more than 70 percent of all card offers. The "preapproved" offers for $100,000 credit lines rarely translated into actual extensions of such limits, however, and the average credit limit on platinum cards was only $9,728.

Service Fees Card issuers commonly charge service fees, including late fees, overlimit fees, and cash advance fees. In late 1983, service fees on Visa and MasterCard cards averaged about $3 annually, and annual fees averaged about $18 (as always, in 2002 dollars). In late 1989, before the entry of AT&T and other large nonbanks, service fees per account had risen to about $11 annually, but annual fees per account had fallen to about $17. Average service fees per account exceeded annual fees in late 1993 ($11 versus $10). By late 1996, average service fees had grown to about $21 per year, whereas annual fees had fallen to about $5. By late 2001, service fees per account had risen to about $38, and annual fees had grown to about $9. Some of the recent annual fee increase could be due to the increased penetration of rewards cards (which often carry annual fees). And recent service fee increases could be partly due to the increased penetration of so-called subprime issuers that target more risky cardholders, who in turn are more likely to make late payments, for instance, and thus get charged service fees more frequently.

As table 9.2 indicates, service fees can vary substantially from issuer to issuer. Service fees are set both to reflect directly related costs (for

Table 9.2
Payment card characteristics across issuers, 2002

Company	Special card name	Interest rate	Grace period (days)	Annual fee	Late fee	Over limit fee	Cash advance fee
Citibank	Platinum Select MasterCard	4.99%	25	none	$15, $25, or $35	$29	3%, $5 min
MBNA	Gold Points Rewards Visa	12.99%	at least 25	none	$15, $25, or $35	$15, $25, or $35	3%, $5 min
First USA/ Bank One	Platinum Visa	9.15%	at least 20	none	$15, $29, or $35	$29	3%, $10 min
Chase Manhattan	Wal-Mart MasterCard	10.99%, 14.99%, or 19.99%	at least 20	none	$15, $29, or $35	$29	3%, $5 min
Capital One Financial	Visa Platinum	8.90%	at least 25	none	$29	$29	3%, $5 min
Bank of America	America West FlightFund Visa	11.24%	at least 20	$75	$15, $29, or $35	$32	4%–5%, $5–$25 min
Providian Financial	Visa Platinum Premium	9.99%	at least 25	none	$0 or $35	$0 or $35	3%, $10 min
Household Bank	Mastercard	19.24%	at least 20	none	$35	$35	5%, $10 min or $20 min
Fleet	Titanium Visa	10.99% or 11.99%	at least 20	none	$35	$15, $29, or $35	4%, $5 min
Direct Merchants	MasterCard	13.24%, 18.24%, or 23.24%	25	none	$35	$35	$5 if =<$100, $15 or 4% (whichever is higher) if >$100

Issuer	Card						
Wells Fargo	Student Visa	10.24% or 19.8%	20–25	none	$30 or $35	$32	4%, $5 min
U.S. Bancorp	Visa Classic	10.24% to 19.24%	20–25	$0 or $203	$29 or $38	$35	4%, $5 min
FNB Omaha	Gold Visa	13.99%	25	none	$29 or $35	$35	3%, $15 min
Target Financial	Visa	9.9%, 12.9%, 15.9%, or 18.9%	at least 25	none	$29	$29	3%, $5 min
Advanta	Platinum Business MasterCard	7.99%	25	none	$35	$35	3%, $5 min
National City	FirstAir Platinum Visa	13.24%	20–25	$59	$29	$29	3%, $5 min
People's Bank	Platinum Mastercard	9.99%	25	none	$35	$35	3%, $5 min
American Express	Rewards Green	NA	NA	$65	Varies: $0 to the greater of $30 or 2.9%	No limit	3%, $5 min
Discover	Platinum	13.99%	at least 25	none	$15, $25, or $35	$15 or $35	3%, $5 min

Note: Late fees for a given card can vary depending on the balance outstanding or the cardholder's payment history within the last twelve months. Overlimit fees for a given card can vary depending on the amount charged over the limit and other factors. Interest rates for some cards float based on the prime rate.
Source: Company Web pages (May 2003).

instance, the costs of making cash advances or, more subtly, the increased default risk associated with late payments) and to help cover common costs (for example, the costs of maintaining the bank's computer systems).

Card Features   Many issuers offer services besides payment and credit. These services, which can be valuable for some cardholders, became increasingly popular during the early 1990s as competition for cardholders intensified. For example, Discover offers a cash-back bonus based on the volume of purchases. Some issuers offer discounts on products sold by affiliates of the card issuers (say, General Motors). Still other issuers, like Citigroup, offer free features on their cards such as protection against telemarketing calls and promotional mail. Some issuers offer travel insurance; others reward users with frequent-flier miles. Some cards allow the cardholder to skip a payment periodically. Other common enhancements include warranty extensions, purchase protection, price protection, collision damage on rental cars, rental discounts, travel rebates, and credit card registration. Minimum payments, the availability of cash advances, and interest charges on cash advances vary across different card plans.

Cards that provide credits for frequent-flier programs have become quite popular. Citigroup offered the first such card in 1987, giving points in American Airlines' Advantage program. Today, its AAdvantage MasterCard program is the largest cobranded airline program. Most airlines now have one or more broadly similar affinity cards with credit card issuers. The Bank One United Mileage Plus Visa card has the second-largest cobranded airline program, with an estimated 4.1 million cardholders by the end of 2002.

Affinity programs come in all shapes and sizes. There are cards that carry the logos of professional sports teams. There are also charity cards that contribute a small percentage of your purchases to a designated charity. While the sponsoring companies establish consumer loyalty and name recognition, consumers are able to earn rewards for card usage or to carry a card bearing a logo with which they identify.

More generally, issuers and payment card systems compete by developing and offering new features and novel packages of existing features, coupled with carefully designed pricing systems—and spend a good deal on marketing, notably on advertising, and direct mail solicitations of prospective customers. And because competing products are not perfect substitutes, individual sellers have some pricing discretion, even when there are many competitors. Credit card issuers are more like restaurants than like wheat farmers: if a bank raised its late-payment fee by a few percentage points, for instance, it would likely retain most of its customers. Because their tastes differ, however, consumers would almost certainly be less well served if there were only a single flavor of payment card and all competition focused on price.

Issuers' Revenues and Costs

For co-opetitive issuers, finance charges account for 70 percent of card revenue on average, penalty and cash-advance fees account for 12 percent, annual fees for 3 percent, and other income for 1 percent. In addition, co-opetitive issuers also receive revenue from interchange fees. Interchange fees accounted for 15 percent of revenue for the average issuer in 2001. The structure of these fees is determined by each association's management, in consultation with its board. Individual issuers can increase their interchange revenue by persuading cardholders—through incentives or marketing—to use their cards more.

Because American Express is a go-it-alone, performing both issuing and acquiring functions, and because it issues both charge and credit cards, its revenue sources are not exactly comparable to those of the bankcard issuers. Merchant discount fees account for 56 percent of American Express card revenues, and card fees and finance charges together account for the rest. (When finance charge revenue is excluded, merchant discount fees account for 82 percent of American Express's revenue.)

Pricing credit and charge cards is an intricate and risky process, as is forecasting revenue. New cardholders may be anywhere on the spectrum between pure transactors and pure revolvers, and their behavior may change over time. Eliminating the annual fee, for example, might attract more cardholders, and finance charges earned from revolvers might offset the corresponding loss in fee revenue. But no-fee cards appeal disproportionately to transactors, for whom the annual fee is the only regular card cost, so incremental finance charge revenue is likely to be low.

Let us turn now to the cost side of issuing. Although issuers incur some fixed costs, most of their cost varies with the number of cards they issue and how these cards are used. For the co-opetitive credit card issuers, the cost of funds for financing revolving debt has historically comprised the largest fraction of cost, though as figure 9.1 shows, in the recession year of 2001, charge-offs accounted for 37 percent of total cost, while the cost of funds accounted for only 30 percent. Charge-off costs vary over the business cycle and with the past aggressiveness of issuers in advancing credit: they have varied from a low of 8 percent of total costs in 1983 to a high of 37 percent in 2001.

The difficulty of predicting charge-offs has been the downfall of many issuers. Credit card lending is especially risky because the loans are usually not secured by any assets and do not have a fixed duration. When cardholders default, payment card issuers undertake collection procedures. These procedures are expensive relative to the size of most loans.

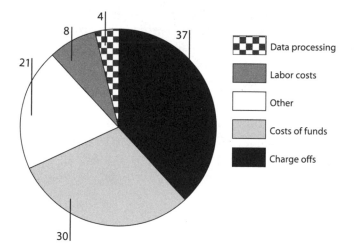

Figure 9.1
Components of issuers' costs, 2001 (%)
Note: This figure includes only the issuing side of the business. Shares are percentages of total issuer costs.
Source: Visa U.S.A.

They are often futile when the cardholder has gone bankrupt. Charge-offs resulting from bankruptcy have increased from 10 percent of all charge-offs in 1982 to 50 percent in 2002.

Although the use of computerized credit scoring, discussed in chapter 4, has increased the ability of issuers to weed out potential deadbeats, it remains hard to predict which consumers will default. In 2001, for instance, the delinquency rate on credit card loans was 4.33 percent. This is substantially above the delinquency rates on other types of loans, such as real estate (2.1 percent), commercial (3.06 percent), or personal (3.27 percent). Credit rationing at the individual level seeks to mitigate these risks. It is thus an important dimension of card program management—and a difficult one.

Competitive Strategies

Successful card issuers are good at "prospecting" for cardholders who will generate long-run profits for the issuer. For finance-oriented cards, that means finding consumers who will carry balances but have little likelihood of defaulting. For transaction-oriented cards, that means finding consumers who will charge a lot yet pay their charges off in full and on time.

The economics of prospecting for profitable new cardholders is simple. There is an initial investment in contacting prospective cardholders either directly through targeted mailings or indirectly through advertisements. That initial investment results in some fraction of prospective cardholders applying for the card. In 2000, new account marketing, on average, cost credit card issuers $25 for every application they processed. Once the application is processed, a decision on whether to accept the applicant is made and, in the case of approval, a card is issued. The cost to complete this entire process averaged $72 per approved credit card application in 2000.

The credit quality of a card portfolio created by an issuer's initial investment will improve over time, all else (including the unemployment rate) remaining constant, because cardholders found not to be good credit risks are dropped over time. Moreover, the issuer will learn about each cardholder's charge and credit habits, and from this information, her profit potential. The most successful issuers obtain a high yield of profitable cardholders from their initial investment, and acquire information about the spending habits and creditworthiness of each active cardholder that they can use themselves or sell to others.

Card portfolios are valuable assets. In fact, there is an active market for buying and selling them. The buyer obtains a group of cardholders whose spending and payment patterns have been observed for some time without the expense of prospecting for customers. The seller can recover at least part of its investment in the portfolio and perhaps earn a return on that investment. In 2002, there were thirty-seven portfolio ownership changes involving $23.8 billion in credit card receivables, second only to the $34.6 billion that changed hands in 1998. The largest deal in 2002 was the sale of Providian Financial Corporation's $8 billion portfolio to J.P. Morgan Chase.

In searching for new customers, credit card issuers often try to persuade people to switch their balances to the new card from one or more of their existing cards. About 60 percent of new solicitations come with an offer to switch balances by doing nothing more than providing information on existing cards. Issuers also try to get their existing customers to transfer balances from other cards. An estimated $96.4 billion of balances were transferred in 2002, about 17.2 percent of the total balances outstanding at the end of that year. Between 1992 and 2002, balance transfers grew at an average annual rate of 38.9 percent. Issuers typically offer a low introductory interest rate—often lasting at least six months and 5 to 10 percentage points below the prevailing rates—to give people an incentive to switch.

Balance transfer offers became popular after Capital One introduced the strategy in 1991 and thereby, according to *Credit Card Management*, "changed card marketing." This tactic has become slightly less popular in recent years (76 percent of solicitations came with this offer in 2001, down from 82 percent in 1998) as issuers have found that some consumers switch again before the low introductory interest rate expires.

Recent efforts by issuers to persuade individuals to carry new cards and to use them illustrate the use of these strategies in practice. Blue from American Express stands out as an interesting recent success story. American Express launched its Blue smart card in September 1999. Even before any applications were developed for its chip, Blue gained relatively wide acceptance among consumers. By mid-2000, about two million Blue Cards were in circulation, many of which had replaced Visa and MasterCard cards. And it was estimated that by early 2003, there were about six million American Express Blue cardholders in the United States.

As mentioned earlier, the main difference at first between Blue and the more traditional payment cards was that Blue came with a card reader that once plugged in to the cardholder's personal computer, offered an extra layer of security for online shopping. While few Blue cardholders even as of late 2002 used this feature, it helped establish a high-tech image. In addition, Blue was the lowest-priced American Express card when it was introduced.

In order to promote its Blue Card, American Express relied on a range of marketing techniques. It hired pop singer Sheryl Crow to attend a press conference and hype the consumer version of the card. It also hired Magic Johnson, the former star guard for the Los Angeles Lakers, to promote the small-business version of Blue. But American Express also used some more innovative approaches. For example, the first one hundred start-up Internet businesses that signed up for Blue received free services from IBM and SmartAge.com. And American Express set up a contest among those one hundred small businesses, with the promise that the winner would receive $100,000 to help finance the business.

To stimulate applications for its chip and thus enhance its value, American Express held a contest that awarded prizes to the people or companies that developed the best Java-based applications for Blue. By early 2003, it had started promoting ID Keeper, a Blue Card application that can store a cardholder's favorite Web site addresses and the user ID/password combinations for accessing those sites.

The Starbucks prepaid card is another success story. Since late 2001, Starbucks has been selling a prepaid card that customers can use to pay at its stores. The card was originally conceived of as a way to save customers time at the counter, but it has also become a device through which Starbucks can get to know their customers better. In the first month of the program, the coffee chain's customers purchased 2.3 million cards worth $32 million, and since then they have acquired an additional 11.3 million cards. The prepaid card already accounts for one out of ten purchases at Starbucks stores, and about one-third of all cardholders are regularly reloading them for further use.

Starbucks employees have been the main channel for the marketing and distribution of the prepaid card. Since late 2002, customers have been able to go online to replace lost cards, reload the ones they currently have, and check their transaction histories. Furthermore, in fall 2003 Starbucks partnered with Visa U.S.A. and Bank One to launch the first dual-purpose credit card for a retailer—it works as a prepaid card at Starbucks stores and as a regular credit card anywhere else. The card's reward system will allow users to accrue coffee credits at the Starbucks chain.

NextCard, on the other hand, was part of the dot.com bubble. Launched in 1996, by the third quarter of 2001 it had built a portfolio of about $2 billion in receivables and 1.2 million accounts. It was considered one of the most successful Internet-based credit card issuers. NextCard's unique feature was that it granted instant credit online to applicants, even before a card had been sent through the mail. Unfortunately, it faced an adverse selection problem that its credit-screening methods did not solve. According to some analysts, NextCard customers were primarily individuals who had been turned down for credit elsewhere. Fraud and charge-offs escalated. NextCard went bankrupt in 2002.

Market Structure

Economists often look at an industry's structure to predict the nature and intensity of competition within it. An extreme market structure is described by the textbook case of perfect competition in which

• a large number of competing firms vie for the consumer's dollar;

• these sellers produce identical products;

• no seller is large enough to affect the market price significantly by itself;

• firms can enter and exit the industry easily without substantial unrecoverable (that is, sunk) costs;

• consumers have good information about the choices available to them; and

• consumers can switch vendors when better offers are available to them.

Payment card vendors do not offer identical products, as we discussed above. Otherwise, however, this description matches the industry well.

A Large Number of Competing Firms

A January 2003 Federal Reserve System survey of 127 of the largest credit card issuers in the United States found that 54 issuers distribute their cards nationally. The same survey reported that 28 additional issuers distribute cards regionally in areas encompassing more than one state, but do not issue them nationally. Moreover, the Federal Reserve System survey excluded many smaller, local banks that also issue credit cards, generally making them available at least to their good depository customers.

No Single Issuer Is Large Relative to the Industry

If a single issuer dominated the industry, it could perhaps act like a monopolist, raising fees above competitive levels, reducing output, and harming consumers. In fact, none of the numerous credit and charge card issuers dominates the industry (see table 9.1 above). Economists are also concerned that if a few leading firms together dominate an industry, they won't compete as aggressively. If a small number of firms account for most of an industry's sales, the industry is said to be "concentrated."

A common measure of industry concentration is the total share of sales accounted for by the four largest firms. (There is no magic in the number four, but it has become a convention.) The four largest credit and charge card issuers have a combined share of between 38 and 51 percent, depending on the measure used. (As we discuss below, debit card issuance is less concentrated at the national level.) This would be about average for manufacturing: in more than 50 percent of manufacturing industries in 1997, the four largest firms accounted for more than 38 percent of the value of shipments in the industry (in more than 30 percent of manufacturing industries, the four largest firms accounted for more than 51 percent of the value of shipments). Less comprehensive data are available for other industries. The four largest securities brokerage firms have a 38 percent share, for instance, and the four largest title insurance companies have a 56 percent share.

Another common measure of industry concentration is the Herfindahl-Hirschman Index (HHI), which can range from almost 0 for a perfectly competitive industry to 10,000 for a pure monopoly. According to the U.S. Department of Justice and the Federal Trade Commission merger guidelines, industries are considered unconcentrated when the HHI is below 1,000; moderately concentrated when the HHI is between 1,000 and 1,800; and highly concentrated when the HHI is above 1,800. In 2002, the HHI for the credit and charge card portion of the payment card industry was 816. This is well within the competitive range, especially when compared to industries such as breakfast cereals (2,446), automobiles (2,863), and household laundry machines (2,870).

As we saw in chapter 3, there was substantial consolidation among issuers in the late 1990s. From 1995 to 2000, the combined share of the top ten credit and charge card issuers increased from 61 to 78 percent, and has since remained at that level.

Entry and Exit Are Easy

Entering the payment card industry as an issuer is fairly easy. Master-Card and Visa are open to all financial institutions that qualify for FDIC deposit insurance—including financial institutions owned by or affiliated with nonbanks such as retailers, investment firms, insurance companies, and automakers. Membership fees amount to a small fraction of revenues—approximately 2 to 2.5 percent for a medium-size issuer and 1.5 to 2 percent for a large issuer, based on data from Visa.

Visa's and MasterCard's open membership policies and low entry costs, together with the expansion of demand for payment cards, resulted in a great deal of entry after the industry's early difficulties were behind it. Figure 9.2 shows the number of Visa issuers from 1971 to 2002. Between 1981 and 1991, the Visa system had a net increase of about 4,200 issuer members, both small and large. Between 1991 and 2001, there was a net increase of about 2,769 issuers—about 90 percent of which joined for the sole purpose of issuing debit cards.

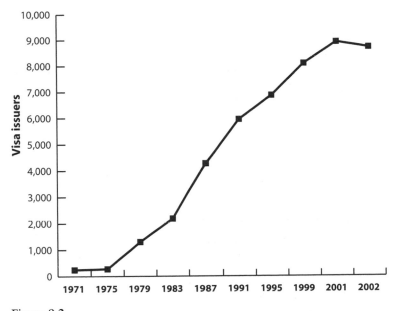

Figure 9.2
Growth of Visa issuers in the United States, 1971–2002
Source: Visa U.S.A.

The development of markets for bankcard portfolios has made exiting less painful—and of course a less painful exit means a less risky entry. Members that wish to exit, for whatever reason, can sell their portfolios to other members. The sale of portfolios helps the owner recoup the cost of acquiring and nurturing cardholders, thereby reducing the amount of sunk and unrecoverable investment costs. In turn, this possibility makes entry into payment cards less risky and, other things being equal, increases the expected profitability of entry.

Information Is Widely Available to Consumers

Consumers have fairly extensive information about payment cards, largely because of issuers' marketing activities. During 2001, issuers sent out about 5 billion direct mail credit card solicitations, an average of approximately 3.9 solicitations per month for each household in the United States (5 solicitations for each household who received offers). With advertising spending by the card systems alone exceeding three-quarters of a billion dollars, consumers are inundated with information. Other sources increase the availability of information to consumers. Newspapers publish lists of low-rate cards, and the Federal Reserve publishes a survey of credit card plans from about 150 issuers. Information is also readily available over the Internet, where one can search for the "best" credit cards available, based on a variety of different criteria.

Consumer Switching Costs

It is easy to switch cards, and people do so all the time. There are two kinds of switching. Among households with cards, about 66 percent have more than one card, and they account for almost 80 percent of credit card transaction volume. These households can switch their transactions easily depending on the relative benefits and costs of using each of their cards. If rewards programs become better, finance charges fall, credit lines expand, or more merchants take a card, millions of cardholders can react by simply pulling one card from their wallet rather than another. The other sort of switching is replacing one card with another, and that is also easy. To add a card often involves just saying yes to an attractive offer that arrives in the mail, though to drop a card with an annual fee it is typically necessary to call or write the issuer. And as we noted above, about 60 percent of solicitations include an offer to switch balances from existing cards.

Market Performance

The payment card industry's performance is consistent with its competitive structure. Consumers have benefited from the rapid expansion of payment card services as well as numerous innovations. As a consequence, the inflation-adjusted price of payment card services has declined.

Output

By any measure, the payment card industry has experienced rapid growth in the last three decades. We focus on credit and charge here, but as we discuss below, the most rapid growth recently has been in debit.

Figure 9.3 shows several key measures of the total output of credit and charge cards between 1971 and 2002. The average annual growth rate of purchase volume (in 2002 dollars, as always) was 13.6 percent in the 1970s, 10.3 percent in the 1980s, and 10.5 percent in the 1990s. The number of cards increased at an average annual rate of 11.7 percent in the 1970s, 7.9 percent in the 1980s, and 6.8 percent in the 1990s. The average growth rate of outstanding balances was 13.9 percent in the 1970s, 15.9 percent in the 1980s, and 10.1 percent in the 1990s.

Figure 9.4 shows that the purchase volume per card and the average outstanding balance per card have risen over time. Between 1971 and 2002, the number of households increased by 69 percent and personal consumption expenditures increased by 187 percent. During the same period, the number of credit and charge cards in circulation increased by 1,021 percent, the purchase volume on credit and charge cards increased by 1,988 percent, outstanding balances increased by 3,146 percent, and total consumer credit outstanding increased by 223 percent,

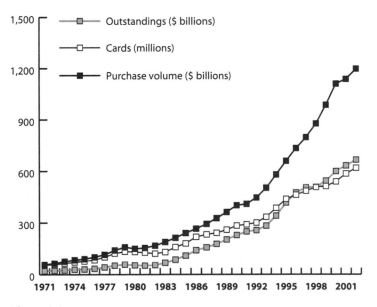

Figure 9.3
Measures of output for credit and charge cards, 1971–2002
Note: Figures are in 2002 dollars.
Sources: *The Nilson Report* (various issues); and Visa U.S.A.

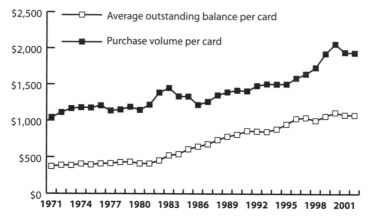

Figure 9.4
Use of credit and charge cards as payment devices and sources of credit, 1971–2002
Note: Figures are in 2002 dollars.
Sources: *The Nilson Report* (various issues); and Visa U.S.A.

as payment cards grew at the expense of other means of payment and sources of credit.

Prices
We estimate that the price received by issuers for credit card services declined by 42 percent between 1984 and 2001. (The choice of period was dictated by data limitations.) The effective price to cardholders declined by only 17 percent over the same time period because the tax deductibility of credit card interest was phased out in the late 1980s. That decline reflects changes in finance charges, annual fees, service charges, the rate of inflation, and other factors. It does not reflect changes in benefits such as frequent-flier mileage or insurance coverage, or other improvements in the quality of cards such as merchant coverage or transaction speed.

Finance charges, annual and other fees, the rate of inflation, the tax deductibility of credit card interest, the nature of the grace period, and the method used for assessing finance charges all affect the true price that consumers pay for payment card services. To see how credit card prices have changed over time, we have constructed a price index that accounts for these and other elements as well as available data permit. (The price index does not factor in card features such as frequent-flier mileage or insurance coverage, or changes in quality over time.)

Both the price that consumers pay for credit cards and the price that issuers receive for them depend on the extent to which consumers actually pay their bills. If a consumer defaults on a credit card loan, the issuer loses not only the consumer's interest payments but the principal as well. The additional cost of these charge-offs decreases the effective price paid by consumers on average for credit. In the most recent recession (2001), the charge-off rate increased from 5.3 to 6.7 percent, leading to a sharp decline in the effective finance rate consumers paid, on average, to issuers.

Consumers pay the after-tax, charge-off-adjusted price on credit card balances, while issuers receive the before-tax, charge-off-adjusted price. These two prices, which are critical for understanding issuer and consumer behavior, are shown in figure 9.5. Given the tremendous

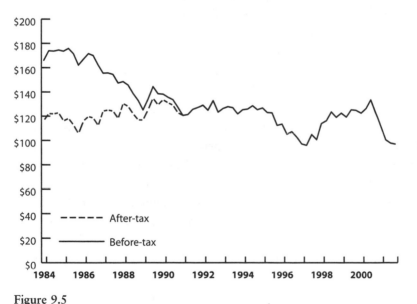

Figure 9.5
Real price index for credit card services, 1984–2001
Note: Figures are in 2002 dollars.
Source: Visa U.S.A.

expansion of the credit card industry during the 1980s and 1990s, it is not surprising that the average price issuers received declined by nearly 42 percent over this period. From 1983 to 2001, the percentage of households carrying at least one bankcard increased from 43 to 73 percent. The increase in credit lines was even more striking. The average credit line in 2002 was over 2.5 times that of 1986 (adjusted for inflation).

Historical Profitability and Market Failure

Economic theory predicts that intense competition will reduce profits on average to the competitive level—the lowest level that will attract the capital the industry needs. The discussion so far of market structure and performance in card issuing suggests intense competition and thus competitive levels of profitability on average. In a provocative article based on evidence from the 1980s, Lawrence Ausubel argued that there was nonetheless a "failure of competition" in the credit card industry that permitted issuers to earn supracompetitive profits.

Unfortunately, measuring profitability accurately in any real industry is notoriously difficult, and the payment card industry has some special problems. Moreover, the only way to see if payment card profitability has been above the competitive level would be to compare it with accurately measured profitability in other industries, adjusting all for the differences in riskiness. Data limitations clearly preclude a definitive treatment of payment card profitability. It does seem clear, however, that Ausubel's claims of a failure of competition leading to persistent supracompetitive profits are not well supported by the available evidence.

Figure 9.6 depicts one measure of the profitability of credit card issuers—the ratio of before-tax profits on credit card operations to outstanding balances for Visa issuers—for the period 1971–2001. This accounting measure is necessarily an imprecise one of real, economic profitability, but it is the best measure available. The difficult years in the early 1970s are plainly visible, as is the dramatic compound impact of rapid inflation, high unemployment, and binding usury laws in the 1979–1981 period. Figure 9.6 shows that credit card profits during the mid-1980s were robust, reflecting a decline in the cost of funds to banks (due to the decline in interest rates) as well as a sharp increase in the

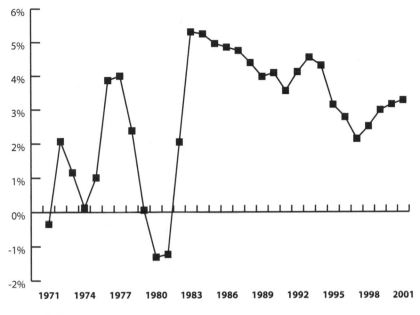

Figure 9.6
Rates of return for credit card lending (before-tax earnings as a percentage of
outstanding balances for Visa issuers), 1971–2001
Source: Visa U.S.A.

demand for payment cards for both payment and finance (due to the
long, robust economic expansion that began in 1982). The Federal
Reserve's *Functional Cost Analysis* similarly reveals that using this
measure of profitability, rates of return on credit card lending exceeded
those in other kinds of bank lending in every year between 1984 and
1988. But as figure 9.6 makes clear, this period was far from typical of
the industry's historical experience.

Table 9.3 illustrates this point using data from the *Functional Cost
Analysis* for 1974–1996—the period for which published data are available. Figures from the *Functional Cost Analysis* need to be viewed with
some caution because the sample is not random and has changed over
time, and the banks in the sample tend to be small and medium size.
(These data are therefore not directly comparable with those reported
above for Visa issuers.) Thus, the largest issuers (and lenders) tend to be
excluded. In addition, of course, the data are for credit cards and do not

Table 9.3
Rates of return for selected types of lending, 1974–1996

Before-tax earnings as a percentage of outstanding balances

Year	Credit card (%)	Installment (%)	Real estate mortgage (%)	Commercial and other (%)
1974	0.77	1.56	2.21	3.49
1975	1.58	2.34	2.74	2.60
1976	2.73	2.45	2.85	1.84
1977	3.09	2.75	3.18	1.86
1978	2.55	2.82	2.70	2.86
1979	1.62	2.32	2.06	4.02
1980	−1.61	1.57	1.65	4.58
1981	1.00	1.69	0.73	5.38
1982	2.32	2.81	0.91	3.26
1983	2.36	3.17	2.16	1.49
1984	3.42	2.81	2.10	1.95
1985	3.97	2.70	2.86	1.40
1986	3.28	2.57	2.37	0.97
1987	3.38	2.31	3.05	1.34
1988	2.53	2.23	2.70	1.96
1989	1.20	2.21	2.67	2.43
1990	1.51	1.92	1.66	0.79
1991	3.12	1.72	2.72	1.12
1992	2.92	2.02	3.16	0.77
1993	4.22	2.14	3.20	1.35
1994	1.44	1.45	3.18	1.90
1995	−2.93	1.01	3.10	2.29
1996	−3.75	0.99	3.06	1.99
Average 1974–1996	*1.77*	*2.15*	*2.48*	*2.25*
Average 1980–1989	*2.19*	*2.41*	*2.12*	*2.48*
Average 1990–1996	*0.93*	*1.61*	*2.87*	*1.46*

Source: Board of Governors of the Federal Reserve System, *The Profitability of Credit Card Operations of Depository Institutions* (August 1997).

include information on charge or debit cards. Finally, it bears repeating that using these accounting rates of return to assess economic profitability is inherently problematic. Nonetheless, we believe these data do provide some indication of the profitability of credit card lending relative to other types of lending. And table 9.3 indicates that even though credit card operations have historically had lower rates of return than other forms of consumer lending on average, the profitability of credit cards has been much more variable than that of other types of consumer lending—in large part because credit card loans are generally not secured.

Let us now consider Ausubel's claims of a failure of competition in more detail. His argument had three main parts. First, he asserted that during the 1980s, interest rates charged by issuers to consumers were sticky—that is, they were relatively unresponsive to changes in banks' cost of funds. Second, he maintained that this stickiness could persist because consumers persistently underestimated the amounts they would borrow on their credit cards and were therefore less sensitive to credit card interest rates than they should rationally have been. Third, he argued that this lack of sensitivity generated consistently supracompetitive profits for issuers even though the credit card industry looked competitive on the surface. In order to measure profitability, Ausubel looked at realized returns on assets (as in figure 9.6) and what he defined as premiums on credit card portfolio sales. Let us examine these in turn.

To begin with Alexander Raskovich and Luke Froeb have shown that rates charged for other bank loans during the 1980s were also relatively insensitive to banks' cost of funds. This is not a surprise since bank lending operations, particularly credit card operations, have other important costs, such as charge-offs, that do not generally vary with the cost of funds. Moreover, credit card interest rates became notably more responsive to the cost of funds in the 1990s. Writing in the *Federal Reserve Bulletin* in 1992, Glenn Canner and Charles Luckett pointed out that credit card interest rates were already becoming more flexible, at least in the sense that considerably lower rates were being offered to certain groups of cardholders. And if we focus on the second half of the 1990s, a regression model like the one Ausubel estimated for 1982–1987 on the basis of Federal Reserve Board rate data shows that credit card interest rates were about ten times more responsive to the cost of fund changes than they were in the period Ausubel covered.

Second, even if Ausubel is right and consumers do systematically underestimate their future borrowing, this is not enough to explain why competition is not in principle sufficient to eliminate excess profits. As we noted above, consumers say that finance charges are important to them, and issuers do compete on the basis of finance charges—just check your mail next week. Even if consumers weren't sensitive to differences in finance charges, competition on annual fees, service charges, rewards programs, and other features would be enough to drive profits to competitive levels on average.

Finally, Ausubel's evidence doesn't show that competition in credit cards isn't in fact sufficient to eliminate excess profits. His measures of profitability are misleading because, as we have indicated above, they cover a period of time (1984–1988) when credit card lending was unusually profitable—both in historical terms and relative to other forms of bank lending. In addition, his discussion of premiums on credit card portfolio sales—which he defines as the amount that the acquirer pays the seller in excess of outstanding balances on the cards involved in the transaction—ignores the basic economics of the business. In order to have built a portfolio of credit card accounts, a seller must have invested in account acquisition and, typically, have lost money on some deadbeats before they could be dropped from the portfolio. Ausubel's premium is basically the seller's return on that investment.

Debit Issuance

Debit cards are issued as part of a total checking account package. Banks don't provide debit cards as a stand-alone product; they offer a bundle that includes checking, teller services, and ATM access in addition to debit cards, and they may also offer other features such as online account access or brokerage services. Banks offer debit cards as one part of the bundle that can be used to both attract and retain customers.

The bundled nature of checking account services complicates pricing. For example, we have all long been familiar with the "free checking" offered by banks. But we also know that the proverbial free lunch does not exist, and if banks don't charge for checks, they must cover their costs in other ways—such as by paying us an interest rate on our deposits that is below the interest they earn on loans. Similarly, "free debit" can be profitable to issuers because of interchange fees. As we've discussed, signature debit has thus far had significantly higher interchange fees than PIN debit. And of course, because of common law precedent, checks have an interchange fee of zero.

Issuer Structure

As we noted earlier in this chapter, credit and charge cards are issued by four types of firms: single-issuer networks, depository institutions, monolines, and nonbanks. Of these, only depository institutions, along with some brokerage firms, currently issue debit cards. These firms are in the business of holding customers' deposits. And since these depository institutions had already issued ATM cards for cash withdrawals, it was natural for them to also allow customers to pay for goods and services using those same cards.

On a national basis, the concentration among debit issuers is much lower than for credit and charge cards. The top ten issuers combined for only 42.8 percent of the signature debit purchase volume and 38.3 percent of the signature debit cards issued. (Data on PIN debit volume at the issuer level are not generally available, but the levels of concentration appear to be lower, probably because some banks may be more selective in issuing signature debit. Every major PIN debit issuer also issues signature debit, and vice versa.) The largest issuer is Bank of America with a 12.4 percent share of the signature debit purchase volume. This is partly a result of its status as the second-largest bank based on deposits, as well as its efforts to issue debit cards and get consumers to use them that we discussed in chapter 1. The rest of the top ten issuers are shown in table 9.4. The only one that is not a traditional depository bank is the number seven issuer, Merrill Lynch, which offers debit cards for its brokerage account customers. Merrill Lynch, like other brokerage firms, issues cards through a relationship with a bank—in this case, Maryland Bank. Debit issuer concentration at the national level is low mainly because national banking concentration is relatively low. The

Table 9.4
Top ten signature debit card issuers, 2002

Purchase volume (%)			Cards (%)	
1	Bank of America	12.41	Bank of America	9.97
2	Wells Fargo	7.36	Wells Fargo	8.00
3	Wachovia	4.47	Washington Mutual	4.58
4	Bank One	3.47	U.S. Bancorp	2.73
5	Washington Mutual	3.44	Wachovia	2.72
6	U.S. Bancorp	3.17	Bank One	2.66
7	Merrill Lynch	2.81	FleetBoston	2.29
8	FleetBoston	2.29	Fifth Third	2.11
9	J.P. Morgan Chase	1.73	Citigroup	1.77
10	Citigroup	1.67	KeyBank	1.49
	Top ten	*42.83*	*Top ten*	*38.32*

Note: Numbers may not add up to totals due to rounding.
Source: The Nilson Report (various 2003 issues).

top ten banks accounted for 28.6 percent of the total deposits in the United States, and their share of consumer deposits is likely lower.

The national picture, however, is not the whole story. Debit cards are mainly issued by depository institutions to their consumer customers, and economists have generally concluded that competition in consumer banking services is local. That is, people want to hold their accounts at a bank that is relatively close to their home or office. Many studies have assumed that the geographic scope of consumer banking markets is roughly coincident with Metropolitan Statistical Areas. Any particular Metropolitan Statistical Area, which generally includes a city or large town and the surrounding communities, may be too broad or narrow, but on average they seem about right, and data are readily available at that level of aggregation. For nonmetropolitan areas, economic studies have often treated a county as the relevant geographic unit.

While regional data on debit issuance are not available, we can look at the regional concentration of banking as a rough proxy. Using the HHI discussed earlier in this chapter, we calculate regional bank HHIs, using deposits in 2002 as a measure of size in computing the shares. The deposit-weighted average HHI across all Metropolitan Statistical Areas is 1,393. Thus, "on average," banking at this level is moderately concentrated. There are 58 Metropolitan Statistical Areas with HHIs below 1,000 (covering 31 percent of the total deposits), 201 with HHIs between 1,000 and 1,800 (covering 56.5 percent of the total deposits), and 77 with HHIs greater than 1,800 (covering 12.5 percent of the total deposits).

Recent changes in technology and banking regulation may, however, result in much broader geographic banking competition. As banking over the Internet and by telephone has become more common, geographic proximity to a bank has become less important for some people. Although the evidence is not conclusive, some economists have suggested that banks may already face effective competition at the statewide level. As regulatory changes have made it easier for banks to operate throughout the country, competition may ultimately operate at the national level, as it does in most other advanced countries. Internet banks such as ING Direct and NetBank as well as banks run by brokerage firms such as E*Trade and Ameritrade have become increasingly popular since the mid-1990s and already compete at this level.

The profile of debit issuers could also change over time. As noted, brokerage firms are currently the only debit issuers that are not traditional depository institutions. As debit cards become more popular, it is possible that other issuers, such as American Express or Discover, may enter. To do so, they would have to gain access to consumers' deposits in order to debit them on transactions, which could be done using the existing ACH system (possibly at slightly higher costs than for Visa or Master-Card issuers) or by contracting directly with banks for access.

Prices and Profitability

As we observed in chapter 8, the interchange fee provided the main incentive for banks to issue and encourage the usage of signature debit cards. Since interchange fees were at least four times higher for signature debit than PIN debit on average, banks had an interest in getting consumers to authorize a debit transaction with a signature rather than a PIN. One way to do this might have been to charge consumers for using PIN debit. But particularly early on, consumers were resistant to paying fees on debit transactions—checks and the use of their bank's

ATMs were often free, after all—and were also frequently uncertain as to the difference between PIN and signature debit. For fear that they would discourage all debit use, most banks did not charge for either type of debit usage, and those that did charge for PIN debit would often exempt their best customers.

As consumers have become more familiar with PIN and signature debit, some issuers have imposed fees on some PIN debit transactions. Banks that chose to charge PIN debit fees applied them selectively to lower-value accounts. Some banks prefer that their customers use signature debit rather than PIN debit because on a stand-alone basis, they at best break even at the margin on those transactions. Without an annual fee, they have to cover all their costs from interchange fees, which have increased in recent years yet still only range from around 10¢ to 29¢ per transaction on average for the major PIN debit networks. The switch fees issuers have to pay the networks for each transaction (which are not netted out from interchange fees) range from 2¢ to 4.5¢. Other expenses, such as transaction processing or responding to customer inquiries, average about 12¢ to 15¢ per transaction. For example, one issuer, Corus Bank in Chicago, reportedly loses about 2.5¢ on every PIN debit transaction; it receives an average of 16.5¢ in interchange fees on a PIN debit transaction, but has to pay 19¢ on average for processing the transaction.

Banks are willing to offer "unprofitable" PIN debit because they make money from the overall banking relationship—which is the same reason they offer free checking. But without the profits that come from signature debit and its higher interchange fee, they would almost certainly not have promoted debit as much as they have in recent years. They might have raised other fees or lowered the rate they pay on deposits to compensate for the costs of offering PIN debit transactions. Going forward, all of this may be affected by the recent settlement in the Wal-Mart litigation, which we explore in chapter 11.

Output
As we discussed in chapter 3, all measures of debit card output have increased dramatically since 1990. Between 1990 and 2002, the number of signature debit cards increased from about 9.1 million to 174.9

million. Purchase volume grew at an even faster rate, from 101.4 million purchases and $7.1 billion in 1990 to 8.2 billion purchases and $317.8 billion in 2002, with almost all of the growth taking place after 1995. Similarly, PIN debit purchase volume grew from $3.5 billion in 1990 to $18.7 billion in 1995 and $162.2 billion in 2002, about 10 percent of the total payment card volume. (Growth in the number of PIN debit cards was less dramatic since ATM cards were already common by 1990.) Today, between the PIN and signature versions, debit accounts for 29 percent of all payment cards and 29 percent of all payment card volume.

As debit cards became increasingly popular, a substantial number of banks joined the co-opetitives solely for the purpose of issuing debit cards. There were nearly 2,500 such Visa debit issuers in 2002, and over two-thirds of their net entry took place after 1995. (We don't have comparable data for MasterCard.)

Product Differentiation and Marketing

Compared to credit and charge cards, debit cards have been relatively undifferentiated products. Since the product is debit, not credit, this means there can be no competition on interest rates or credit lines. The fact that consumers are generally not solicited by mail or advertising for debit cards means that issuers have not developed debit-specific marketing techniques to push their cards. And since issuers cannot directly affect merchant acceptance, they cannot compete along that dimension either, at least within a system.

Differentiation does exist at the level of the banking relationship. Banks compete for customers on the availability of branches, their own EFT networks (where customers are typically not surcharged for cash withdrawals), their hours of operation, and other service quality dimensions. Banks may also offer add-on features such as telephone or Internet account access, which allows depositors to monitor transactions, including debit card usage. Banks compete on the overall package they offer to customers, not on the debit card component alone.

The absence of revenues from annual fees or finance charges on debit cards also means there is less to fund the rewards benefits that are common on credit and charge cards. Even so, banks have started to offer debit-based rewards programs. J.P. Morgan Chase introduced the first frequent-flier program, partnering with Continental Airlines, in February 1999. In September 1999, Bank of America introduced three separate debit cobranding deals with Alaska Airlines, America West, and US Airways. And in January 2002, Citigroup offered an American Airlines debit card. These banks' customers have the option to pay more for these rewards cards or to pay nothing for a standard card. The mileage debit cards typically charge an annual fee of $25 to $30 (compared to $50 to $60 on mileage credit cards) and offer one mile for every $2 charged (compared to a one-to-one ratio on mileage credit cards). Some programs award miles on all transactions, while others award them only on signature debit.

Smaller banks have also started to offer rewards programs. For example, Harbor Bank of Maryland, a local bank in Baltimore, offers its customers a card on which they can receive rebates of up to 10 percent at certain local retailers. These rebates, less an administrative fee, are then split between the cardholder and a church or charity the cardholder designates. Visa also announced a system-level rewards program on both credit and debit cards in November 2002, making it easier for smaller banks to offer their own rewards programs. Consumers accumulate points in the Visa program that can be redeemed for merchandise from a catalog or benefits such as movie tickets or video rentals.

Banks offer rewards programs in part because they hope they provide benefits for the customer relationship as a whole. For example, Bank of America said it believed its frequent-flier cards have helped it to attract new checking account customers. Customers who are happy with their rewards programs may also be less likely to leave a bank since they would have to give up their rewards program balances to do so.

10

Backroom Battles

People don't see us . . . but we have a huge behind-the-scenes impact.
—Henry C. Duques, CEO of FDC (1994)

A lot goes on behind the scenes in the payment card industry. First Data Corporation (FDC) is involved in many of these activities, so let's begin with a tour of this sprawling firm.

FDC processes card transactions that take place at merchants. That usually means that it receives a request from a merchant to authorize payment by a customer with a card. Using its computers and telecommunications systems, FDC contacts the credit or debit system that corresponds to the customer's card and conveys the system's response back to the merchant. If the transaction is authorized, FDC takes care of paying the merchant on behalf of the bank acquirer as well as generating a periodic statement of accounts. FDC was the largest merchant processor in 2002 with at least 32 percent of the total merchant transaction volume and 38 percent of co-opetitive merchant transaction volume.

FDC isn't formally the acquirer—the business that enters into contracts with the merchant on behalf of one or more of the card systems—for any of the merchants whose transactions it processes. In theory, only a co-opetitive member can serve as an acquirer for the Visa or MasterCard systems, so FDC can only be a third-party processor in general. (A small portion of FDC's volume goes through its subsidiary, First Financial Bank, which is a co-opetitive member.) In practice, FDC and similar firms are so sufficiently in control of the acquiring process for at least some of their merchant business that many industry experts and

investment analysts view them as the actual acquirers for those merchants. On this basis, FDC (including Cardservice International, a wholly
owned subsidiary) is the acquirer for about 12 percent of merchant locations and 7.7 percent of merchant transaction volume, making it the
sixth-largest acquirer in the United States in 2002.

FDC is also a major player in the other side of the payment card business. Many banks that issue cards subcontract the work of sending
monthly statements and collecting money from cardholders to third-
party cardholder processors. In 2002, FDC was the largest such processor, servicing 33 percent of all U.S. cardholder accounts and 41 percent
of co-opetitive cardholder accounts. (The go-it-alones currently do all
their own cardholder processing.) As in the case of merchant processing,
FDC remains invisible to the ultimate customer—so you have no idea
whether FDC, one of its competitors, or the bank that issued you the
card has generated your statement.

To operate as a merchant processor, FDC links into the MasterCard
or Visa systems for signature-based transactions (and for Maestro and
Interlink) and into one of the EFT networks for PIN debit transactions.
And that leads us to a potentially important part of FDC's business. Following the merger with Concord EFS, it owns the STAR EFT network.
STAR accounted for 53 percent of all PIN debit transaction volume in
2002. That would make FDC by far the largest PIN debit system, with
Interlink (Visa's PIN debit system) a distant second with 16 percent of
the business.

The growth of FDC, especially after the merger with Concord, may
influence the evolution of the industry. To understand this, it is useful to
begin with some history of the back room.

The Evolution of the Payment Processing Business

FDC illustrates two seemingly opposite trends in the payment card industry: increased specialization, and greater integration. Over the years,
banks have come to specialize in issuing cards. They have hived off tasks
that weren't central to developing relationships with cardholders. Companies like FDC have found that these tasks have economies of scale and
scope—or perhaps that the combination of these tasks yields strategic

advantages. The result has been the emergence of a small number of large and increasingly vertically integrated businesses that so far at least, live entirely in the back room.

The go-it-alones have always done their own issuing and processing on the cardholder side, and most of their own acquiring and processing on the merchant side. Most members of MasterCard and Visa also began by soliciting both cardholders and merchants. Since they operated within a single locality or state and served both consumers and businesses, it was natural for them to serve both sides of the payment card industry. Indeed, in the early years of the bankcard systems, many banks found that a large portion of their transactions were between their cardholder and merchant customers; these were called "on-us" transactions, and meant that the bank was paying the interchange fees to itself.

Some Visa and MasterCard members, especially smaller banks, relied on third parties to provide processing services on both the cardholder and merchant sides. A smaller bank could do this by joining one of the regional bankcard processing cooperatives—such as the Eastern States Bankcard Association, the Southwestern Bankcard Association, or the Atlantic States Bankcard Association—that provided processing for their bank members. Alternatively, it could purchase processing services from third-party firms, either nonbanks such as FDC or larger banks such as Bank One. By 1981, about 36 percent of co-opetitive cardholder accounts were subcontracted out for processing. A significant proportion of merchant volume was also processed by third parties, although quantitative estimates are unavailable.

During the 1980s, banks also began to cede control of the acquiring part of the business to third parties. Many banks got out of the acquiring business altogether following Chase Manhattan's sale of its merchant portfolio to NaBanco in 1981. As the competition from specialist firms and the go-it-alones began to intensify, more banks found that merchant acquiring was less profitable than other lines of business, including issuing cards. Following this trend, Chemical, Manufacturers Hanover, Security Pacific, and many other banks exited the merchant acquiring business in the late 1980s. As a part of strategic reassessments and restructurings, the banks concluded that the merchant side of the business was best left to processing specialists such as NaBanco and National

Data Corporation. The share of co-opetitive acquiring accounted for by nonbank acquirers increased from effectively zero in the 1970s, to 9 percent in 1988, to 36 percent in 2002. As noted, only bank members of Visa and MasterCard can formally be acquirers, so nonbank "acquirers" must still rely on a silent bank partner that is a member.

In addition, as we discuss below, many of the banks that currently remain in acquiring do so as part of alliances with firms like FDC, relying on them for processing services. As merchant processing relied increasingly on new technologies—such as electronic point-of-sale systems, and networks for transaction authorization, capture, accounting, and charge-back functions that became increasingly sophisticated—it became a prohibitively expensive activity for all but the largest banks. (A charge-back is a transaction disputed by the cardholder.) In addition, the growth of major national retail chains such as Wal-Mart intensified buyer pressure on merchant discounts.

Some banks that chose to stay in the merchant processing and acquiring businesses turned to the equity markets to fund their technology units, sometimes spinning them off wholly or in part to public ownership. Bank of America did this with its BA Merchant Services unit; National City Corporation did the same with National Processing Company, as did First U.S.A. with Paymentech. This suggests there was little value from integrating merchant processing and other bank activities. There was apparently no more reason for banks to provide their own processing than their own computer equipment or office supplies. Many banks could not, or chose not to, sustain the capital investments required to stay in the processing business, and they opted out entirely. This trend, which occurred mostly in the mid-1980s to mid-1990s, led to a blitz of mergers and a large consolidation as merchant processors sought economies of scale and scope. By 2002, third-party firms came to take over merchant processing, accounting for over 70 percent of merchant processing volume. Over roughly this same period, and for much the same reasons, many banks opted out of processing on the issuing side of the business. The share of third-party firms in cardholder processing increased from 36 percent in 1981 to over 71 percent in 2002.

The existence of scale economies in merchant acquiring and processing is not surprising since transactions processing is a highly data-intensive activity that is accomplished most efficiently with large centralized computer and telecommunications systems. As a consequence of these economies, firms specializing in acquiring developed, as did firms that focused on merchant processing. The acquiring specialists included independent sales organizations that focused just on signing up merchants and then passing them off to other firms that processed transactions and maintained the merchant relationship.

During the 1990s, mergers, acquisitions, and internal growth changed the back room dramatically. The best way to see this is to consider the recent evolution of the major players.

Who's Who in the Back Room

Table 10.1 shows the leading firms in each part of the back room and, as a prelude to our later discussion of integration between back rooms and networks, entities that provide network services. These network services include EFT network processing, money transfers, and electronic bill payment. As we saw in chapter 8, EFT networks facilitate ATM and PIN debit transactions. Money transfers include wiring money and money orders, both of which transfer funds without going through banks. Electronic bill payment involves the electronic collection, presentment, and payment of bills instead of the traditional mailing of bills and payments. (The table includes acquiring and merchant processing together because many of the reports on this subject do not distinguish between the two.)

Here, we briefly describe five entities that have a significant presence in at least one part of the back room and that illustrate different business models: FDC, Alliance Data Systems, Certegy, Bank of America, and Total Systems.

First Data Corporation

FDC, based in Denver, Colorado, specializes in processing payments between consumers and businesses, and its interests extend beyond cards. It owns Western Union—the company that was the dominant telegraph firm in the mid-nineteenth century and never managed the transition to telephones—which has a 75 percent share of money transfers. Many of

Table 10.1
The major players in the payment card back room

	Acquiring merchant processing	Check authorization	Cardholder processing	ATM processing	EFT network ownership	Money transfers	Electronic bill payment
Alliance Data Systems	■						
Certegy	■	■	■				
CheckFree							■
Concord EFS	■			■	■		
Efunds		■		■			
FDC	■	■	■	■	■	■	
Global Payments							
Intercept	■	■		■		■	
National Processing							
Total Systems	■		■				

Note: Total Systems owns a 50 percent interest in merchant processor Vital Processing, a joint venture with Visa U.S.A.
Source: Merrill Lynch, "The Payment Processing Industry" (November 15, 2002).

these transfers are between members of immigrant communities around the world and involve people who do not have bank accounts. FDC also has a majority stake in a holding company—eONE Global—that invests in a portfolio of firms specializing in emerging payment systems. The eONE Global firms supply electronic, wireless, and Internet payment and processing solutions as well as electronic tax payment capabilities for governments, enterprises, and mobile phone providers. Of immediate interest here, FDC processed 10.2 billion merchant transactions and handled 227 million payment card accounts in 2002; as a result of the merger with Concord EFS, it also owns the STAR EFT system, which has 254,700 ATM machines and can be accessed by 132 million ATM cards. (With the exception of STAR, the FDC data we report do not include the impact of the Concord merger.)

FDC is the product of a series of mergers and acquisitions. Immediately after it was founded in 1969, it took over processing duties for the Mid-America Bankcard Association (a bankcard processing cooperative). During its first eleven years, FDC took over two additional regional bankcard processing associations. American Express purchased FDC in 1980 when FDC was processing 250 million transactions annually. After the acquisition, FDC was able to take over processing duties for several more regional bankcard associations, including the Eastern States Bankcard Association in 1988. (It was not, however, involved in processing American Express transactions.) By 1992, FDC was processing transactions for one million merchants.

Since being spun off by American Express in 1992, FDC has continued with an aggressive series of mergers and acquisitions. In 1995, it merged with the First Financial Management Corporation, which included most of what is now FDC's merchant services division as well as Western Union. First Financial Management Corporation was the parent company of NaBanco, the largest merchant acquirer at the time and one of the characters in chapter 11's antitrust war stories. During that same year, FDC also acquired Card Establishment Services (formerly the merchant acquiring unit of Citigroup), the third-largest merchant acquirer at the time. These acquisitions catapulted FDC to the number one position in both merchant acquiring and processing. It then bought a majority stake in the second-largest EFT network, NYCE, in 2001. As we mentioned earlier, FDC had to agree to divest its ownership interest in NYCE to obtain Justice Department clearance for its merger in 2004 with Concord EFS, including Concord's STAR network. FDC complemented this network in 2002 by acquiring PayPoint, one of the largest processors of PIN debit transactions.

FDC has also entered into a series of joint ventures with banks. Each party contributes merchant relationships to the venture. Then the venture's or the bank's sales force solicits new relationships. The banks contribute their relationships with the card co-opetitives (since only members can formally acquire) and sometimes clearing and settlement services. FDC puts in some of its merchant accounts (from its NaBanco and Card Establishment Services acquisitions) and provides core processing services, such as certain authorization, transaction capture, and settlement services, as well as processing for Internet-based and prepaid card transactions. The banks gain the opportunity to enhance their relationships with merchants without a heavy investment in processing. FDC, by relinquishing some of its direct relationships with merchants and competing less directly with its bank partners, gains merchant volume for its processing platform, with the potential for additional economies of scale. As of 2002, FDC had formed ventures with twenty-four banks, including two of the top ten acquirers in that year. Together, FDC's bank partners accounted for 28.5 percent of the merchant business in 2002; adding in FDC's 7.7 percent, FDC and its partners accounted for 36.2 percent that year. (We'll have more to say about FDC's alliance strategy below.)

Alliance Data Systems

The Dallas, Texas–based Alliance Data Systems has three major businesses. It operated more than fifty store card programs in 2003 for retailers such as Limited Brands, Crate and Barrel, and Ann Taylor, thereby helping retailers to find and retain cardholders as well as process transactions. These generated $2.8 billion in card outstandings in 2002, roughly equal to the outstandings held by the eighteenth-largest co-opetitive issuer. Alliance is the fourth-largest store card processor based on transaction volume and the second-largest based on accounts. (The largest is GE Consumer Finance based on volume and accounts.) Lastly,

Alliance has a significant presence in merchant acquiring and processing. Unlike FDC, it does not operate a card network, money transfer business, or EFT network.

Alliance was created in 1996 through the merger of BSI Business Services, the transaction processing and credit services business of J.C. Penney, and World Financial Network National Bank, the private-label credit card issuer and processor for The Limited. Prior to this merger, Alliance's predecessor company, J.C. Penney Business Services (which later became BSI Business Services), brought end-to-end credit processing services to the retail, petroleum, and casual dining industries. In 1989, another of Alliance's predecessor companies, The Limited, created the first monoline bank for a retailer, World Financial National Bank, to handle issuing its store cards. After the merger of these companies, Alliance was the second-largest third-party, private-label processing operator in the United States.

Alliance has subsequently grown through a series of acquisitions. In 1998, it acquired Loyalty Management Group, which had created and managed the Air Miles Reward program, a loyalty mileage program in Canada. During that same year, Alliance also acquired Harmonic Systems, a provider of merchant processing and loyalty card programs. Alliance added 180 new processing clients through the 1999 acquisition of the Network Transaction Services unit of Associates First Capital Corporation's SPS Payments subsidiary. In 2001, Alliance entered into the utility billing industry by acquiring Utilipro, which provided account processing and servicing to companies that compete in deregulated utility markets. That same year, Alliance also acquired Mail Box Capital Corporation, a company that supplied statement generation and data processing services for a wide range of clients, including firms in the utilities, financial, telecommunications, and retail industries, as well as government entities. In 2002, Alliance acquired Frequency Marketing, a company specializing in the design and operation of loyalty marketing programs, and Enlogix Group, which offered Alliance an entrance into the Canadian utility market along with the opportunity to provide services such as customer care, customer information system hosting, billing, and marketing to utility companies.

Certegy

Certegy, based near Atlanta, Georgia, provides credit and debit card holder processing and check risk management. In 2002, Certegy processed over two billion payment transactions. Certegy is the third-largest third-party cardholder processor, with a 2 percent share in 2002. It handles thirteen million payment card accounts for thousands of financial institutions. Certegy does not do any acquiring, instead focusing on its processing business and check authorization services. In the check authorization business, Certegy is the second-largest firm with 12 percent of total volume.

Certegy started in 1961 as Telecredit, a company in the check risk-management industry. Telecredit created the first centralized electronic database that tracked and delivered check authorization decisions to merchants at the point of sale. In 1974, Telecredit acquired a card services business, which it expanded through alliances with the Independent Community Bankers of America and Card Services for Credit Unions. Telecredit was a partner offering cardholder processing services to the associations' members. Equifax acquired Telecredit in 1990. Equifax expanded the business through a series of international acquisitions. In 1994, Equifax acquired First Bankcard Systems, a developer of cardholder processing software. In 1996, it acquired the largest European check risk-management company, Transax. Equifax acquired a controlling interest in UNNISA, a large cardholder processing business in Brazil, in 1998, and acquired the remaining interest in 2001. In 1999, the company began cardholder processing operations in the United Kingdom. Equifax acquired Procard, the second-largest credit card holder processing company in Chile, in 2000. In 2001, these processing businesses were spun off as Certegy, while Equifax retained nonprocessing businesses that focused primarily on providing information-based services, such as credit reporting.

Bank of America

As we have discussed, Bank of America is a large commercial bank—at one time the largest in the nation. Initially based in San Francisco, it moved its headquarters in 1998 to Charlotte, North Carolina, following its merger with NationsBank. It issues credit and debit cards and acquires merchants. In 2002, Bank of America was the seventh-largest credit and charge card issuer with $62 billion by volume. It was the largest debit card issuer in the United States with 12 percent of the total industry volume. Bank of America outsources its cardholder processing to Total Systems. With nearly $71 billion in processing volume and 190,000 merchant locations, Bank of America is the ninth-largest merchant acquirer. Finally, Bank of America has 13,000 ATMs in the United States—more than any other bank.

Total Systems

Total Systems consists of a company that does mainly cardholder processing and a joint venture with Visa, called Vital, which mainly does merchant processing. As a cardholder processor, Total Systems is the second largest in the United States with an 18 percent share in 2002. Total Systems handles 148 million cardholder accounts. Vital doesn't do any acquiring, instead focusing on processing for three hundred acquiring banks that subcontract this activity.

Total Systems began in 1959 as a small division of Columbus Bank and Trust Company, a Georgia bank that is now owned by Synovus, when it started offering CB&T charge accounts. The CB&T charge system relied on manual posting machines and was accepted by three thousand merchants in the Columbus area. Columbus's bankcard processing system, Total Systems, provided Visa and MasterCard members across the country with merchant processing services in 1974 and cardholder processing in 1975. It spun this business off as Total Systems in 1983.

Total Systems is a subsidiary of Synovus, which owns 81 percent of its equity. In 1992, Total Systems acquired Mailtek, which processed Delta's frequent-flier program, and Lincoln Marketing, which specialized in correspondence for financial institutions and credit application processing. Total Systems formed Vital with Visa in 1996. In 2000, Synovus, Total Systems's parent company, acquired ProCard, a commercial card data manager. Synovus planned to use the acquisition to expand Total Systems's services to clients who want to build commercial card portfolios. In 2003, Total Systems acquired Enhancement Services Corporation, a provider of loyalty and marketing services for payment cards.

The genesis of Vital offers some insight into the dynamics of this business. In 1996, Visa's merchant processing affiliate, Merchant Bank Services, merged with Total Systems's merchant processing business to form Vital. Visa's Merchant Bank Services was the largest provider of electronic authorization and data capture, while Total Systems contributed modern merchant accounting, billing options, and reporting systems. In 1997, Vital partnered with Golden Retriever Systems, a database management company specializing in custom merchant reporting and risk management, and signed a merchant processing contract with the National Processing Company, the second-largest merchant processor at that time. Vital contracted with Bank of America for point-of-sale processing in 1998. In 2002, Vital authorized over 6.5 billion electronic payment transactions and settled more than 2.6 billion transactions on its system.

Market Structure and Performance

Although several firms have integrated across various segments of the back room, it is useful to consider the three main parts separately. Here, we examine the structure and performance of the acquiring, merchant processing, and cardholder processing businesses. The main message is that these industries have become increasingly concentrated. Yet industry observers frequently describe them as highly competitive businesses with thin margins. There's no contradiction: the successful firms have invested aggressively to reduce their costs by exploiting scale and scope economies and realizing efficiencies. Having a few such firms supplying nearly identical services and vying for customers mainly on the basis of price has proven sufficient to put enormous pressure on margins.

Acquiring

Acquirers compete for new and existing merchant accounts. They sometimes work with independent sales organizations to help them recruit merchants. This is a prospecting business: acquirers incur fixed costs in recruiting merchants and recover these costs from the fees they earn from successful relationships. Recent data suggest that the average cost for acquiring a new merchant ranges from $100 to $1,500. The number varies depending on whether the merchant is signed by an independent sales organization, a telemarketer, or a bank's in-house staff. The cost is also likely to depend significantly on the size and type of merchant.

The main weapons in recruiting merchants are price and service. Both are much affected by the merchant processor the acquirer uses for handling day-to-day transactions, so the lines between acquirer and processor quickly blur. The best way to think of the acquirer is as the account representative—the person who works with the retailer to handle its card transactions. For new businesses, this person works with the store to obtain equipment for taking cards (as we all know from shopping, this equipment varies in sophistication from merchant to merchant), deciding what cards to accept, and choosing among various methods for reporting and summarizing transactions and integrating these methods into the merchant's accounting system. For ongoing businesses, the acquirer is the point of contact for the merchant for changes in the card equipment or service offerings and for dealing with any problems.

For banks, being in the acquiring business helps them fill out the bundle of services they can offer to merchants—from checking accounts to business loans. They also value the direct, personal relationship with the merchant because it helps them sell other services, even if they subcontract out most of the relevant tasks to specialists. (The merchant may have Discover bundled in with the package from a Visa/MasterCard acquirer, but it must obtain a separate relationship with American Express, which acts as its own acquirer and processor. As we noted in chapter 7, however, the merchant can use the same terminals for all cards.) Accepting that the bank cares most about the merchant relationship has been the secret of FDC's success in the merchant processing business; FDC's joint ventures with banks cede control of the merchant relationship to the bank.

Merchants receive several key services from the acquirer directly or indirectly. With terminals installed and an account established, the merchant is ready to take payment by card. A clerk enters the transaction information and swipes the card. The resulting transaction and card information is sent over a telecommunications network to the merchant processor, which working through the relevant card network, secures authorization from the bank or the go-it-alone that issued the customer's card and secures payment for the merchant. The merchant usually receives detailed accounting of transactions at the end of each month, although there is a quicker and tighter integration with the accounting systems of larger merchants. Detailed reports and analyses may accompany the basic accounting information, and the acquirer may provide a help desk or other merchant support.

Although acquirers can differentiate themselves by providing more sophisticated accounting services, the business is mainly about offering reliable transaction processing services at the lowest possible price. A fee arrangement between an acquirer and a merchant may have a gross discount fee of 1.5 to 2 percent of the transaction's value and a fixed fee of 5¢ to 25¢ for each transaction. These numbers are illustrative, as merchant agreements vary substantially. For example, major merchants pay significantly less than small ones. The acquirer in turn pays an assessment fee—which may be around 0.05 to 0.10 percent of the transaction's value—to Visa or MasterCard, and an interchange fee—which may be around 1.5 percent—to the card issuer. In addition, if the acquirer is not formally the acquiring bank, it also pays the acquiring bank a small service fee. For those acquirers that subcontract almost everything but maintaining the relationship, virtually all these costs are determined by the prices they have to pay their suppliers. The largest of these costs is the interchange fee paid to the bank that issued the customer's card. For this reason, some acquirers' statements show their own fees and the interchange fee separately. The interchange fee is determined by the card network, and it varies across categories of merchants and attributes of the transaction (such as whether the transaction was processed electronically).

The level of concentration in the acquiring business differs depending on how the FDC alliances are viewed. Because the details of how the FDC alliances are run—such as the relative control of FDC over pricing and other competitive decisions—are not public, the degree to which the alliance partners are true competitors is unclear. It is nonetheless instructive to consider the two possible extremes. If the alliance partners and FDC are regarded as wholly separate competitive entities, the industry is relatively unconcentrated; the top acquirer, Chase Merchant Services, has only a 13 percent share of the volume and the HHI for acquiring (as a reminder, a measure of industry concentration discussed in chapter 9) is only 709. If FDC and its alliance partners are considered a single competitive entity, however, the industry appears significantly more concentrated; the top acquirer under this methodology is then FDC and its partners, with a 36 percent share of the volume, and the acquiring HHI is 1,702.

In any event, there is evidently intense competition for merchant accounts, and it is common for merchants to switch among acquirers in an effort to get the best possible price. According to one trade press account, "Merchants are notorious for jumping from one portfolio to another whenever a better price comes along." Another industry study comments that merchants "are often willing to switch from one bankcard processor to another simply to save a few hundredths of a percentage point on fees." Large national merchants, in particular, have a lot of bargaining power since their volume provides acquirers with scale efficiencies. The bidding process and the threat of switching have helped drive down the prices paid by major merchants.

Competition, scale economies, and rapid reductions in data processing and telecommunications costs have come together to reduce the net merchant discount—the difference between the total merchant discount and the interchange fee, which goes to issuers—that merchants pay acquirers for their services. These reductions mainly reflect cheaper merchant processing services. Figure 10.1 shows the precipitous drop in the average net merchant discount over the last two decades. It declined at an annual rate of 2.68 percent during the 1980s, and at an annual rate of 2.66 percent from 1990 to 2002. (On a per transaction basis, as opposed to a percent age of the volume, the decline is greater in recent years because the average transaction size has fallen due to the growth of debit, which has a smaller transaction size than credit.)

Merchant Processing

Merchant processors compete for the business of acquirers. (Even merchant processors that also acquire compete for the merchant processing business of acquirers that do not also process transactions.) Selections from marketing material illustrate their selling points: FDC markets its

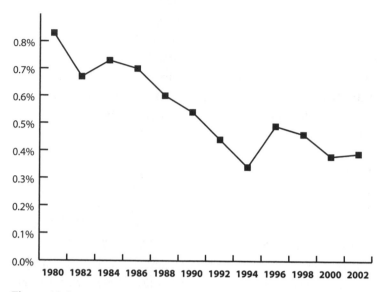

Figure 10.1
Average net merchant discount, 1980–2002
Note: Net merchant discount is the merchant discount rate net of the interchange fee.
Source: Visa U.S.A.

alliance programs to banks by focusing on "stability," "flexibility," "commitment," and "vision." Stability relates to FDC's economies of scale in merchant processing, allowing the acquirer to offer merchants competitive pricing. Flexibility involves the company's state-of-the-art technologies. Commitment refers to its full-service support. And vision relates to the processor's investments in new technologies, and allowing acquirers to seek out new clients while FDC is handling back-office functions. Vital, a merchant processor that does not acquire, promotes itself as a "pure" merchant processor with a "single-minded dedication to acquirers." The company positions itself as a partner, not a competitor, allowing acquirers to focus on their relationships with merchants without the threat of competition from their processors. Vital promotes service, technology, and partnership to acquirers. To merchants, it promotes compatibility and simplicity.

Merchant processing is now a highly concentrated business. Although precise data are not available, we know that the concentration in merchant processing is comparable to that in the acquiring business with alliance partners treated as a single entity because all partners typically use the same processor. Based on the acquirer data, the processing HHI is 1,590. (This is slightly lower than the acquiring HHI given above because Paymentech processes half of its own acquiring volume even though it is an alliance partner with FDC.) Despite this relatively high concentration, the merchant processing business is known for intense competition and razor-thin margins.

The costs have come down as the volumes have increased. As we would expect in a competitive market, these savings have been passed on to the merchants. For example, from 1996 (the earliest year with available comparable data) to 2002, FDC's revenues from its Merchant Services division have increased at an average annual rate of 13 percent, from $1.3 billion (as always, in 2002 dollars) to $2.8 billion. Over this period, FDC's Merchant Services division's operating margins have decreased slightly from 28.9 to 26.7 percent. Although FDC's expenses per transaction have fallen significantly, by 25.8 percent, from 26.7¢ to 19.8¢, its revenue per transaction has fallen by even more, by 27.7 percent, from 37.5¢ to 27.1¢. (FDC's Merchant Services division is comprised primarily of its merchant processing business, but also includes the NYCE system and other nonmerchant processing operations. Thus, while these numbers should be indicative of profitability in FDC's merchant processing, they are affected to some extent by the profitability of these other operations.)

Major merchant processors have grown because spending on payment cards has grown, and because their increased scale and scope efficiencies have allowed them to gain a greater share of the business. This growth has resulted in significant increases in merchant processors' profits. For example, from 1996 to 2002, FDC's and National Processing Company's profits from their respective merchant processing divisions increased from $419 million to $815 million.

Cardholder Processing

Cardholder processors compete for the business of financial institutions that issue cards. Issuers are about evenly split between handling cardholder accounts internally and subcontracting these tasks to specialists.

Size matters. Most smaller issuers rely on companies like Certegy to do everything from printing embossed cards, to risk management, collecting billing information, and sending out statements. Credit unions, savings and loans, and other smaller banks issue credit cards as part of a bundle of services for their customers; so long as they own and manage the customer relationship, they are happy to have a specialist take care of the messy backroom details for them. Some larger banks such as Bank of America, Providian, and First Tennessee also find that their comparative advantage lies in prospecting for cardholders and maintaining relationships with them—thus, they subcontract backroom activities to one of the processors.

Cardholder processing, like merchant processing, makes intensive use of data processing and telecommunication services. Not surprisingly, this is another concentrated business, with 62 percent of all cardholder processing and 77 percent of co-opetitive cardholder processing done by four firms: FDC, Certegy, Total Systems, and Visa DPS. The industry HHIs are at least 1,600 for the processing of all cardholder accounts and 2,400 for the processing of co-opetitive cardholder accounts. These statistics significantly understate the degree of competition, however, since large banks can do cardholder processing efficiently themselves, and many in fact do so. In-house processing accounts for 43 percent of the transaction volume in the United States and 93 percent internationally. "We see the bank as our competitor," said Tom Walsh, vice president for marketing at FDC. "It's the in-house systems we're bidding against." Contracts are fiercely contested, and the larger banks are willing to bring processing back in-house. For example, Bank One recently announced that it would transition its cardholder processing to an in-house system once its current contract with FDC ends.

Cardholder processors typically charge a flat fee for each account managed during the year. In addition, the cardholder processor receives a per transaction authorization fee. Industry experts estimate that banks pay a per account fee of $2 to $5 per year, covering services such as mailing statements and processing cardholder payments, and an authorization fee ranging from 5¢ to 20¢ per transaction. Competition, together with increased scale economies and improved technology, has helped reduce card processing prices. For instance, from 1996 to 2002, FDC's Card Issuer Services division lowered its expenses per account managed by 22 percent, from $6.12 to $4.77. Competition, though, has generally passed these savings on to banks. FDC's average revenue per account fell even more, by 23.8 percent, over the same period, from $7.77 to $5.92. As a result, FDC's operating margin fell slightly, from 21.2 percent in 1996 to 19.4 percent in 2002. (As with the financial data for merchant processing, FDC's Card Issuer Services division includes some businesses that are not directly related to cardholder processing.)

As in merchant processing, leading firms have increased profits through growth. FDC, for example, increased its operating profits from cardholder processing from $252 million to $373 million between 1996 and 2002. Revenues grew from $1.2 billion to $1.9 billion over the same time period.

Integration

The back room has become increasingly integrated over the last two decades, as banks have come to rely on specialist firms to perform a broad array of processing functions. The 1980s saw an increased reliance on outside firms to provide both cardholder and merchant processing, as well as acquiring, and this trend has continued to the present. Another development over the past decade has been the integration of these specialist firms, especially FDC, into other parts of the back room. When FDC was spun off from American Express in 1992, it was mainly involved in merchant and card processing. It also had a small telemarketing business, and provided processing for American Express money orders, health-care institutions, cable television, and mutual fund shareholders. Over the next decade, FDC exited from these ancillary businesses and integrated into two more segments of the payment system back room: EFT processing, and EFT network ownership.

There are several possible explanations for this integration. There may be economies of scope from providing these tasks jointly. Certainly, American Express has found that it is better to do most things itself; these economies may be based on either sharing technology or using experience in one area to make things function better in another. It may be that the skills that make a firm an efficient merchant processor also make it an efficient cardholder processor, but further research needs to consider the real importance of these explanations.

There may also be strategic considerations. FDC appears to be emerging as another keystone in the payment card world as a result of assembling pieces of the action that no one else seemed to want: the unglamorous jobs of merchant and cardholder processing. Consider the possibilities. It provides services to banks on both the cardholder and the merchant sides of the system. It wants to cut out the Visa and MasterCard systems on those transactions that flow between the customer accounts of its acquirers and issuers. FDC has offered such a service to Visa and MasterCard banks. Visa has argued that this would degrade the performance of the Visa system, and the matter is in litigation.

It doesn't take much imagination to write an interesting ending to this story: FDC could create a new for-profit payment system—particularly now that its merger with Concord has been consummated—that is somewhere between American Express's closed system and the co-opetitives' open ones. If its bank partners became equity participants it would be equivalent to a go-it-alone system in almost all respects. It will be interesting to see how this develops.

11

The Antitrust Wars

People of the same trade seldom meet together, even for merriment and diversion, but the conversation ends in a conspiracy against the public, or in some contrivance to raise prices.

—Adam Smith, *The Wealth of Nations* (1776)

The investigating economist or government agent sees price policies that seem to him predatory and restrictions of output that seem to him synonymous with loss of opportunities to produce. He does not see that restrictions of this type are, in the conditions of the perennial gale [of creative destruction], incidents, often unavoidable incidents, of a long-run process of expansion which they protect rather than impede.

—Joseph Schumpeter, *Capitalism, Socialism and Democracy* (1942)

Two thousand and three was a pivotal year in the payment card industry's decades-long antitrust wars. A lawsuit brought by Wal-Mart and other retailers in 1996 was settled in April 2003 on the eve of a jury trial in Brooklyn. In that settlement, MasterCard and Visa agreed to pay around $2.2 to $2.6 billion (in present discounted value) and to allow merchants to take their debit cards without taking their credit cards or vice versa. A borough away and a few weeks later, MasterCard and Visa asked a federal appeals court in Manhattan to overturn a lower court decision that would allow their members to issue American Express and Discover cards in addition to the co-opetitive cards—and incidentally, would establish duality in signature debit cards. That court refused to do so in September 2003, and unless the Supreme Court reverses the appeals court, the go-it-alones will be able to enlist co-opetitive members to issue go-it-alone cards.

In fall 2003, another class action case stood pending in Manhattan. The plaintiffs argued that the fees cardholders are charged for exchanging foreign currency into dollars when they used their cards abroad were set anticompetitively by the co-opetitives. On the other side of the country, a state court in San Francisco had already chastised the associations for not disclosing those currency exchange fees more effectively and ordered the associations to pay cardholders about $800 million. (The decision is under appeal.) Copycat lawsuits were filed against American Express.

Meanwhile, as we noted in the preceding chapter, FDC and Visa filed dueling claims over FDC's efforts to offer processing services that bypassed Visa's network: Visa sued FDC for contractual violations that Visa says jeopardized the reliability of the Visa system, while FDC sued Visa for antitrust violations.

Across the Pacific, MasterCard and Visa lowered their interchange fees in accordance with an Australian decision requiring an interchange reduction to a cost-based benchmark. Visa decided to drop its appeal even as MasterCard continued its own. Across the Atlantic, an antitrust complaint by European retailers to the European Commission (the European Union's antitrust authority) had led Visa to agree in 2002 to lower its interchange fees on cross-country purchases. The European Commission formally issued similar objections to MasterCard in a letter to the organization in late 2003, apparently following failed private negotiations. Competition authorities in several European countries, such as the Office of Fair Trading in the United Kingdom, were nonetheless pursuing similar cases.

Figure 11.1 shows that antitrust warfare over association membership began in the early 1970s, soon after the birth of the co-opetitives, and has continued ever since. Worthen Bank and Trust wanted to participate in the Visa association as well as the MasterCard association, and it filed an antitrust lawsuit against Visa in April 1971. That was the first shot in a series of battles that continue to this day over membership in the co-opetitives. Can (or must) an association require its members to dedicate themselves to that association's card brand? Can (or must) it permit its members to participate in other associations or work with the go-it-alone systems? Those questions were at the heart of Worthen's complaint (which led to the Justice Department's first consideration of association membership); Sears's complaint in *Mountain West* that MasterCard and

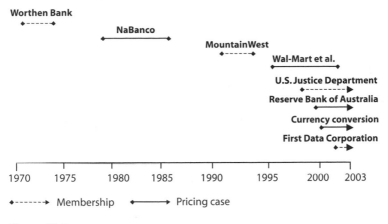

Figure 11.1
Major court battles, 1970–2003

Visa wouldn't let it join their associations because Sears operated the competing Discover Card system; American Express's complaint to the Justice Department that MasterCard and Visa wouldn't let their members also issue American Express cards; the Justice Department's complaint that MasterCard and Visa violated the antitrust laws by allowing their members to have governance roles in both associations and by preventing their members from issuing the cards of competing go-it-alone systems; and FDC's complaint that Visa's rule requiring members to process Visa transactions on the Visa system violates the antitrust laws.

Another series of battles, having to do with pricing, began in June 1979 when the National Bancard Corporation (NaBanco) claimed that the Visa co-opetitive engaged in illegal price-fixing when it determined the interchange fee between acquiring and issuing members. Should the co-opetitives be allowed to establish an interchange fee? If so, should the government place any restrictions on how that fee is set? Those questions were addressed in NaBanco's lawsuit, and are at the center of the similar cases in Australia and Europe mentioned above. The *Wal-Mart* case was about pricing as well: the retailers claimed that they were injured because signature debit cards would be as inexpensive to them as PIN debit cards if the co-opetitives didn't tie their signature debit cards to their credit cards and require merchants to take both or neither.

During its first two decades, the payment card industry had no significant antitrust skirmishes. Only Citigroup's purchase of Carte Blanche in 1965 and its subsequent sale in 1968 in response to Justice Department pressure merits a note. But the co-opetitives have been flypaper for antitrust challenges almost since their birth, and that has led to the wars that have raged—often over familiar territory—for more than thirty years. And with no obvious end in sight: the issues being litigated today will likely endure at least through the decade as appeals are made and follow-on cases are brought to the courts.

In one sense, it is easy to see why the co-opetitives must spend so much time defending themselves against antitrust charges. Legal and economic thinking on antitrust policy has been shaped by Adam Smith's famous observation, made in his 1776 book *The Wealth of Nations*, that "people of the same trade seldom meet together, even for merriment and diversion, but the conversation ends in a conspiracy against the public, or in some contrivance to raise prices." What would he have thought about MasterCard and Visa? Tens of thousands of financial institutions work together to provide services that have become essential to the daily economic lives of millions of consumers and merchants around the world. Representatives of these institutions meet several times a year to talk business—as members of the boards or other working committees of the card associations. Without knowing more, the author of *The Wealth of Nations* might view the co-opetitives with the same cynicism he afforded the local blacksmith club.

For the last thirty years, competition authorities and the courts have struggled with the role of the co-opetitives and the two-sided nature of the payment card industry. The complexity and difficulty of these issues is best evidenced by the different conclusions that authorities and courts reached at different times and places. The Justice Department favored dual membership in the mid-1970s because it thought duality would increase competition among issuers, but disliked aspects of dual membership in the late 1990s because it thought they suppressed competition among systems. A federal appeals court in the mid-1980s concluded that the co-opetitives needed to establish interchange fees to balance the two sides of the market and to operate efficient payment card systems. The Reserve Bank of Australia (which regulates commercial banks) decided that the co-opetitives' interchange fees were too high, resulted in too much card use, and penalized cash users. A federal appeals court decided in 1994 that Visa wasn't violating the antitrust laws by refusing to allow the owner of a competing system to become a member, while another federal appeals court in 2003 found that Visa violated the antitrust laws by refusing to allow its owner-members to join forces with a competing go-it-alone system.

From another perspective, though, it is hard to understand why the payment card industry has received such intense antitrust scrutiny. The same federal district court judge who found that MasterCard and Visa violated the antitrust laws by not letting American Express enter into deals with members to issue American Express cards also found that card issuing was a competitive industry facilitated by the associations, noting that

It was not until the 1970s that the growth of the payment card industry was significantly facilitated by the formation and growth of what would become the Visa and MasterCard associations. Before the existence of these joint ventures there were no national credit cards, and charge cards were available only from three national issuers: American Express, Diners Club and Carte Blanche. Even those cards could be used only at a limited group of merchants. Today, credit and debit cards that can be used nationally and internationally at millions of merchants are issued by thousands of association members. Minimum financial qualifications required for a credit card have declined dramatically so that even consumers with lower incomes are readily able to obtain payment cards.

Even without adjusting for the increased quality of services provided, prices to consumers have decreased 20 percent from 1984 to 1999. The associations have also fostered rapid innovation in systems, product offerings and services. Fraud rates have also decreased through a number of technological innovations. Consumers have access to products that combine dozens of features available through the associations with features and services developed by the individual issuers. Cardholders today can choose from thousands of different card products with varying terms and features. Consumers in the United States also have extensive information available to them about card offerings and can readily switch cards and issuers.

There are fewer competitors at the system level, but the intense competition among them is evident from their television ads and new product introductions. Antitrust scrutiny is commonly triggered when a firm has few significant competitors in the marketplace and there seems to be no realistic process of competitive entry. AT&T and IBM attracted almost continuous attention for this reason during a good part of the twentieth century, as has Microsoft since Windows became the leading personal computer operating system in the early 1990s. But there is no single dominant player in payment systems. Even when viewed only at the system level, Visa's share of purchase volume never exceeded 50 percent. And one sees the results of vibrant competition at the system level in fluctuations in systems' relative volumes.

Historically, the card industry is one in which leading systems are regularly displaced. American Express took over from Diners Club in the early 1960s, MasterCard took over from American Express in the late 1960s, Visa took over from MasterCard in the late 1970s, and MasterCard has recently caught up to Visa in credit cards (although not in debit cards). Of course, intense competition does not mean that companies don't try to evade the antitrust laws. Some of the most egregious price-fixing behavior has taken place in industries that are so competitive—such as construction—that executives are willing to risk jail to soften the brutal rule of the market. But that doesn't appear to be the case in the card industry: the controversial membership rules and pricing policies have been followed during years in which aggressive competition has resulted in rapid expansions in output, reductions in cost, and improvements in product quality—the hallmarks of a healthy industry.

Harm to Competitors or Harm to Consumers?

The enduring principles of U.S. antitrust policy were established in the final years of the nineteenth century and the early years of the twentieth. (These principles have influenced competition laws adopted later in the twentieth century by other nations as well as the European Union.) After the passage of the Sherman Act in 1890, the U.S. Supreme Court created a framework for distinguishing between permissible and impermissible competitive behavior by firms with "market power"—the ability to affect marketwide prices and output. Congress then filled some perceived loopholes in the Sherman Act, and the Court's interpretation of it, with the passage of the Clayton Act and the Federal Trade Commission Act in 1914. Nonetheless, the Sherman Act defined the battlefield on which the co-opetitives have fought their most important antitrust battles.

The Sherman Act has two key sections:

Section 1: Every contract, combination in the form of trust or otherwise, or conspiracy, in restraint of trade or commerce among the several States, or with foreign nations, is hereby declared to be illegal. . . .

Section 2: Every person who shall monopolize, or attempt to monopolize, or combine or conspire with any other person or persons, to monopolize any part of the trade or commerce among the several States, or with foreign nations, shall be deemed guilty of a felony.

After 1890, it was up to the courts, particularly the U.S. Supreme Court, to infuse meaning into this mess of unfamiliar words and phrases.

Adam Smith's view of collaboration among competitors is perhaps best reflected in the "per se rule" against price-fixing—a rule that had its origins in Justice Rufus Peckham's 1897 majority decision for the Supreme Court. In the *United States v. Trans-Missouri Freight* case, a railroad association had agreed to fix rates. The railroads argued that they had set reasonable rates. Peckham would hear none of it. He found against the railroads on the grounds that an agreement to fix prices is itself an unreasonable restraint of trade, no matter what sort of prices the agreement produces. Any other rule of law, he contended, would force courts to regulate thousands of prices throughout the economy. He thus found that agreements to fix prices are unlawful per se—illegal by their nature, regardless of their effects and regardless of whether their participants have market power.

One year after *Trans-Missouri*, Judge William Howard Taft (the future president and chief justice) issued an opinion that suggested an interesting dichotomy of business practices. In *United States v. Addyston Pipe and Steel*, Taft supported the application of the per se rule when an agreement plainly serves no legitimate business purpose and only restrains competition. He maintained, however, that "ancillary" restraints— restraints that are subordinate to a legitimate business purpose and exist to further that purpose—should not be subject to the per se rule. For example, members of a law partnership would have a legitimate interest in agreeing not to compete with the partnership because such competition would undermine the partnership's purpose. This restraint on the partners, Taft asserted, is ancillary to the legitimate goal of forming a successful business venture.

Ancillary restraints are not necessarily legal, though. Rather, the courts have treated them on a case-by-case basis under what is now known as the "rule of reason." This approach had its origins in Chief Justice Edward Douglass White's opinions in cases against Standard Oil and American Tobacco, both decided in 1911. The Court found that certain practices could be harmful depending on their "inherent effect" and "evident purpose." Only practices by firms with market power that "unreasonably" restrain trade are unlawful. For business practices that are not illegal per se, courts must consider both why they were adopted and what effect they had. That basic approach has become the cornerstone of modern antitrust analysis under the Sherman Act.

Over the course of the twentieth century, the courts, influenced by the writings of legal and economic scholars, have developed some overarching principles that help them apply the per se rule and the rule of reason to the particular cases with which they are confronted. Most important, there is now broad agreement among courts, legal scholars, and economists that antitrust policy should "protect competition, not competitors," and that consumer welfare is the fundamental standard for evaluating competitive effects. As Robert Litan and Carl Shapiro put it, "For at least 20 years a broad, bipartisan consensus has prevailed regarding the goal of U.S. antitrust policy: to foster competitive markets and to control monopoly power, not to protect smaller firms from tough competition by larger corporations. The interests of consumers in lower prices and improved products are paramount." The focus on consumers may seem obvious now, but for decades many courts and commentators suggested that antitrust enforcement had multiple objectives, including the preservation of small businesses.

There is also broad agreement on another principle that both tempers the focus on consumer welfare and prevents the courts from becoming the regulatory agency feared by Justice Peckham: the courts should substitute their judgment about how to maximize consumer welfare for the results of market forces only when there is evidence that businesses are engaging in practices that significantly harm consumer welfare. Market practices—particularly those of firms that lack market power—are presumed innocent until proven guilty. And while one usually doesn't need to establish guilt beyond a reasonable doubt because most antitrust litigation involves civil cases, not criminal cases, the courts often set the bar fairly high. One reason is that the courts have determined that the cost of convicting the innocent (condemning procompetitive practices) may exceed the cost of exonerating the guilty (acquitting anticompetitive practices). As the Supreme Court noted in an influential 1986 decision on predatory pricing, "Mistaken inferences [in predation cases] are especially costly, because they chill the very conduct [vigorous price competition] the antitrust laws are designed to protect."

The movement by the courts from the mechanistic application of formal legal rules to a serious examination of consumer welfare led in 1979 to an important decision establishing that even agreements to fix prices are not automatically per se violations. It depends on "whether the practice facially appears to be one that would always or almost always tend to restrict competition and decrease output . . . or instead one designed to 'increase economic efficiency and render markets more, rather than less, competitive.' " The case involved Broadcast Music, Inc., which offered blanket licenses that gave radio or television stations the right to perform music copyrighted by artists who belonged to Broadcast Music. Columbia Broadcasting System claimed that this amounted to an agreement among the artists to fix prices. In *Broadcast Music, Inc. v. CBS*, the Supreme Court found that "a middleman with a blanket license was an obvious necessity if the thousands of individual negotiations, a virtual impossibility, were to be avoided," and thus that the practice was not illegal per se. The Court reasoned that users benefited from "unplanned, rapid, and indemnified access to any and all of the repertory of compositions," and that sellers benefited from "a reliable method of collecting for the use of their copyrights."

Who's In, Who's Out?

Soon after the formation of the bankcard associations, there was a debate about whether banks should dedicate themselves to a single co-opetitive or whether they should be able to participate in both. As Visa's former CEO Dee Hock, a strong opponent of multiple membership, put it,

"There were compelling arguments on both sides of the issue." Although Hock was speaking about dual membership in the card co-opetitives, his point is true for many of the membership controversies we consider here. Co-opetitive members may benefit from being able to work with multiple systems and having those systems compete for the banks' business. But as we saw in chapter 7, the co-opetitives may perform poorly if they can't count on the loyalty of their members. And since the members benefit from systems that provide a valuable brand and an efficient network, they may find it in their collective interests to insist that members dedicate themselves. The delicate balance between these benefits and costs is evidenced by the different choices that co-opetitives and their members have made at different times, for various geographies, and for issuing and acquiring.

Competition authorities, courts, and some commentators have focused on somewhat different trade-offs. On the one hand, letting banks belong to several systems may increase competition among the banks. Banks may also benefit from being able to sell several different card brands; they can use that to appeal to various cardholder segments or to provide a better service to merchants who benefit from having a single acquirer for all cards. On the other hand, letting banks belong to several systems may reduce competition among the systems. Members with investments in multiple systems may not want one system to which they belong to compete too much with another system to which they also belong. That is especially true for system activities that mainly take a share away from another system rather than growing the market; then the member may find itself paying for marketing or product development efforts that simply shift demand among its own products. Although there is an element of truth in these views, reality is complex and interesting, as we will see below.

Worthen

The first antitrust battle was over whether banks should be able to belong to both co-opetitives. In April 1971, a Visa member, Worthen Bank and Trust Company, applied for and was admitted into MasterCard, which was then much larger than Visa. Six months later, Visa passed a bylaw that prohibited dual membership—one of the first of several exclusivity rules we discuss here. Worthen, which wanted to be able to offer both card brands to merchants, sued.

Visa argued that duality would reduce competition between Master-Card and Visa and result in higher costs for consumers and merchants. The trial judge in *Worthen Bank and Trust Co. v. National Bank Americard* found that Visa's exclusivity rule was a per se violation of the antitrust laws, and he was persuaded that cardholders and merchants would be better off if they could do business with banks that handled both cards.

The actions by the U.S. Department of Justice in the wake of Visa's defeat illustrate the competing views on duality and exclusivity. Visa appealed, and the Justice Department filed a brief with the court to express its views. On balance, the Justice Department seemed to believe that the trial judge was right that exclusivity was harmful to competition. It suggested that the card systems were primarily service organizations for banks. A multibrand bank would want to maximize sales of both brands, and it would not want either system to "limit its advertisement, promotion, and enrollment of new members in other areas, since the more widespread each system becomes, the more attractive it is to consumers and merchants." The Justice Department was skeptical of Visa's claims that system competition was important or that duality would harm system competition. Nevertheless, the Justice Department thought it was possible that a full trial might reveal some procompetitive benefits of exclusivity. It therefore urged the U.S. Court of Appeals for the Eighth Circuit to reverse the per se finding and order a new trial under the rule of reason. The Eighth Circuit agreed, but the case was settled before a trial took place.

Without a decision in its favor, Visa risked further lawsuits. Although the members and governors of Visa had mixed feelings about duality, they tried to reduce Visa's litigation risks by seeking a favorable review of their exclusivity rule from the Justice Department. In a 1974 letter seeking this review, Visa's lawyers noted that "because dual membership has increased steadily for several years causing increased pressure from non-dual banks to become dual with effects which [Visa] believes are seriously anticompetitive; and because we believe that a final resolution of the matter is in the best interest of the public as well as all banks, we request that the [Justice] Department expedite its consideration of this matter." Visa also let the Justice Department know that without its support, management would not be able to persuade the board and members to continue the exclusivity rule.

Almost a year later, the Justice Department decided not to support either duality or exclusivity. It concluded that there was not enough information to decide whether duality was anticompetitive or not. In fact, although the Justice Department said that it was not concerned about exclusivity in issuance at that time, it expressly left open the possibility that it would be in the future. It also expressed concern about the effect of exclusivity on the development of debit cards and other electronic funds transfer systems.

In response, the Visa board reaffirmed its view that "system-to-system competition should be preserved and enhanced and that participation in competing systems be prohibited." It limited this prohibition to issuance and permitted members to acquire for both systems. But Visa soon concluded that this approach raised "irresolvable, definitional, operational and legal problems," and the board eliminated all restrictions on duality in May 1976.

Visa's observation that banks faced pressures to become dual issuers proved correct once the bylaw was abandoned. In a letter to the Justice Department in February 1977, Visa alerted the Justice Department that 75 percent of its new members were MasterCard members, and many of them were large issuers. It noted that these dual members were starting to use common advertisements for their dual cards, expressed concern over the leakage of confidential information, and maintained that members were questioning the desirability of having two separate systems.

This summary of the origins of duality offers two lessons. First, in the 1970s there was a great deal of uncertainty over whether exclusivity was on balance good or bad for competition. The two associations reached different conclusions; there was dissension within the associations; and the antitrust enforcers were not sure either. Second, it was generally recognized as early as the beginning of the 1970s that duality increases bank-to-bank competition while potentially inhibiting some forms of competition between the two systems. Decisions on whether to prohibit duality were based on which form of competition was perceived as more important. The Justice Department was aware that duality could reduce promotion and other forms of competition between the dual systems. It decided that the benefits of duality outweighed those of exclusivity.

Many of the predictions made by proponents and opponents of duality in the early 1970s came true. As Visa had foreseen, the banks were driven by cost considerations to set up single back rooms for their card operations. The banks also resisted efforts by the co-opetitives' managements to introduce systems that would require the back rooms to treat MasterCard and Visa transactions differently. On occasion, they also resisted attempts by the co-opetitives to invest in advertising that would shift shares between the brands. As the Justice Department had predicted in its amicus brief in *Worthen*, however, the banks also encouraged the management of the associations to maximize sales of both brands.

MountainWest

As mentioned earlier, Sears launched the Discover Card in 1985. (After the trial in the case discussed in this section, Sears spun off Discover with its Dean Witter subsidiary, which then merged with Morgan Stanley in 1997. Throughout this chapter, we refer to the plaintiff as Sears for simplicity.) The Discover Card soon became both popular and profitable, and it garnered 5.3 percent of all payment card volume five years after its introduction.

In late 1988, Sears sought membership in Visa. Visa refused and then passed a membership rule—bylaw 2.06—that denied Visa membership to any applicant that is issuing, directly or indirectly, Discover Cards or American Express cards, or any other cards deemed competitive by Visa's board of directors. (The parent, subsidiary, affiliate, or issuer were also covered. Visa did not deem Diners Club and Carte Blanche—by then, two tiny T&E-oriented charge card brands both owned by Citibank—competitive.)

In May 1990, Sears purchased an insolvent thrift institution, MountainWest, that had a Visa membership and a small payment card portfolio. Sears was going to use this membership for launching its Prime Option card. Visa found out about these plans after learning that a thrift institution with a few thousand accounts had requested the production of 1.5 million new cards and it prevented Sears from going forward. Sears filed an antitrust lawsuit, and asked the court to force Visa to admit MountainWest as a member and to eliminate bylaw 2.06. While multiple issues were raised at trial, our discussion here focuses on the debate that ensued around issuer and system competition.

Sears argued that its entry would increase competition among issuers. Its business plans showed that it expected that it would have a 5 percent share of credit cards within seven years. Moreover, Sears said that its new card provided an innovative and low-cost offering to cardholders. Visa countered that adding another issuer to an unconcentrated and highly competitive market would not lead to lower prices or significantly higher output; whatever share Sears garnered would come from other card issuers. Visa also alleged that letting the owners of competing card systems become members of Visa would reduce system competition: with Discover as a large member, Visa would not be able to compete as aggressively against it; and with a stake in Visa (and perhaps MasterCard), Discover would not compete as aggressively against Visa. Sears responded that new systems would enter only if they could also issue the co-opetitive cards (and claimed that had been its plan from the start—to be a go-it-alone system with a foot in the co-opetitives).

The jury in *SCFC ILC, Inc. v. Visa U.S.A.* (generally referred to as the *MountainWest* case) found for Sears, and Visa appealed. Both parties sought to frame the appeal in terms of how the antitrust laws should treat memberships in joint ventures (the phrase "joint ventures" is the term both sides used for what we have called associations or co-opetitives). Visa asserted that it should not have to admit Sears, unless Sears could prove that it could not compete successfully without membership. Sears argued that joint ventures should not be allowed to restrict membership or adopt other rules that have the purpose as well as effect of restraining competition unless those rules or restrictions can be proven to be ancillary to a legitimate association purpose.

In September 1994, a federal appeals court decided for Visa under a rule-of-reason analysis. It said that the issue was whether the membership restrictions "increase price, decrease output, or otherwise capitalize on barriers to entry that potential rivals cannot overcome." It found that there was no evidence that preventing Sears from being a Visa issuer would have any of those harmful effects. It also noted that Sears was not excluded from the payment card industry and could issue its new card through Discover. The Supreme Court declined Sears's request for a review.

United States v. Visa

Shortly after the appeals court decision in the *MountainWest* case, the Justice Department began an investigation of the co-opetitives' rules that permitted members to belong to the other co-opetitive, but prohibited members from issuing cards of competing go-it-alone systems. One might expect the Justice Department to have been concerned about the apparent contradiction between these rules: why permit dual membership with one system but not others? Surprisingly, as the inquiry gathered steam the Justice Department complained about *both* duality *and* exclusivity, though historically moving away from one has amounted to moving toward the other. After failing to reach a settlement with the co-opetitives, the Justice Department filed a lawsuit in October 1998.

A trial judge heard the case, United States v. Visa U.S.A. et al., in summer 2000 and issued a decision in October 2001 in which she rejected the Justice Department's claims against duality, but accepted its claims against exclusivity. MasterCard and Visa appealed. The U.S. Court of Appeals for the Second Circuit upheld the lower court's decision in September 2003. The co-opetitives have asked the U.S. Supreme Court to consider a further appeal; the Court, which takes about 1 percent of all requests for review, has not said whether it will consider the case as we go to press.

The Justice Department's case against duality was based on a distinction between duality in governance and in issuance. The government said that it was fine to have banks issuing multiple card brands; in fact, it wanted to encourage that through the elimination of the exclusivity rule. But it said that it was harmful to have banks that issued multiple card brands on the board of directors or other governing committees of the co-opetitives. It argued that overlapping governance had reduced the incentives of the two associations to compete with each other. It offered four examples of this over a period of about a quarter century.

MasterCard and Visa found themselves defending a business practice that by the time of the trial, was almost moribund. The co-opetitives—especially Visa—had decided that member loyalty was important to their effectiveness, and they had entered into agreements with many members to dedicate themselves to their systems. Nevertheless, they argued that the Justice Department had not presented credible evidence that duality had reduced system competition by deterring innovation. For instance, the Justice Department had claimed that MasterCard had delayed the introduction of smart cards in the United States because MasterCard's governing members also belong to Visa, and Visa was not ready to support smart cards. MasterCard and Visa countered that both had studied smart cards and found that there was no business justification for introducing these cards during the period considered by the government. Smart cards were perhaps worth their extra cost in European countries that had unreliable and expensive phone systems, but without a compelling application, or substantially lower costs, they did not make economic sense in the United States, where merchants had reliable and fast connections to the card systems.

The trial judge agreed with MasterCard and Visa on duality. She said the only evidence she found that duality had affected competition involved MasterCard's failure to respond more aggressively to Visa's "It's Everywhere You Want to Be" advertising campaign. But she maintained that there was no evidence that suppression of competition was the result of duality in governance rather than in issuance, and she noted that the decision by the associations to reduce duality made this issue moot.

The Justice Department also contended that exclusivity harmed consumers because it made the go-it-alones weaker system competitors. Exclusivity prevented them from gaining additional scale by issuing cards through banks. Moreover, without bank relationships the go-it-alones could not offer debit cards. The government claimed argued that banks generally benefited from issuing multiple card brands, that banks were uniquely situated to issue payment cards, and that a number of banks had expressed a specific interest in issuing American Express cards. Exclusivity, according to the government, also harmed banks and their consumers by effectively prohibiting bank-issued American Express cards, thus reducing product variety. The government claimed that in other countries without the exclusivity rules, consumers had benefited from additional card options.

MasterCard and Visa countered that the government did not have factual support for these statements. American Express was only a little smaller than MasterCard, and there was no evidence that MasterCard's smaller size at the time kept it from being cost competitive with Visa. MasterCard and Visa also pointed out that American Express itself denied that it was at any significant disadvantage because of scale. The co-opetitives also said that there was no evidence that the go-it-alones wanted to issue debit cards. Furthermore, even if they did want to issue debit cards, banks were unlikely to give the go-it-alones access to their checking account customers, who were the banks' major asset. As for increased variety, MasterCard and Visa observed that the government, unlike Sears in the *Mountain West* case discussed above, had not introduced any evidence that would enable the court to determine whether there would be a significant increase in output, decrease in price, or increase in quality. Most significantly, the co-opetitives argued that American Express was not excluded in any way from the payment card industry; it operated a successful system and was the largest card issuer. MasterCard and Visa also asserted that the output from American Express partnerships with banks in other countries was trivial.

The trial judge sided with the government on exclusivity. She required the co-opetitives to end their rules that prohibited members from issuing cards on behalf of the go-it-alones. She also required them to allow members to rescind their existing loyalty agreements with the associations in order to sign agreements with the go-it-alones, though the associations were free to negotiate new ones. And though debit cards were not explicitly considered in the case, she also required Visa to repeal a rule that prohibited Visa Check issuers from also issuing other debit brands. (MasterCard had no such rule.) This part of the decision brought duality to signature debit. The appeals court upheld the trial judge's decision. Barring a final-second save by the U.S. Supreme Court, the go-it-alones will be able to compete with the co-opetitives for issuers' attention by the time you are reading this.

The trial judge's decision highlights the difficulty that the courts have had with the co-opetitives and their membership rules. The government and the co-opetitives agreed that duality tended to reduce competition between the systems. Their only disagreement was whether this tempering was the result of overlaps in governance or in issuance. The judge recognized that there were some harmful effects from duality—that duality "has led to some blunting of competitive incentives"—but she could not ascribe the effects solely to dual governance rather than dual issuance. Yet the court's solution will force the payment card systems to become more integrated in several ways.

Allowing co-opetitive members to rescind their loyalty agreements to sign up with the go-it-alones reverses the efforts that the associations have made to unwind duality, as does ending nonduality in signature debit. And allowing the go-it-alones to solicit issuers gives those financial institutions that are allied with the go-it-alones incentives to lobby the co-opetitives to temper competition with the go-it-alones. As Visa pointed out at trial, American Express has incentives to form strategic alliances to reduce co-opetitive competition in advertising, merchant discounts, and corporate cards. And as we explained in chapter 8, these were the areas of Visa's competitive activity that American Express Chair Harvey Golub tried to persuade banks were not really in their interest.

A central premise of the government's case looked doubtful within a year after the court's decision. One of the government's key arguments was that it was not possible for the go-it-alones either to persuade banks to switch from the co-opetitives to them or to buy their card portfolios. One of the reasons given was that it would be too difficult for either the banks or American Express to persuade co-opetitive cardholders to switch to cards issued on the American Express system. Near the trial's end, however, American Express announced a deal to buy the ShopRite MasterCard portfolio and two other portfolio deals, with Bank of Hawaii and BSB Bank, before the end of the following year. American Express has since stated that it faced no significant problems in converting those portfolios to American Express cards. Even though American Express is technically the issuer, Bank of Hawaii offers "Bank of Hawaii Credit Cards from American Express" on its Web site.

Who Pays for Plastic?

The debate over who should pay for payment card services is as old as the payment card industry. As we have seen, merchants have complained about the fees they pay to take payment cards since the early days of the industry. Sometimes these complaints led to group boycotts. On other occasions, on which we focus here, these complaints were made to courts or antitrust authorities. Yet even without the urging of merchants, antitrust enforcers are naturally concerned about fees that are established through an agreement among competitors. For that reason the co-opetitives, rather than the go-it-alones, have borne the brunt of the litigation over who pays.

In their defense of the interchange fee and related practices, the co-opetitives have emphasized the two-sided nature of payment systems. They observe that interchange fees help them balance the interests of cardholders and merchants. A lower fee for merchants means higher fees for cardholders; in the case of a highly competitive industry, as in the United States, almost all of the interchange fee revenue received by issuers will get passed on to cardholders. Moreover, the co-opetitives note that interchange fees enable them to compete with the go-it-alone systems. American Express can determine its cardholder and merchant pricing directly, so it can charge merchants more than the co-opetitives without an interchange fee. The co-opetitives—whose members compete for cardholders and merchants—can only influence the relative prices paid by merchants and consumers through the interchange fee. Interchange fees also provide incentives for various systemwide initiatives. Without interchange fee revenue, for instance, banks would not have found it profitable to issue signature debit cards.

The oldest concern about the interchange fee is that competitors should not be allowed to set prices. All the courts and regulators that have looked at this question have recognized that the co-opetitive systems must have an interchange fee. If thousands of acquirers and issuers had to negotiate individually over their obligations and fees, there would be chaos, or at least large transactions costs. So the issue has been whether the co-opetitives can be trusted to set the fee themselves, whether the government should set the fee, or whether the government should impose guidelines on how the co-opetitives set the fee.

And that brings us back to the more recently expressed concern, which we discussed in chapter 5, that the co-opetitives set interchange fees that are too high. Interchange fees encourage banks to issue cards and to give cardholders incentives to use those cards. But as the argument goes, cardholders do not bear the additional cost the merchant pays when they use their cards rather than another method of payment that is less costly for the merchant. Merchants cannot charge cardholders the extra cost that cards impose either because their card system contracts don't permit them to or because it is too hard for them to do so. Merchants accept cards not because they reduce the cost of transactions, so the assertion goes, but in order to take business from other merchants—a zero-sum game with no social benefit. As a result, payment cards displace cheaper payment methods and, since merchants pass their costs on to their customers, cash users end up subsidizing card users. Although these newer concerns are often aimed at the co-opetitives and interchange fees, what matters to the merchant is the merchant discount, so these issues logically apply with equal force to the go-it-alone systems.

The interchange fee controversy is much like the exclusivity debate we just explored. The "right" interchange fee, like the "right" level of exclusivity, is hard to describe in theory and even harder to determine in practice. Both debates reflect trade-offs between worthwhile objectives— from the standpoint of both the businesses involved and society. The question then becomes whether we believe government regulators are more likely than the co-opetitives to make the right trade-off.

Interchange Fees Are Procompetitive: *NaBanco v. Visa*

In a case filed in 1979, National Bancard Corporation (NaBanco) claimed that the interchange fee constituted a price-fixing agreement that violated section 1 of the Sherman Act. NaBanco specialized in signing up merchants and processing card transactions. When it acquired a card transaction from a merchant, NaBanco was obliged by association rules to pay an interchange fee to the card-issuing bank. It noted that this was unlike check clearing; we indicated in chapter 2 that checks are exchanged at par as a result of the efforts of the Federal Reserve.

NaBanco argued that the interchange fee was set by the Visa board acting on behalf of issuing banks and was therefore illegal per se.

NaBanco also contended that collective determination of the interchange fee was illegal under the rule of reason because the interchange fee put banks that specialized in acquiring merchant accounts at an unfair disadvantage compared to banks that both serviced merchants and issued cards. It maintained that integrated issuer-acquirer banks could offer merchants a lower discount since these banks did not have to pay an interchange fee on transactions involving their own cardholders.

Visa did not deny that in a literal sense, interchange fees established a price among members. Nevertheless, it relied on the *Broadcast Music, Inc.* decision, in which the Supreme Court found that even though blanket royalty licenses were literally price-fixing, they were permissible under the rule of reason because of the efficiencies created. Visa argued that following *Broadcast Music*, the collective decision to set the interchange fee should be evaluated under the rule of reason. NaBanco rejected the application of *Broadcast Music* on the grounds that card association members had the practical option of negotiating interchange fees bilaterally.

Visa countered by explaining the role of the interchange fee in terms of what we would now call a two-sided market. It portrayed the association as a joint venture of banks. The joint venture wanted to maximize the use of Visa by both cardholders and merchants. Visa asserted that the purpose of the interchange fee was to provide a "mechanism to distribute and share the costs of the joint venture in relation to prospective benefits, thereby encouraging members to provide the Visa service to a competitively maximum extent on both the cardholder and merchant 'sides' of the business." It also argued that the interchange fee was necessary for the joint venture to offer credit card services. The alternative to having some interchange fee (even zero) would be a chaotic system involving literally thousands of bilateral negotiations among issuing and acquiring banks, with the viability of the system in question. Unlike classic price-fixing, where ending collusion leads to higher output and lower prices, the outcome would probably involve lower output and possibly higher overall prices.

The district court and the U.S. Court of Appeals for the Eleventh Circuit agreed with Visa. The Eleventh Circuit upheld the district court's rule-of-reason approach in the case, explicitly relying on the two-sided nature of the industry:

Another justification for evaluating the [interchange fee] under the rule of reason is because it is a potentially efficiency creating agreement among members of a joint enterprise. There are two possible sources of revenue in the VISA system: the cardholders and the merchants. As a practical matter, the card-issuing and merchant-signing members have a mutually dependent relationship. If the revenue produced by the cardholders is insufficient to cover the card-issuers' costs, the service will be cut back or eliminated. The result would be a decline in card use and a concomitant reduction in merchant-signing banks' revenues. In short, the cardholder cannot use his card unless the merchant accepts it and the merchant cannot accept the card unless the cardholder uses one. Hence, the [interchange fee] accompanies "the coordination of other productive or distributive efforts of the parties" that is "capable of increasing the integration's efficiency and no broader than required for that purpose."

The Eleventh Circuit went on to find that "an abundance of evidence was submitted from which the district court plausibly and logically could conclude that the [interchange fee] on balance is procompetitive because it was necessary to achieve stability and thus ensure the one element vital to the survival of the VISA system—universality of acceptance." The Supreme Court declined to review the Eleventh Circuit's decision.

The Reserve Bank of Australia Demurs

The Reserve Bank of Australia (RBA) reached a different conclusion, in a different, regulatory setting, in a finding issued in 2002. Visa and MasterCard's initial appeal to the Australian courts was heard in June 2003 and rejected in September 2003. MasterCard was further appealing this decision as of this writing, while Visa dropped its own appeal in late 2003. Harkening back to Adam Smith, the RBA viewed Visa's interchange fee as inherently suspect because it is set by a horizontal agreement among competitors: "Co-operative behaviour between competitors which involves the collective setting of prices is rarely permitted in market economies. Prima facie, such behaviour is anti-competitive and, where it is allowed, it typically requires some form of dispensation by competition authorities on the basis that there are offsetting benefits to the public."

The RBA, however, did not appear to consider eliminating interchange fees, recognizing that "interchange fees can play a role in redressing imbalances between the costs and revenues of issuers and acquirers in four party credit card schemes." Instead, it wanted to regulate the interchange fee because it was "not convinced that community welfare would be maximized if the setting of interchange fees . . . were left entirely to the schemes and their members in Australia."

Specifically, the RBA was concerned that Visa's interchange fees were set too high, thereby encouraging the excessive use of credit cards as an alternative to other payment methods. (We looked at this basic argument in chapter 5.) The RBA relied on the findings from theoretical models showing that firms may have private incentives to set interchange fees that are higher than the rate that maximizes the value of card transactions to society as a whole. The models suggested that individual merchants have an incentive to accept Visa cards if they expect to take sufficient incremental sales from other merchants, even if accepting Visa cards would raise the merchant's costs. The RBA then claimed that the private benefits to individual merchants associated with such incremental sales did not constitute a social benefit, as they came at the expense of sales by other merchants.

The RBA proposed to cure this through a regulatory scheme for interchange fees that was based on cost factors. Moreover, it wanted to consider only costs on the issuer side and yet exclude many issuer-side costs from consideration without providing an economic basis for such exclusion. Visa and MasterCard have challenged this decision in court.

In a similar matter, the European Commission, acting on complaints made by associations of retailers, reached a preliminary determination that Visa's interchange fee violated European laws against collective price setting. On further reflection, the European Commission decided there was no feasible alternative to a collectively determined interchange fee, but it was unwilling to leave the determination in the hands of Visa. It reached an agreement with Visa in 2002 requiring Visa to lower its interchange fee and conduct cost studies, which would be reviewed by the European Commission and would form the basis of cost-based benchmarks for the interchange fee. We focus on the RBA investigation rather than the European Commission's because there are more publicly available documents discussing the RBA's approach. Visa has argued that there are at least three fundamental economic problems with the RBA's approach.

First, the RBA failed to demonstrate that interchange fees in fact exceeded the socially optimal level or led to significant consumer harm. The RBA relied on theoretical models that showed the fees *could* be too high. But the same models also indicated that privately set interchange fees *could* be at the socially optimal level—or *could* be too low.

Second, there is no support in economic theory for setting interchange fees based solely on costs. As economist Michael Katz, who was hired by the RBA to study the issue, noted, "There is little reason to believe that it is optimal to set the interchange fee equal to either an issuer's marginal costs of a card transaction or zero." In short, because the socially optimal interchange fee depends in a complex way on both demand and cost factors, regulation based on costs alone will not produce efficient pricing—except by pure chance. The RBA plan would set a benchmark for interchange fees by allocating costs based on functionality, ignoring demand conditions entirely—even though, as Katz explicitly stated, "efficient pricing must be based in part on demand conditions."

A third problem with the RBA's approach is its exemption of proprietary systems, such as American Express and Diners Club, from the proposed regulatory scheme: "American Express and Diners Club, on the other hand, do not have collectively determined interchange fees. Whether they have an internal transfer mechanism or 'implicit' interchange fee is not relevant; the three party card schemes do not have a process under which competitors collectively agree to set a price which then affects, in a uniform way, the prices each of the competitors charges to third parties."

Visa argued that this reflects a lack of understanding of two-sided markets and places the co-opetitives at a disadvantage relative to the go-it-alone systems. If the concern is that merchants pay too much compared to cardholders (and this encourages the overuse of cards), the matter should be of even greater concern to the American Express system. American Express merchant discounts are generally steeper than Visa discounts—by about a third in the United States.

As of late 2003, the preliminary evidence suggested that one immediate effect of the regulation had been to increase cardholder fees and decrease cardholder benefits. One study found that cardholder prices had increased as much as 25 to 50 percent at some banks. And some banks reduced the number of rewards points earned or imposed new caps on the total. Another effect was to make American Express and Diners Club more attractive to issuers since the proprietary systems were not subject to the regulation. For example, ANZ Bank, one of the major issuers that had placed new rewards restrictions on its co-opetitive cards, reached an arrangement with Diners Club whereby ANZ's cardholders could retain their rewards, but only by paying an additional $200 in annual fees for a Diners Club card.

Wal-Mart and the Honor-All-Cards Rule

In a lawsuit filed in the United States in 1996, a large group of retailers claimed that making them take signature debit cards as well as credit cards—a consequence of the honor-all-cards rule in the co-opetitives' contracts with merchants—violated antitrust prohibitions against tying the sale of one product to another. The group of retailers was led by Wal-Mart and included Sears, The Limited, Safeway, Circuit City, the National Retail Federation, the International Mass Retail Association, the Food Marketing Institute, and thirteen other large and small retailers. The group sought to represent all merchants who took MasterCard and Visa cards. A federal court agreed and certified a plaintiff class of about 4 million merchants. (The count of merchants was an estimate and grew over time—an estimated four million were in the class when certified, with over five million estimated to be in the class by the time of settlement.) The plaintiff class in the case, *In re: Visa Check/MasterMoney Antitrust Litigation* (commonly referred to as the *Wal-Mart* case), claimed treble damages of as much as $100 billion. MasterCard and Visa settled on the eve of trial by agreeing to apply their honor-all-cards rules separately to credit cards versus debit cards and paying the retailers about $2.2 to $2.6 billion (this is the present discounted value at the time of the settlement of cash payments that were to be made over ten years). Some merchants, including Best Buy, opted out of the class and have filed their own suits.

Although the case centered on the honor-all-cards rule and was based on the allegation that this rule effects an unlawful tie between debit and credit cards, the retailers' basic concern was that the rule enabled the co-opetitives to charge significantly higher interchange fees for signature debit than the PIN debit systems. The retailers argued that without the rule, the co-opetitives would be forced to lower their interchange fees to the same level as the PIN debit systems. Retailers would therefore pay lower interchange fees when cardholders use their cards with signatures at merchants who have PIN pads as well as at merchants who do not have PIN pads. Our discussion focuses on this critical claim. (As we pointed out in chapter 5, the honor-all-cards rule appears to have been used by all systems throughout the history of the industry. It ensures the cardholder side of the market that their cards will be accepted on the merchant side. Had the case gone to trial, a key issue would have been whether the honor-all-cards rule was an anticompetitive tie or an efficiency-enhancing rule. In August 2001, the European Commission found that the Visa honor-all-cards rule in the European Union was not anticompetitive.)

We saw earlier that U.S. banks, unlike their counterparts in Europe, had little interest in issuing debit cards until the early 1990s. As we described in chapter 8, this changed because the co-opetitives (Visa in particular) and the EFT networks made investments that helped get critical masses of cardholders and merchants to use their platforms for debit cards—the co-opetitives got cardholders on board while the EFT networks got merchants on board. The co-opetitives were able to offer debit card holders access to their base of merchants because of the honor-all-cards rule. Merchants had signed contracts in which they agreed to take all cards with the co-opetitive brand on them.

Wal-Mart and the other merchants in the original lawsuit said that without the honor-all-cards rule, the debit card industry would have evolved as it did except that the co-opetitive interchange fees would have been the same as the PIN debit systems. Under this scenario, the co-opetitive banks would have realized $2.4 billion less in interchange revenue between 1996 and 1998, but they would have nevertheless issued the same number of signature debit cards to their checking account customers. Assuming this scenario, the retailers were able to assert that all merchants who took debit cards were injured by the honor-all-cards rule—so merchants who did not have PIN pads and had customers who used signature debit cards were harmed in the same way as PIN pad merchants—and the amount of damages done by the honor-all-cards rule could be computed as the difference in the interchange fees times the volume of signature debit transactions. This argument was instrumental in persuading the trial court to certify a class of all merchants.

But this argument ignores the business realities of two-sided markets. To establish the debit card platform, the co-opetitives had to be able to get a critical mass of cardholders and merchants on board their systems. At the time, neither banks nor cardholders had any demonstrated demand for the product, and without a base of cardholders, merchants had no reason to take the card. The retailers claimed that the co-opetitives not only would have succeeded in getting both sides on board but would have recruited all the merchants who took debit cards under the honor-all-cards agreement as well as all the cardholders who the banks had recruited at the higher interchange fee, and that those cardholders would have used their cards to the same degree. That is somewhat like saying that one can take a weight off one side of a delicately balanced scale and nothing else will change. Businesses don't experience $2.5 billion losses in revenues without something changing. And in a multisided market, how that recalibration occurs can be quite complex.

Two more plausible scenarios are worth considering. One is that with much lower revenues from signature debit, the co-opetitives and their members would not have invested in signature debit cards when they did, while the EFT systems would have invested as they actually did. (On the one hand, the EFT systems might have had greater potential without competition from signature debit cards; on the other hand, the EFT systems benefited from, as discussed in chapter 8, the increased incentives to install PIN pads due to the growth of signature debit and the interchange differential between signature debit and PIN debit. In addition, the EFT systems were helped by the co-opetitives' efforts to popularize debit cards through advertisements.) Then PIN debit systems would have grown while signature debit systems would have started later and on a smaller scale, if they started at all. Another scenario is that the banks would have imposed fees on debit card holders, or they would have increased the total cost to the cardholder of a checking account to make up for the interchange fee revenues they wouldn't have gotten. It is likely that banks would have issued fewer debit cards since—unlike the actual situation in which they get interchange fee revenues—higher consumer fees would have reduced demand. Many other scenarios are possible, and the evolution of cardholder fees, merchant fees, and debit card volume would depend on the rates at which the two sides of the system would come on board.

Square Pegs and Round Holes

The courts and regulatory authorities have had trouble fitting the square pegs of the payment card industry into the round holes of the competition laws. The co-opetitive organization has stumped them repeatedly. And even when the co-opetitives have prevailed—as they did in *NaBanco* and *MountainWest* in the United States, or in the honor-all-cards investigation before the European Commission—it is only after highly contentious proceedings. The co-opetitives face two problems. The first is the understandable suspicion that courts and authorities have of competitors who make decisions together. The second and very much related problem is a lack of comprehension of how the co-opetitives differ from business organizations with which the courts are more familiar.

Some courts and authorities treat the co-opetitives as if they were merely associations of competing businesses—like the eighteenth-century blacksmith guild that so exercised Adam Smith or the dental associations that have gotten into antitrust hot water in recent years. The difference is that typical guilds or associations are not really essential to their members; they provide some nice services and a professional community, but their members can shoe horses or do root canals without them. The co-opetitives provide a core set of services that are essential for their members to be in the payment system business at all. And while the cost of these services is, as we have seen, low relative to the size of the industry, the co-opetitive cards could not exist without them. Most important, the intense competition that courts have acknowledged in the United States results from the existence of the co-opetitives. Without the co-opetitives, only a few firms would have competed for cardholders and merchants—as was the case for most of the industry's first two decades.

Other courts and authorities want to treat the co-opetitive card systems as if they were like manufacturer-distributor systems (like automobile manufacturers and automobile dealers) or like franchise organizations (like the McDonald's corporation and the McDonald's franchisees). That was particularly apparent in the trial court decision concerning the exclusivity case brought by the Justice Department. For example, the court noted that "member banks provide networks with an effective distribution system," and that without the exclusivity rules, "American Express would be able to utilize the banks' distribution channels." The court accepted the notion that the co-opetitives were suppliers of network services to banks; from that premise, it then made the leap that the banks would benefit from having more suppliers. But as we saw in chapter 7, the co-opetitives are more complex organisms than these analogies indicate. The members are the co-opetitives, and the co-opetitives are the members. That is unlike manufacturers or franchisors, which have an arm's-length relationship with separately owned distributors and franchisees. Unfortunately, ignoring the organic nature of the co-opetitives—and their similarity to partnerships, clubs, and families—leads the courts and authorities to underemphasize the importance of loyalty and shared purpose.

Many courts and authorities have also had difficulty understanding the two-sided aspect of the payment card industry along with its implications for pricing, investment, and other business decisions, and the different capabilities of co-opetitives and go-it-alones to balance the two sides. That is perhaps best seen in the RBA's decision, which missed the point that everything it disliked about interchange fees was equally true for the go-it-alones' merchant discounts. The judge in the retailers' case who ruled on class certification also didn't get the interdependence of pricing and investment on the two sides of the market.

Co-opetition and two-sided markets make issues such as exclusivity and pricing difficult to grapple with for both the businesses involved and the competition authorities and courts who are asked to consider these practices. That is why MasterCard and Visa reached different judgments in the early 1970s on whether they should be exclusive. And that is why the Justice Department, from its *NaBanco* brief in the early 1980s to its tortured analysis in the late 1990s, had such difficulty deciding what position to take on duality. The complexities of pricing are also why different card systems have chosen different pricing strategies. Payment card systems coexist with merchant discounts that range from 34¢ per $100 for PIN debit cards to $2.64 per $100 for American Express.

These complexities make it especially hard for outsiders to second-guess the payment card systems. One can come up with good arguments for why the co-opetitives should have more or less exclusivity, and one can debate about how social welfare might change if interchange fees were higher or lower. But as a practical matter, nobody has enough information to prove they are right in any such debate. Under these conditions, general views about when and how governments should intervene in markets are necessarily an important factor in reaching judgments about the payment card industry. If one believes that government regulators can often wade through economic complexity, as well as remain immune from political pressures such as from card systems or merchant associations, and arrive at better answers than markets, then one might favor allowing regulators to decide on membership rules and interchange fee setting. That is apparently the view of the RBA. If on the other hand, one believes that governments are likely to do better than markets only when there is substantial evidence that markets are not working well and when economic analysis points clearly to a remedy that will make them work better, then one should be cautious about substituting the judgments of regulators for market outcomes in the payment card industry. This is a vibrantly competitive industry, largely because of the co-opetitives, not despite them.

The antitrust wars altered two major co-opetitive rules in 2003. The *Wal-Mart* settlement has altered debit card competition by ending the application of the honor-all-cards rule. The Justice Department lawsuit is poised to eliminate rules that prevented the go-it-alones from having co-opetitive members issue their cards, and it has jeopardized some of the partnership agreements that the co-opetitives used to secure more member loyalty and to distance themselves from each other. The decision in the case would also establish duality in signature debit. These losses for the co-opetitives will alter the landscape in ways we discuss in our next chapter.

12

On the Brink

A strategic inflection point is when the balance of force shifts from the old structure, from the old ways of doing business and the old ways of competing, to the
new. Before the strategic inflection point, the industry simply was more like the
old. After it, it is more like the new. It is a point where the curve has subtly but
profoundly changed, never to change back again.
—Andrew S. Grove, *Only the Paranoid Survive* (1999)

Looking back at the history of payment cards we see two inflection
points where the gradual evolution of the industry was disrupted, where
there was a discontinuity between the past and the future. McNamara's
insight into getting cardholders and merchants on board a single platform seems obvious now. Not then—stores had charge programs and
gave customers cards for decades, but no one had seen either the promise
of a two-sided market platform or how to create one. How people pay
for things was different after 1950 than before. The second discontinuity came with the creation of the co-opetitives in the late 1960s. Born
more of necessity than invention perhaps, the card associations provided
a business model that quickly spread around the world, and at least in
the United States, it resulted in intense competition despite extensive
network and scale economies. Co-opetition shook up the sleepy card
industry of the 1960s, dominated by American Express, and resulted in
the explosive growth of card issuance and acceptance. And it changed
how consumers borrowed money and managed their finances.

Another break in the evolutionary path of the payment card industry
may follow developments in 2003. Or not—it is impossible to observe
an inflection point when you are on it. It often takes years for hindsight

to become sharp enough to reveal that a fundamental change has occurred. Yet consider the events. FDC is trying to compete with Visa for processing its members' transactions and has a competing PIN debit system. An appeals court has agreed that co-opetitive members can also issue cards on behalf of the go-it-alones, and American Express appears ready to pursue deals with several large banks. The debit card business was shaken up by the *Wal-Mart* settlement. The co-opetitives can no longer require merchants to accept debit cards if they want to accept credit cards. With the ink barely dry on this settlement, one can almost hear the tectonic plates of the card industry grinding away. And a host of new technologies and business models seem poised to enter the fray, from the emergence of things like fingerprint verification to making purchases with your mobile phone. We think the card industry is more likely to be transformed than destroyed, but checks seem to be at an increasing risk of going the way of the typewriter.

In a few years, the dust from all these struggles will have settled. Only then will we know whether we're witnessing the end of an era, whether the card industry has merely continued to evolve or has made a quantum leap.

Technologies from the Exotic to the Merely Smart

The forward march of technology has carried the payments industry rapidly along with it. All indications are that the next few years promise more technological progress that will serve to make cashless payment convenient, secure, rapid, and digital than ever before.

The history of the payment card industry is partly the history of technology. Increasingly complex behind-the-scenes technical wizardry has made the transaction process increasingly easy and rapid for consumers. At the same time, it has helped the card systems, banks, and retailers by enhancing efficiency, transaction security, and antifraud efforts, and by increasing the ubiquity of payment cards. But now the payments industry stands on the brink of technology-driven change, and as technology moves rapidly from the exotic to the commonplace, the future of the payments industry is one in which the plastic card may play a very different role—greater in some respects and lesser in others. The technological ferment is perhaps best seen by considering a technology that many of us have seen in one spy thriller or another: fingerprint identification.

Biometrics

When Phillip Patten arrived at the cash register of the West Seattle Thriftway supermarket on May 1, 2002, with his intended purchase—a soy fudge bar—he didn't pull out cash, a checkbook, or a payment card. He paid for the fudge bar with his fingerprint. It was the first day of a new era at the grocery, which became one of the first in the nation to let customers pay by touching their finger to an electronic sensor that scans their fingerprints and links them to their payment card or checking account number.

Store owner Paul Kapioski said the biometric system provided a convenient and secure option for customers to pay for their purchases. Patten was one of several customers who enrolled in the system by scanning his finger, entering his phone number on a keypad, sliding his payment card through a reader, and entering an authorization number (such as his PIN debit number). The system, provided by Indivos, stores the information in its database, which is then accessed to authorize transactions. To complete a purchase once enrolled, Patten needs only to place his finger on the sensor and enter his phone number and authorization number. (Visa ran trials of the Indivos system for about three years in its company cafeteria in San Francisco. Indivos says the system handled more than 12,500 transactions, and the correct payment card account was billed every time.)

Fingerprints aren't the only body part that biometrics may use. Another biometric approach to payment card authorization is based on the unique movements of a cardholder's hand as they sign their receipt. The *New York Times* reported in March 2003 that biometric handwriting recognition "could eventually free shoppers from carrying credit or debit cards," or at the least make stolen cards useless and possibly reduce fraud in several other ways. "Signatures are a biometric. The dance of your hand on the paper is unique to you," said Thomas G. Zimmerman, a computer scientist at the IBM Almaden Research Center in San Jose, California. Legislation that gave electronic signatures legal validity gave signature-verification biometrics a boost, though using the technology as a payment mechanism is still only in the research phase.

Biometric methods are just starting to be used by merchants. Interestingly, at the forefront of adoption are not the technologically savvy national retailers like Wal-Mart but the little stores with many indigent customers who unfortunately pose high risks of fraud. According to the *Los Angeles Times* in 2002,

> You might not peg La Playa Market, a cramped Inglewood bodega with a single checkout lane, as an early adopter of technology. But the store was among the first in the nation to install a groundbreaking and controversial personal-identification system that uses unique physical characteristics such as an individual's fingerprint to identify customers and crack down on check-cashing fraud. Although large supermarket chains and major discount retailers have been slow to introduce the system, mom-and-pop food markets and small urban grocery chains are rushing to biometric technology.

Smart Cards

Smart cards have been around since the mid-1980s, but there has been little demand for their intelligence in the United States. The millions of chip-based cards in circulation overseas have a rudimentary application for which there has been little need in the United States. Each chip carries a PIN, which is not as easy to steal as that on a magnetic stripe card. Merchants abroad avoid having to make a phone call to authorize a purchase by having the customer enter their PIN, which a terminal then checks against that in the chip. Other applications are being developed that make more use of the chip, which itself is getting smarter. In the last four years, chip memory has more than doubled and is predicted to double again within the next year. Plus, prices for smart card chips decreased by 30 percent from 2002 to 2003.

Smart cards have an operating system installed on the chip, similar to those for personal computers, personal digital assistants, and mobile telephones. The power of the card comes from the applications written for its operating system. Many businesses could write these applications— the card systems, banks, merchants, and entrepreneurs with bright ideas, to name a few. There is, however, the usual chicken-and-egg problem that affects two-sided market platforms. Building businesses around new applications makes more sense if more people carry chip-based cards;

card issuers would have more incentives to provide smart cards if there were more interesting applications that made these more expensive cards more valuable to consumers. It appears to have taken a long time for smart cards to spread in the United States, partly because there has been a weak business justification for them—in some sense, they have been a technology in search of a problem—and partly because no one has developed the kind of "killer app" that has ignited other software platforms. Smart cards now appear to have some potential in the United States, although their immediate future is uncertain. Here are some examples of what's happening in 2003.

American Express offered the first general-purpose smart card—the Blue Card—in the United States in 1999. As of today, the card does little more than a traditional card, at least in traditional stores. For Internet applications, though, the Blue Card combined with a PC-compatible smart card reader offers greater security and electronic wallet features for online shopping. When a user inserts their Blue Card into the smart card reader and enters their PIN, an included application allows the user to store personal information, URLs, and Web site log-in information directly on the card's chip. The program then allows the user to access Web sites directly, and enters log-in, purchasing, and shipping information automatically. Around six million Blue Cards were in circulation by spring 2003. This large cadre of cardholders is likely to attract more applications writers.

The Target Visa card, a relationship card, illustrates both the potential that some see in smart cards, as well as the difficulty of finding a successful business care for them. In September 2001, Target started mailing its Visa chip card to individuals that held the Target proprietary card and began installing smart card readers in almost all of its stores. The megaretailer planned to use smart card technology for sophisticated loyalty programs, allowing for personalized rewards that go to the best customers. The card was useful initially for managing customers' accounts through Target's Web site. To make this possible, Target provided free chip card readers to its customers. Electronic coupons were the newest chip-based technology on the card; Target started testing them in early 2003 and expected to roll out the program to all the stores in its chain by the year's end. Consumers went online on their home computers to download the coupons onto their Target Visa card, and Target redeemed the coupons at the point of sale.

By 2003, Target had about nine million smart card holders, representing the lion's share of Visa's twelve million chip cards. Being a major national merchant allowed Target to offer an instant base of stores where consumers could use their smart cards. Despite these advantages, Target announced in March 2004 that it was phasing out its smart card program because of "limited use" of the chip feature.

In some other countries, smart cards are much further along. Master-Card has been particularly active in smart cards, with over 150 million in circulation globally in 2003. In France and Russia, smart cards are already broadly accepted. The single domestic French card system, Cartes Bancaires, has been fully based on smart cards since the late 1980s, primarily to deal with its fraud problems. Russia followed the French model in the early 1990s, also to limit fraud. Asia and South America are not on par with Europe yet, but smart cards are well accepted there for transit systems and pay phones.

Wireless Technology

The ability to transmit card information wirelessly is likely to alter the payments landscape dramatically. A major application of wireless technology, which we discuss below, involves commerce conducted with mobile phones. Another application involves waving cards at the point of sale and thereby reducing transaction costs by saving time. Many people are now familiar with several variants of this technology. Highway tollbooths and subway stations have been outfitted to interact with a wireless device and make a deduction automatically from a prespecified account—often an account tied to a credit or debit card number.

A recent and important variant incorporates this ability into the card itself. "Contactless" smart cards—such as the MasterCard PayPass, which was introduced in December 2002—have both a chip and a radio transmitter embedded in the card. Waving the card at the point of sale results in account information being sent wirelessly to a specially equipped merchant terminal, which then transmits all transaction information to the system involved. Contactless systems are "ideal for traditional cash-only environments where speed is essential, such as quick serve and casual restaurants, gas stations and movie theaters," says MasterCard. In Japan, contactless card developers gained acceptance in a national convenience store chain in late 2002; they are now aiming for all the places that consumers currently use coins, such as parking lots, taxis, and vending machines.

This new technology also provides a good example of how technological change has made entry into payment devices easier. Speedpass is a small black plastic wand that initially just enabled wand holders to pay for gas at Exxon and Mobil gasoline stations. And early in 2003, shoppers could also use Speedpass to buy groceries at three Greater Boston Stop and Shop supermarkets. These Boston shoppers can link Speedpass to their store's membership card and their checking, credit, or debit account, allowing them to both pay with Speedpass and also get the discounts given to customers who carry the store's loyalty cards. In addition, Speedpass allows users to manage their Speedpass account online—viewing lists of their Speedpass purchases and changing which checking, credit, or debit account their Speedpass draws from. Cards are still in the picture, but it doesn't require much imagination to realize that this is a potential way to bypass the card systems.

A2A Payments

An important competitor to payment cards for online payments outside the United States are account-to-account (A2A) transfers. With A2A transactions, money is electronically transferred from the payer's account to the payee's account (somewhat like ACH transactions in the United States). In the United States, payment cards continue to capture virtually all Internet retail volume. A2A transactions have become quite popular in Europe, however, and appear to be moving in that direction in Japan and Canada. For example, A2A payments ("credit transfers") accounted for 33 percent of all noncash payments in Europe in 2000.

A2A transfers offer some benefits over payment cards, especially abroad. They are generally cheaper than credit cards for non-U.S. merchants to accept. For consumers, A2A transfers eliminate the need to finance nonbank, third-party accounts such as PayPal. Plus, outside the United States where customers are more accustomed to paying through debit than credit, A2A transfers provide an additional debit payment option. Nevertheless, they can increase the cost of payments for consumers since overseas banks typically charge the payer a flat fee that ranges from a few cents to about $1.50 for each A2A transfer.

In the United States, only a handful of banks are offering A2A transfer services to their customers. At First Internet Bank of Indiana, for example, about 30 percent of the ten thousand checking account customers use the A2A payment service. The bank's customers use the service 1.5 times a month, on average. A payee may use the service for free, but the payer is assessed a $5 charge per transfer.

E-Commerce, E-Payments, and M-Commerce

Some of the most interesting developments in payment systems are occurring because of two gales of innovation that came from outside the payment card industry: the rise of the Internet, the spread of mobile phones, and the convergence of the two.

First some statistics. Most Americans have access to the Internet from their computers at home or work. The fraction of Americans with Internet access at home has more than doubled from 27 percent in 1999 to 60 percent in 2003, and 36 percent of home Internet users had broadband connections in 2003, up 49 percent from the previous year. Then there are mobile phones. There are about 130 million subscriptions registered in the United States—covering about 60 percent of the adult population. But this is a technology that is very much driven by developments in Asia and Europe with spillover to the States, as we shall see. There are an estimated 1.2 billion mobile phone subscribers in the world. Of particular importance are the phones that can handle substantial streams of data; these are known as 3G, for "third-generation" mobile phone technology. (A somewhat less powerful technology, known as 2.5G, has also been important.) In Japan in particular, access to data services including Internet access has been available on mobile phones since February 1999, when NTT DoCoMo's "i-mode" service debuted. As of May 2003, there were 38 million subscribers to mobile data services in Japan, along with 35 million in Europe.

Every computer, mobile phone, and personal digital assistant that is connected to a communications network—the Internet, the telephone system, or as is increasingly the case, both—provides a platform for making purchases. As Malcolm Williamson, the chair of Visa International, put it in 2000:

Just as we were beginning to understand e-commerce, wireless technology was born. It didn't take long to figure out how the Internet could be delivered over a huge distributed base of cell phones, palm computers, pagers and other devices. So in addition to e-commerce, we had a brand new channel—mobile, or "m-commerce." And the potential number of access points for payment cards jumped from 400 million PCs to something approaching a billion wireless devices that will soon exist in the global marketplace.

E-Commerce

The volume of Internet commerce has grown at an average rate of 22 percent annually over the last three years. During 2002, Americans bought $43 billion worth of retail goods over the Internet, or 1.3 percent of all U.S. retail sales. All signs point toward the further rapid growth of electronic commerce. As we discussed in chapter 5, there are three major kinds of e-commerce transactions: person-to-person (P2P), business-to-consumer (B2C), and business-to-business (B2B). Electronic payments are important for Internet transactions of each sort.

B2C transactions are similar to most card purchases. Customers pay with cards, and merchants have an acquiring relationship that allows them to get reimbursed. This is now routine on the Web. The vast majority of B2C purchases in the United States are paid for with cards.

As transactions move from brick-and-mortar stores to the Web, the importance of cards will increase, and cash and checks will continue to decline. At physical bookstores and newsstands, 45 percent of purchases are made with payment cards, and the rest mainly with cash and checks; at music stores, 48 percent of purchases are made with payment cards. In contrast, almost all book and record purchases at Amazon.com are made with cards.

The main wrinkle in the Web-based use of cards concerns security. Americans have been less wary of their cards being stolen over the Web than people expected when the Web was started. Nevertheless, cardholders, merchants, and systems have taken some precautions. A selling point of American Express's Blue Card was that it was more secure for online transactions because the card could be swiped in a reader attached to a computer, avoiding the need to type in account information (though few people actually use this feature). Another option is password protection for standard payment cards, where Internet merchants prompt cardholders to authorize their card purchase with a unique password. Both Visa and MasterCard have password programs—Verified by Visa and SecureCode, respectively—and both provide incentives for Web merchants to use them. Merchants who prompt Visa cardholders for a password are not liable for fraud-related charge-backs (transactions disputed by the cardholder), for instance, even if the customer never enters the password. As with the American Express special card readers for Blue, however, password protection has thus far garnered relatively few users, although this may change. MasterCard had signed up nearly 2,500 issuers and over 9,000 merchants on a global basis for SecureCode by late 2003.

Similar to B2C transactions, payment cards are also a natural payment medium for online B2B transactions. As we discussed in chapter 5, purchasing cards are used by businesses to buy goods and services from each other in brick-and-mortar environments. Business transactions can involve a lot of "paperwork," such as tax forms, filings on usage of minority- and women-owned businesses, and a company's own accounting reports. For Internet B2B transactions, the combination of electronic transactions with an electronic payment method offers the potential for greater efficiency processing and analyzing this information. The employee clicks a button to buy supplies, and all the forms are routed electronically to the right places. Visa, for example, markets its purchasing card as potentially cutting the order and fulfillment cycle from seven to two days or less, and reducing administrative costs from as much as $103 to as low as $4 on a transaction.

P2P payments amounted to about $725 billion in the United States in 2001. These range from paying the babysitter, to reimbursing a friend for lunch, to sending money to a relative. Most are typically made with cash or sometimes check. We saw earlier that Western Union has made a big business out of wire transfers mainly between the unbanked. P2P exchanges on the Net today are a small subset of P2P payments overall; they mainly involve people selling secondhand items—some collectible, some utilitarian—to each other. We identify this with eBay, which succeeded by developing an exchange model that got both sides on board and has kept them there. Goods and services valued at $15 billion were exchanged on eBay in 2002. Most people who sell on eBay don't directly accept payment cards, and cash and checks are at least as cumbersome for online transactions as they are for mail order. They can also lead to considerable delays in completing a transaction and raise the risks for the parties involved. Other sites had similar issues. The void was quickly filled by a number of businesses that tried to create "Internet currency," as we discuss in the section on e-payments below.

E-Payments

The emergence of the World Wide Web in the 1990s attracted a variety of entrepreneurs and companies aiming to turn the Web into a medium for financial transactions. None, so far, has succeeded as spectacularly as PayPal, now a subsidiary of online auctions giant eBay, which built a global online payments platform from scratch virtually overnight. It grew large by making a virtue of simplicity and taking full advantage of the viral nature of the Internet.

Unlike some new ventures designed for the Web, PayPal did not try to create a new currency for the online environment. Virtually all those companies that did—like Flooz and Beenz—failed. PayPal, on the other hand, merely built an online tool for transferring funds within the existing payments infrastructure of payment cards and checking accounts.

All it takes to set up a PayPal account is your name, an e-mail address, and a credit, debit, or checking account number. Once enrolled, you can send and receive money via the service. Seeded initially by PayPal's promise of $10 for opening an account and $10 for referrals of new accounts, PayPal benefited from viral proliferation. "The service's simplicity and low cost attract people seeking payment," said *Wired* magazine in September 2001. "They persuade payers to open their own accounts, and when these new users want to receive funds, they, too, ask others to get on board."

PayPal's formula succeeded where others had failed. According to *Wired*:

The emoney graveyard was already strewn with headstones when PayPal came along. Services like DigiCash and CyberCash, which launched in the mid- and late '90s with complicated schemes involving encryption-software downloads and electronic certificates, amassed little volume. More recent attempts such as Beenz made it easy to open an account, but their novel currencies—sort of gift certificates, sort of frequent-flier points—proved too hard to get and spend.

PayPal was acquired in October 2002 by eBay for $1.5 billion in stock. According to eBay's March 31, 2003, quarterly report, PayPal had 27.2 million accounts at the end of the first quarter of 2003 and processed 50.5 million payments in the quarter, with a total payment volume of $2.6 billion. This is a pittance when compared to the general-purpose payment card volume of $1.7 trillion in the United States, but it seems sure to grow.

PayPal is both a complement and a competitor to the card systems. It helps increase the use of cards because it provides a convenient way for people to exchange things among themselves using the existing card systems. It is particularly helpful to those individuals and microbusinesses that sell things on eBay, but aren't able to accept payment by card directly. Without PayPal or a similar service, individuals would probably have to rely on their old standby, checks—even though checks from strangers are risky. PayPal is also competition for cards. It makes it easy for people to avoid payment cards altogether by using their checking account. Once PayPal verifies a user's checking account, that user can then fund their PayPal account through the ACH system. Likewise, a user receiving funds over PayPal can withdraw the newly received funds to their checking account through ACH. More important, it is a payment platform used by an increasing number of individuals and businesses. We'll return to it below when we talk about competitive threats to the existing card systems.

M-Commerce

Purchases made with mobile phones will likely increase substantially as more subscribers have mobile phones and as mobile operators offer easier ways of buying more things. The coordination required among the players—banks, mobile operators, and content providers—has proved problematic, however, and the wide-scale introduction of m-commerce systems still seems years off. Asia and Europe have led the way, and the experiences there provide some useful insights.

In Japan, service provider NTT DoCoMo employs an advanced internal billing system that i-mode content providers can utilize to charge subscribers tiny monthly fees for using their services. Because i-mode is offered over a packet-switched data network, it can charge end users based on the amount of data they download, instead of the time they are online (as with a traditional circuit-switched telephone network). Both providers and users of mobile data services benefit from these technically sophisticated billing and payment systems tailored to specific uses; this innovation has undoubtedly contributed to i-mode's rapid adoption. Cards play no role—in effect, DoCoMo is like a shopping mall where you pay once on your way out, with the mall paying the stores in turn.

In Europe, advanced mobile data services have been deployed more slowly. Service providers have realized the significance of mobile payment systems to m-commerce and are now attempting to stimulate the development of payment methods. In 2002, Vodafone, the largest mobile phone operator in the world, introduced a billing system called M-Pay Card that enables customers to pay for data services with a payment card. Users register once and then receive a "personal wallet." Transactions are confirmed by entering a one-time security code sent to a mobile phone via text messaging. By handling the transaction itself, Vodafone retains the relationship with the customer. The cost to the end user for using this billing system is simply the charge for the text message.

Another service offered by Vodafone, M-Pay Bill, allows users to download services like ring tones and games with the charges going directly to their mobile phone bill. No payment cards are involved (unless, of course, customers pay their monthly bill with one). Prepaid customers pay with the credit they have on their prepaid card, while contract customers' charge for the M-Pay bill is listed as part of their monthly mobile phone bill.

Developments in m-commerce continue: mobile operators Vodafone, Telefónica Móviles, Orange, and T-Mobile recently announced the creation of a new m-commerce platform called Simpay to be launched in 2004. Simpay will enable mobile phone users to purchase goods and services across all operator networks, and as with payment cards, will charge retailers a percentage or fixed fee per transaction. The mobile operator handles small purchase billing for items like ring tones and MP3 downloads (typically involving amounts of up to $10) so these charges appear directly on consumers' phone bills. For more expensive purchases, like concert tickets, payment cards are required and charges are billed on the card issuer's statement.

Shaking Up the Marketplace

At a basic level, the payments card marketplace has been fairly stable for a long time. There have been two major types of ecosystems. The go-it-alones, from Diners Club in 1950 to Discover in 1985, look very much alike, as do the MasterCard and Visa co-opetitives. One variety of ecosystem had a short life: the franchise system, which made an appearance in the mid-1960s.

The ground started moving underfoot around 1995. The commercial Web was born with the proliferation of browsers, modems, and Web sites. FDC started the series of mergers and acquisitions that have made it an integrated system, although still apparently a work in progress. As we saw in chapter 8, the EFT networks also started changing, going from a number of regional, member-owned associations to the effectively national STAR system now owned by FDC. Wal-Mart and a number of other retailers filed a lawsuit in 1996 to get the co-opetitives to allow them to accept credit cards without also taking debit cards. The Justice Department filed its lawsuit against duality and exclusivity in 1998. International standards for 3G services were created in 1996, paving the way for the recent introduction of high-bandwidth services in Asia and Europe.

In evolutionary biology, what corresponds to an inflection point is a "punctuated equilibrium"—one in which stability gives way to radical change, typically with one species replacing another. The co-opetitive card ecosystems appear robust, though they are clearly challenged by the changes in their environments. It is too soon to tell whether the EFT networks, FDC, payment systems specifically designed for e-commerce and m-commerce, and a possible American Express hybrid system that combines a go-it-alone approach with a franchise system will become permanent fixtures; whether they will be absorbed into the existing business models; or whether they will go the way of the National Credit Card or Universal Travelcard systems that never made it out of the 1950s.

The Role of Litigation in Reshaping the Marketplace
Several court decisions have altered the business strategies available to the payment card systems. As of this writing, at least some of the partnership agreements that MasterCard and Visa struck with members appear to be in trouble as a result of the lawsuit filed by the Justice Department, although the matter is still being appealed by the co-opetitives. In their attempts to build member loyalty, the co-opetitives will probably now need to go back to the beginning, but with an important twist: American Express and Discover can compete with the co-opetitive hubs for the business of co-opetitive members. This will tend to weaken the co-opetitives for the same reason uncertainty over fidelity weakens any relationship. The members of the co-opetitives have no assurance that their fellow members will remain committed to the venture. That makes each one less willing to commit, especially for long-run investments. The go-it-alones face a less serious problem: their own business isn't up for grabs, but instead, only the additional relationships they obtain with co-opetitive members. Only time will tell how the co-opetitives deal with divided loyalties among their members. It will also be interesting to see whether MasterCard's reorganization as a stock corporation, in which ownership is not automatically linked to issuing and acquiring, leads it to different strategies or results than Visa, which remains a membership corporation.

As a result of the *Wal-Mart* settlement, as noted earlier, MasterCard and Visa can no longer require merchants who want to take credit cards to accept signature debit cards as well. It is interesting that soon after the settlement, MasterCard and Visa both raised their credit card interchange fees, especially for small- and medium-size merchants. Several of the PIN debit networks have also raised their interchange fees recently. Most claim the increases were necessary for issuers to recover their costs and had nothing to do with the *Wal-Mart* settlement. In fact, one EFT network representative stated that PIN debit interchange fees are sure to keep going up, within the constraints of the two-sided market: "We believe it's getting closer to covering costs, but it's not there yet. . . . We try to balance the needs of issuers and acquirers."

The *Wal-Mart* settlement does appear to be the key driver behind some recent issuers' announcements, however. U.S. Bancorp and TCF Bank both announced that they are considering removing PIN debit capabilities from some of their debit cards. While some consumers may lose the service altogether, others may face transaction fees for PIN debit. As of mid-2003, 20 percent of banks had begun to charge a per-transaction fee of some sort for PIN debit, ranging from 25¢ to $1.

The U.S. judicial system sometimes leads to a feeding frenzy of lawsuits against corporate giants. Lawsuit begets lawsuit, each one raising the specter of crippling payouts. In the wake of *Wal-Mart*, ten lawsuits have been filed so far against MasterCard and Visa by individuals seeking damages from the actions the retailers complained about, and several merchants who hadn't joined the *Wal-Mart* class have also sued. These cases illustrate what Judge Richard Posner has called "the cluster-bomb effect." When a major antitrust case is filed against a large enterprise, especially if that company loses or settles the case, it is almost always subjected to a host of follow-on suits, sometimes with devastating effects. In light of *Wal-Mart* and other cases discussed in chapter 11, the co-opetitives increasingly face this risk.

The Go-It-Alone Challenge

The co-opetitives also face greater rivalry from the integrated for-profit systems than ever before. There is the rejuvenated Methuselah of payment systems: the hipper American Express is almost two-thirds the size of MasterCard based on credit and charge volume, and its share of the credit card business has stabilized even as Visa's appears to be contracting. Then there are the EFT systems, many of which were transformed from co-opetitive to franchise-style systems in the last few years and merged to form an EFT giant, STAR. And FDC is a formidable go-it-alone competitor in processing and, with ownership of STAR, seems to have the potential to become a competitive payment system. Of less significance at the moment, but not to be lightly dismissed, is PayPal.

At the same time, the co-opetitives face an increasing risk of new antitrust-related constraints that the others don't. The various divisions of the integrated go-it-alones can enter into arrangements with each other to balance the two sides of the market with no risk of antitrust scrutiny. That would remain true even for a go-it-alone that became dominant because the courts almost always stay out of internal firm affairs. Similarly, franchise-style systems can announce terms to issuers and acquirers with no more worry about antitrust liability than any ordinary business announcing prices. On the other hand, the unintegrated co-opetitives face antitrust risks whenever their members adopt rules or policies because those members are competitors. Several examples from chapter 11 highlight the asymmetry. The RBA concluded that it was anticompetitive for MasterCard (with a 22.7 percent share of cards in Australia, based on the RBA's data) to determine the interchange fee for its members and thus affect merchant discounts; American Express (with a 6.5 percent share of cards in Australia) faces no antitrust scrutiny in directly setting its merchant discount or internal transfers between its issuing and acquiring divisions. The U.S. Court of Appeals for the Second Circuit affirmed that it is anticompetitive for MasterCard (with a 26 percent share of purchase volume in the United States, based on the record in the case) to prohibit its members from also issuing the cards of the go-it-alone systems. On the other hand, American Express (with a 20 percent share of purchase volume in the United States) can enter into an agreement with a member of MasterCard that requires that bank to issue exclusively American Express cards. The FDC-Visa lawsuit will pose a related issue. Can Visa be prohibited from requiring its members to use its authorization and settlement systems, while FDC can insist that the parts of its company that acquire merchants use only its system for processing transactions?

The Formation of New Ecosystems

Four interesting new types of ecosystems seem to be emerging in the payment card world. The first is the return of an extinct type: the franchise system. The government's successful exclusivity case has made it more likely that American Express will develop another franchise system in the United States. American Express plans to enter into contracts with a number of banks that issue co-opetitive cards to have them issue American Express cards as well. The Banco Popular card in Puerto Rico is a potential model. The twist is that unlike normal franchises, it seems that only businesses that have a relationship with a competing system need apply. (This is like McDonald's only giving franchises to entrepreneurs who also maintain a Burger King franchise.) It also appears that American Express is only targeting some major issuers, not aiming to have a large number of franchisees or become an open system.

The second new type is a bit like Frankenstein's monster—an analogy that the co-opetitives may appreciate, but that isn't meant to be pejorative. The keystone in this new ecosystem is FDC. It has been putting all the parts in place. It isn't a full-fledged system yet. But it is getting close, and the interchange system at the center of its lawsuit with Visa demonstrates just how close. According to FDC, it has relationships with both the acquiring bank and the cardholder bank for 17 percent of its transactions. FDC claims it can replace Visa in processing those transactions. Together with its alliance partners, FDC could develop a new payment system—a pure go-it-alone, a franchise system, or a network services company.

The third new type is related to, but somewhat different from FDC. The EFT systems could become full-fledged ecosystems, well-rounded competitors to the existing systems. At the moment, the EFT systems focus on online transactions for the subset of merchants who have PIN pads. Things could go in two interesting directions from there. PIN-based transactions could become more popular as a result of people getting used to them, technological change making the equipment less costly, and the expansion of PIN-based card use for e-commerce and m-commerce. Or the EFT systems could integrate into signature-based services just as the co-opetitives have integrated into PIN-based services. Or of course, both could happen.

The fourth newcomer is not far along in its evolution and could go in many directions: e-based and m-based payment systems. These systems provide a currency for a community of traders on Internet- and mobile phone–based platforms. They could just become extensions of the card systems—almost the case for PayPal now. Or they could build a critical mass of individuals and merchants, and thus give birth to a new card system.

Weakened by litigation and handicapped by antitrust laws, the co-opetitives could find these new types of payment systems formidable rivals. Or these systems could go the way of Beenz and Flooz—two Internet payment systems that some incorrectly predicted would seriously wound plastic cards on the Web. As we said at the start of this discussion, whether we are at an inflection point and will find ourselves with wholly different payment card ecosystems in a few years, or whether the co-opetitives will be able to say, like Mark Twain, that the reports of their death were greatly exaggerated, remains to be seen.

13

And They Don't Take Cash

Cash died today in Winsted and may eventually die everywhere because it simply didn't keep up with the modern world.
—Editorial (following Diners Club experiment in Winsted, Connecticut), *Winsted Evening Citizen* (March 13, 1963)

Everybody has talked about the checkless, cashless society. They said it would be here 10 years from now. We think it's here today.
—John G. McCoy, chair of City National Bank and Trust, Columbus, Ohio (1973)

You can order your groceries, stamps, and the latest DVDs from online supermarkets in many urban areas. It's an exaggeration to say that you can buy just about every retail product from Internet merchants, but it's a smaller one every day. Soon your mobile phone will provide another way to buy a wide range of things, from movie tickets to a Frappuccino. You can't use cash or checks in this rapidly growing virtual world of commerce. If you venture into brick-and-mortar stores, almost all will take payment electronically over one of several networks. Today that mainly involves using a plastic card, but fingerprints, eyeballs, or some other personal identifier may one day substitute for the only function the card itself supplies: associating your purchase with a set of digits that computers can use to move other digits into and out of accounts. And when cards aren't taken—say, for paying your mortgage—it is increasingly possible to have those payments also done electronically.

You could nearly live without checks today, and almost without cash, though you still need cash for P2P exchanges and the odd few places that don't take cards. New technologies are making checks and cash less and less necessary over time. People use smart cards to pay for parking in France, and that is coming to the United States as well. As the Internet becomes even more important, you may find that babysitters are happier getting deposits in their PayPal accounts instead of cash.

As we mentioned earlier, people have been talking about the cashless society being right around the corner for several decades now. The checkless society is a real possibility now. The number of checks written has declined by about 20 percent from 1995 to 2002 in the United States. We know from the experience of other countries that checks aren't necessary; they have persisted in the United States because government intervention and major subsidies made them an attractive system for a long time. The cashless society may be a generation or two away, and even then, it may be that cash continues to be used for some transactions—perhaps mainly between people, or among the poorest segments of society.

The guaranteed data that Visa's Dee Hock described as the emerging core feature of money (see chapter 1) may yet become the coin of the realm, even if the plastic cards that today embody them become less crucial. Even if that takes until the centennial of the payment card industry in 2050, it will be remarkable nonetheless. In the space of a century, virtual money (bits of information that exist only on computer media and travel the world at the speed of light) would have supplanted physical money (coins, paper, and checks) after a 2,500-plus year reign.

That virtual money is even a contender for the throne is a testament to the suppleness of competitive markets in handling complex coordination problems through the development of novel business organizations and arrangements. McNamara figured out how to establish a profitable two-sided market platform for coordinating merchants and cardholders. He found the right pricing structure for getting both sides on board. Many have fine-tuned his business model in the last fifty years; no one has discovered anything fundamentally better. Many others realized that banks needed co-opetition to obtain the critical mass of cardholders and merchants necessary to succeed in this new payments business—and to work around the web of federal and state regulations that kept banks small and local. But the founders of what became

MasterCard and Visa perfected the mixtures of cooperation and competition. They created organizations—most important, a set of rules that determine relationships among members and allocate voting rights—that turned out to be robust and scalable. These organizations are the keystones for a global payment card industry that connects people, merchants, and banks worldwide. Explosive industry growth in the United States followed the creation of the bank co-opetitives and the introduction of a product that Americans devoured—a card providing immediate access to revolving credit.

Over time, entrepreneurs have discovered that they can integrate other products and services into payment cards, thereby making these cards more valuable for consumers and merchants. Combining payment and lending services on the same card was by far the most significant innovation along these lines. It gave consumers a new ability to take out instant loans to make purchases, helped the many merchants who lacked the size or sophistication to extend consumers credit by themselves efficiently, and provided banks with a convenient method for lending money to an ever expanding set of households and small businesses. Combining cash withdrawal and payment services on the same card was another critical innovation, and it has underpinned the popularity of PIN debit cards. As payment cards become smarter—as more cards have chips, and as those chips pack more speed and memory—they will have more features built in. At the other end of the technology spectrum, biometric identification systems may make cards unnecessary for many transactions.

Whether you think of payment cards as pieces of plastic, small computer platforms, or just sequences of numbers in banks' computers, they truly are much more than money. And because payment cards open up so many more possibilities than cash or checks, it is by no means implausible that the $20 bill will go the way of wampum before the middle of this century. That doesn't mean that fifty years from now people will be carrying plastic or that any of the businesses that are now synonymous with payment cards will matter much. At any time discontinuous change may occur. A gale of innovation may sweep away firms and industry structures that now seem invulnerable. Or a wave of litigation may do the same.

The first few years of this decade suggest that the rest will be filled with turmoil and change in the payment card industry. Maybe we will soon see the first signs of a discontinuity, or maybe not. But whatever happens in the next few years, the history of the payment card industry makes it almost certain that the next few decades will be at least as full of discontinuities as the last few have been. And both consumers and merchants will benefit—likely in ways we can't even imagine now.

Sources and Notes

We have prepared notes and source cites for each chapter, as well as a selected bibliography. We start by making some general comments on definitions and conventions used in the book. All dollar figures are adjusted (using the GDP implicit price deflator) to reflect purchasing power in 2002. While this practice may seem unusual to noneconomists, it is a useful way of comparing dollar figures from different time periods and putting them in context for the reader, at least as of the early 2000s. We place occasional reminders about this convention throughout the book.

One of our main sources was *The Nilson Report*, a commonly used industry newsletter that includes payment card statistics. In addition, we relied on several other books, surveys, and press articles on card ownership usage throughout this book, including David S. Evans and Richard L. Schmalensee, *The Economics of the Payment Card Industry* (1993); the Federal Reserve Board, *Survey of Consumer Finances* (various years); Paul Chutkow, *Visa: The Power of an Idea* (2001); Joseph Nocera, *A Piece of the Action: How the Middle Class Joined the Money Class* (1994); and various press articles from *American Banker* and *Credit Card Management*, among others.

Chapter 1

For a good introduction to developments in payment devices, see Martin Mayer, *The Bankers: The Next Generation* (1998), which quotes Visa's founder Dee Hock extensively. A discussion of prepaid cards can be found in Lavonne Kuykendall, "Users and Uses of Payroll Cards Proliferate," *American Banker* (July 24, 2002).

For the statistics reported in this chapter, we rely primarily on two sources. Current payment card usage and acceptance is documented in *The Nilson Report* (various 2003 issues). The U.S. Bureau of the Census, *Current Population Survey* (various years) provides data for the number of households and household income.

The economic literature on two-sided markets includes David S. Evans, "The Antitrust Economics of Multi-Sided Platform Markets," *Yale Journal on*

Regulation (2003); David S. Evans, "Some Empirical Aspects of Multi-Sided Platform Industries," *Review of Network Economics* (2003); Jean-Charles Rochet and Jean Tirole, "Platform Competition in Two-Sided Markets," *Journal of the European Economic Association* (2003); and Bernard Caillaud and Bruno Jullien, "Chicken and Egg: Competition among Intermediation Service Providers," *RAND Journal of Economics* (2003).

Global payment card ownership, usage, and acceptance can be found in *The Nilson Report*, no. 786 (April 2003). Other sources for international information include Peter Lucas, "How the Rest of the World Does Web Payments," *Credit Card Management* (April 2003); Ronald J. Mann, "Credit Cards and Debit Cards in the United States and Japan," *Monetary and Economic Studies* (2002); Lafferty's *Cards Europe* (2001), and *Cards Asia-Pacific* (2001); and Visa International. The Web sites of JCB, MasterCard International, Visa International, Cartes Bancaires, American Express, and Diners Club are also good sources of worldwide payment card information. The origins of coins, checks, and paper money are documented in Glyn Davies, *A History of Money: From Ancient Times to the Present Day* (2002). Sources used for information on the EFT networks include Faulkner and Gray, *Debit Card Directory* (various years); and *The Nilson Report*, no. 785 (April 2003). Recent data on individual general-purpose card issuers is available in *The Nilson Report*, no. 780 (January 2003); and *The Nilson Report*, no. 784 (March 2003). Recent data on acquirers for general-purpose cards is available in *The Nilson Report*, no. 783 (March 2003). Store card ownership and usage can be found in *The Nilson Report*, no. 790 (June 2003).

Although the origin of the term "co-opetition" is unclear—some attribute it to Novell's founder, Ray Noorda—its widespread use began with the publishing of Adam M. Brandenburger and Barry J. Nalebuff, *Co-opetition* (1996).

Since 1990, the Federal Reserve has published a survey every six months of credit card terms offered by financial institutions. The *Survey of Credit Card Plans* is available at <http://www.federalreserve.gov/pubs/shop/tablwb.pdf>. Information on individual payment card plans is also readily available over the Internet at individual issuers' Web sites.

For more on the history of American Express, see John Friedman and John Meehan, *House of Cards: Inside the Troubled Empire of American Express* (1992); and Peter Z. Grossman, *American Express: The Unofficial History of the People Who Built the Great Financial Empire* (1987). The press release for the U.S. launch of American Express's smart card, Blue, is available at <http://home3.americanexpress.com/corp/latestnews/blue.asp>.

A selection of other key sources used for this chapter include "Charge It, Please," *Time* (April 9, 1951); "Dining on the Cuff," *Newsweek* (January 29, 1951); Robert A. Bennet, "Toughing It out at Dean Witter," *New York Times* (October 5, 1986); Timothy Wolters, " 'Carry Your Credit in Your Pocket': The Early History of the Credit Card at Bank of America and Chase Manhattan," *Enterprise and Society* (2000); Stephen Holden, "What's That You Say Now, Mrs. Robinson?" *New York Times* (February 9, 1997); Jan Jaben Eilon, "Smart

Cards Make Their Move," *Bank Technology News* (February 2002); Steve Swartz, "American Express to Raise Fees on Green and Gold Cards," *Wall Street Journal* (November 4, 1988); Steve Weiner, "The Rise of Discover," *Forbes* (May 4, 1987); Lavonne Kuykendall, "MC Overtakes Visa in Some Market Metrics," *American Banker* (December 20, 2002); David Breitkopf, "B of A: Early Debit Effort Made Us No. 1," *American Banker* (April 11, 2002); U.S. Bureau of the Census, *Statistical Abstract of the United States: 2000* (2000); 1987 issues of *The Nilson Report*; Citigroup, *Annual Report* (2002); MBNA Corporation, *Annual Report* (2002); First Data Corporation, *Annual Report* (2002); and information provided by Visa U.S.A.

Chapter 2

See Antoine-Augustin Cournot, *Researches into the Mathematical Principles of the Theory of Wealth* (1986) for a discussion of the nature of currency. The history of early mediums of exchange and barter is described in Milton Friedman, *Money Mischief: Episodes in Monetary History* (1994); John Kenneth Galbraith, *Money: Whence It Came, Where It Went* (2001); Jack Weatherford, *The History of Money* (1997); B. Eichengreen and M. Flandreau, eds., *The Gold Standard in Theory and History* (1997); and Glyn Davies, *A History of Money: From Ancient Times to the Present Day* (2002). The revolution resulting in the use of paper bills for exchange is summed up in Weatherford, *The History of Money*; and Davies, *A History of Money*. The progression toward the advent of paper money is discussed in Galbraith, *Money*; and Davies, *A History of Money*. The latest developments in payment means are addressed in "Dining on the Cuff," *Newsweek* (January 29, 1951); Andrew K. Rose, "One Money, One Market: The Effect of Common Currencies on Trade," *Economic Policy* (2000); and Paul Chutkow, *Visa: The Power of an Idea* (2001). The origins of banking panics in the United States is discussed in C. Calomiris, *U.S. Bank Deregulation in Historical Perspective* (2000). A comparison of payment instruments, including payment cards, is provided in Daniel D. Garcia Swartz, Robert W. Hahn, and Anne Layne-Farrar, "The Economics of a Cashless Society: Some New Evidence on the Costs and Benefits of Payment Instruments," AEI-Brookings working paper (2003). Data on the use of various payment methods in 2000 are available in Visa U.S.A., *International Country Overviews* (2001); and *The Nilson Report*, no. 753 (December 2001). We have reported data on shares of different payment methods as a proportion of "consumer expenditures," which we have estimated by subtracting consumption items that involve implicit payments (such as the rent you pay yourself on your own home) from total personal consumption expenditures as reported by the government. We have reported data as consistently as possible, although there are slight discrepancies among different data sources, primarily because data are not centrally collected on cash and check payments for consumer expenditures.

The history of banking in the United States is based on Jonathan Hughes and Louis P. Cain, *American Economic History* (1998); Joao Cabral dos Santos,

"Glass-Steagall and the Regulatory Dialectic: Economic Commentary," *Federal Reserve Bank of Cleveland* (1996); and Harry D. Hutchinson, *Money, Banking, and the United States Economy* (1988). Historical banking legislation pertaining to geographic expansion can be found at Federal Deposit Insurance Corporation, *Important Banking Legislation* <http://www.fdic.gov/regulations/laws/important/>. Statistics on the number of banks in the United States can be found in U.S. Bureau of the Census, *Historical Statistics of the United States: Colonial Times to 1970* (1975); Federal Deposit Insurance Corporation, *Historical Statistics on Banking*; and Credit Union Administration, *Annual Report* (various years). Data on the number of banks in the leading industrialized countries can be found in Bank for International Settlements, *Statistics on Payment and Settlement Systems in Selected Countries* (April 2003).

The history of the U.S. monetary system is described in Milton Friedman and Anna Jacobson Schwartz, *A Monetary History of the United States, 1867–1960* (1993); Friedman, *Money Mischief*; Hughes and Cain, *American Economic History*; and Jason Goodwin, *Greenback: The Almighty Dollar and the Invention of America* (2003). Information on the establishment of the Federal Reserve System is available on the Federal Reserve Board Web site, <http://www.federalreserve.gov/GeneralInfo/fract/sect02.htm>.

Statistics on the use of checks as a payment instrument in the United States and other countries can be found in *The Nilson Report*, no. 761 (April 2002); and Bank for International Settlements, *Payment and Settlement Systems* (April 2003). *Retail Payments Research Project* published by the Federal Reserve Board is a more reliable source on check usage generally, but we have relied on estimates from *The Nilson Report* in some cases to permit comparisons across time, which the Fed data do not permit. Statistics on the use of checks in U.S. supermarkets and grocery stores were calculated based on the *Visa Payment Systems Panel Study*. The history of check clearing is available in James Cannon, *Clearing-Houses: Their History, Methods, and Administration* (1908); Walter Spahr, *The Clearing and Collection of Checks* (1926); Leonard Watkins, *Bankers' Balances: A Study of the Effects of the Federal Reserve System of Banking Relationships* (1929); and William Baxter, "Bank Interchange of Transactional Paper: Legal and Economic Perspectives," *Journal of Law and Economics* (1983). Discussions of nonpar banks are available in Melvin C. Miller, *The Par Check Collection and Absorption of Exchange Controversies* (1949); Paul Jessup, *The Theory and Practice of Nonpar Banking* (1967); and Ed Stevens, "Non-Par Banking: Competition and Monopoly in Markets for Payment Services," *Federal Reserve Bank of Cleveland Working Paper* (1998). A discussion of the Giro system is provided in David B. Humphrey, "The Evolution of Payments in Europe, Japan, and the United States: Lessons for Emerging Market Economies," *World Bank Policy Research Working Paper* (1996).

Statistics on the substitution of other payment methods for checks, including the debit card and ACH, can be found in Bank for International Settlements, *Statistics on Payment Systems in Eleven Developed Countries: Figures for 1990* (1991); *The Nilson Report*, no. 759 (March 2002); *The Nilson Report*, no. 760

(March 2002); *The Nilson Report*, no. 761 (April 2002); and Bank for International Settlements, *Payment and Settlement Systems* (April 2003).

We draw our discussion of lending and interest rates from Sidney Homer and Richard Sylla, *A History of Interest Rates* (1996); and Weatherford, *The History of Money*. The Conference of State Bank Supervisors, *A Profile of State-Chartered Banking* (1988, 2002) contains information on interest rate caps.

Lendol Calder, *Financing the American Dream: A Cultural History of Consumer Credit* (1999) provides a comprehensive overview of the origination and development of installment credit, and attitudes toward borrowing. Data on the growth of consumer credit overtime can be found on the Board of Governors of the Federal Reserve System's Web site <http://www.federalreserve.gov/releases/>. Other sources on the evolution of credit include Joseph Nocera, *A Piece of the Action: How the Middle Class Joined the Money Class* (1994); and numerous press articles.

Chapter 3

The quote at the beginning of the chapter comes from Edward Bellamy, *Looking Backward: 2000–1887* (1888). Many credit Bellamy's novel for conceiving of the term "credit card" long before credit cards were invented.

We relied on several books and articles about the history of the payment card industry and consumer credit throughout this chapter. These include Lewis Mandell, *The Credit Card Industry: A History* (1990); Gavin Spofford and Robert H. Grant, *A History of Bank Credit Cards* (1975); Joseph Nocera, *A Piece of the Action: How the Middle Class Joined the Money Class* (1994); Lendol Calder, *Financing the American Dream: A Cultural History of Consumer Credit* (1999); and David S. Evans, "More Than Money: The Development of a Competitive Electronic Payments Industry in the United States," *Payment Card Economics Review* (2004). American Express's payment card history is documented in John Friedman and John Meehan, *House of Cards: Inside the Troubled Empire of American Express* (1992); and Peter Z. Grossman, *American Express: The Unofficial History of the People Who Built the Great Financial Empire* (1987). For a good account of Visa's technological history, see Paul Chutkow, *Visa: The Power of an Idea* (2001). A detailed account of the early history of credit at Sears can be found in Boris Emmet and John E. Jeuck, *Catalogues and Counters: A History of Sears, Roebuck and Company* (1950).

In addition to these history books, the launch of Diners Club and its early history were pieced together through various press accounts, including "Charge It, Please," *Time* (April 9, 1951); "Credit Card for Diners," *New York Times* (March 30, 1950); Charles Grutzner, "Living High without Money," *New York Times* (December 2, 1956); and Dave Jones, "Credit Card Climb," *Wall Street Journal* (February 21, 1958).

The early histories of Diners Club, American Express, and various short-lived payment card programs are documented in "On-the-Cuff Travel Speeds Up," *Business Week* (August 16, 1958); "National Credit Card, Inc. Files a

Bankruptcy Petition," *Wall Street Journal* (March 24, 1954); "Charge Everything," *Newsweek* (January 3, 1955); "Esquire Club Buys Signet Club," *Wall Street Journal* (March 4, 1957); "American Express Gets Gourmet Guest Club's Credit Card Members," *Wall Street Journal* (June 26, 1958); "Hotel Group Expands Own Credit System, Declares War on Other Charge-It Outfits," *Business Week* (October 20, 1954); Charles Grutzner, "American Express Newest Competitor in Booming Credit Card Field," *New York Times* (August 10, 1958); "Credit Card System: Child of the Century," *New York Times* (June 1, 1977); "American Express Finds New Ways to Make Money," *Business Week* (November 26, 1960); "That's about It. . . . Is Cash Obsolete All Over?" *Newsweek* (July 28, 1958); "Tougher Going for Credit Cards," *Business Week* (September 10, 1960); Edwin McDowell, "How Seymour Flug Wants to Remake Diners Club," *New York Times* (January 27, 1980); "Make-Up Artist," *Forbes* (September 15, 1968); and "Shuffling Cards at Diners' Club," *Business Week* (December 27, 1969).

The individual Bank of America branches in California in 1958 are listed in *Polk's Bank Directory* (1958). Additional historical information on Bank of America can be found in Timothy Wolters, " 'Carry Your Credit in Your Pocket': The Early History of the Credit Card at Bank of America and Chase Manhattan," *Enterprise and Society* (2000); National BankAmericard, *Annual Report* (1973); and "Bank of America Plans Nationwide Licensing of Its Credit Cards," *Wall Street Journal* (May 25, 1966). The early history of Carte Blanche and Citigroup's card program is documented in "Hilton, Diner's Club Draft a Stock Deal to Allow Hotel Chain to Control Latter," *New York Times* (September 17, 1958); "Credit Card Revolt: More Restaurants Drop National Firms, Set Up Own Charge Systems," *Wall Street Journal* (June 11, 1959); "Bill Dodgers," *Newsweek* (February 22, 1963); Alexander R. Hammer, "Hilton Credit Will Show Deficit of about 4 Million for Fiscal '61," *New York Times* (April 19, 1961); Edward Cowan, "Citicorp Clear in Bid to Rebuy Carte Blanche," *New York Times* (April 1, 1978); and "First National City Bank to Drop Everything Card," *New York Times* (November 7, 1968).

Information in "The Birth of Co-opetition" section was drawn from the payment card history books noted above and various press accounts, including "Carte Blanche Offering Its Credit Card System to Banks on Franchise," *Wall Street Journal* (July 7, 1966); "American Express, Like Rivals, Will Offer Franchises to Banks for Its Credit Cards," *Wall Street Journal* (July 15, 1966); "Card Franchises Offered by Four Major Firms," *Burroughs Clearing House* (September 1966); "Uni-Serv Plans to License Its Card for Nation's Banks," *New York Times* (July 11, 1968); H. Erich Heinemann, "Charter Revisions Weighed by Banks," *New York Times* (June 21, 1968); "Chase Buying Back Uni-Card," *New York Times* (December 19, 1968); Robert D. Hershey Jr., "BankAmericard to Chase: Operating Net Is off 3.3%," *New York Times* (January 20, 1972); "The Santa Claus That Makes You Pay," *Business Week* (December 20, 1969); "Stores Honor Many Banks' Cards under Midwest Plan," *Wall Street Journal* (January 17, 1967); "Michigan Banks Launch Credit Card Cooperative," *Burroughs*

Clearing House (January 1966); "Bank Credit Cards: Implications for the Future," *Bankers Monthly Magazine* (January 15, 1967); "Cards Won't Replace Currency—Yet," *New York Times* (July 28, 1968); "New Credit Card Plan Set to Start March 1 in at Least 7 States," *Wall Street Journal* (February 8, 1968); "Bankers Reshuffle Their Credit Cards," *Business Week* (December 7, 1968); "The Credit Card's Painful Coming-of-Age," *Fortune* (October 1971); Arnold H. Lozowick, "Compatible Bank Credit Cards (Second in a Series)," *Bankers Monthly Magazine* (October 15, 1967); and "Many Banks Asking to Join 2 Big Credit Card Systems," *New York Times* (December 8, 1976).

Other than the articles and books already mentioned, the information in the "Regulation and Stagflation" section relied on some additional sources, including "American Express: Why Everybody Wants a Piece of Its Business," *Business Week* (December 19, 1977); Christopher C. DeMuth, "The Case against Credit Card Interest Rate Regulation," *Yale Journal on Regulation* (1986); Conference of State Bank Supervisors, *A Profile of State-Chartered Banking* (1988, 2002); *Marquette v. First of Omaha* (1978); Jeff Gerth, "Law Freeing Banks near in Delaware," *New York Times* (February 4, 1981); Al Neuharth, "Delaware; Mighty Midget: Haven for Banks, Corporations," *USA Today* (August 10, 1987); Robert A. Bennett, "Citibank Sets $15 Fee on Its 2 Credit Cards; Loans to Cost 19.8%," *New York Times* (December 18, 1980); "BankAmerica and Citicorp: The New Banking Forces New Strategies," *Business Week* (July 13, 1981); Thomas P. Fitch, "The New World of Credit; Is This a Route to Interstate Banking?" *U.S. Banker* (March 1985); Michael Weinstein, "Chase's Consumer Banking Chief Views Role of Smooth Operations," *American Banker* (June 3, 1985); "Credit Card Banking," *Bankers Monthly Magazine* (November 15, 1966); Phillip Brooke, "Banks Reappraise Cards as Losses Mount," *American Banker* (May 18, 1971); and James R. Hambelton, "Size No Sure Road to Success in Card Field, Large Banks Learn," *American Banker* (July 21, 1966).

Additional sources used for "The 1980s' Spending and Debt Spree" section include Mark Furletti, "An Overview and History of Credit Reporting," Federal Reserve Bank of Philadelphia Payment Cards Center discussion paper (June 2002); "Citibank Sets $15 Fee on Its 2 Credit Cards; Loans to Cost 19.8%," *New York Times* (December 18, 1980); "Creditors Tighten Their Terms," *New York Times* (March 27, 1980); James E. Ellis, "Mighty Sears Tests Its Clout in Credit Cards," *Business Week* (September 2, 1985); Jeff Bailey, "Plastic Pitfall: Sears Is Discovering Discover Credit Card Isn't Hitting Pay Dirt," *Wall Street Journal* (February 10, 1987); Janice Castro, "Charge of the Plastic Brigade," *Time* (March 23, 1987); Leah Nathans Spiro, "Behind the Bombshell from Amex," *Business Week* (October 21, 1991); Steven Lipin, "Net Falls 93% at American Express Co.," *Wall Street Journal* (October 25, 1991); James J. Daly, "AmEx's Improving Progress Report," *Credit Card Management* (May 1995); Peter Pae, "Optima Backfires on American Express," *Wall Street Journal* (October 3, 1991); W. A. Lee, "GM + Chase a Minus for Household," *American Banker* (May 16, 2003); Lisa Fickenscher, "Citicorp Exec Returns with $14B AT&T Portfolio," *American Banker* (April 3, 1998); "On a Plastic Canvas,"

ABA Banking Journal (September 1989); Laura Gross, "Citibank Joins American Airlines in Affinity Credit Card Program," *American Banker* (April 13, 1987); and U.S. Bureau of the Census, *Statistical Abstract of the United States* (various years).

Additional sources used for "The 1990s and the Rise of the Debit Card" section include Ronald J. Mann, "Credit Cards and Debit Cards in the United States and Japan," *Monetary and Economic Studies* (2002); Bank for International Settlements, *Statistics on Payment and Settlement Systems in Selected Countries* (1993); John P. Caskey and Gordon H. Sellon Jr., "Is the Debit Card Revolution Finally Here?" *Federal Reserve Bank of Kansas City Economic Review* (1994); James J. McAndrews, "The Evolution of Shared ATM Networks," *Federal Reserve Bank of Philadelphia Business Review* (1991); Susan Pulliam, Paul Beckett, and Carrick Mollenkamp, "Bank Regulators Examine 'Securitizations' in Wake of Enron's Accounting Debacle," *Wall Street Journal* (February 14, 2002); "Bank of America Deal Seen Spurring More Bank Mergers," *Reuters News* (October 27, 2003); William Plasencia, "Chase and Chemical Building a Force to Be Reckoned With," *American Banker* (January 31, 1996); Antoinette Coulton, "As Big Issuers Plan Mergers, Card Portfolios a Hot Item," *American Banker* (April 15, 1998); Lisa Fickenscher, "Citicorp Exec Returns with $14B AT&T Portfolio," *American Banker* (April 3, 1998); Miriam Kreinin Souccar, "Bank Card Portfolio Sales Rebound with Two Deals," *American Banker* (October 18, 1999); Jennifer Kingson Bloom and Lisa Fickenscher, "Visa Rewarding Banks for Snubbing MasterCard," *American Banker* (September 7, 1999); and Peter Lucas, "How the Rest of the World Does Web Payments," *Credit Card Management* (April 2003).

A selection of other sources used throughout this chapter include American Express, *Annual Report* (various years); Board of Governors of the Federal Reserve System, *Survey of Consumer Finances* (various years); *The Nilson Report* (various years); National Bureau of Economic Research, *U.S. Business Cycle Expansions and Contractions*; U.S. Department of Labor, Bureau of Labor Statistics; MasterCard International Web site; and information provided by Visa U.S.A.

Chapter 4

The quotes at the beginning of the chapter come from Irving Bachellar, *Charge It!* (1912), cited in Lendol Calder, *Financing the American Dream: A Cultural History of Consumer Credit* (1999); and Paul Chutkow, *Visa: The Power of an Idea* (2001).

Throughout this chapter, we used data obtained from the *Survey of Consumer Finances (SCF)* available on the Board of the Federal Reserve System's Web site. The Federal Reserve Board has conducted the *SCF* since the end of World War II. The *SCF* is a highly regarded and often-cited source of information on the saving, spending, and financing habits of U.S. households. The *SCF* started including detailed questions on credit card use in 1970; the last *SCF* for which data were available for our research was conducted in 2001. The *SCF*'s chief strength is that it provides data on the use of payment cards from a representative sample of households, along with extensive detail on those households. Its main weakness is one shared by all surveys: people give survey takers information that is not always reliable. For instance, and not surprisingly, people tend to understate the amount of debt they have. As a result, the *SCF* is not the best source of data on the total credit card debt of the U.S. public; Visa and MasterCard have more reliable information. There are inconsistencies between the numbers reported in this chapter and those in other chapters on, for example, the average charge volume per household, but the *SCF* is the best source available for making comparisons among different segments of the population. Ana M. Aizcorbe, Arthur B. Kennickell, and Kevin B. Moore, "Recent Changes in U.S. Family Finances: Evidence from the 1998 and 2001 Survey of Consumer Finances," *Federal Reserve Bulletin* (2003) summarizes certain conclusions that can be drawn from the most recent *SCF* data.

"The Growth and Diffusion of Payment Cards among U.S. Households" section is based on the *SCF* data and the following press articles: Gerald Walker, "Life a la Carte," *New York Times* (November 8, 1959); Richard Rutter, "Personal Finance: The Era of the Credit Card," *New York Times* (February 8, 1965); "Here Come the Bank Cards!" *Forbes* (February 15, 1969); and "Whoopee on the Calf," *National Affairs* (October 19, 1959). The discussion of prepaid cards at the end of this section is documented in Cathy Bowen, "Welfare Agencies Seek Aid from Smart Cards," *Card Technology* (October 1, 2002); and Lavonne Kuykendall, "Users and Uses of Payroll Cards Proliferate," *American Banker Online* (July 24, 2002).

The discussion in "Time Savings in Completing Transactions" is based on data from Idaho Credit Union League, *Give Members Convenience of Debit Cards*, press release (September 1999); and *The Nilson Report*, no. 761 (April 2002).

The increase in available credit is documented in *The Nilson Report* (various 1970–2002 issues); and data provided by Visa U.S.A. The section on "The Growth and Democratization of Credit" is based on the *SCF* data; and the data on consumer credit available on the Board of the Federal Reserve System's Web site.

The discussion of human borrowing behavior is provided in Drazen Prelec and George Loewenstein, "The Red and the Black: Mental Accounting of Savings and Debt," *Marketing Science* (1998); Lawrence M. Ausubel, "Credit Card Defaults, Credit Card Profiles, and Bankruptcy," *American Bankruptcy Law Journal* (1997); George-Marios Angeletos et al., "The Hyperbolic Consumption Model: Calibration, Simulation, and Empirical Evaluation," *Journal of Economic Perspectives* (2001); and Shane Frederick, George Loewenstein, and Ted O'Donoghue, "Time Discounting and Time Preference: A Critical Review," *Journal of Economic Literature* (2002).

The problem of debt accumulation explored in "Goes a Sorrowing" is based on Ausubel, "Credit Card Defaults"; Calder, *Financing the American Dream*; and various press articles: "Debt May Be Drag on Recovery," *Seattle Times*

(2002); "People Are Borrowing to Maintain Lifestyles; Debt Could Swallow up Consumer, Say Experts," *San Francisco Chronicle* (2001); and "Paying the Piper: Hangover May Loom for Americans Who Enjoyed Credit Boom," *Wall Street Journal* (2000). The statistics in this section are from the *SCF*; and the data are available on the Board of the Federal Reserve System's Web site; from the Bureau of Economic Analysis; and in *The Nilson Report* (various issues). It should be noted that statistics on credit card debt commonly include balances that are held only during the billing and grace periods, and on which finance charges are not paid.

The classic theoretical treatment of credit rationing is Joseph E. Stiglitz and Andrew Weiss, "Credit Rationing in Markets with Imperfect Information," *American Economic Review* (1981). A useful summary of the subsequent literature is provided by Xavier Freixas and Jean-Charles Rochet, *Microeconomics of Banking* (1997). For examples of studies on liquidity constraint in households, see Tullio Jappelli, "Who Is Credit Constrained in the U.S. Economy?" *Quarterly Journal of Economics* (1990); Giouanni Ferri and Peter Simon, "Constrained Consumer Lending: Exploring Business Cycle Patterns Using the Survey of Consumer Finances," mimeograph (1997); and David Gross and Nicholas Souleles, "Do Liquidity Constraints and Interest Rates Matter for Consumer Behavior? Evidence from Credit Card Data," *Quarterly Journal of Economics* (2002).

Credit-scoring techniques are documented in Bill Rayburn, "Home Lenders Need Scoring Method for Collateral Risk," *American Banker* (July 12, 2002); W. A. Lee, "Bringing Scoring Tasks In-House: U.S. Bancorp Says a New System Makes It a Better Judge of Risk," *American Banker* (August 26, 2002); and other *American Banker* articles.

The examples of small businesses using credit cards to finance operations were compiled from a variety of sources, including Kenneth Klee, "The Money Chase," *Fortune Small Business* (2001); Bridget McCrea, "Masters of Survival," *Fortune Small Business* (December 21, 2002); and other press articles. Statistics on small businesses can be found in Small Business Administration, *The State of Small Business: A Report of the President* (1997), and *Small Business Economic Indicators for 2001* (2003).

The 2002 value of venture capital expenditures comes from VentureOne, *Industry Information: Statistics*, <http://www.ventureone.com/index.html>. For an analysis of liquidity constraints and entrepreneurship, see David S. Evans and Boyan Jovanovic, "An Estimated Model of Entrepreneurial Choice under Liquidity Constraints," *Journal of Political Economy* (1989); David G. Blanchflower and Andrew J. Oswald, "What Makes an Entrepreneur?" *Journal of Labor Economics* (1998); and Thomas Dunn and Douglas Holtz-Eakin, "Financial Capital, Human Capital, and the Transition to Self-Employment: Evidence from Intergenerational Links," *Journal of Labor Economics* (2000).

The sections "The Use of Credit Cards by the Self-Employed" and "Credit Card Use by Firms with Fewer than Five Hundred Employees" are based on data from the *Survey of Small Business Finances* (1998), available on the Federal Reserve System's Web site; and the *SCF*.

Chapter 5

The quotes of two merchants' contrary perspectives on accepting payment cards come from "On-the-Cuff Travel Speeds Up," *Business Week* (August 16, 1958); and Joseph Nocera, *A Piece of the Action: How the Middle Class Joined the Money Class* (1994). Merchant revolts against payment cards are documented in "Hotel Trade Issues Its Own Credit Card," *New York Times* (October 16, 1956); Paul J. C. Friedlander, "Agents versus Credit Cards," *New York Times* (November 9, 1958); William R. Clarry, "Credit Card Revolt: More Restaurants Drop National Firms, Set up Own Charge System," *Wall Street Journal* (June 11, 1959); "Credit Cards: Not So Clubby," *Newsweek* (January 19, 1959); and Elsa C. Arnett, "Restaurateurs Take on American Express," *Boston Globe* (March 29, 1991).

The history of merchant acceptance was drawn from various payment card history books and press articles, including "Dining on the Cuff," *Newsweek* (January 29, 1951); Charles Grutzner, "Living High without Money," *New York Times* (December 2, 1956); "The Santa Claus That Makes You Pay," *Business Week* (December 20, 1969); "Saks to Take American Express Card," *New York Times* (September 28, 1977); Isadore Barmash, "Two Macy Divisions to Honor American Express Cards," *New York Times* (November 6, 1972); Jeffrey Kutler, "1% of Penney Sales on Visa," *American Banker* (March 24, 1980); "Wanted, Dead or Alive," *Economist* (September 25, 2003); Kevin T. Higgins, "Priming the Supermarket Pump," *Credit Card Management* (March 1996); Lavonne Kuykendall, "A Golden (Arches) Test Case for Micropayment Processing," *American Banker* (December 16, 2002); Peter Lucas, "Online Debit's Revised Sales Pitch," *Credit Card Management* (January 2002); Peter Lucas, "How the Rest of the World Does Web Payments," *Credit Card Management* (April 2003); Nocera, *A Piece of the Action*; "Toward an Ever-Fuller Life on Credit Cards," *Newsweek* (September 28, 1959); and Gerald Walker, "Life a la Carte," *New York Times* (November 8, 1959).

For a discussion on the economics of interchange fees, see Julian Wright, "The Determinants of Optimal Interchange Fees in Payment Systems," *Journal of Industrial Economics* (2004). A recent cost-benefit analysis on accepting payment cards can be found in Daniel D. Garcia Swartz, Robert W. Hahn, and Anne Layne-Farrar, "The Economics of a Cashless Society: Some New Evidence on the Costs and Benefits of Payment Instruments," AEI-Brookings working paper (2003). Other economics literature on payment cards include Alan S. Frankel, "Monopoly and Competition in the Supply and Exchange of Money," *Antitrust Law Journal* (1998); David S. Evans and Richard Schmalensee, "Economic Aspects of Payment Card Systems and Antitrust Policy toward Joint Ventures," *Antitrust Law Journal* (1995); Julian Wright, "Optimal Card Payment Systems," *European Economic Review* (2003); and Jean-Charles Rochet and Jean Tirole, "Cooperation among Competitors: Some Economics of Payment Card Associations," *RAND Journal of Economics* (2002).

The Board of Governors of the Federal Reserve System, *Survey of Consumer Finances* has data on credit card ownership from 1970–2001. Data on the decrease in the cost of merchant terminals are documented in Peter Lucas, "Online Debit's Revised Sales Pitch," *Credit Card Management* (January 2002). The U.S. Postal Service's acceptance of payment cards is reported in "Post Office to Accept All Major Cards," *American Banker* (March 29, 1995); and Leslie Beyer, "A Stamp of Approval for the Post Office," *Credit Card Management* (April 1999). Merchant interchange fee incentives for MasterCard are reported in Miriam Kreinin Souccar, "Interchange Fees an Obstacle for Procurement Cards," *American Banker* (April 28, 2000).

The information on the *Wal-Mart* lawsuit in this chapter was drawn from *In re: Visa Check/MasterMoney Antitrust Litigation*, 192 F.R.D. 68 (E.D.N.Y. 2000), *aff'd.*, 280 F.3d 124 (2d Cir. 2001), *cert. denied*, 122 S. Ct. 2382 (2002); W. A. Lee and Lavonne Kuykendall, "What Debit Settlements Really Mean to Issuers," *American Banker* (May 2, 2003); and W. A. Lee, "Settlements in Hand, Lawyers in Debit Suit Lighten up in Court," *American Banker* (May 5, 2003).

A selection of other sources used throughout this chapter include U.S. Bureau of the Census, *Statistical Abstract of the United States* (various years); Frederick H. Lowe, "Cards Make the Fast-Food Menu," *Credit Card Management* (April 2001); U.S. Department of Labor, Bureau of Labor Statistics; various articles on CNet News, <http://news.com.com/>; and information provided by Visa U.S.A. In addition, we relied on information and data posted on various companies' Web sites, including Visa U.S.A., MasterCard International, Bank of America, American Express, and Wells Fargo.

Chapter 6

The quote at the beginning of the chapter comes from Joseph Nocera, *A Piece of the Action: How the Middle Class Joined the Money Class* (1994), 26–27. The story of the Tu-Ba Cafe is reported in Howard W. French, "Osaka Journal: Japanese Date Clubs Take the Muss out of Mating," *New York Times* (February 13, 2001).

Information and data on Microsoft can be found in Martin Campbell-Kelly, "Not Only Microsoft: The Maturing of the Personal Computer Software Industry, 1982–1995," *Business History Review* (2001); *United States v. Microsoft*, 253 F.3d 34 (2001); and Josh Lerner, "Did Microsoft Deter Software Innovation?" working paper (2002).

The 1958 quote on Diners Club came from "Credit-Card Game," *Time* (September 22, 1958). Additional historical information on Diners Club and American Express for this chapter can be found in John Friedman and John Meehan, *House of Cards: Inside the Troubled Empire of American Express* (1992); "Credit Cards for Diners," *New York Times* (March 30, 1950); and "Dining on the Cuff," *Newsweek* (January 29, 1951). Information on Bloomberg came from Michael Bloomberg, *Bloomberg by Bloomberg* (1997). Press articles documenting viewers deserting Internet publications that attempted to charge users include Michael Liedtke, "Online Subscriptions Herald the End of Web Freedom," *Associated Press* (March 18, 2002); Thomas E. Weber, "Web Users Balk at New Fee

Services That Deliver Little Value," *Wall Street Journal* (April 8, 2002); and Timothy J. Mullaney, "Sites Worth Paying For?" *Business Week* (May 14, 2001). The quote by Brian Arthur is from Joel Kurtzman, "An Interview with W. Brian Arthur," *Strategy+Business* (1998). The *Houston Chronicle's* share of newspaper readers was calculated from data in SRDS Media Solutions, *Circulation 2003* (2002). The typical markup rates for retail stores came from Stephen C. Harper, *The McGraw-Hill Guide to Starting Your Own Business* (2003); and Jan Kingaard, *Start Your Own Successful Retail Business* (2002).

Historical merchant discount fees are documented in "On-the-Cuff Travel Speeds Up," *Business Week* (August 16, 1958); Peter Z. Grossman, *American Express: The Unofficial History of the People Who Built the Great Financial Empire* (1987); Friedman and Meehan, *House of Cards*; and Timothy Wolters, "'Carry Your Credit in Your Pocket': The Early History of the Credit Card at Bank of America and Chase Manhattan," *Enterprise and Society* (2000). Merchant acceptance for American Express and Discover came from various issues of *The Nilson Report*. Information on the early efforts of the Bank of America franchise system can be found in Nocera, *A Piece of the Action*; Gavin Spofford and Robert H. Grant, *A History of Bank Credit Cards* (1975); and from information provided by Visa U.S.A.

See Brian Arthur, *Increasing Returns and Path Dependence in the Economy* (1994) for information on network economics. Other economic literature on two-Sided markets include David S. Evans, "The Antitrust Economics of Multi-Sided Platform Markets," *Yale Journal on Regulation* (2003); David S. Evans, "Some Empirical Aspects of Multi-Sided Platform Industries," *Review of Network Economics* (2003); Jean-Charles Rochet and Jean Tirole, "Platform Competition in Two-Sided Markets," *Journal of the European Economic Association* (2003); and Bernard Caillaud and Bruno Jullien, "Chicken and Egg: Competition among Intermediation Service Providers," *RAND Journal of Economics* (2003).

Sources used to create the figures cited in this chapter include American Express, *Annual Report* (various years); Bernstein Research, *The Future of the Credit Card Industry: Part II* (January 1996); "On-the-Cuff Travel Speeds Up," *Business Week* (August 16, 1958); "The Santa Claus That Makes You Pay," *Business Week* (December 20, 1969); "The Trick Is Managing Money," *Business Week* (June 6, 1970); "American Express: Why Everybody Wants a Piece of Its Business," *Business Week* (December 19, 1977); "Visa Takes Aim at American Express," *Forbes* (April 16, 1979); and information provided by Visa U.S.A.

A selection of other sources used throughout this chapter include Saul Hansell, "Red Face for the Internet's Blue Chip," *New York Times* (March 11, 2001); Lendol Calder, *Financing the American Dream: A Cultural History of Consumer Credit* (1999); and Boris Emmet and John E. Jeuck, *Catalogues and Counters: A History of Sears, Roebuck and Company* (1950). In addition, we relied on various online trade press sources, including CNet News, <http://news.com .com/>; Enterprise News and Reviews, <http://www.eweek.com/>; Internet News, <http://www.internetnews.com/>; Mercury News, <http://www.siliconvalley .com/mld/siliconvalley/>; and ZDNet News, <http://www.zdnet.com>.

Chapter 7

The quote at the beginning of the chapter comes from Adam M. Brandenburger and Barry J. Nalebuff, *Co-opetition* (1996). Although the origin of the term "co-opetition" is unclear—some credit it to Novell's founder, Ray Noorda—its widespread use began with the publication of Brandenburger and Nalebuff's book.

Discover was launched in Atlanta, Georgia, and San Diego, California, in September 1985, and went nationwide in January 1986. This is documented in *The Nilson Report*, no. 364 (September 1985); James E. Ellis, "Mighty Sears Tests Its Clout in Credit Cards," *Business Week* (September 2, 1985); and "New Sears Credit Card," *New York Times* (January 21, 1986).

The history of the standardization of payment cards can be found in Almarin Phillips, "The Role of Standardization in Shared Bank Card Systems," in *Product Standardization and Competitive Strategy*, ed. H. Landis Gabel (1987). For further reading on the history of standardization in other industries, see Irwin Dorros, "Standards, Innovation, and ISDN," *Public Utilities Fortnightly* (March 7, 1985); Robert M. Grant, "The Effects of Product Standardization on Competition: Octane Grading in the UK," in *Product Standardization and Competitive Strategy*, ed. H. Landis Gabel (1987); and the American National Standards Institute, *ANSI Accredited Standards*.

Further reading on VHS's triumph over Betamax include Michael A. Cusumano, Yiorgos Mylonadis, and Richard S. Rosenbloom, "Strategic Maneuvering and Mass-Market Dynamics: The Triumph of VHS over Beta," *Business History Review* (1992); Stan J. Liebowitz and Stephen E. Margolis, "Network Externality: An Uncommon Tragedy," *Journal of Economic Perspectives* (1994); and Stan J. Liebowitz and Stephen E. Margolis, *Winners, Losers, and Microsoft: Competition and Antitrust in High Technology* (1999).

The information on the organizational setup of the different payment card systems came from the Web sites of American Express, MasterCard International, Visa U.S.A., and Visa International; Lewis Mandell, *The Credit Card Industry: A History* (1990); Paul Chutkow, *Visa: The Power of an Idea* (2001); and Gifford Pinchot, *Intrapreneuring* (1985), 59–61. The information provided by Visa U.S.A. Citigroup's rift with Visa in the late 1990s is reported in "The Big Banks Aren't Happy with the Associations' Rules," *Credit Card News* (February 1, 1999); and Miriam Kreinin Souccar, "Antitrust Testimony Recalls Breakaway Effort Led by Citi," *American Banker* (August 8, 2000).

Articles on companies leaving New York City and the Chicago Bears football team threatening to leave Chicago include Mark McCain, "A Sweetener to Stay in New York Stirs Controversy," *New York Times* (September 18, 1988); "Morgan Site in Stamford," *New York Times* (December 18, 1990); Steven Prokesch, "Promises Aside, States in Region Fight with One Another for Jobs," *New York Times* (November 30, 1992); "Republic National Gets Tax Break, Will Keep Data Jobs in New York," *American Banker* (May 26, 1994); Charles V. Bagli, "Pledge to Stay in City Wins Bear Stearns a Tax Break," *New York Times* (August 28, 1997); Charles V. Bagli, "Wall Street Plays Relocation Card, and City Pays," *New York Times* (November 8, 1998); Liam Ford, "Soldier Field

Getting First Reviews," *Chicago Tribune* (June 15, 2003); Liam Ford and Karen Mellen, "Soldier Field Suit Rejected," *Chicago Tribune* (February 22, 2003); Andrew Martin, Liam Ford, and Laurie Cohen, "Bears Play, Public Pays," *Chicago Tribune* (April 21, 2002); and Ray Long and Gary Washburn, "Bears Would Pay More, Get More under Stadium Deal," *Chicago Tribune* (November 23, 2000).

The data on joint ventures and cooperatives came from Bruce Kogut, "The Stability of Joint Ventures: Reciprocity and Competitive Rivalry," *Journal of Industrial Economics* (1989); and T. K. Das and Bing-Sheng Teng, "Instabilities of Strategic Alliances: An Internal Tensions Perspective," *Organization Science* (2000). Patrick Rey and Jean Tirole, "Loyalty and Investment in Cooperatives," working paper (2000) provided information of cooperatives and the tragedy of the commons. The quote on the similarities of biological ecosystems to business networks can be found in Marco Iansiti and Roy Levien, *The Keystone Advantage* (2004). The quote by Bennett Katz is from Chutkow, *Visa: The Power of an Idea*, 117.

Figure 7.1 was constructed from data in various issues of *The Nilson Report* from 1992 through 2003. Figure 7.2 used data from American Express, *Form 10-K* (year-end 2002); MasterCard, Inc., *Form 10-K* (year-end 2002); and the Web-sites of Discover, Visa International, and Visa U.S.A. Current payment card usage and acceptance is documented in *The Nilson Report* (various 2003 issues).

The information on the go-it-alones' ecosystems came from various press and journal articles, including Marc Abbey, "National Merchants Revisited," *Credit Card Management* (December 27, 2002); "Amex President Pleased with Card Trend," *Reuters News* (February 27, 1997); "Nonbank Competition for Small Business: The Race Is On," *Journal of Lending and Credit Risk Management* (1996); "American Express and AT&T (New York) Announce Joint Initiative for Small Business," *PR Newswire* (March 23, 1992); Catherine Fredman, "American Express Nets the Future," *NYSE Magazine* (2000); Mike Tharp, "American Express Enters Japan," *New York Times* (August 25, 1980); American Express, *Annual Report* (2002); and American Express's Web site. The quote by Harvey Golub is from Harvey Golub, "The American Express Experience: Remarks by Harvey Golub," Joseph I. Lubin Memorial Lecture, Stern School of Business.

A selection of other sources used throughout this chapter include *The Nilson Report* (various years); Garrett Hardin, "The Tragedy of the Commons," *Science* (December 13, 1968); *Tri-State Generation and Transmission Association v. Shoshone River Power, Inc.*, 805 F.2d 351 (1986); *Cajun Electric Power Cooperative in the City of Morgan City v. South Louisiana Elec.*, 837 F. Supp. 194 (1993); "Survey: Amex Cobranded Flier Card Tops Citi's," *American Banker* (January 23, 1998); and information provided by Visa U.S.A.

Chapter 8

The opening quote is representative of Visa's advertising campaign that visited popular restaurants, bars, and vacation spots that "don't take American

Express." The campaign aimed at lessening the prestige attached to American Express by showing its relative lack of acceptance. It was quite successful, hastening American Express' decline and increasing Visa's share of the credit card market.

Economic data from Boston in the early 1990s came from the U.S. Department of Labor, Bureau of Labor Statistics; the Regional Economic Information System at the University of Virginia, <http://fisher.lib.virginia.edu/reis/>; and the New England Electronic Economic Data Center, <http://www.bos.frb.org/economic/neei/neeidata/mp.txt>. Our discussion of the Boston Fee Party attempts to paint a picture of some of the economic issues confronting merchants, from their perspective, at that time. It is not intended to provide a complete analysis of the relative costs and benefits to them from the acceptance of American Express cards. The following sources provided information on the merchant discounts charged by American Express and its sources of revenue: "The Pressure Is Building on AmEx Discount Rates," *Credit Card News* (April 15, 1991); "Restaurateurs Take on American Express," *Boston Globe* (March 29, 1991); "Peers Join Hub Restaurateur to Derail American Express," *Boston Globe* (April 20, 1991); "American Express Keeps the Heat on Its Merchants," *Credit Card News* (February 1, 1992); "American Express' Golub Takes Aim at Bank Cards," *American Banker* (October 7, 1992); and American Express, *Form 10-K* (year-end 1993). We relied on a variety of sources for the details of American Express's relations with Boston-area merchants, including John Friedman and John Meehan, *House of Cards: Inside the Troubled Empire of American Express* (1992).

The data for figure 8.1, "Systems' shares of payment card purchases," come *The Nilson Report* (various issues). The system advertising information comes from "Savior of the Smart Card," *Credit Card Management* (September 1, 2001); Hilary Cassidy, "Credit Cards," *Adweek* (April 21, 2003); "Megabrands," <http://www.adage.com>; Laura Gross, "Visa Ad Campaign Emphasizes Wide Acceptance," *American Banker* (September 27, 1985); W. A. Lee, "Key Marketing Quarter for Visa," *American Banker* (September 30, 2003); and Barry Janoff, "New Campaigns," *Brandweek* (June 2, 2003).

The "And They Don't Take American Express" section relies on Peter Z. Grossman, *American Express: The Unofficial History of the People Who Built the Great Financial Empire* (1987); and Friedman and Meehan, *House of Cards*. For contemporary accounts, we used the following articles (along with others): A. F. Ehrbar, "Hazards Down the Track for American Express," *Fortune* (November 6, 1978); John Merwin, "Visa Takes Aim at American Express," *Forbes* (April 16, 1979); Jeffrey Kutler, "Mastercard Challenges Amer. Express," *American Banker* (March 6, 1981); "American Express Applies for a New Line of Credit," *New York Times* (July 30, 1995); "AmEx on the Offensive," *Credit Card Management* (May 1997); "AmEx One-ups the Bank Cards in Warehouse Stores," *Credit Card News* (August 15, 1999); "Blue's Beauty Is in the Minds of Its Cardholders," *Card Technology* (October 5, 2000); and Jane Adler, "Banco Popular Eyes the Mainland," *Credit Card Management* (November 1998). Other sources include the American Express Web site; and Harvey Golub's (American Express CEO at the time) and Philip Heasley's (president and chief operating officer of U.S. Bancorp) testimony in *United States v. Visa U.S.A. et al.* (2001). The data for this section come from *The Nilson Report* (various issues).

For information on the birth of Discover, see James E. Ellis, "Mighty Sears Tests Its Clout in Credit Cards," *Business Week* (September 2, 1985); Steve Weiner, "The Rise of Discover," *Forbes* (May 4, 1987); "New Sears Credit Card," *New York Times* (January 27, 1986); and *The Nilson Report*, no. 364 (September 1985).

Information on Visa's main target in its "everywhere you want to be" campaign comes from Visa U.S.A., *Cardholder Tracking Study*; Jeffrey Kutler, "Poll: Consumers Prefer Visa to MasterCard," *American Banker* (September 26, 1988); Visa U.S.A., "Meeting of the Product Development and Marketing Committee of the Board of Directors" (June 16–17, 1985); and *United States v. Visa et al.*, 163 F. Supp. 2d 322, 356–58 (2001). MasterCard's response can be found in Brian Moran, " 'Possibilities' Drive Touts Basics," *Advertising Age* (February 24, 1986); and Michael Weinstein, "Visa Outranks MasterCard, Survey Finds," *American Banker* (September 9, 1986). MasterCard's resurgence in the 1990s is documented in Saul Hansell, "The Man Who Charged up MasterCard," *New York Times* (March 7, 1993); Yvette D. Kantrow, "AT&T's Entry into Credit Cards Seen Secure from Bank Protests," *American Banker* (May 21, 1990); and Yvette D. Kantrow, "MasterCard's GM Card Gambit Rekindles Dispute with Visa," *American Banker* (September 16, 1992). The competition between Visa and MasterCard, including their efforts to get issuers to dedicate to one system, is detailed in Lisa Fickenscher, "Citicorp Exec Returns with $14B AT&T Portfolio," *American Banker* (April 3, 1998); Jennifer Kingson Bloom and Lisa Fickenscher, "Visa Rewarding Banks for Snubbing MasterCard," *American Banker* (September 7, 1999); Timothy O'Brien, "Détente over, Visa Faces Industry Shake-Up," *New York Times* (February 11, 1999); and "Citi's Tilt to Master-Card: High Stakes, High Risk," *American Banker* (February 11, 1999).

The data on debit card growth in the 1990s come from *The Nilson Report* (various issues). The rise of signature debit is detailed in the following press articles: "Visa Uses ATM Fees as Bait as It Goes after Big Off-Line Debit Fish," *Bank Network News* (March 26, 1997); "Visa Adds Marketing Muscle to Debit POS," *Bank Network News* (June 11, 1993); "As Debit Evolves, So Do the Words That Consumers Use to Name It," *Debit Card News* (April 27, 1998); "Untapping the Benefits of Check Cards," *U.S. Banker* (February 1994); Charles Keenan, "Ads Promote Debit without Mentioning the D-Word," *American Banker* (July 8, 1997); and "Shirley MacLaine Films Visa Debit Card Ad," *American Banker* (October 7, 1997). The emergence of PIN debit is detailed in Faulkner and Gray, *Debit Card Directory* (various years); *The Nilson Report* (various years); and an assortment of press articles, including "Interchange Fee Hikes Test Merchants' Muscle," *Debit Card News* (June 28, 1998); "Offline Debit, ATM Fees Give Online Networks a Promo Boost," *Debit Card News* (March 16, 1999); " 'Regional' Disappearing from EFT Network Lexicon,"

American Banker (February 14, 2002); and Alan Kline, "Small Banks Brace for Drop in Interchange Fees," *American Banker* (July 22, 2003). Web sites such as those of STAR and Pulse were used, as were annual reports from Fiserv and Pulse.

Chapter 9

Andrew Carnegie is quoted from his article "Wealth," *North American Review* (1889). The data on the top fifty issuers and single-issuer networks can be found in *The Nilson Report* (various 1998 and 2003 issues). Our discussion of non-banks is based on the following press articles: Lavonne Kuykendall, "In Brief: Corvette Takes Brand Ride with Household," *American Banker* (May 30, 2002); Lisa Fickenscher, "Citicorp Exec Returns with $14B AT&T Portfolio," *American Banker* (April 3, 1998); and Lavonne Kuykendall, "Citi to Add Sears Book to Its Card Catalogue," *American Banker* (July 16, 2003).

The statistics on transactors and revolvers came from the Board of Governors of the Federal Reserve System, *Survey of Consumer Finances* (various years). The information on various credit cards was collected from issuers' Web sites in May 2003. The discussion of various card features is based on "Most People Use Few Cards, a Study Shows," *Card Marketing* (2001); Andrew Davidson, "One Man's Platinum Journey," *Credit Card Management* (2002); "United Miles," *Card-Track Online* (December 9, 2002); and issuers' Web sites. The service fees are calculated based on the data provided by Visa U.S.A.

The data on co-opetitive issuers' costs and revenues are provided by Visa U.S.A. American Express's revenues come from American Express, *Annual Report* (2002). The information on charge-offs is based on Burney Simpson, "The Forecast: Still Shaky," *Credit Card Management* (December 2002); and Donald Shoultz, "New TRW System Prescreens Credit Card Solicitation Lists," *American Banker* (March 31, 1987).

The average cost to issuers for new applications is based on information provided by Visa U.S.A. The data on portfolio ownership changes came from Kate Gobson, "Portfolio Deals at Highest Level since Mid-1980s," *American Banker* (January 6, 2003). The discussion of marketing techniques employed by issuers to attract customers draws on "The Card's in the Mail," *Marketing Management* (2003); and Libby Wells, "Balance Transfers Become Costly," *Bankrate* (January 14, 2002). The information on American Express Blue comes from numerous press articles. The story of Starbucks prepaid card is taken from Rob Howe, "At Starbucks, the Future Is in Plastic," *Business 2.0* (August 2003). Next Card's rise and fall is documented in Linda Punch, "The Pure-Play Meltdown," *Credit Card Management* (January 1, 2002); and Lavonne Kuykendall, "After NextBank, Doubts on Internet-Only Model," *American Banker* (February 11, 2002).

On different measures of industry concentration, see Dennis W. Carlton and Jeffrey M. Perloff, *Modern Industrial Organization* (2000). The data on concentration within the manufacturing industry are based on the U.S. Bureau of the Census, *Concentration Ratios in Manufacturing* (1997) and U.S. Bureau of the Census, *Concentration Ratios in Finance and Insurance* (1997); the data on concentration within the credit and charge card industry come from *The Nilson Report* (various 2003 issues). The U.S. Department of Justice and Federal Trade Commission *1992 Horizontal Merger Guidelines* are at <http://www.ftc.gov/bc/docs/horizmer.htm>.

The data on measures of output for the credit and charge card industry can be found in *The Nilson Report* (various issues). The comparative statistics for households, consumer expenditures, and consumer credit outstanding come from the Bureau of Economic Analysis; and the U.S. Census Bureau. The price index was calculated based on the data provided by Visa U.S.A. The growth in credit lines is documented in David Breitkopf, "After Year of Scrutiny, Subprime Reconsidered," *American Banker* (November 14, 2002); and Christopher Farrell and Gary Weiss, "Credit-Card Wars: Profits Are Taking a Direct Hit—Savage Competition and Hair-Raising Default Rates Are Zapping Issuers," *Business Week* (November 17, 1986).

The "Historical Profitability and Market Failure" section is based on Franklin Fisher and John McGowan, "On the Misuse of Accounting Rates of Return to Infer Monopoly Profits," *American Economic Review* (1983); Lawrence Ausubel, "The Failure of Competition in the Credit Card Market," *American Economic Review* (1991); and Glenn Canner C____ Luckett "Developments in the Pricing of Credit Card Services," *Federal Reserve Bulletin* (1992). The rates of return for various types of lending come from Visa U.S.A.; and Federal Reserve Board, *Functional Cost Analysis*.

The data on the top ten signature debit issuers come from *The Nilson Report*, no. 784 (March 2003); and *The Nilson Report*, no. 785 (April 2003). The data on PIN debit issuers come from the Thomson Corporation. We calculated regional bank HHIs using the FDIC data on bank deposits. The discussion of interchange fees for signature debit and PIN debit draws on "Study Shows Issuers Have Different Views on PIN Fees," *ATM and Debit News* (August 22, 2002); David Breitkopf, "Study: PIN Fees Are up but Won't Become Norm," *American Banker* (August 19, 2002); and David Breitkopf, "PIN Debit Fees Becoming a Math Problem for Banks," *American Banker* (July 23, 2003). The data on measures of output for the debit card industry come from *The Nilson Report* (various years).

Chapter 10

Henry C. Duques is quoted in Veronica Byrd, "Hello, Western Union? First Data Calling," *Business Week* (August 29, 1994). The information on the FDC can be found in *The Nilson Report*, no. 783 (March 2003); *The Nilson Report*, no. 784 (March 2003); *The Nilson Report*, no. 785 (April 2003); and First Data Corporation, *Annual Report* (2002). It should be noted that data on merchant acquiring and processing are typically less precise than data on the issuing side. In addition, many of the details of the various alliances in the business are not public and it is therefore not always possible to know how volume should be apportioned among alliance members.

For information on the issuing and acquiring of the go-it-alones, see "Rulings Have Discover Set to Partner with Banks," *American Banker* (May 28, 2003); and "Funny Thing about ISOs: Independent Sales Organizations Control about 75% of the Acquiring Business," *Credit Card Management* (November 1, 1994). For information on the issuing and acquiring of the co-opetitive members, see Arnold H. Lozowick, "Compatible Bank Credit Cards," *Bankers Monthly Magazine* (October 15, 1967); "Defendants Trial Brief," *National Bancard Corp. v. Visa U.S.A.*; and *The Nilson Report* (various 1981 issues). Numerous press articles (1980s) and *The Nilson Report* (various 1980s' issues) provide an overview of the acquiring side of the payment card business in 1980s. For the consolidation of merchant processors, see the following press releases. (See, for example, "First Data Signs Long-Term Merchant Processing Agreement with Certified Merchant Services" FDC press release [April 27, 2003]; "NOVA Renews Alliance with KeyCorp for Key Merchant Services" [Key Corp press release] (March 12, 2002); and "Vital Processing Services Signs Contract with Electronic Merchant Systems" vital press release [May 12, 2000].)

The discussion on First Data Corporation is based on *The Nilson Report*, no. 267 (September 1981); *The Nilson Report*, no. 783 (March 2003); First Data Corporation, *Annual Report* (2002); Alan Levinsohn, "The Rise and Sprawl of a Card Services Empire," *ABA Banking Journal* (July 1998); and Mickey Meece, "First Data Strengthens Position in Card Processing," *American Banker* (December 21, 1993).

The discussion on Alliance Data Systems is based on *The Nilson Report*, no. 790 (June 2003); *The Nilson Report*, no. 628 (September 1996); *The Nilson Report*, no. 647 (July 1997); Alliance Data Systems, *Form 10-K* (various years); and numerous Alliance Data Systems press releases.

The section on Cartegy is based on *The Nilson Report*, no. 791 (July 2003); Cartegy's Web site, <http://www.certegy.com/AC_CertegyAtAGlance.html>; and Equifax, *Form 10-K* (various years). The section on Bank of America is based on *The Nilson Report* (various 2003 issues); Bank of America's Web site, <http://www.bankofamerica.com/index.cfm>; and Debora Vrana, "Charlotte: A New U.S. Behemoth of Banking," *Los Angeles Times* (May 28, 1998).

The section on Total Systems is based on TSYS's Web site, <http://www.tsys.com/company/index.cfm?pageID=255>; CB&T's Web site, <http://www.columbusbankandtrust.com/index.cfm?catID=5&subject=1&page=2>; Vital press releases; Jeremy Quittner, "Visa and Total System Launch Merchant Processing Partnership," *American Banker* (May 21, 1996); and Helen Stock, "Total System's Parent Agrees to Buy ProCard," *American Banker* (March 7, 2000). The average cost for acquiring new merchants comes from Linda Punch, "Predicting Attrition," *Credit Card Management* (May 2001). The discussion of acquiring is based on First Data Corporation, *CSFB Equity Research* (August 22, 2002); Merrill Lynch, *The Payment Processing Industry* (November 15, 2002); *The Nilson Report* (various 2003 issues); and numerous press articles.

(See, for example, "Merchant-Acquirers and ISOs Mirroring Each Other in Fees," *American Banker* [July 16, 2001]; and Charles Marc Abbey, "National Merchants Revisited," *Credit Card Management* [December 27, 2002].)

For our discussion of merchant processing and cardholder processing, we used First Data Corporation, *Form 10-K* (1998); First Data Corporation, *Annual Report* (2000, 2002); and Merrill Lynch, *The Payment Processing Industry*. The discussion of merchant processing is also based on National Processing, *Form 10-K* (various years); and press articles. (See, for example, "Finding Profits in Acquiring," *Credit Card Management* [December 1, 1999].) The discussion of cardholder processing is also based on Total Systems, *Annual Report* (2002); Cartegy, *Annual Report* (2002); Lavonne Kuykendall, "First Data–Bank One Split Hits a Pothole," *American Banker* (August 28, 2003); and David Satterfield, "Efficient Card Processors Find Market from Mergers Consolidation," *American Banker* (September 21, 1987).

Chapter 11

The introductory quotes were taken from Adam Smith, *An Inquiry into the Nature and Causes of the Wealth of Nations* (1776) and Joseph Schumpeter, *Capitalism, Socialism, and Democracy* (1942).

For information on legal suits filed against Visa, MasterCard, and American Express, see "The Retailers' Home Run," *Credit Card Management* (June 26, 2003); "Visa and MasterCard Lose Appeal on DOJ Lawsuit but Legal Battle Is Likely to Continue," *Card News* (October 1, 2003); "Visa, MasterCard Must Face Antitrust Claims—Judge," *Reuters News* (July 7, 2003); and "American Express Sued in Purported Class Action in California," *Dow Jones Corporate Filings Alert* (April 10, 2003). Information on litigation outside the United States can be found in "Visa to Appeal Crt Ruling on Ctrl Bk Credit Card Reforms," *Dow Jones International News* (September 10, 2003); and "Interchange Rate Battle Now Spreading to UK," *American Banker* (February 12, 2003). The amount of the settlement in the *Wal-Mart* case is reported as the present discounted value of the settlement of $3 billion over ten years, using discount rates of 4 to 8 percent. The bank prime loan rate was around 4 percent.

On the history of the U.S. antitrust laws, see "Antitrust Law Basics; Background," Bowie and Jenson Web site, <http://www.bowie-jensen.com/articles/antitrust.html>. Dee Hock's quote pertaining to dual membership in the card coopetitives comes from Dee Hock, *Birth of the Chaordic Age* (1999). Our discussion of the *Worthen* case draws on court decisions rendered in this case; *Brief for the United States*; National BankAmericard, Inc., *Meeting of the Board of Directors* (various years), and *Bylaws* (1975); and correspondence between the attorneys for National BankAmericard, Inc. and the deputy assistant attorney general. See the court decisions in *MountainWest* for a discussion of this case; and the court decisions in *United States v. Visa U.S.A. et al.* for the most recent legal actions taken against Visa and MasterCard.

Our discussion of the *NaBanco* case draws on court decisions in this case; *Broadcast Music, Inc. v. CBS*, 441 U.S. 1 (1979); and William F. Baxter, "Bank Interchange of Transactional Paper: Legal and Economic Perspectives," *Journal of Law and Economics* (1983). For information on legal actions taken in Australia, see Reserve Bank of Australia, *Reform of Credit Card Schemes in Australia: A Consultation Document* (December 2001); "Credit Card Schemes in Australia: A Response to the Reserve Bank of Australia and Australian Competition and Consumer Joint Study," *Visa International Service Association* (January, 2001); and Michael Katz, *Network Effects, Interchange Fees, and No-Surcharge Rules in the Credit and Charge Card Industry in Australia* (2001). Information on the *Wal-Mart* case can be found in *In re: Visa Check/ MasterMoney Antitrust Litigation*, 192 F.R.D. 68 (E.D.N.Y. 2000); "In a Battle of Titans, Debit Card Lawsuit May Reshape Financial Services Space, $100 Billion in Antitrust Damages Possible," *Item Processing Report* (January 30, 2003); and Lavonne Kuykendall, "Best Buy Suing Visa, MC; Other Retailers to Follow?" *American Banker* (June 20, 2003).

Some other cases that were referenced in the text, but are not directly related to payment cards, include *Brooke Group Ltd. v. Brown and Williamson Tobacco Corp.*, 509 U.S. 209 (1993); *Brown Shoe Co. v. United States*, 370 U.S. 294 (1962); *Matsushita v. Zenith*, 475 U.S. 574 (1986); and *Standard Oil v. United States*, 221 U.S. 1 (1911).

Chapter 12

The introductory quote is from Andrew S. Grove, *Only the Paranoid Survive: How to Exploit the Crisis Points That Challenge Every Company* (1999). The early developments in the payment card industry are discussed in Lewis Mandell, *The Credit Card Industry: A History* (1990); and "Towards a Cashless Society," *Time* (November 5, 1965).

Our discussion of payment technologies draws on numerous press articles. Biometric technology is explored in Lorrie Grant, "Retailers Test Paying by Fingerprint," *USA Today* (July 29, 2002); and Melinda Fulmer, "Grocery Stores Checking out Fingerprints: Small Shops Are Using Biometric Technology That Retrieves Customers' Data to Cut Losses from Fraud, *Los Angeles Times* (November 25, 2002). For information on smart cards, see "A Smart Card for Everyone?" *Information Security Magazine Online* (March 2002); and Donald Davis, "How Chips, and Suppliers, Are Changing," *Card Technology* (May 1, 2002). For information on Target Visa, see Lavonne Kuykendall, "Target Aims to Break Chip Card Impasse," *American Banker* (June 20, 2001); and "Target Finds Use for Chips: Industry Awaits the Results," *Card Marketing* (May 1, 2002). Examples of the acceptance of smart cards around the world are described in Jeffrey Kutler, "French-U.S. Consensus Could Advance Smart Card Dialogue," *American Banker* (June 29, 1998); and Donald Davis, "2003 Industry Outlook: Chip Cards Break New Ground," *Card Technology* (December 1, 2002). The use of wireless payment technology is discussed in "No Cash? No Card? No Problem! New Speedpass Features Allow Stop and Shop Customers to Pay and Save All in One," Exxon/Mobil press release (February 12, 2003). Information on A2A transfers is provided in Peter Lucas, "How the Rest of the World Does Web Payments," *Credit Card Management* (April 2003). The growth of e-commerce and the use of payment cards to pay for online purchases are documented in U.S. Bureau of the Census, *Retail 1Q: 2003 E-Commerce Report* (May 23, 2003); Tom Franklin, "E-Business and E-Payments: How? Who? How Much?" *Business Communications Company, Inc.* (2002); and Peter Lucas, "How the Rest of the World Does Web Payments," *Credit Card Management* (April 2003). For information on PayPal, see "Money Shot," *Wired* (2001). The discussion of m-commerce draws on Matthew Karnitschnig, "Stuck in Its Tracks," *Wall Street Journal Europe* (January 31, 2003); and Alain Lefebvre, "Not All Kilobytes Are Equal," *Telecommunications International* (March 1, 2002).

The discussion of FDC mergers and acquisitions can be found in "First Data Corp. Completes Buy of Card Establishment," *Dow Jones News Service* (March 9, 1995); and "First Data and First Financial Management Close Merger Transaction," *Business Wire* (October 27, 1995). Information on the *Wal-Mart* and the Department of Justice legal actions is available in "Retailers Once Again Challenge the Associations' 'Honor-All-Cards' Rule," *Credit Card News* (November 15, 1996); "MasterCard, Visa Antitrust Trial Date Set," *American Banker* (December 21, 1998); and W. A. Lee, "Settlements in Hand, Lawyers in Debit Suit Lighten up in Court," *American Banker* (May 5, 2003).

"The Role of Litigation in Reshaping the Marketplace" section is based on Lavonne Kuykendall, "Visa to Raise Interchange, Aiming Squarely at MC," *American Banker* (June 27, 2003); David Breitkopf, "Pulse: Processing Tab Main Reason for Hike," *American Banker* (July 7, 2003); and "Maryland Man Seeks $115 Trillion from Card Industry," *CardFlash* (July 2, 2003). See also Reserve Bank of Australia, *Reform of Credit Card Schemes in Australia: A Consultation Document*; and "Brief for Appellee United States of America," *United States v. Visa U.S.A. et al.* (2001).

Chapter 13

Introductory quotes are taken from William K. Zinsser, "The Day There Was No Money," *Reporter* (September 12, 1963); and "It's Getting Hard to Live without a Credit Card," *U.S. News and World Report* (October 8, 1973).

For developments in biometric technology, see Rob Blackwell, "Stronger Body of Evidence for Biometrics," *American Banker* (March 19, 2002); and Will Wade, "Fingerprint Payment Systems Going Live at U.S. Retailers," *American Banker* (March 25, 2003). For examples of the use of smart cards in France and the United States, see Jane Adams, "The Key to the City Is on a Chip Card," *Card Technology* (October 5, 2000); Kim Housego, "France Prepares Nationwide Launch of Smart Cards," *Associated Press* (February 3, 2003); and Donald Davis, "Building Blocks of the U.S. Smart Card Market," *Card Technology* (May 1, 2003).

For data on the number of checks written in the United States, see "Federal Reserve Banks Announce Changes to Increase Efficiency in Check Services as Check Volumes Decline Nationwide," Federal Reserve Financial Services Policy Committee press release (February 6, 2003). Dee Hock is quoted in Martin Mayer, *The Bankers: The Next Generation* (1998). Glyn Davies, *A History of Money: From Ancient Times to the Present Day* (2002) provides a comprehensive overview of the history of payment means.

Selected Bibliography

Books

Arthur, B. *Increasing Returns and Path Dependence in the Economy*. Ann Arbor: University of Michigan Press, 1994.

Bloomberg, M. *Bloomberg by Bloomberg*. New York: John Wiley and Sons, 1997.

Brandenburger, A. M., and B. J. Nalebuff. *Co-opetition*. New York: Doubleday, 1996.

Calder, L. *Financing the American Dream: A Cultural History of Consumer Credit*. Princeton, NJ: Princeton University Press, 1999.

Calomiris, C. W. *U.S. Bank Deregulation in Historical Perspective*. Cambridge: Cambridge University Press, 2000.

Carlton, D., and J. Perloff. *Modern Industrial Organization*. 3d ed. Reading, MA: Addison-Wesley, 2000.

Chutkow, P. *Visa: The Power of an Idea*. Chicago: Harcourt, 2001.

Cournot, A.-A. *Researches into the Mathematical Principles of the Theory of Wealth*. Homewood, IL: R. D. Irwin, 1986.

Davies, G. *A History of Money: From Ancient Times to the Present Day*. Cardiff: University of Wales Press, 2002.

Eichengreen, B., and M. Flandreau, eds. *The Gold Standard in Theory and History*. New York: Routledge, 1997.

Emmet, B., and J. E. Jeuck. *Catalogues and Counters: A History of Sears, Roebuck and Company*. Chicago: University of Chicago Press, 1950.

Evans, D. S., and R. Schmalensee. *The Economics of the Payment Card Industry*. Cambridge, MA: National Economic Research Associates, 1993.

Freixas, X., and J.-C. Rochet. *Microeconomics of Banking*. Cambridge: MIT Press, 1997.

Friedman, J., and J. Meehan. *House of Cards: Inside the Troubled Empire of American Express*. New York: Kensington, 1992.

Friedman, M. *Money Mischief: Episodes in Monetary History.* San Diego: Harvest Books, 1994.

Galbraith, J. K. *Money: Whence It Came, Where It Went.* Bridgewater, NJ: Replica Books, 2001.

Grossman, P. Z. *American Express: The Unofficial History of the People Who Built the Great Financial Empire.* New York: Crown Publishers, 1987.

Grove, A. S. *Only the Paranoid Survive: How to Exploit the Crisis Points That Challenge Every Company.* New York: Doubleday, 1999.

Hock, D. *Birth of the Chaordic Age.* San Francisco: Berrett-Koehler Publishers, 1999.

Homer, S., and R. Sylla. *A History of Interest Rates.* New Brunswick, NJ: Rutgers University Press, 1996.

Hughes, J., and L. P. Cain. *American Economic History.* 5th ed. Reading, MA: Addison-Wesley, 1998.

Hutchinson, H. D. *Money, Banking, and the United States Economy.* Englewood Cliffs, NJ: Prentice Hall, 1988.

Iansiti, M., and R. Levien. *The Keystone Advantage.* Boston: Harvard Business School Press, 2004.

Liebowitz, S. J., and S. E. Margolis. *Winners, Losers, and Microsoft: Competition and Antitrust in High Technology.* Oakland, CA: Independent Institute, 1999.

Mandell, L. *The Credit Card Industry: A History.* Boston: Twayne Publishers, 1990.

Mayer, M. *The Bankers: The Next Generation.* New York: Truman Talley Books/Plume, 1998.

Nocera, J. *A Piece of the Action: How the Middle Class Joined the Money Class.* New York: Simon and Schuster, 1994.

Pinchot, G. *Intrapreneuring.* New York: Harper and Row Publishers, 1985.

Schumpeter, J. A. *Capitalism, Socialism, and Democracy.* New York: Harper Perennial, 1942.

Smith, A. *An Inquiry into the Nature and Causes of the Wealth of Nations.* Edited by R. H. Campbell and A. S. Skinner. Oxford, UK: Clarendon Press, 1970.

Spofford, G., and R. H. Grant. *A History of Bank Credit Cards.* Washington, DC: Federal Home Loan Bank Board, 1975.

Weatherford, J. *The History of Money.* New York: Three Rivers Press, 1997.

Articles

Aizcorbe, A. M., A. B. Kennickell, and K. B. Moore. "Recent Changes in U.S. Family Finances: Evidence from the 1998 and 2001 Survey of Consumer Finances." *Federal Reserve Bulletin* 89 (2003): 1–39.

Angeletos, G., D. Laibson, A. Repetto, J. Tobacman, and S. Weinberg. "The Hyperbolic Consumption Model: Calibration, Simulation, and Empirical Evaluation." *Journal of Economic Perspectives* 15 (2001): 47–68.

Ausubel, L. M. "The Failure of Competition in the Credit Card Market." *American Economic Review* 81 (1991): 50–81.

Ausubel, L. M. "Credit Card Defaults, Credit Card Profiles, and Bankruptcy." *American Bankruptcy Law Journal* 71 (1997): 249–270.

Baxter, W. F. "Bank Interchange of Transactional Paper: Legal and Economic Perspectives." *Journal of Law and Economics* 26 (1983): 541–588.

Blanchflower, D. G., D. S. Evans, and A. J. Oswald. "Credit Cards and Consumers." Unpublished manuscript, 1998.

Blanchflower, D. G., and A. J. Oswald. "What Makes an Entrepreneur?" *Journal of Labor Economics* 16 (1998): 26–60.

Caillaud, B., and B. Jullien. "Chicken and Egg: Competition among Intermediation Service Providers." *RAND Journal of Economics* 34 (2003): 309–328.

Campbell-Kelly, M. "Not Only Microsoft: The Maturing of the Personal Computer Software Industry, 1982–1995." *Business History Review* 75 (2001): 103–145.

Canner, G. B., and C. A. Luckett. "Developments in the Pricing of Credit Card Services." *Federal Reserve Bulletin* 78 (1992): 652–666.

Carnegie, A. "Wealth." *North American Review* 148 (1889): 653–664.

Caskey, J. P., and G. H. Sellon Jr. "Is the Debit Card Revolution Finally Here?" *Federal Reserve Bank of Kansas City Economic Review* 79 (1994): 79–95.

Cusumano, M. A., Y. Mylonadis, and R. S. Rosenbloom. "Strategic Maneuvering and Mass-Market Dynamics: The Triumph of VHS over Beta." *Business History Review* 66 (1992): 51–94.

Das, T. K., and B. Teng. "Instabilities of Strategic Alliances: An Internal Tensions Perspective." *Organization Science* 11 (2000): 77–101.

DeMuth, C. C. "The Case against Credit Card Interest Rate Regulation." *Yale Journal on Regulation* 3 (1986): 201–242.

Dunn, T., and D. Holtz-Eakin. "Financial Capital, Human Capital, and the Transition to Self-Employment: Evidence from Intergenerational Links." *Journal of Labor Economics* 18 (2000): 282–305.

Evans, D. S. "The Antitrust Economics of Multi-Sided Platform Markets." *Yale Journal on Regulation* 20 (2003): 325–381.

Evans, D. S. "More Than Money: The Development of a Competitive Electronic Payments Industry in the United States." *Payment Card Economics Review*, 2 (2004): 1–27.

Evans, D. S. "Some Empirical Aspects of Multi-Sided Platform Industries." *Review of Network Economics* 2 (2003): 191–209.

Evans, D. S., and B. Jovanovic. "An Estimated Model of Entrepreneurial Choice under Liquidity Constraints." *Journal of Political Economy* 97 (1989): 808–827.

Evans, D. S., and R. Schmalensee. "Economic Aspects of Payment Card Systems and Antitrust Policy toward Joint Ventures." *Antitrust Law Journal* 63 (1995): 861–901.

Ferri, G., and P. Simon. "Constrained Consumer Lending: Exploring Business Cycle Patterns Using the Survey of Consumer Finances." Mimeograph, Princeton University, 1997.

Fisher, F. M., and J. J. McGowan. "On the Misuse of Accounting Rates of Return to Infer Monopoly Profits." *American Economic Review* 73 (1983): 82–97.

Frankel, A. S. "Monopoly and Competition in the Supply and Exchange of Money." *Antitrust Law Journal* 66 (1998): 313–361.

Frederick, S., G. Loewenstein, and T. O'Donoghue. "Time Discounting and Time Preference: A Critical Review." *Journal of Economic Literature* 40 (2002): 351–401.

Garcia Swartz, D. D., R. W. Hahn, and A. Layne-Farrar. "The Economics of a Cashless Society: Some New Evidence on the Costs and Benefits of Payment Instruments." AEI-Brookings working paper, 2003.

Gross, D., and N. Souleles. "Do Liquidity Constraints and Interest Rates Matter for Consumer Behavior? Evidence from Credit Card Data." *Quarterly Journal of Economics* 117 (2002): 149–185.

Hardin, G. "The Tragedy of the Commons." *Science* 162 (1968): 1243–1248.

Kogut, B. "The Stability of Joint Ventures: Reciprocity and Competitive Rivalry." *Journal of Industrial Economics* 38 (1989): 183–198.

Liebowitz, S. J., and S. E. Margolis. "Network Externality: An Uncommon Tragedy." *Journal of Economic Perspectives* 8 (1994): 133–150.

Litan, R. E., and C. Shapiro. "Antitrust Policy during the Clinton Administration." In *American Economic Policy in the 1990s*, edited by J. Frankel and P. Orzag. Cambridge: MIT Press, 2002.

Lerner, J. "Did Microsoft Deter Software Innovation?" Working paper, 2002.

Mann, R. J. "Credit Cards and Debit Cards in the United States and Japan." *Monetary and Economic Studies* 20 (2002): 123–160.

McAndrews, J. J. "The Evolution of Shared ATM Networks." *Federal Reserve Bank of Philadelphia Business Review* (May/June 1991): 3–16.

Phillips, A. "The Role of Standardization in Shared Bank Card Systems." In *Product Standardization and Competitive Strategy*, edited by H. Landis Gabel. Amsterdam, Netherlands: Elsevier Science, 1987.

Prelec, D., and G. Loewenstein. "The Red and the Black: Mental Accounting of Savings and Debt." *Marketing Science* 17 (1998): 4–28.

Raskovich, A., and L. Froeb. "Has Competition Failed in the Credit Card Market?" Economic Analysis Group discussion paper, U.S. Department of Justice, Washington, DC, 1992.

Rey, P., and J. Tirole. "Loyalty and Investment in Cooperatives." Working paper (2000).

Rochet, J.-C., and J. Tirole. "Cooperation among Competitors: Some Economics of Payment Card Associations." *RAND Journal of Economics* 33 (2002): 549–570.

Rochet, J.-C., and J. Tirole. "Platform Competition in Two-Sided Markets." *Journal of the European Economic Association* 1 (2003): 990–1029.

Rose, A. K. "One Money, One Market: The Effect of Common Currencies on Trade." *Economic Policy* 30 (2000): 9–45.

Stiglitz, J., and A. Weiss. "Credit Rationing in Markets with Imperfect Information." *American Economic Review* 71 (1981): 393–411.

Wolters, T. " 'Carry Your Credit in Your Pocket': The Early History of the Credit Card at Bank of America and Chase Manhattan." *Enterprise and Society* 1 (2000): 315–354.

Wright, J. "The Determinants of Optimal Interchange Fees in Payment Systems." *Journal of Industrial Economics* LII (2004): 1–26.

Wright, J. "Optimal Card Payment Systems." *European Economic Review* 47 (2003): 587–612.

Government Publications

Board of Governors of the Federal Reserve System. *The Profitability of Credit Card Operations of Depository Institutions.* August 1997. <http://www.federalreserve.gov/boarddocs/rptcongress/creditcard/1997/>.

Board of Governors of the Federal Reserve System. *Statistics: Releases and Historical Data.* <http://www.federalreserve.gov/releases/>.

Board of Governors of the Federal Reserve System. *Survey of Consumer Finances.* Washington, DC: Federal Reserve Bank, various years.

Board of Governors of the Federal Reserve System. *Survey of Credit Card Plans.* <http://www.federalreserve.gov/pubs/shop/tablwb.pdf>.

Board of Governors of the Federal Reserve System. *Survey of Small Business Finances.* Various years. <http://www.federalreserve.gov/pubs/oss/oss3/nssbftoc.htm>.

Bureau of Economic Analysis. National income and product accounts tables. <http://www.bea.doc.gov/bea/dn/nipaweb/index.asp>.

Department of Justice and Federal Trade Commission. *1992 Horizontal Merger Guidelines.* April 1997. <http://www.ftc.gov/bc/docs/horizmer.htm>.

Federal Deposit Insurance Corporation. *Historical Statistics on Banking.* <http://www2.fdic.gov/hsob/>.

Federal Deposit Insurance Corporation. *Important Banking Legislation.* <http://www.fdic.gov/regulations/laws/important/>.

Small Business Administration. *Small Business Economic Indicators for 2001.* February 2003. <http://www.sba.gov/advo/stats/sbei01.pdf>.

Small Business Administration. *The State of Small Business: A Report of the President.* Washington, DC: U.S. Government Printing Office, 1997.

U.S. Bureau of the Census. *Concentration Ratios in Finance and Insurance.* 1997. <http://www.census.gov/epcd/www/concentration.html>.

U.S. Bureau of the Census. *Concentration Ratios in Manufacturing.* 1997. <http://www.census.gov/epcd/www/concentration.html>.

U.S. Bureau of the Census. *Current Population Survey.* Various dates. <http://www.bls.census.gov/cps/cpsmain.htm>.

U.S. Bureau of the Census. *Retail 1Q: 2003 E-Commerce Report.* May 23, 2003. <http://www.census.gov/mrts/www/current.html>.

U.S. Bureau of the Census. *Statistical Abstract of the United States: 1992.* Washington, DC: U.S. Government Printing Office, 1992.

U.S. Bureau of the Census. *Statistical Abstract of the United States: 2000.* Washington, DC: U.S. Government Printing Office, 2000.

U.S. Bureau of the Census. *Statistical Abstract of the United States: 2001.* Washington, DC: U.S. Government Printing Office, 2001.

U.S. Bureau of the Census. *Statistical Abstract of the United States: 2002.* Washington, DC: U.S. Government Printing Office, 2002.

U.S. Department of Labor. Bureau of Labor Statistics. <http://www.bls.gov/>.

Legal Cases

Broadcast Music, Inc. v. CBS, 441 U.S. 1 (1979).

Brooke Group Ltd. v. Brown and Williamson Tobacco Corp., 509 U.S. 209 (1993).

Brown Shoe Co. v. United States, 370 U.S. 294 (1962).

Cajun Electric Power Cooperative in the City of Morgan City v. South Louisiana Elec., 837 F. Supp. 194 (1993).

In re: Visa Check/MasterMoney Antitrust Litigation, 192 F.R.D. 68 (E.D.N.Y. 2000), *aff'd.*, 280 F.3d 124 (2d Cir. 2001), *cert. denied*, 122 S. Ct. 2382 (2002).

Marquette National Bank of Minneapolis v. First of Omaha Service Corp. et al., 439 U.S. 299 (1978).

Matsushita v. Zenith, 475 U.S. 574 (1986).

National Bancard Corp. (NaBanco) v. Visa U.S.A., Inc., 596 F. Supp. 1231, 1265 (S.D. Fla. 1984), *aff'd.*, 779 F.2d 592 (11th Cir. 1986), *cert. denied*, 479 U.S. 923 (1986).

SCFC ILC, Inc. v. Visa U.S.A., Inc., 819 F. Supp. 956 (D. Utah 1993), *rev'd. in part and aff'd. in part*, 36 F.3d 958 (10th Cir. 1994), *cert. denied*, 515 U.S. 1152 (1995). (This case is generally referred to as *MountainWest*.)

Standard Oil v. United States, 221 U.S. 1 (1911).

Tri-State Generation and Transmission Association v. Shoshone River Power, Inc., 805 F.2d 351 (1986).

United States v. Addyston Pipe and Steel Co., 85 F.271 (6th Cir. 1898), *aff'd.*, 175 U.S. 211 (1899).

United States v. Microsoft, 253 F.3d 34 (2001).

United States v. Trans-Missouri Freight Assn., 166 U.S. 290 (1897).

United States v. Visa U.S.A. et al., 163 F. Supp. 2d 322 (2001).

Worthen Bank and Trust Co. v. National BankAmericard Inc., 345 F. Supp. 1309 (E. D. Ark. 1972), *rev'd.*, 485 F.2d 119 (8th Cir. Ark. 1973), *cert. denied*, 415 U.S. 918 (1974).

Other Sources

Alliance Data Systems. *Annual Report*. Various years.

American Express. *Annual Report*. Various years.

American National Standards Institute. *ANSI Accredited Standards Developers*. <http://www.ansi.org/>.

Bank for International Settlements. *Statistics on Payment and Settlement Systems in Selected Countries*. Basel, Switzerland: BIS/CPSS, various years.

Bernstein Research. *The Future of the Credit Card Industry: Part II*. New York: Bernstein Research, January 1996.

Citigroup. *Annual Report*. Various years.

Conference of State Bank Supervisors. *A Profile of State-Chartered Banking*. 12th ed. Washington, DC: Conference of State Bank Supervisors, 1988.

Conference of State Bank Supervisors. *A Profile of State-Chartered Banking*. 19th ed. Washington, DC: Conference of State Bank Supervisors, 2002.

First Data Corporation. *Annual Report*. Various years.

Franklin, T. "E-Business and E-Payments: How? Who? How Much?" Business Communications Company, Inc. January 2002.

Katz, M. *Network Effects, Interchange Fees, and No-Surcharge Rules in the Credit and Charge Card Industry in Australia*. Reserve Bank of Australia. 2001.

MBNA Corporation. *Annual Report*. Various years.

National BankAmericard. *Annual Report*. 1973.

National Bureau of Economic Research. *U.S. Business Cycle Expansions and Contractions*. <http://www.nber.org/cycles/>.

National Credit Union Administration. *Annual Report*. Various years.

National Processing. *Annual Report*. Various years.

The Nilson Report. Oxnard, CA: HSN Consultants, various dates.

Polk's Bank Directory. 127th ed. Nashville, TN: R. L. Polk and Co., 1958.

Reserve Bank of Australia. *Reform of Credit Card Schemes in Australia: A Consultation Document.* December 2001.

Visa International.

Visa U.S.A.

Index

A2A payments. *See* Account-to-account (A2A) payments
AAdvantage program, 80, 222, 246
Accel system, 209, 211
Account number on payment cards, 9
Account-to-account (A2A) payments, 84, 303–304
ACH. *See* Automated Clearinghouse
Acquirers
  competition among, 258–261
  co-opetition and, 17
  merchants and, 119, 258–261
  in 1980s, 77
  services of, 119, 121–122
  third-party firms and, 18
  in transaction example of payment cards, 10–11
Adobe, 139, 177
Advertising
  competition in payment industry and, 190–193, 199–205
  by merchants, 123
  Visa, 185, 190–193, 199–205
Affinity programs, 79–80, 169, 202, 222–223
Air Miles Reward program, 255
Alliance Data Systems, 254–255
American Dream, financing, 48–50
American Express
  account numbers, 9
  Banco Popular de Puerto Rico and, 198, 314

Blue Card, 13, 160, 227, 301, 305
  cardholder fees, 151
  competition in payment card industry and, 190–199
  corporate program, 194–195
  Costco and, 196–197
  creation of, 4, 13, 57–59
  Diners Club and, 7, 58–61
  First Data Corporation and, 253
  as go-it-alone, 7, 17, 181–184
  government regulation and, 67
  Green Card, 13, 186, 192
  historical perspective of, 13, 57–59
  interchange fee and, 156
  lending experience of, 51
  as major-brand payment card, 12–14
  MasterCard and, 22
  Membership Miles program, 195–196
  organization of, 164
  purchase example using, 12
  restaurants and, 185–187
  service fees, 150
  Visa and, 22
American National Standards Institute, 160
American Tobacco, 274
Ameritrade, 243
Ancillary restraints, 273–274
Antitrust issues
  ancillary restraints and, 273–274

Antitrust issues (cont.)
costs of payment cards and,
285–294
duality, 70–71, 84, 276–284
honor-all-cards rule and, 291–294
MountainWest and, 279–281, 283
NaBanco v. Visa, 286–288
payment card industry and,
294–296
per se rule and, 273–274
Reserve Bank of Australia,
288–291
U.S. policy and, 272–275, 294–296
U.S. v. Visa and, 281–284
Wal-Mart case and, 23, 211,
291–294, 296, 298, 311–312
Worthen Bank and Trust Company
and, 70, 170, 276–279
Apple Computer, 145, 177, 183
Aquinas, Thomas, 47
Aristotle, 45, 47
Arkansas, 68–70
Arthur, Brian, 142
Arthur Andersen, 154
AT&T, 78–79, 125, 182, 202, 216,
271–272
AT&T Universal, 79, 83, 202
Athenian coins, 27–28
ATM. *See* Automated Teller Machine
ATM cards. *See* Automated Teller
Machine cards
Audience makers, 138
Australia, 20, 84
Ausubel, Lawrence, 99, 236,
239–240
Automated Clearinghouse (ACH), 44,
308
Automated Teller Machine (ATM), 2,
81–82
Automated Teller Machine (ATM)
cards, 81

B2B. *See* Business to business
B2C. *See* Business to consumer

Bachellar, Irving, 87
Backroom competition
Alliance Data System in, 254–255
Bank of America in, 256–257
Certegy in, 256
First Data Corporation in, 251–254
integration and, 265–266
market performance and, 258–266
market structure and, 258–266
players in, 251–258
processing business and, 248–251
Total Systems in, 257–258
BA Merchant Services, 250
Banco Popular de Puerto Rico, 198,
314
Bank of America
in backroom competition, 256–257
franchises, 7, 61–64
frequent flier programs of, 17, 246
as go-it-alone, 153
growth of, 16–17
historical perspective of, 16–17,
56–57
Nationsbank merger and, 83
processing business of, 250
Visa and, creation of, 7
BankAmericard
co-opetition and, 61, 152
creation of, 2
in foreign countries, 62
franchises, 61–64
historical perspective of, 56–57
merchants and, 52
Visa and, 61, 66
Bankcard, 20
Bankers Trust, 64
Banking industry
checks and, 36–39, 41–43
Civil War and, 35–36
consolidation in, 33–34, 83
evolution of, 32–44
Federal Reserve System and, 36,
41–42
growth of, 33–34

historical perspective of, 33–36
laws regulating, 32–34, 61, 64
BankNet system, 74
Bank notes, 35, 38
Bank One, 83, 222, 228, 264
Bankruptcy, 102–103
Banks. *See also specific names*
  checking accounts at, 36–39, 91–93
  clearinghouses for, 39–44
  consolidation of, 33–34, 83
  co-opetition and, 63–64
  co-opetitives and competition
    among, 166
  divergent interests of, 170–174
  Internet banks, 243
  lending (historical), 51
  with local or regional payment
    cards, 17
  monoline, 16, 215–216
  national credit card campaigns and,
    70
  paper money conversion and, to
    coins, 29
  payment cards and, 55–56, 61–67
  per capita, among leading industrial
    countries, 34
  term of, 32
Bartering system, 25–26
BASE-I system, 74
BASE-II system, 74
Bellamy, Edward, 53
BHR credit card, 56
Bill of exchange, 28
Billing cycles of credit cards, 11
Biometrics, 299–300
Bloomberg services, 139
Blue Card, 13, 160, 227, 301, 305
Borrowing. *See also* Usury
  American Dream and, 48–50
  consumer debt and, 49, 75–80,
    101–102
  credit cards and, 52
  democratization of, 95–97
  growth of, 95–97

historical perspective of, 48–50
installment plans and, 48
joys of, 97–100
morality and, 46–47, 100–101
objections to, 50–51
revolution in, 44–45
revolving credit and, 57
societal acceptance of, 51–52
sorrows of, 100–104
Boston Fee Party, 186–189
Brandenburger, Adam, 159
Broadcast Music, 275
Broadcast Music, Inc. v. CBS, 275,
  287
Brokerage firms, 243. *See also specific
  names*
Business to business (B2B), 126–128,
  143, 305–306
Business to consumer (B2C),
  126–127, 305

Caillaud, Bernard, 144
Calder, Lendol, 48, 100–101
Calvin, John, 47
Canner, Glenn, 239
Capital. *See* Cash; Money
Capitularies of Charlemagne (800
  CE), 46
Card associations, 8
Card Establishment Services, 253
Cardholder fees, 151, 218
Cardholder processing business,
  18–19, 263–265. *See also*
  Processing payment cards
Card Services for Credit Unions, 256
Carnegie, Andrew, 213
Carte Blanche
  account numbers, 9
  Citigroup and, 15, 60, 63
  competitors of, 7
  creation of, 4
  decline of, 78
  historical perspective of, 59–60
Cartes Bancaires, 20, 302

Cash. *See also* Money
 balances, 91–93
 in payments, various, 31–32
 prevalence of, 31
 return on, 45
 in small transactions, 120–121
Cashless society, 24, 44, 113,
 317–320
Cash price, 48–49
Cash Station system, 209
Certegy, 256, 264
Charge-offs, 68–69, 73, 235–236
Chase Manhattan, 83, 249
Checking accounts, 36–39, 91–93
Checks
 banking industry and, 37–39
 bill of exchange and, 28
 checking accounts and, 36–39,
 91–93
 clearinghouses for, 39–44
 decline in use of, 43–44
 EFT networks and, 44
 in exchanges, 28, 38
 fees for processing, 41, 43
 invention of, 28
 for large transactions, 121
 in payments, various, 31–32
 prevalence of, 37–39
Chemical Bank, 64, 83
Chicago Bears football stadium, 173
China, 20–21, 27
Chutkow, Paul, 87
Citigroup
 AAdvantage program, 80, 222
 AT&T card program and, 216
 Carte Blanche and, 15, 60, 63
 Diners Club and, 15
 Everything card and, 63–64
 heterogeneity and, 171
 MasterCard and, 14, 64, 172–173
 national network of, 32
 negative externalities and, 169
 U.S. usury laws and, 69–70
Civil War, 35–36
Clayton Act, 272

Clearinghouses for banks, 39–44
CNet, 138
Coca-Cola, 136–137
Coins, 26–29, 35–36. *See also* Money
Columbia Broadcasting System, 275
Commodity exchanges, 34
Competition in payment card
 industry. *See also* Backroom
 competition; Issuer competition
 acquirers, 258–261
 advertising and, 190, 199–205
 American Express example of,
 190–199
 Boston Fee Party and, 185–189
 cost reduction, 177
 debit cards and, 205–208
 for innovation, 177
 merchants, 122–124
 mixture of, 6–7, 22
 nonprice, 123
 pricing strategies and, 189
 product quality and, 189–190
 strategies, 225–228
Consolidation in banking industry,
 32–34, 83
Consumer Price Index, 125
Consumers
 commitments and, 99–100
 credit card use by, 98–100
 debt of, 49, 75–80, 100–104
 information about payment cards
 and, 231–232
 multisided platform businesses and,
 141
 switching costs charged to, 232
Contactless systems, 302–303
Cooperation in payment card
 industry, 5–7, 22, 160–161
Cooperatives, 167, 169, 174–175
Co-opetition
 acquirers and, 17
 BankAmericard and, 61, 152
 banks and, 63–65
 birth of, 7, 61–62
 concept of, basic, 65–66

interchange fees and, 66, 152–156
MasterCard and, 66
partnership programs and, 83–84
in payment card industry, 7, 22,
  160, 297
term of, 7
Visa and, 66
Co-opetitives
  competition among banks and, 166
  differences from go-it-alones,
    162–163
  divergent interests of banks and,
    170–174
  ecosystems of, 179–181
  examples of, 161–162
  free riding and, 169
  go-it-alones and, 175–184
  loyalty issues and, 169–170
  negative externalities and, 169
  opportunism and, 167–170, 172
  organization of, 163–165
  problems facing, 167–175, 294
Correspondence relationships, 39–40
Costco, 196–197
Cost reduction from competition, 177
Cournot, Antoine-Augustin, 25
Credit. *See* Borrowing; Credit cards
Credit Card Forum (1996), 198
Credit cards. *See also specific types*
  banks and, 70, 76
  billing cycle of, 11
  borrowing and, 51
  consumers' use of, 98–100
  credit line and, 98, 219, 236
  debt problem of, consumer, 102–103
  defaults, 102–103
  entrepreneurship and, 107–113
  firms with fewer than 500
    employees and, 111–113
  growth of, 8
  lending and, 51, 95–107
  logos on, 1–2, 159
  mass mailings of, banning of, 73
  mental accounting and budgeting
    and, 99

of nonfinancial firms and, 78–79
percentage of households with, 89
self-employed and, 110–111
small-business financing and,
  107–110
"temptation" cost of, 100
top ten (2002), 15–18
Credit line, 98, 219, 236
Credit rationing, 105
Credit-scoring systems, 87, 106–107

Dark Ages, 46
"Dead Mall" concept, 145
Debit cards. *See also specific types*
  ATM cards and, 81
  competition in payment card
    industry and, 205–208
  frequent flier programs and, 246
  growth of, 8, 43–44, 80–84
  issuers of, 240–246
  logos on, 1
  marketing of, 245–246
  MasterCard and, 81
  output of, 244–245
  PIN and, 11, 210, 243–244
  prices of, 243–244
  product differentiation among,
    245–246
  profitability of, 243–244
  rewards programs for, 245–246
  signature on, personal, 11–12
  Visa and, 81, 206–208
Debt, consumer, 49, 75–80, 101–104
Decentralization, 177
Defaults, credit card, 102–103
Delaware, 7, 69
Demand coordinators, 138–139
Demand depository account, 36–39
Depository institutions, 215
Diners Club
  account numbers, 9
  acquisitions by, 56
  American Express and, 7, 58–61
  business model of, 157
  cardholder fee of, 151

Diners Club (cont.)
  Citibank and, 15
  creation of, 4, 115
  decline of, 78
  in foreign countries, 56
  historical perspective of, 54–55, 143
  merchant discount and, 115, 129
  paper trail of, 30
  success of, 190
  workings of, 133–134
Direct network externalities, 135–136
Discover Card
  account numbers, 9
  creation of, 77
  as go-it-alone, 192–193
  growth of, 77–78
  historical perspective of, 13
  as major-brand payment card,
    12–13
  organization of, 164
  purchase example using, 12
"Divide-and-conquer" strategy, 144
DoCoMo's i-mode service, 304
Drafts as media of exchange, 38
Duality, 70–71, 84, 276–284
Duques, Henry C., 247

eBay, 128, 145, 306–308
E-commerce, 304–307
Economics
  behavioral, 99–100
  innovations in, major, 5, 21
  of merchants taking payment cards,
    120–124
  multisided platforms, 134–135,
    148–149
  real versus nominal interest rates
    and, 68
Economies of scale, 177, 250–251
Ecosystems
  business, 176–179
  co-opetitive, 179–181
  go-it-alone, 181–184
  new, forming, 313–315

payment card, 175–184
EFT networks
  business model of, 157–158
  checks and, 43
  creation of, 12–13
  interchange fees and, 206
  logos, 1
  merchants and, 81–82
  payment card industry and,
    205–206
  PIN and, 11, 117, 208–211
  structural transformation of,
    210–211
Electronic fund transfers. *See* EFT
  networks
Electronic money. *See* Money
Entrepreneurship and credit cards
  financing small businesses, 107–
    113
  firms with fewer than 500
    employees, 111–113
  self-employed and, 107–110
eONE Global, 253
E-payments, 307–308
Equifax, 256
Esquire's card program, 56
E*Trade, 243
EuroCard, 56, 62
European Commission, 129
Everything card, 63–64
Exchanges. *See also* Money
  bank notes, 35, 38
  bartering system, 25–26
  bill of exchange and, 28, 46
  checks, 28, 37–38
  commodities, 34
  drafts, 38
  electronic money, 25–27, 30–31
  historical perspective of, 25–31
  metallic coins, 26–28, 35–36
  money, 26
  multi-sided platform markets and,
    30
  oxen, 26

paper money, 28–29
precious metal, 26–27
tobacco, 34–35
Experian, 106

Fair, Isaac and Co., 106
Fasciano, Mark, 107
FatWire, 107
FDC. *See* First Data Corporation
Federal Reserve Board, 36, 41, 88
Federal Reserve System, 36–37,
  41–42, 103
Federal Trade Commission, 73
Federal Trade Commission Act
  (1914), 272
Fees
  cardholder, 151, 218
  check processing, 39–42
  payment card service, 150
  service, 150, 219–222
Finance charges, 218, 219
Financing the American Dream
  (Calder), 48
Fingerprinting, 299
First Bankcard Systems, 256
First Chicago, 83
First Data Corporation (FDC)
  American Express and, 253
  in backroom competition, 251–254
  in payment card industry, rise of,
    19, 298, 310, 314
  STAR system and, 14
  workings of, 247–248
First Internet Bank of Indiana, 304
First USA, 83, 250
"Floor limit," 153–154
For-profit firms, 174–175
Four Hands (furniture importing
  business), 107
France, 7, 9, 20, 302
Franchise issues and opportunities,
  61–66, 154
Franklin, Benjamin, 50, 100
Free riding, 169

Frequent flier programs, 80,
  195–196, 222, 246, 255
Froeb, Luke, 239
Fukuda, Hiromoto, 133
Functional Cost Analysis (Federal
  Reserve), 237
Future of payment card industry,
  23–24, 317–320

Garcia Swartz, Daniel, 130–131
Gates, Bill, 134
General Electric, 78–79
General Motors, 78–79, 137, 166,
  176, 216
Georgia, 68
Giannini, A. P., 56
Giro (consolidated bill payment
  scheme), 43
Go-it-alones
  American Express as, 7, 17,
    181–184
  Bank of America as, 153
  business model of, 157
  challenge from, 312–313
  co-opetitives and, 175–184
  Discover Card as, 192–193
  ecosystems of, 181–184
  in issuer competition, 214–215
  issuers as, 17
  pricing strategies of, 150–152
  shares in, 162–163
Gold-dollar standard, 35–36
Gold money, 27, 29, 35
Golub, Harvey, 182, 195, 198–199,
  284
Gourmet Magazine Club card, 56
Great Depression (1930s), 35, 48
Greenbacks, 35
Green Card (American Express), 13,
  186, 192
Grove, Andrew, 297

Hahn, Robert, 130–131
Hamilton, Alexander, 35

Hammurabi's code of laws, 45
Harbor Bank of Maryland, 246
Hatton, Brett, 107
Health Passport Project, 90
Herfindahl-Hirschman Index (HHI), 230, 242, 263
Herodotus, 27
HHI. *See* Herfindahl-Hirschman Index
Hilton Hotels, 59
Hock, Dee, 1, 5, 275–276, 318
Honor-all-cards rule, 291–294
Hubs, 177–178
"Hyperbolic discounting" literature, 99–100

Iansiti, Marco, 176–177
IBM, 145, 227, 271–272
i-mode service, 304
Independent Community Bankers of America, 256
Independent sales organizations (ISOs), 18
India, 20–21, 27
Indirect network, externalizing and internalizing, 135–136, 142
I-Net system, 74
Inflation tax, 26, 29
ING Direct, 243
Installment plans, 48
Interbank, 64
Interchange fees
  American Express and, 156
  co-opetition and, 152–156
  debate about, 285–286
  EFT networks and, 206
  on-us transactions and, 249
  Visa and, 129–130, 154–155, 286–288
Interest
  nominal, 68
  rates, 68–70
  real, 68
  return on cash, 45
  savings, 91–93

Interlink system, 209, 211
Internet
  auctions, 128, 145, 306–307
  banks, 243
  e-commerce and, 304–307
  e-payments and, 307–308
  money, 307
Interstate banking regulations, 32–33, 61, 64
ISOs. *See* Independent sales organizations
Issuer competition
  depository institutions in, 215
  go-it-alones in, 214–215
  market performance and, 232–240
  market segmentation and, 216–225
  market structure and, 228–232
  monoline banks in, 215–216
  nonbanks in, 216
  players, 213–216
  product differentiation and, 216–225
  strategies, 225–228
Issuers. *See also* Go-it-alones; Payment cards
  costs of, 223–225
  credit-scoring systems and, 87, 106
  debit card, 240–246
  duality and, 70–71
  go-it-alone, 17, 214–216
  growth of Visa issuers, 231
  historical profitability of, 236–240
  losses incurred by (1970s), 71–74
  market failure and, 236–240
  market performance of, 232–240
  nonbank, 79, 216
  output of, 232–234
  pricing strategies of, 234–235
  revenues of, 223–225
  risk undertaken by, 105
  structure of, 241–243
  in transaction example of payment cards, 9–11

Japan, 303
Jasper's (restaurant), 185–187
JCB, 3, 19–20
J.P. Morgan Chase, 17, 226, 246
Jullien, Bruno, 144
JVC's VHS, 161

Kahn, Ari, 107
Kapioski, Paul, 299
Katz, Bennett, 179
Katz, Michael, 290
Keystones (hubs), 177–178

Larking, Kenneth, 52
Laws and litigation. *See* Antitrust
  issues; *specific laws*
Layne-Farrar, Anne, 130–131
Lending
  American Express's experience, 51
  banks and, 51
  Calder's study on, 48, 100–101
  credit cards and, 51, 95–107
  credit rationing and, 105
  joys and sorrows of, 104–107
  merchants and, 51–52
  payment cards and, 45
  rates of return on select, 237–238
  revolution in, 45
  risks of, 105
  to small businesses, 107–110
Levien, Roy, 177
Litan, Robert, 274
Loans. *See* Credit cards; Lending
Logos on payment cards, 1–2, 159
Loyalty issues, 169–170
Loyalty Management Group, 255
Luckett, Charles, 239
Lydians, 26–27, 31

Maestro system, 209
Magic Line system, 209
Magnetic stripe on payment cards, 9,
  159
Mail Box Capital Corporation, 255
Mailtek, 257

Major's Cabin Grill (birthplace of
  Diners Club), 115
Manufacturers Hanover, 64
Market failure, 236–240
Market makers, 137–138
Market performance
  backroom competition and,
    258–266
  of payment card industry, 232–240
Market segmentation, 216–223
Market structure
  backroom competition and,
    258–266
  issuer competition and, 228–232
"Marquee buyers," 144–145
*Marquette National Bank v. First of
  Omaha Service Corp.* (1978), 7, 69
MasterCard
  AAdvantage program, 80, 222
  account numbers, 9
  American Express and, 22
  Citigroup and, 14, 64, 172–173
  computer systems of, 74
  co-opetition and, 66
  co-opetitive ecosystem of, 179–181
  creation of, 7
  debit cards and, 81
  duality and, 281–284
  in foreign countries, 62
  historical perspective of, 14
  loyalty issues and, 170
  as major-brand payment card,
    12–14
  organization of, 163–165
  password programs, 306
  PayPass, 302
  purchase example using, 6
  Reserve Bank of Australia and,
    288–291, 313
  service fees, 150, 219–222
  Visa and, 6, 23, 199–205
MBNA, 16, 83
McCoy, John G., 317
McNamara, Frank, 4, 30, 53–54,
  133–134, 149–150, 297, 318

M-commerce, 308–310
Membership Miles Program
  (American Express), 195–196
Mental accounting and budgeting, 99
Merchant Bank Services, 258
Merchants. *See also specific names*
  acceptance of payment cards by, 115
  acquirers and, 119, 258–261
  advertising by, 123
  BankAmericard and, 52
  competition among, 122–124
  cost improvements of payment cards
    and, 125–126
  Diners Club card discounts to, 115,
    129
  duality and, 70–71
  economics of payment cards and,
    120–124
  EFT networks and, 81–82
  independent sales organizations and,
    18
  installment plans and, 48
  lending and, 51–52
  payment card industry and, 22, 143
  performance improvements of
    payment cards and, 124–125
  processing businesses and, 261–263
  in transaction example of payment
    cards, 9–11
  volume of payment cards by
    category, 118
Mergers and acquisitions in banking
  industry, 32–34, 83
Metallic coins, 26–31, 35–36
Metropolitan Statistical Areas, 242
Microsoft, 134, 139, 143, 145–146,
  177
Middle Ages, 46–47
Mint Act (April 1792), 35
Mobile phone technology, 304–305
Money. *See also* Cash; Exchanges
  Athenian coins, 28–29
  electronic, 25–27, 30–31
  exchanges, 26
  gold, 27, 29

greenbacks, 34–35
  inflation tax and, 26, 29
  innovations involving, 27–31
  Internet, 307
  management, 91–93
  metallic coins, 26–31, 35–36
  Native American, 34
  paper, 27–31, 35–36
  resources needed to produce, 26, 30
  return on, 45
  silver, 28, 29
  wampum, 34
Money orders, 58
Monoline banks, 16, 215–216
Montgomery Ward, 48
Monthly statements of payment
  cards, 2
Mountain Farms Mall
  (Massachusetts), 145
MountainWest, 279–281, 283
M-Pay Card, 309
Multihoming, 146
Multisided platform businesses
  categories of, 137–139
  consumers and, 141
  economics of, 134–135
  externalities and, internalizing,
    135–136
  market characteristics of, 134–135
  multiple products and, 141–142
  pricing balancing act and, 139–141
  revenue in, 140–141
  single-sided businesses and,
    136–137, 139
Multisided platform markets
  balancing interests in, 144–146
  business models in, 142–149
  characteristics of, 134–135
  competition among nonoverlapping
    platforms, 157–158
  economics in, 148–149
  exchanges and, 30–31
  making a living in, 148–149
  multihoming and, 146–148
  price discrimination and, 141

price setting in payment cards,
149–158, 289–290
pricing strategies in, 144–146
scaling and, 146, 148

NaBanco. *See* National Bancard
Corporation
NaBanco v. Visa, 286–288
Nalebuff, Barry, 159
NASDAQ, 137
National Bancard Corporation
(NaBanco), 249, 269, 286–288
National BankAmericard (NBI),
64–65, 154
National checking network, 39–45
National City Corporation, 250
National Data Corporation, 249–250
National Football League, 161
National Processing Company, 250
National Restaurant Association, 55,
60
Nationsbank, 83
Native American money, 34
NBI. *See* National BankAmericard
Negative externalities, 169
NetBank, 243
Netscape, 143
Network effects, 142
Network Transaction Services, 255
NextCard, 228
Nixon, Richard, 36
Nocera, Joseph, 52, 95, 133
Nominal interest rates, 68
Nonbanks, 78–79, 216
Nonfinancial firms, 78–79, 216
Nonprice competition, 123
NYCE system, 11, 210–211,
253–254

Ocean Spray cooperative, 162
"On-us" transactions, 249
Opportunism, 168–170, 172
Optima card (American Express),
13
Oxen exchanges, 26

P2P. *See* Person to person
Palm and Palm Pilot, 134, 136,
138–139, 144, 145, 148
Paper money. *See* Checks; Money
"Par list" of nonmember Reserve
Banks, 42
Partnership programs, 83–84
Password programs, 306
Payment card industry. *See also*
Acquirers; Competition in payment
card industry; Issuers; Merchants
A2A payments and, 84, 303–304
agreements within, 5
antitrust issues and, 23, 294–296
biometrics and, 299–300
business ecosystems in, 178
consolidation in banking industry
and, 32–33, 83
cooperation in, 6–7, 22, 160–161
co-opetition in, 7, 22, 160, 297
credit rationing and, 105
credit-scoring systems and, 87,
106–107
critical period of (1966–1970), 65
disruption in, 297–298
duality and, 70–71, 84
e-commerce and, 304–307
EFT networks and, 205–206
entering, 230
e-payments and, 307–308
exiting, 175, 231
First Data Corporation in, 19, 298,
310, 314
future of, 23–24, 317–320
government regulation of, 67–69
growth of, 76–77, 80–84
historical profitability and, 236–240
honor-all-cards rule and, 291–294
litigation reshaping, 311–312
losses incurred by (1970s), 71–74
market failure and, 236–240
market performance, 232–240
marketplace and, 310–315
market structure of, 228–232,
310–315

Payment card industry. (cont.)
  m-commerce and, 308–310
  merchants and, 22, 143
  network of, 5–6
  output, 232–234
  partnership programs and, 83–84
  pivotal year (2003) for, 267–268
  prices, 234–236
  revenue in, 8
  revolution of, 5
  securitization and, 82–83
  smart cards and, 300–302
  spending spree of consumers and
    (1980s), 75–80
  standardization of equipment and
    technology and, 66, 159–161
  technological changes and, 21, 24,
    85, 298–304
  third-party firms and, 17–19, 23
  transaction volume in 2002, 15–18
  two-sided platform markets and, 3,
    6–7
  wireless technology and, 302–303
Payment cards. *See also* Credit cards;
  Debit cards; *specific names*
  account numbers on, 9
  affinity programs, 79–80, 222–223
  banks and, 55–56, 61–67
  benefits of, 91–94
  card fees, 218
  charge-offs and, 68–69, 73,
    235–236
  chicken-and-egg problem of, 22
  computer systems of, 74
  convenience of, 52
  costs, 129–132, 223–225, 285–294
  credit line, 98, 219, 236
  diffusion of, 88–90
  economic characteristics of, 22
  economics of merchants taking,
    120–124
  ecosystems of, 175–184
  evolution of, 4
  features, 222–223
  finances charges, 218, 219
  in foreign countries, 19–21
  franchise opportunities of, 62–66
  frequent flier programs and, 80,
    195–196, 222, 246, 255
  function of, 2
  general-purpose, 60–61, 84–85
  global scope of, 4–5
  golden anniversary of, 84–85
  growth of, 21, 44, 88–90, 113–114
  historical perspective of, 53–54
  interest savings from, 91–93
  for large transactions, 121
  lending and, 45–47
  logos on, 1–2, 159
  magnetic stripe on, 9, 159
  major-brand, 12–14
  monthly statements of, 2
  network involving, 5–8
  new products and services from, 94
  of nonfinancial firms, 78–79, 216
  prevalence of, 1–2, 4, 21, 31, 113
  price setting in, 149–158, 289–290
  product differentiation and,
    217–223
  purchase examples, 6, 9–12
  revenues, 223–225
  salaries received on, 2
  secondary players, 14–18
  service fees, 150, 219–222
  shares in, 162
  switching costs, 232
  time-saving factor of, 93–94
  transaction process and, 6, 9–12,
    90–91
  types of, 1–2
  for welfare benefits, 90
Paymentech, 250
PayPal, 128, 307–308
PayPass, 302
PDA. *See* Personal digital assistant
Peckham, Rufus, 273–274
Per se rule, 273
Personal digital assistant (PDA), 136
Personal identification number. *See*
  PIN

Person to person (P2P), 126, 128, 305–306
PIN
  debit cards and, 11, 210, 243–244
  EFT networks and, 11, 117, 208–211
  smart cards and, 7, 300–301
Plastic money. *See* Payment cards
Precious metal exchanges, 26–27
Predatory pricing, 275
Pricing strategies
  balancing act, 139–141
  competition in payment card industry and, 189
  of go-it-alones, 150–152
  of issuers, 234–235
  in multisided platform markets, 144–146
  predatory pricing and, 275
  price discrimination and, 141
  price setting, 149–158, 289–290
  in two-sided platform markets, 150–152
Procard, 256
Processing payment cards, 18–19, 248–251, 261–263
Product differentiation
  of debit cards, 245–246
  issuer competition and, 216–223
  in payment cards, 217–223
Product quality and competition in payment card industry, 189–190
Pulse system, 11, 211
Punctuated equilibrium, 310

Raskovich, Alexander, 239
RBA. *See* Reserve Bank of Australia
Real interest rates, 68
Reformation, 47
Renaissance, 47
Reserve Bank of Australia (RBA), 288–291, 313
Reserve Banks, 36–37, 42
Respondent-correspondent system, 40
Returns, 45–46

Revolving credit, 57
Rey, Patrick, 175
Rochet, Jean-Charles, 144
Rosen, Philip, 115
Rudolph, Sidney J., 55

Salaries received on payment cards, 2
Scaling strategy, 146, 148
SCFC ILC, Inc. v. Visa U.S.A., 280
Schneider, Ralph, 54
Schumpeter, Joseph, 267
Sears, Roebuck & Co., 13, 48, 51, 77, 216, 279–281
SecureCode, 306
Securitization, 82–83
Security and e-commerce, 305–306
Seigniorage, 27
Self-employed and credit cards, 110–111
Service fees, 150, 219–222
Shapiro, Carl, 274
Sherman Act, 272, 274, 286
Signatures, personal, 11–12, 299–300
Silver money, 28–29
Simpay platform for m-commerce, 309–310
Singer, I. M., 48
Single-sided businesses, 136–137, 139
Single-sided markets, 136–137, 139, 141
Small businesses
  financing, 107–110
  firms with fewer than 500 employees, 111–113
  self-employed, 110–111
SmartAge.com, 227
Smart cards
  American Express Blue Card, 13, 160, 227, 301, 305
  French, 9
  PIN and, 7, 300–301
  Target and, 301–302
  technology of, 300–302
  for welfare benefits, 90

Smith, Adam, 267, 270, 273, 294
Sony's Betamax, 161
Sorrowing problem, 100–104
Sotheby's, 137
South Dakota, 70
Speedpass, 303
Spending spree (1980s), 75–80
Stagflation, 67–68
Standardization of equipment and
  technology, 66, 159–161
Standard Oil, 274
Starbucks prepaid card, 227–228
STAR system, 1, 11, 13–14,
  209–211, 310
"Stranded assets," 175
Strategic behavior, 172
SureView system, 106
Switching costs, 232
Synovus, 257

T&E cards. *See* Travel &
  entertainment cards
Taft, William Howard, 273–274
Target (retail chain), 301–302
TCF Bank, 312
Technological changes
 A2A payments, 84, 303–304
 biometrics, 299–300
 mobile phone, 304–305
 payment card industry and, 21, 24,
   85, 298–304
 smart cards, 7, 9, 13, 90, 160,
   300–302
 wireless technology, 302–303
Telecredit, 256
Third-party firms, 17–19, 23
Time price, 48
Tipping theory, 142
Tirole, Jean, 144, 175
Tobacco exchanges, 34–35
Total Systems, 257–258
Tragedy of the commons, 168
Transaction volume of payment card
  industry in 2002, 15–18
Travel & entertainment (T&E) cards,
  9, 56, 61

Travel Related Services, 184
Trip-Charge, 56
Tu-Ba Cafe, 133
Two-sided platform markets
 payment card industry and, 3, 6–8
 pricing strategies in, 150–152

Uni-Card, 60, 67
*United States v. Addyston Pipe and
  Steel*, 273
*United States v. Trans-Missouri
  Freight*, 273
United States v. Visa, 281–284
Universal Travelcard, 56, 191
U.S. Bancorp, 195, 312
U.S. Constitution, 35
U.S. Court of Appeals for the
  Eleventh Circuit, 288
U.S. Court of Appeals for the Second
  Circuit, 313
U.S. Justice Department, 60, 270,
  277–279, 281–282
U.S. Post Office money order, 58
U.S. Treasury, 36
U.S. Treasury Bill, 68
Usury. *See also* Borrowing
 European laws, 47
 historical perspective of, 46–47
 U.S. laws, 47, 68–70

VCR designs, 161
Virginia Credit Union (Indiana), 17
Visa
 account numbers, 9
 advertising, 185, 193, 199–201,
   204–205
 American Express and, 22, 160
 BankAmericard and, 66
 computer system of, 74
 co-opetitive ecosystem of, 179–181
 creation of, 7
 debit cards and, 81, 206–208
 duality and, 278–284
 in foreign countries, 19–20
 franchising issues and, 154
 free riding and, 169

historical perspective of, 13–14
interchange fees and, 129–132,
154–156, 286–288
loyalty issues and, 170
as major-brand payment card,
12–14
MasterCard and, 6, 23, 199–205
membership of, 162
Merchant Bank Services and, 258
MountainWest and, 279–281, 283
organization of, 163–164
password programs, 306
purchase example using, 10–11
Reserve Bank of Australia and,
288–291, 313
Sears and, 279–281
service fees, 150
Target and, 301–302
Worthen Bank and Trust Company
and, 276–279
Visa Check, 81, 207–208, 210
Vital (merchant processor), 257–258,
263
Vodafone, 309
Vogue, 138

Wall Street Journal, 138
Wal-Mart case, 23, 211, 291–294,
296, 298, 311–312
Walsh, Tom, 264
Wampum, 34
Waters, George, 59
Weak exit penalties, 175
Wealth of Nations, The (Smith), 267,
270
Welfare benefits and payment cards,
90
White, Edward Douglass, 274
White, Jasper, 185–187
Williamson, Malcolm, 305
Wireless technology, 302–303
*Worthen Bank and Trust Co. v.
National Bank Americard*,
276–279
WPIX, 138

Xbox, 143

Yahoo!, 137, 145, 148
Yellow Pages, 138

Zayre, 145
Zimmerman, Thomas G., 299